MW01254006

ENTREPRENEURSHIP, GROWTH, AND INNOVATION

THE DYNAMICS OF
FIRMS AND INDUSTRIES

INTERNATIONAL STUDIES IN ENTREPRENEURSHIP

Series Editors:
Zoltan J. Acs
University of Baltimore
Baltimore, Maryland USA

David B. Audretsch
Max-Planck-Institute for Research into Economic Systems
Jena, Germany

ENTREPRENEURSHIP, GROWTH, AND INNOVATION

THE DYNAMICS OF FIRMS AND INDUSTRIES

edited by

Enrico Santarelli
University of Bologna,
and Max Planck Institute of Economics, Jena

 Springer

Library of Congress Control Number: 2006920113
ISBN-10: 0-387-28868-6   e-ISBN 0-387-32314-7
ISBN-13: 978-0387-28868-0

Printed on acid-free paper.

Printed in the United States of America.

9 8 7 6 5 4 3 2 1

springeronline.com

CONTENTS

LIST OF CONTRIBUTORS

Zoltan J. Acs is the Doris and Robert McCurdy Distinguished Professor of Entrepreneurship and Innovation, Professor of Economics and Director of the Entrepreneurship Program in the Robert G. Merrick School of Business, University of Baltimore. He is also a Census Research Fellow at the U.S. Bureau of the Census and Research Professor at the Max Planck Institute of Economics (Jena, Germany). His research focuses on technical change, entrepreneurship, small business economics, regional science and industrial organization. He is the Editor and founder of *Small Business Economics*.
University of Baltimore, Merrick School of Business – Baltimore, MD 21204 (USA); E-mail: zacs@ubalt.edu

David B. Audretsch is the Director of the Department "Entrepreneurship, Growth and Public Policy" at the Max Planck Institute of Economics (Jena, Germany) and serves as Ameritech Chair of Economic Development and Director of the Institute for Development Strategies at Indiana University (Bloomington, USA). He is also a Research Fellow of the Centre for Economic Policy Research (London). His research focuses on the links between entrepreneurship, government policy, innovation, economic development and global competitiveness. He is the Editor and founder of *Small Business Economics*.
Indiana University, Institute for Development Strategies, SPEA, Suite 201 – Bloomington, IN 47405-2100 (USA) and *Max Planck Institute of Economics – Entrepreneurship, Growth and Public Policy Group - Kahlaische Str. 1007745, Jena (Germany)*; E-mail: audrets@indiana.edu

Rui Baptista is Associate Professor of Strategy and Organizations at the Department of Engineering Management of Instituto Superior Técnico, Technical University of Lisbon and Senior Research Fellow at the Max Planck Institute of Economics (Jena, Germany). His research interests focus on the subjects of entrepreneurship, technological innovation, firm and labor mobility, and their relationship with economic growth and regional development. He is Associate Editor of *Small Business Economics*.
Technical University of Lisbon, Department of Engineering Management of Instituto Superior Tecnico - Av. Rovisco Pais, 1049-001, Lisbon (Portugal); E-mail: rui.baptista@ist.utl.pt

Elena Cefis is Assistant Professor in Organisational Economics and in Economic Policy respectively at the Utrecht School of Economics, Utrecht

University (since 2003) and at the Department of Economics, University of Bergamo (since 2000). Her main areas of research are industrial dynamics and economics of innovation.
Utrecht University, School of Economics – Vredenburg 138, 3511 BG Utrecht (The Netherlands); E-mail: E.Cefis@econ.uu.nl

Julie Ann Elston is Assistant Professor of International Business at Oregon State University Cascades and Research Fellow at the Max Planck Institute of Economics (Jena, Germany). She is a regular contributor to the field of entrepreneurship and small firm studies serving as Review Editor of *Small Business Economics*.
Oregon State University - 228 Cascades Hall, 2600 NW College Way, Bend OR, 97701-5998 (USA); E-mail: Julie.Elston@osucascades.edu

Isabel Grilo works in the Enterprise and Industry Directorate-General of the European Commission. She is also an associate professor (on leave) of the Université de Lille 3. Her research interests are in industrial organization, applied game theory and more recently in the determinants of entrepreneurship.
European Commission, Directorate General Enterprise and Industry – BREY 5/150 B - 1049 Brussels (Belgium); E-mail: Isabel.Grilo@cec.eu.int

Ali Güneş is Researcher at the State Institute of Statistics (Ankara, Turkey), where his duties include annual surveys of manufacturing industries, structural business statistics, and short term statistics. He conducted research on small and medium-sized enterprises, firm dynamics and measurement of productivity and technology indicators.
State Institute of Statistics (DIE) - Necatibey cad. No: 114 Yücetepe, Ankara, 06100 (Turkey); E-mail: ali.gunes@die.gov.tr

Yuri (Yuriy) Kaniovski (Kaniovskyi) is Professor of Mathematics for Economists at the School of Economics and Management of the Free University of Bozen-Bolzano. His research interests are in Evolutionary Economics, in particular in mathematical modelling of firm and industry dynamics, stochastic increasing returns, path-dependence.
Free University of Bozen/Bolzano, School of Economics and Management - Via Sernesi, 1, 39100 Bolzano (Italy); E-mail: YKaniovskyi@unibz.it

Luuk Klomp is Unit Manager of the Research, Monitoring & Evaluations section of the Directorate General for Enterprise and Innovation at the Dutch Ministry of Economic Affairs (The Hague). His current research interests are productivity, the knowledge-based economy and the economics of innovation.

Ministry of Economic Affairs, Directorate General for Enterprise and Innovation – P.O. Box 20101 2500 EC The Hague (The Netherlands); E-mail: l.klomp@minez.nl

Luca Lambertini is Professor of Economics at the Department of Economics of the University of Bologna, and Research Fellow of ENCORE (Amsterdam). His main research fields are differential game theory and applications, industrial organization, and intraindustry trade. He is Associate Editor of *Networks & Spatial Economics*.
Università di Bologna, Dipartimento di Scienze Economiche – Strada Maggiore, 45, 40125 Bologna (Italy); E-mail: lamberti@spbo.unibo.it

Francesca Lotti is Researcher at the Bank of Italy, Economics Research Department. Her duties include the analysis of the evolution of market structure in different industries. Her research interests focus on firm and industry dynamics, and the analysis of competition and industrial policy in the European Union.
Bank of Italy, Economic Research Department - via Nazionale 91, 00184 Roma (Italy); E-mail: francesca.lotti@bancaditalia.it

Helen Louri is Professor of Economics at the Department of Economics of the Athens University of Economics and Business, and Director of the Prime Minister's Economic Office. Her research interests are in industrial organization and especially in foreign direct investment, location, technology diffusion, productivity, market dynamics, entry and exit, firm survival.
Athens University of Economics and Business, Department of Economics – 76 Patission Street, 10434 Athens (Greece); E-mail: lourie@aueb.gr

Orietta Marsili is Assistant Professor of Entrepreneurship at the Rotterdam School of Management, Erasmus University. Her main research interest concerns the links between innovation, entrepreneurship and industry evolution.
Erasmus University Rotterdam, Rotterdam School of Management – P.O.Box 1738, 3000 DR Rotterdam (The Netherlands);
E-mail: omarsili@rsm.nl

Kenan Orhan is Researcher at the State Institute of Statistics (Ankara, Turkey), where his duties include annual surveys of manufacturing industries, structural business statistics and regional industry statistics. He participated in various research projects on regional development, industrial concentration, industrial subcontracting and labor market dynamics.
State Institute of Statistics (DIE) - Necatibey cad. No: 114 Yücetepe, Ankara, 06531 (Turkey); E-mail: kenan.orhan@die.gov.tr

Costas Peppas is a Ph.D. student at the Department of Economics of the Athens University of Economics and Business.
Athens University of Economics and Business, Department of Economics – 76 Patission Street, 10434 Athens (Greece); E-mail: peppas@aueb.gr

Roberta Piergiovanni is Researcher at Statistics Italy (ISTAT), where her duties include the evaluation of the main aggregates in the national and regional accounts (value added, production, intermediate costs, and prices), in particular for the construction and distributive sectors. Her research interests focus on new-firm entry and growth, measurement of well-being, and the development of methodologies for national and regional accounts.
ISTAT - Direzione Centrale della Contabilità Nazionale - Via A. Depretis 74/b 00100 Rom (Italy); E-mail: piergiov@istat.it

Enrico Santarelli is Professor of Economics at the Department of Economics of the University of Bologna, and Research Professor at the Max Planck Institute of Economics (Jena, Germany). He is also a Research Fellow of ENCORE (Amsterdam). His research interests are in industrial organization, and especially in firm and industry dynamics, entrepreneurship, measurement and determinants of technological change, industrial policy. He serves on the Editorial Board of *Small Business Economics*.
Università di Bologna, Dipartimento di Scienze Economiche – Strada Maggiore, 45, 40125 Bologna (Italy); E-mail: santarel@spbo.unibo.it

Erol Taymaz is Professor of Industrial Economics at the Middle East Technical University (Ankara, Turkey), where he also taught Technology and Industrial Dynamics. He is currently working on the economics of technology and innovation, industrial dynamics, and micro-simulation modeling.
Middle East Technical University, Department of Economics - Ankara 06531 (Turkey); E-mail: etaymaz@metu.edu.tr

A. Roy Thurik is Professor of Economics and Entrepreneurship at Erasmus University Rotterdam and Professor of Entrepreneurship at the Free University in Amsterdam. He is also Scientific Advisor at EIM Business and Policy Research and Research Professor at the Max Planck Institute of Economics (Jena, Germany). His research focuses on the role of small firms in markets, on the role of business owners in firms and on the consequences and causes of entrepreneurship in economies. He is Associate Editor of *Small Business Economics*.
Erasmus University Rotterdam, Rotterdam School of Economics, Centre for Advanced Small Business Economics, P.O.Box 1738, 3000 DR Rotterdam (The Netherlands): E-mail: thurik@few.eur.nl

Efthymios Tsionas is Assistant Professor at the Department of Economics of the Athens University of Economics and Business, His research interests are in theoretical and applied econometrics, and efficiency analysis using both sampling-theory and Bayesian estimators.
Athens University of Economics and Business, Department of Economics – 76 Patission Street, 10434 Athens (Greece); E-mail: tsionas@aueb.gr

André van Stel is Researcher at EIM Business and Policy Research in Zoetermeer (The Netherlands). His main research interests are in the areas of the determinants and consequences of entrepreneurship.
EIM Business and Policy Research - P.O. Box 7001 2701 AA Zoetermeer (The Netherlands); E-mail: AST@eim.nl

Marco Vivarelli is Professor of Economics at the Catholic University of Piacenza, and Research Professor at the Max Planck Institute of Economics (Jena, Germany). He is also a member of IZA (Bonn). His research interests focus on firm and industry dynamics, skill-biased technological change, and income inequality. He is Associate Editor of *Small Business Economics*.
Catholic University, Department of Economic and Social Sciences - Via Emilia Parmense 84, 29100 Piacenza (Italy);
E-mail: marco.vivarelli@unicatt.it

INTRODUCTION

Enrico Santarelli
University of Bologna, and Max Planck Institute of Economics, Jena

Although the role of entrepreneurial decision making as a factor which revolutionizes production patterns by exploiting inventions was clearly identified by Joseph Alois Schumpeter (1908, 1911; cf. Acs and Phillips, 2002) in his early German writings, nearly one century later entrepreneurship has still to be fully integrated into economic theory. It was only after developments in the field of empirical industrial organization, with the emergence of the new branch of small business economics in the 1980s - following David Birch's (1979) finding of the superior job creation performance of small firms - that economists started systematically to explore the determinants and the impact of entrepreneurship in the modern economies (cf. Geroski, 1995).

Recent studies have identified a U-shaped relationship between a country's rate of entrepreneurial dynamics and its level of economic development (Wennekers *et al.*, 2005). They thus support the idea that among the driving forces of structural change a crucial role is played by those entrepreneurially active individuals that Schumpeter labeled "energetic types" and who display their "essential features" by introducing the "new" into various activities and by "breaking with the established routines" usually adhered to by managers. In fact, according to Schumpeter (1911, p. 171, as translated in Santarelli and Pesciarelli, 1990, pp. 682-683) "it is only in contemporary economy that the energetic type has developed to such a significant extent in the economic field as to constitute a special class of economic subject and be given his own name: entrepreneur".

Schumpeter's vision has been recently reappraised by David Audretsch and Roy Thurik (2000), who have aptly pointed out that the economic challenge of the twenty-first century is transition from the managed to the entrepreneurial society, the purpose being to take full advantage of the knowledge-based society brought about by the diffusion of information and communication technologies (ICT). Thus, identification of determinants and effects of the uneven patterns of entrepreneurship that characterize different countries is crucial for the design of public policies accelerating such transition. The present book takes up this suggestion by bringing together thirteen contributions by leading scholars who explore from both a theoretical and an empirical viewpoint the factors that combine with entrepreneurship and innovation to influence firm and industry dynamics in general, and with regard to a selected number of countries including the United States, Germany, Greece, Italy, Portugal, The Netherlands, and Turkey, besides the 25 member states of the European Union as a whole.

Some of the papers collected in the book conduct both theoretical and empirical discussion of whether and to what extent *Gibrat's Law* of proportionate effect is a useful analytical device for the study of firm growth. As well known, *Gibrat's Law* was originally formulated by the French statistician Robert Gibrat (1931), who found that the growth rate of a given firm is independent of its size at the beginning of the period examined. This means that "the probability of a given proportionate change in size during a specified period is the same for all firms in a given industry - regardless of their size at the beginning of the period" (Mansfield, 1962, p. 1031). *Gibrat's Law* proves enlightening when applied to the study of market structure, because it explains in stochastic terms the skewed pattern observed in the size distribution of firms within most industries. In general, it cannot be rejected if *a)* firm growth follows a random pattern and is independent of initial size, and *b)* the resulting distributions of firms' size are approximately lognormal; whereas it cannot be accepted if an overall negative relationship between initial size and post-entry rate of growth is found (Lotti and Santarelli, 2004). Needless to say, acceptance/rejection of the *Law* is consistent with contrasting patterns of industry dynamics.

The first two chapters of the book are theoretical in nature. They introduce and develop in a formalized manner original approaches to firm and industry dynamics which can be inserted respectively within the evolutionary and the neoclassical paradigms.

In Chapter 1, Yuri Kaniovski summarizes the results of current models of industry evolution. These are analytical tools which can be usefully employed to explain theoretically the variety of real-life industries and their historical trajectories assuming that firms are 'heterogeneous' and differ in some fundamental and measurable characteristics like size, capital and labor productivity. In order to assess the impact of management on these dynamics, Kaniovski observes how a number of production decisions have been treated by the leading evolutionary models: investment routines, learning regimes (in particular, search for innovations as well as imitation of the existing best practice), entry and exit rules. On the basis of random variables, these models generate industry trajectories which are realizations of stochastic processes. Typically, the state of the industry at each moment of time carries the seeds of its state in the next period with the consequence that the corresponding random process proves to be Markovian. When the transition probabilities do not depend on time, one can determine a long-run equilibrium of the industry using the averaging method. In a situation with boundedly rational entry, the existence of a unique long-run equilibrium is proved for a variant of the stochastic model of industrial evolution introduced in Winter *et al.* (2003). Firms are heterogeneous in their labor and capital efficiencies as well as in their entry and investment rules. The equilibrium obtains as a rest point in a deterministic counterpart of the Markov process with time-homogeneous transition probabilities governing the dynamics of industry outputs. The chapter compares the predictions of the standard theory of perfect competition with this structure, and it also considers the extreme case of a vanishing flow of entrants.

In Chapter 2, in order to verify the theoretical consistency of *Gibrat's Law* with recent developments in the mainstream approach to the theory of the firm, Luca Lambertini introduces a dynamic oligopoly game where firms enter simultaneously but compete hierarchically *à la* Stackelberg at each instant over time. They are assumed to accumulate capacity through costly investment, with capital accumulation dynamics being affected by an additive stock the mean and variance of which are known. The main findings in this chapter are the following: first, the Stackelberg game is uncontrollable by the leader, i.e. it is time consistent; second, the leaders invest more than the followers, with the result that, in steady state, the leaders' capacity and profits are larger than the followers'. The analysis carried out in this chapter does not confirm *Gibrat's Law*, since the individual growth rate of the firms is determined by the timing of moves.

The next ten chapters of the book are mostly empirical. They show how alternative methodologies can be employed to estimate the effects of, among other factors, entrepreneurship, firm size, level of human capital, labor market characteristics, and innovation on firm growth and survival.

In Chapter 3, Luuk Klomp, Enrico Santarelli and Roy Thurik conduct an exhaustive survey of about 60 empirical papers testing *Gibrat's Law*, and compare them in terms of characteristics of the data employed, research methods, and main findings. The Authors regretfully acknowledge that comparison cannot always be conducted straightforwardly, because the studies surveyed differ widely in terms of the samples used and the methods applied. Therefore, for the purposes of this chapter the studies examined are divided into groups of which the results can be compared, taking two characteristics into account when forming them. Firstly, several studies, like Mansfield (1962), carry out static analysis while other studies, like Chesher (1979), deal with the persistence of growth. Secondly, the Authors develop their survey following Mansfield (1962) who tests three versions of *Gibrat's Law*: in version 1 all firms are included, also those leaving the industry during the observation period; in version 2 only the survivors are analyzed; in version 3 only large surviving firms operating at or above the minimum efficient scale (MES) are included. Both static and temporal analysis of the three versions should produce six types of empirical growth studies. However, the first version of *Gibrat's Law* cannot be studied in the case of persistence of growth: for it is not possible to analyse the persistence of growth for firms that leave the industry during the observation period. Recently, a certain amount of attention has been paid to the post-entry growth of new firms. The Authors add these studies as the sixth group to their review.

In Chapter 4, Isabel Grilo and Roy Thurik focus on the transition economies of Eastern Europe. They observe that developing a dynamic sector of Small and Medium Sized Enterprises (SMEs) is essential for countries transforming their centrally-planned economies into market-oriented ones. Following Schumpeter, they assume that, because new firm formation is the main driver of this transition, entrepreneurial *energy* is a necessary condition for new firm formation. Grilo and Thurik use 2004 survey data from the 25 E.U. member states and the U.S. to explain country differences in entrepreneurial energy, captured as latent and actual entrepreneurship. Latent entrepreneurship is measured by the probability of a declared preference for self-employment over employment. Besides demographic variables such as gender, age, education level and whether parents are self-employed, the set of explanatory variables used includes country specific effects, measures of risk tolerance, internal and external locus of control and four perceptions of 'obstacles'. The 'obstacle' variables include the perception by respondents of administrative complexities, of availability of financial support, of accessibility of information for start-up and whether the current economic climate is favorable. Specific attention is paid to differences among the eight former communist member states and the 17 other E.U. member states. The most striking result is the greater influence of risk tolerance in shaping both latent and actual entrepreneurship in transition economies relative to market economies.

In Chapter 5 Zoltan Acs examines regional variation in entrepreneurial activity in light of theoretical developments in the fields of new economic geography (Krugman, 1991) and new growth theory (Romer, 1990). The transformation of new knowledge into economic knowledge requires a set of skills, aptitudes, insights and circumstances that is neither uniformly nor widely distributed in the population. Thus, according to Acs, a closer connection between endogenous growth models and models of entrepreneurship is necessary, and for this purpose he studies entrepreneurship using firm formation data annually from 1991 to 1998. These microdata facilitate research on the dynamics of American Businesses, and especially their patterns of formation, employment change and mergers. The major finding is that higher rates of entrepreneurial activity are strongly associated with faster growth of local economies.

In Chapter 6 David Audretsch and Julie Ann Elston explore the relationship between firm size and growth as shaped by the context of country-specific institutions and industries. The purpose of the chapter is to suggest that the literature testing *Gibrat's Law* may have focused on the wrong question. Rather than asking whether or not the *Law* holds, Audretsch and Elston argue that the more relevant question is in "what contexts is the empirical evidence compatible with *Gibrat's Law* and in what contexts is it not?" They suggest that the relationship between firm size and growth is shaped by the context, and this reflects the country, time period and particular industry. Accordingly, whereas studies for North America have found that either the *Law* holds or that a negative relationship exists between firm size and growth, these Authors find a positive relationship between firm size and growth in Germany, which may reflect differences in institutions such as, in particular, the system of finance.

In Chapter 7 Francesca Lotti, Enrico Santarelli and Marco Vivarelli introduce an innovative approach to the empirical estimation of *Gibrat's Law*. In contrast to the previous literature on the subject, they seek to test the *Law* by taking account of both the entry process and the role of survival/failure in reshaping a given population of firms over time. They do so by focusing on the entire population of firms (including newborn ones) in a medium-tech industry, and tracking them over seven years. Consistently with the previous literature, they find that - in general - *Gibrat's Law* is to be rejected, since smaller firms tend to grow faster than their larger counterparts. However, the chapter's main finding is that this rejection of *Gibrat's Law* is due to market dynamics and selection, that is to the entry process and the presence of transient smaller firms. Indeed, whilst *Gibrat's Law* has to be rejected over a seven-year period during which both incumbent and newborn firms are considered, for both sub-populations of surviving firms a convergence towards Gibrat-like behavior over time can be detected. Thus, market selection 'cleans' the original population of firms and the resulting industrial 'core' (mature, larger, well-established and most efficient firms) does not seem to depart from a Gibrat-like pattern of growth.

In Chapter 8 Enrico Santarelli investigates some aspects of the development of industrial districts in the Emilia Romagna region of Italy, where this type of spatial agglomeration of industrial firms has flourished since the period immediately after the Second World War. In particular, this chapter compares the economic performance and technological competitiveness of innovative firms located within and outside industrial districts specializing in selected manufacturing productions. From a methodological viewpoint, it combines case studies – to investigate why location in districts may or may not help firms' innovative activities – and econometric estimates – to investigate whether location in clusters is associated to superior innovative performance. The main finding is that agglomeration economies of the district type may not improve the innovative performance at the firm level and non-district firms are not less innovative than district ones. This may be consequent upon the fact that the industries of specialization in the regional economy are increasingly becoming *traded* industries (Porter, 2003) which sell products across regions and, mostly, to other countries. Accordingly, they do not base their decision to locate within or outside the narrowly-defined industrial district on resource availability but on broader competitive considerations, with the consequence that the relationship between district location and innovative performance tends to weaken.

In Chapter 9 Elena Cefis and Orietta Marsili study the effects of innovation on the survival of manufacturing firms in different technological environments in the Netherlands. They capture the determinants of firms' survival probability by combining firm-level and industry-level features. In particular, the chapter examines the role of innovation within the firm in shaping its survival probability across high-tech and low-tech industries. In addition, the Authors control for the two characteristics of the firm, size and age, generally pointed to in the literature as being important for survival. This allows account also to be taken of the distinction between entrepreneurial and established firms in an industry.

In Chapter 10 Helen Louri, Costas Peppas and Efthymios Tsionas explain how firm- and sectoral-level characteristics such as size, age, financial profile, capital intensity, technical efficiency, market concentration, foreign penetration etc. affect the probability of exit, using for this purpose data on the Greek manufacturing industry in 1997-2003. They focus on the role of technical efficiency and foreign spillover effects on survival, employing a CES translog production function to estimate technical efficiency and then using the hazard function as well as a simple Cox model to estimate the effect that firm- and sectoral-level variables exert on the survival probabilities of Greek manufacturing firms. Firstly, they find that foreign spillovers exercise a positive impact on hazard, possibly revealing the increased competitive pressure existing in sectors where foreign firms have a stronger presence, and reduces survival probabilities. Technical efficiency is instead found to affect a firm's hazard negatively: that is, it positively influences survival.

In Chapter 11 Rui Baptista, André van Stel and Roy Thurik focus on the interrelations between self-employment and unemployment rates for Portugal in the period 1974-2002, comparing them with the pattern observed for OECD countries. The basic features of Portuguese industrial dynamics – a prevalence of micro-businesses and a high significance of necessity-based entrepreneurial activity – suggest that a model estimated using data on 23 OECD countries should systematically over-estimate the (negative) effects of the self-employment rate on the unemployment rate. However, this does not occur for 1990 and 1994. The Authors argue that these counter-intuitive results are due to the external shock associated with Portugal's entry into the E.U.

In Chapter 12 the analysis by Ali Günes, Kenan Orhan and Erol Taymaz starts from certain stylized facts put forward by the previous literature: namely that new firms start small, and small and young firms are less likely to survive or survive only a few years. They expect that entrepreneurs are also aware of these stylized facts, and take measures to reduce the costs of (potential) exit. The study described in the chapter focuses on three mechanisms that entrepreneurs can use to transfer the risks of failure: borrowing from external sources (transferring the risk to creditors), reducing sunk costs (by renting/leasing building, machinery and equipment, transferring the risk to investors), and lowering the regular wage and compensating workers with bonus-type payments (transferring the risk to workers). Analysis of the evolution of these measures over the life cycle of new firms shows that they are negatively correlated with survival probability in Turkish manufacturing, which is indicative that entrepreneurs are able to transfer some of the risks of failure.

Some of the topics studied in the chapters already summarized are not directly amenable to policy intervention. However, in Chapter 13 Enrico Santarelli and Roberta Piergiovanni show that not only can the concepts of innovation, entrepreneurship, and human capital be used to sharpen our understanding of some crucial features of the productive system of a medium-technology country such as Italy, but they can also prove helpful in identifying areas that represent goals and intermediate objectives of industrial policies. The policy prescriptions put forward in this chapter point to the introduction of schemes which jointly promote innovation and entrepreneurship in order to bring about structural change and relocation from traditional consumer good industries to the most knowledge-intensive ones.

The contributors to this book are friends and co-authors of mine with whom I have carried out joint research and engaged in stimulating discussions over the last ten years. Some of them are members of the network that has grown up since 2004 within and around the Entrepreneurship, Growth and Public Policy Group at the Max Planck Institute of Economics in Jena, where David Audretsch has created a unique laboratory for the study of entrepreneurship and its interaction with economic growth and innovation. Needless to say, the climate of intellectual ferment at 'the Institute', as we call it, has proved greatly beneficial to the conception and production of this book.

Bologna, January 2006

REFERENCES

Acs, Z. J. and R. J. Phillips (2002), "Entrepreneurship and Philanthropy in American Capitalism", *Small Business Economics*, 19(3), 189-204.

Audretsch, D. B. and A. R. Thurik (2000), "Capitalism and Democracy in the 21st Century: From the Managed to the Entrepreneurial Economy", *Journal of Evolutionary Economics*, 10(1), 17-34.

Birch, D. (1979), *The Job Generation Process*, Cambridge (MA), MIT Programme on Neighborhood and Regional Change.

Chesher, A. (1979), "Testing the Law of Proportionate Effect", *Journal of Industrial Economics*, 27(4), 403-411.

Geroski, P. A. (1995), "What Do We Know about Entry?", *International Journal of Industrial Organization*, 13(4), 421-440.

Gibrat, R. (1931), *Les Inegalites Economiques*, Paris, Librairie du Recueil Sirey.

Krugman, P. (1991), *Geography and Trade,* Cambridge (MA), The MIT Press.

Lotti, F. and E. Santarelli (2004), "Industry Dynamics and the Distribution of Firm Sizes: A Nonparametric Approach", *Southern Economic Journal*, 70(3), 443-466.

Mansfield, E. (1962), "Entry, Gibrat's Law, Innovation, and the Growth of Firms", *American Economic Review*, 52(5), 1023-1051.

Porter, M. E. (2003) "The Economic Performance of Regions", *Regional Studies*, 37(6&7), 549-578.

Romer, P. (1990), "Endogenous Technological Change," *Journal of Political Economy,* 98(5, part 2), S71-S102.

Santarelli, E. and E. Pesciarelli (1990), "The Emergence of a Vision: The Development of Schumpeter's Theory of Entrepreneurship", *History of Political Economy*, 22(4), 677-696.

Schumpeter, J. A. (1908), *Das Wesen und Der Hauptinhalt der Theoretischen Nationalökonomie*, Leipzig, Duncker and Humblot.

Schumpeter, J. A. (1911), *Theorie der Wirtschaftlichen Entwicklung*, Leipzig, Duncker and Humblot.

Wennekers, S., A. van Stel, A. R. Thurik and P. D. Reynolds (2005), "Nascent Entrepreneurship and the Level of Economic Development", *Small Business Economics*, 24(3), 293-309.

Winter S. G., G. Dosi and Y. M. Kaniovski (2003), "A Baseline Model of Industry Evolution", *Journal of Evolutionary Economics*, 13(2), 355-383.

Chapter 1
A MARKET MODEL OF PERFECT COMPETITION UNDER UNCERTAINTY: HETEROGENEOUS FIRMS AND TECHNOLOGIES

Yuri M. Kaniovski
Free University of Bozen-Bolzano

1. INTRODUCTION

Uncertainty and risk are intrinsic to any entrepreneurial activity. Economic models account for them by involving randomness. In the case of industrial evolution, stochasticity becomes, in addition, the most suitable metaphor for capturing the 'mechanics' of this economic phenomenon. A brilliant explanation of its nature is given by Richard Nelson and Sidney Winter in the seminal book of 1982 on evolutionary economics. On p. 19. they wrote: "what the industry condition of a particular period really *determines* is the probability distribution of its condition in the following period. If we add the important proviso that the condition of the industry in periods prior to period t has no influence on the transition probabilities between t and $t+1$, we have assumed precisely that the variation over time of the industry's condition – or 'state' – is a Markov process."

Many of stochastic industrial dynamic models developed so far represent, in fact, Markov processes. For the corresponding examples see Jovanovic (1982), Hopenhayn (1992), Ericson and Pakes (1995), Bottazzi, Dosi and Rocchetti (2001), Winter, Dosi and Kaniovski (2000 and 2003). Nelson and Winter underline the methodological importance of Markov processes, comparing them, as a mathematical instrument, with calculus. "Just as some orthodox ideas seem to find their most natural mathematical expression in the calculus, the ... economic evolution seems to translate naturally into a description of a Markov process – though one in a rather complicated state space." See Nelson and Winter (1982), p. 19. In fact, even if a stochastic industrial dynamics was not originally presented as a Markov process, with a suitable choice of the state space, it may be turned into a

Markov process. See chapter 5 in Neveu (1965) for a mathematical theory of such transformations. Unfortunately, this modification, may render the dynamics to become too complicated for an analytical treatment or even for computer simulations. Thus, the minimal complexity of the corresponding state space is an important particular problem to address. In fact, given a list of conceptual questions concerning an industry and its evolution, one tends to use a model which would be the simplest possible for both, a mathematical analysis and numeric simulations.

The believe of some economists "that the appropriate time scale for a selection process increases with the size of organizations under consideration (which is another way of saying that mortality rates fall with size)", see Carroll and Hannan (2000) p. 313, justifies the focus here on the long-run properties, firms size distribution and entry rules. In particular, the paper seeks for new notions of long-run equilibria and technical means to analyze them.

The industry consists of firms having different capital and labour productivities. Further heterogeneity of the pool is due to a variety of boundedly rational entry rules and investment routines employed by the firms. The analysis concentrates on the structure of the corresponding equilibria in a modification of the stochastic industrial dynamics model suggested in Winter, Dosi and Kaniovski (2003). Like in many similar contemporaneous studies, see among others Jovanovic (1982), Hopenhayn (1992), Ericson and Pakes (1995), Luo (1995), Hashemi (2000), Bottazzi, Dosi and Rocchetti (2001), the equilibria turn out to be deterministic. Under natural assumptions concerning the model, the existence of a unique deterministic equilibrium is proved. Its structure is studied against variations of intensity of inflow of production capacity due to entry. Two extreme cases are considered: when the inflow vanishes and when it increases without bound.

Arguing about the main problems associated with reshaping the neoclassical theory of industrial organization, based on profit maximization, into an evolutionary theory, resting on a 'survivor principle', J. Sutton (1991) stresses "two things. First, it requires that firms earn non-negative profits at equilibrium. This is nonproblematic, for it is precisely this result that is generated either as an approximation, or in some appropriate limit, by any appeal to a survivor principle. The second element is more controversial: this requires that, should any profit opportunity exist, it will be exploited." See p. 320. This paper demonstrates that the model in Winter, Dosi and Kaniovski (2003) meets these requirements. First, it turns out that the most efficient firms may earn positive expected profits in the long run. They fall as the intensity of inflow of productive capacity due to entry rises. Whether the less efficient firms enjoy or not positive profits depends upon the parameters governing the industry evolution. However, these profits are not sufficient to offset the effect of depreciation. Thus, firms present at this equilibrium do not expand. In other words, the standard textbook treatment of perfect competition extends to a dynamic situation when depreciation of physical capital is taken into account explicitly. Second, at every time instant all profit opportunities available at this moment are exploited. Indeed, on the one hand, every incumbent produces exclusively when a positive profit may be earned, on the other hand, a new firm enters the industry only when a positive profit may be expected. Moreover, the incumbents are profit maximizers. In other words, the 'survival principle' employed in Winter, Dosi and Kaniovski (2003) rests on the neoclassical (orthodox) microfoundations.

Within the approach adopted in Sutton (1991), the equilibrium presented here may be used as a yardstick along with the standard settings by Cournot, Bertrand, etc.

2. BASIC ASSUMPTIONS CONCERNING ENTRY AND INVESTMENTS ROUTINES

The conventional textbook treatment of perfect competition, like, for example, in Carlton and Perloff (1999), will be the benchmark for the analysis given in this paper. To facilitate future analyses and comparisons, let us first formulate and discuss all main model hypotheses employed in Winter, Dosi and Kaniovski (2003). In some cases, possible modifications of these assumptions are also given.

PRODUCT, FIRMS, INDUSTRY AND MARKET. Our basic object is an industry producing a (single) homogeneous and perfectly divisible output. There is a continuous non-increasing inverse demand function, $p = h(q)$, such that $h(0) < \infty$ and $h(q) \to 0$ as $q \to \infty$. As usual, p stands for price and q for demand. Time is discrete, $t = 0,1,\dots$. At $t = 0$ there are no active (that is, ready to manufacture) firms, but a random number of firms are drawn from the pool of potential entrants. They may start manufacturing at $t = 1$. Their (initial) physical capitals are assigned randomly. As a particular case, the initial number of firms and their physical capitals may be set deterministically by the modeler. In this situation the evolution starts from a predetermined initial condition. For example, this may be the current state of the industry whose future development one wants to simulate. Set v for the price (identical for all firms) of physical capital. A generalization to the situation when this price differs across efficiency classes is straightforward.

Assuming a random number of entrants and assigning to them randomly initial capitals, the model takes the approach of the most empirical work in corporate demography – the so-called 'population-level analysis'. It "does not attempt to explain the origin of the organizational population. Instead, it addresses the variation in the flow of entries that follow the first appearance of the population (the first entry)." See p. 104 in Carroll and Hannan (2000), who explain also that "this choice reflects the difficulty of assigning a meaningful starting time of the process." But, unlike an empirical study that deals with a unique process, the actually observed one, a model, when it is run repeatedly, may produce several industry paths. They may give rise to 'what if' arguments in the spirit of the lock-in effects discussed in the literature on path dependence. See David (1985), Arthur, Ermoliev and Kaniovski (1987), Arthur (1989).

The market clears at every time instant $t \geq 1$. When the total productive capacity of the industry equals Q_t, the market clearing price is $p_t^* = h(Q_t)$. At the beginning of period t this value becomes known to all active firms constituting the industry as well as to potential entrants. The incumbents base their production decisions on this value. The potential entrants at t, if they are rational enough, may also rely their entry decisions on the instantaneous profit opportunities that are determined by p_t^*. In fact, having entered at t, it may start manufacturing at $t+1$. The corresponding output decision would be based on p_{t+1}^*. Unfortunately this value is not known at t. In boundedly rational deciding on whether production at $t+1$ will be profitable or not and, consequently, on entering or not at t, the value p_t^* may be used instead of p_{t+1}^* as a proxy. In sum, at every time instant both the production decisions and entry decisions depend upon the same information.

Note that Q_t is the total productive capacity of the industry at the beginning of period t. It may exceed the actual output of the industry at period t. This is the case when some active firms refrain from production because the revealed price p_t^* does not allow them to earn a positive profits. The actual output of the industry at time t becomes known at the end of this period, when all active firms have produced their outputs. (Those are positive or zero depending upon whether the firms manufacture or refrain from manufacturing.) Thus, although p_t^* represents the scenario with the lowest possible profit for everybody present in the industry, it may not be ruled out. At least, without introducing some kind of strategic behaviour or coordination among firms deciding on their outputs. Since perfect competition usually is understood as lack of such coordination, p_t^* has to be taken as the price determining the decisions of all participants of the market at time t.

At time $t \geq 1$ the industry consists of n_t active firms and new firms that enter at t and will be active from $t+1$ onward. Typically, the number n_t is defined endogenously as a result of the entry and exit processes, if the latter is foreseen by the model. Consequently, n_t is commonly a random value.

Consider active firms at time $t \geq 1$. Let they be indexed by i, $1 \leq i \leq n_t$. Each of them is characterized by two efficiency parameters: a capital ratio, $a^{(i)}$, and variable costs per unit of output, $m^{(i)}$. These values are assigned to a firm upon its entry and remain the same during its life time. There are $L \geq 1$ possibilities, $A_1 < A_2 < ... < A_L$, for the capital ratio and $J \geq 1$ available levels, $M_1 < M_2 < ... < M_J$, for variable costs in the industry. That is, a firm, whose capital ratio equals A_l, needs A_l units of physical capital produce a unit of output. In other words, the production function of firm i is
$$q^{(i)} = \frac{1}{a^{(i)}} K^{(i)},$$ where $q^{(i)}$ and $K^{(i)}$ are its output and physical capital correspondingly. A smaller capital ratio means more efficient use of physical capital, while a lower variable costs per unit output may correspond to a higher labour efficiency. Since price may not exceed $h(0)$, it is natural to assume that $M_J < h(0)$. Otherwise, a firm whose variable costs equal M_J, would never be able to earn a positive profit.

ENTRY PROCESS. There are $L \times J$ combinations, or efficiency classes, for capital and labour productivities: $(A_l; M_j)$, $l = 1,2,...,L$, $j = 1,2,...,J$. In the simplest case, for each of them only one firm enters the industry at every time instant $t \geq 0$. If no exit possibility is foreseen, this assumption leads to $n_t = LJt$.

The physical capitals of entrants are assigned randomly according to a distribution. It remains the same for all time instants. (Correspondingly, for all but $t = 0$ time instants, if the initial state of the industry is set deterministically by the modeler.) Denote by θ a random variable distributed over $[a,b]$, $0 < a < b < \infty$. Then $\theta_t^{l,j}$ stands for the realization of θ that would become, if the entry actually occurs, the initial physical capital of the entrant at t whose capital ratio is A_l and whose variable costs are M_j.

The random variables $\theta_t^{l,j}$ are statistically independent in all their indexes.

That is, a and b correspond to a single plant of the minimum efficient scale and to a single plant of the maximum possible size, respectively. Following the tradition in the neoclassical industrial organization literature, one may set $a = b$, but this would eliminate an important source of heterogeneity in the industry.

It is more realistic to assume that the distribution of initial physical capital depends upon the efficiency class. Then one may need $L \times J$ random variables $\theta^{l,j}$ distributed over corresponding intervals $[a^{l,j}, b^{l,j}]$,

$0 < a^{l,j} < b^{l,j} < \infty$ (or $a^{l,j} = b^{l,j}$, if the minimum and maximum sizes coincide for the efficiency class characterized by A_l and M_j).

In an attempt to match the real life situation, one may envisage a random number of entrants. Then, in the simplest case of at most one entrant at a time instant, for any combination $(A_l; M_j)$, there is a probability $p_{l,j}$ that a firm with these efficiency characteristics enters the industry. The probabilities do not depend on t. Varying the values of $p_{l,j}$, one may obtain a mixture of firms with different efficiency characteristics that mimics the dynamics of the real industry of interest. In particular, a relatively small probability corresponding to the firms with the smallest capital ratio and the smallest variable costs may reflect the empirically plausible situation when less efficient firms are more common than more efficient ones. Moreover, since the corresponding waiting time increases as $p_{l,j}$ decreases, the industry will originally consist of less efficient firms and then, as time goes on, better ones will appear.

To describe the event that a firm with the efficiency characteristics $(A_l; M_j)$ enters the industry at time instant t, consider Bernoulli random variables $i_t^{l,j}(p)$ that are statistically independent in all their indexes. The number $p \in [0,1]$ here is a numerical parameter, $P\{i_t^{l,j}(p) = 1\} = p$ and $P\{i_t^{l,j}(p) = 0\} = 1 - p$. Then $i_t^{l,j}(p) = 1$ if and only if a firm with the efficiency characteristics $(A_l; M_j)$ enters the industry at time t, while $i_t^{l,j}(p) = 0$ means that such firm does not enter at t. When $p_{l,j} = 1$, a firm with the corresponding efficiency characteristics enters the industry at every time instant. This particular situation differs from the one with deterministic entry process considered first, because the deterministic entry rule may apply to some, rather than to all, of the efficiency classes.

Even a more realistic picture obtains when at any time t the probabilities to enter depend upon the instantaneous profit margins. This possibility is sketched in Winter, Dosi and Kaniovski (2003) at pp. 363-364. In particular, one may define the above probabilities $p_{l,j}$ as $f_{l,j}(\max(p_t^* - M_j, 0))$. Here $f_{l,j}$ denotes a non-decreasing function, an *entry schedule*, such that $f_{l,j}(x) > 0$ when $x > 0$. Indeed, a potential entrant at t regards p_t^* as a proxy for the price at $t + 1$. Consequently, if the corresponding variable costs equal M_j, it would expect to earn $p_t^* - M_j$ of profit per unit of output during the first production cycle upon entry. The value $f_{l,j}(0)$ may have a straightforward conceptual interpretation. When $f_{l,j}(0) = 0$, the *agent does not enter the industry unless it anticipates a positive profit*. When $f_{l,j}(0) > 0$, entry may take place even if the given above boundedly rational expectation does not promise a positive profit. Since p_t^* may not exceed $h(0)$, one must require that $f_{l,j}(h(0) - M_j) \le 1$.

Potential entrants may be even more sophisticated and risk averse in their decisions. In particular, they may measure the anticipated profit against an *aspiration level*. See Kahneman and Tversky (1979). The latter may account, in particular, for the 'setup costs'. See a discussion concerning this term in Sutton (1991) on p. 8. In our case, at time t the outlays are given by $\theta_t^{l,j} v$. Indeed, since price per unit of physical capital is v, to start a business involving $\theta_t^{l,j}$ units of physical capital, one has to pay $\theta_t^{l,j} v$. To formalize this entry rule, fix non-negative numbers $c^{l,j}$. Then the corresponding firm enters or not at time t depending on whether its anticipated profit exceeds or not $c^{l,j}$ times the setup costs. This conceptual statement implies the following threshold

$$(p_t^* - M_j) \frac{\theta_t^{l,j}}{A_l} > c^{l,j} \theta_t^{l,j} v \text{ or } p_t^* - M_j - c^{l,j} v A_l > 0.$$

Consequently, the corresponding probability to enter at t becomes $f_{l,j}(\max[p_t^* - M_j - c^{l,j} v A_l, 0])$. Note that it depends only on the margins of the instantaneously anticipated profit. (Rather than on $\theta_t^{l,j}$.) When $c^{l,j} = 0$, this entry rule reduces to the previous one.

In a similar way, one may formalize a situation with multiple entrants for each of the efficiency classes. The corresponding maximum feasible numbers of entrants may vary across these classes. See Winter, Dosi and Kaniovski (2003) for details.

OUTPUT DECISION AND PROFIT OF AN ACTIVE FIRM. Because at every time instant price is given, the incumbents make their output decisions like price-takers. When the current price is p_t^*, solving the optimization problem $[p_t^* - m^{(i)}]q \to \max_{q \ge 0}$, a firm with variable costs $m^{(i)}$ either does not produce anything or produces at its maximum capacity available at the moment. This decision depends on whether $p_t^* \le m^{(i)}$ or $p_t^* > m^{(i)}$. In other words, it does not produce when no positive profit may be earned, or it manufactures at the full capacity, if it is profitable. Thus, *all incumbents, making their output decisions at a time instant, exploit all profit opportunities available at this moment.*

Set $q_t^{(i)}$ for the (maximum) productive capacity of firm i at the beginning of period t. Then the profit $\pi_t^{(i)}$ earned by this firm at time t reads $\pi_t^{(i)} = \max[p_t^* - m^{(i)}, 0] q_t^{(i)}$.

INVESTMENT DECISION AND EVOLUTION OF PRODUCTIVE CAPACITY OF AN INCUMBENT. The physical capital of an active firm depreciates regardless of whether it produces or not. Let us assume that the depreciation rate is the same for all firms and that this rate does not depend on whether they manufacture or not. In fact, let a unit of physical capital of any active firm at the beginning of a time period reduces to $1-d$ units by the end of this period. Here d, $d \in (0,1]$, denotes the depreciation rate. Like in the situation with the price for physical capital, a generalization to the situation when depreciation varies across efficiency classes is straightforward.

Consider an active firm i. If $q_t^{(i)}$ stands for its (maximum) productive capacity at the beginning of period t, the corresponding physical capital $K_t^{(i)}$ equals $a^{(i)}q_t^{(i)}$. By the end of this period, the physical capital depreciates to $K_t^{(i)}(1-d)$. To compensate this outflow of physical capital and, consequently, of productive capacity, the firm invests a share $\lambda^{(i)}$, $\lambda^{(i)} \in (0,1]$, of its profit in renewing the physical capital. Then the profit $\pi_t^{(i)}$ earned in period t, allows firm i to purchase $\dfrac{\lambda^{(i)}\pi_t^{(i)}}{v}$ units of physical capital. In sum, the physical capital of firm i at the end of period t reads $K_t^{(i)}(1-d)+\dfrac{\lambda^{(i)}\pi_t^{(i)}}{v}$. If no exit possibility foreseen in the industry, this value equals to $K_{t+1}^{(i)} = q_{t+1}^{(i)}a^{(i)}$, the physical capital of firm i at the beginning of period $t+1$. Consequently, the following balance equation $K_{t+1}^{(i)} = K_t^{(i)}(1-d)+\dfrac{\lambda^{(i)}\pi_t^{(i)}}{v}$ holds true. Since $K_t^{(i)} = q_t^{(i)}a^{(i)}$ for every time instant t when the firm is active, dividing both sides of the previous expression by $a^{(i)}$, one gets a balance equation for the corresponding (maximum) productive capacities

$$q_{t+1}^{(i)} = q_t^{(i)}(1-d)+\frac{\lambda^{(i)}\pi_t^{(i)}}{va^{(i)}} = q_t^{(i)}\left\{1-d+\frac{\lambda^{(i)}}{va^{(i)}}\max[p_t^* - m^{(i)},0]\right\}, \quad t \geq t_0^{(i)}. \quad (1)$$

Here $t_0^{(i)}$ stands for the time instant when the firm in question became active.

The remaining profit, $[1-\lambda^{(i)}]\pi_t^{(i)}$, may be used to pay shareholders' dividends, to pay back the setup costs if a loan was used, etc.

In the simplest case, $\lambda^{(i)}$ remains the same for all active firms and all time instants. That is, $\lambda^{(i)} = \lambda$, $i=1,2,...,n_t$, $t \geq 1$. However, it is more interesting to assume that the share of the gross profit which does not leak out as shareholders' dividends and the interest payments varies across efficiency classes. That is, let $\lambda^{(i)} = \lambda^{l,j}$, if A_l and M_j are the efficiency characteristics of the firm indexed by i. Even more realistic would be to relate this shares with the currently available profit margins. The corresponding *investment schedule* would be $\lambda^{l,j}(\max[p_t^* - M_j, 0])$, where $\lambda^{l,j}$ are non-decreasing functions taking values in $(0,1]$. Indeed, when the profit margin shrinks, the firm may not be able to sustain the same level of investment in physical capital as in a situation with a higher profit per unit of output.

With the assumptions done so far the simplest possible variant of stochastic industrial dynamics may be suggested. It describes the evolution of the total productive capacities of all firms belonging to an efficiency class. The fate of a given firm is not traced within this modelling approach. In particular, firms never exit this industry.

3. EVOLUTION OF EFFICIENCY CLASSES

At the highest level of aggregation, one may regard all firms belonging to an efficiency class as a single agent. Correspondingly, the productive capacity brought by entry may be interpreted as inflow of productive capacity to the corresponding efficiency class. Since the evolution of a particular firm is not traced, one does not need an exit rule.

Set $Q_t^{l,j}$ for the total productive capacity of all active firms whose productivity characteristics are A_l and M_j. Summing up the right hand sides of all equations (1) corresponding to an efficiency class, one gets

$$Q_t^{l,j}\{1 - d + \lambda^{l,j}(\max[p_t^* - M_j, 0])v^{-1}A_l^{-1}\max[p_t^* - M_j, 0]\}, \quad t \geq 0, \quad Q_0^{l,j} = 0.$$

Remark that some of $Q_0^{l,j}$ may be positive, if the initial state of the industry is set by the modeler. This particular situation is not considered next.

First of all, note that $Q_t = \sum_{l=1}^{L}\sum_{j=1}^{J}Q_t^{l,j}$ and $p_t^* = h(Q_t)$. Then the above equations become:

$$Q_t^{l,j}\{1 - d + \lambda^{l,j}\left(\max\left[h\left(\sum_{l=1}^{L}\sum_{j=1}^{J}Q_t^{l,j}\right) - M_j, 0\right]\right)v^{-1}A_l^{-1}\max\left[h\left(\sum_{l=1}^{L}\sum_{j=1}^{J}Q_t^{l,j}\right) - M_j, 0\right]\},$$
$$t \geq 0, \quad Q_0^{l,j} = 0.$$

These expressions give the total productive capacities at $t+1$ of firms that are active in the corresponding class at time t. To obtain the total productive capacities of all firms in this class at time $t+1$, one has to add the productive capacity of the corresponding entrants at t. Then the following recursion obtains:

$$Q_{t+1}^{l,j} = Q_t^{l,j} \left\{ 1 - d + \lambda^{l,j} \left(\max\left[h\left(\sum_{l=1}^{L} \sum_{j=1}^{J} Q_t^{l,j} \right) - M_j, 0 \right] \right) \right.$$
$$v^{-1} A_l^{-1} \max\left[h\left(\sum_{l=1}^{L} \sum_{j=1}^{J} Q_t^{l,j} \right) - M_j, 0 \right] \right\} +$$
$$+ i_t^{l,j} \left(f_{l,j} \left(\max\left[h\left(\sum_{l=1}^{L} \sum_{j=1}^{J} x^{l,j} \right) - M_j - c^{l,j} v A_l, 0 \right] \right) \right) \theta_t^{l,j}$$

$t \geq 0,\ Q_0^{l,j} = 0.$

In the $L \times J$ dimensional Euclidean space $\mathbf{R}^{L \times J}$, these relations define a Markov process with time homogeneous transition probabilities. In fact, when $Q_t^{l,j} = x^{l,j}$, $l = 1,2,...,L$, $j = 1,2,...J$, one has that:

$$Q_{t+1}^{l,j} = x^{l,j} \left\{ 1 - d + \lambda^{l,j} \left(\max\left[h\left(\sum_{l=1}^{L} \sum_{j=1}^{J} x^{l,j} \right) - \right. \right. \right.$$
$$- M_j, 0 \right]) v^{-1} A_l^{-1} \max\left[h\left(\sum_{l=1}^{L} J \sum_{j=1}^{J} x^{l,j} \right) - M_j, 0 \right] \right\} + \qquad (2)$$
$$+ i_t^{l,j} \left(f_{l,j} \left(\max\left[h\left(\sum_{l=1}^{L} \sum_{j=1}^{J} x^{l,j} \right) - M_j - c^{l,j} v A_l, 0 \right] \right) \right) \theta_t^{l,j},\ t \geq 0.$$

The right hand side is a sum of the deterministic function

$$x^{l,j} \left\{ 1 - d + \lambda^{l,j} \left(\max\left[\left(\sum_{l=1}^{L} \sum_{j=1}^{J} x^{l,j} \right) - \right. \right. \right.$$
$$- M_j, 0)] v^{-1} A_l^{-1} \max\left[h\left(\sum_{l=1}^{L} \sum_{j=1}^{J} x^{l,j} \right) - M_j, 0 \right] \right\}$$

and the random variable:

$$i_t^{l,j} \left(f_{l,j} \left(\max\left[h\left(\sum_{l=1}^{L} \sum_{j=1}^{J} x^{l,j} \right) - M_j - c^{l,j} v A_l, 0 \right] \right) \right) \theta_t^{l,j}$$

that does not depend upon the industry evolution prior time t.

STOCHASTIC DYNAMICS OF OUTPUTS. Instead of indexing the productivity classes by two numbers, a single index may be used. In fact, let us number first the total outputs of firms with the smallest capital ratio, starting from the smallest variable costs up to the largest ones. Then with the second smallest level of capital ratio, again from the smallest variable costs to the largest ones. The same principle applies up to the firms with the largest possible capital ratio and variable costs. Set $\vec{q}(t)$ for the $L \times J$ dimensional vector whose coordinates $q_s(t)$ are given by the following relations

$$q_s(t) = Q_t^{l,j} \text{ if } s = J(l-1) + j.$$

Then a vector counterpart of equations (2) reads

$$\vec{q}(t+1) = \vec{q}(t) + \vec{R}(\vec{q}(t)) + \vec{I}(t,\vec{q}(t)), \ t \ge 0, \ \vec{q}(0) = \vec{0}. \tag{3}$$

Here $\vec{0}$ stands for the $L \times J$ dimensional zero-vector. Also, $\vec{R}(\vec{q}(t))$ denotes a $L \times J$ dimensional deterministic vector-function and $\vec{I}(t,\vec{q}(t))$ stands for a $L \times J$ dimensional random vector. Their coordinates are defined by the following relations

$$R_s(\vec{y}) = W_s\left(\sum_{p=1}^{L \times J} y_p\right) y_s - dy_s \text{ with } W_s\left(\sum_{p=1}^{L \times J} y_p\right) =$$
$$= \lambda^{l,j}\left(\max\left[h\left(\sum_{p=1}^{L \times J} y_p\right) - M_j, 0\right]\right) v^{-1} A_l^{-1} \max\left[h\left(\sum_{p=1}^{L \times J} y_p\right) - M_j, 0\right],$$
$$I_s(t,\vec{y}) = i_t^{l,j}\left(f_{l,j}\left(\max\left[k\left(\sum_{p=1}^{L \times J} y_p\right) - M_j - c^{l,j} v A_l, 0\right]\right)\right) \theta_t^{l,j},$$

where $s = J(l-1) + j$. Here $\vec{y}$ stands for a $L \times J$ dimensional (deterministic) vector with non-negative coordinates, y_p.

In formal terms, relation (3) defines a *stochastic discrete time dynamics*. A standard way to grasp an idea of its asymptotic behaviour is to study a deterministic equivalent. This approach goes along with the so-called *averaging method* traditionally used in applied studies of nonlinear systems. The most recent areas of research involve mathematical biology and economics. For example, Aghion and Howitt (1992) used this approach analyzing economic growth, while Lux (1995) applied it studying dynamics of a population of financial speculators.

DETERMINISTIC COUNTERPART AND ITS ANALYSIS. Set $\vec{r}(\vec{y})$ for $E\vec{I}(t,\vec{y})$. Note that

$$r_s(y) = V_s\left(\sum_{p=1}^{L \times J} y_p\right) = f_{l,j}\left(\max\left[h\left(\sum_{p=1}^{L \times J} y_p\right) - M_j - c^{l,j} v A_l, 0\right]\right) E\theta^{l,j},$$

where $s = J(l-1) + j$. The dynamics:

$$\vec{x}(t+1) = \vec{x}(t) + \vec{R}\vec{x}(t) + \vec{r}(\vec{x}(t)), \ \vec{x}(0) = \vec{0} \tag{4}$$

may be regarded as a *deterministic counterpart* of the stochastic dynamical system (3).

Let us characterize singleton stationary (or rest) points of this deterministic dynamics. A stationary point $\overset{\rightarrow\bullet}{x} = (x_1^{\bullet}, x_2^{\bullet}, ..., x_{L\times J}^{\bullet})$ must satisfy the equations $R_s\left(\overset{\rightarrow\bullet}{x}\right) + r_s\left(\overset{\rightarrow\bullet}{x}\right) = 0$ or

$$\left[d - W_s\left(\sum_{p=1}^{L\times J} x_p^{\bullet}\right)\right] x_s^{\bullet} = V_s\left(\sum_{p=1}^{L\times J} x_p^{\bullet}\right), \tag{5}$$

where $s = 1, 2, ..., L \times J$. Conceptually, the coordinates of $\overset{\rightarrow\bullet}{x}$ are outputs. Consequently, they must be non-negative. That is, $x_p^{\bullet} \geq 0$ for all p. Since V_s are non-negative functions, relations (5) imply that:

1) $x_s^{\bullet} > 0$ for some s, then either $V_s\left(\sum_{p=1}^{L\times J} x_p^{\bullet}\right) > 0$, and $d > W_s\left(\sum_{p=1}^{L\times J} x_p^{\bullet}\right)$ or $V_s\left(\sum_{p=1}^{L\times J} x_p^{\bullet}\right) = 0$ and $W_s\left(\sum_{p=1}^{L\times J} x_p^{\bullet}\right) = d$;

2) if $x_s^{\bullet} = 0$ for an index s, then $V_s\left(\sum_{p=1}^{L\times J} x_p^{\bullet}\right) = 0$.

One may interpret $\overset{\rightarrow\bullet}{x}$ as a *long-run equilibrium* of the industrial dynamics in question. Indeed, once $\vec{x}(t) = \overset{\rightarrow\bullet}{x}$ for some time instant t, one sees by (4) that $\vec{x}(t') = \overset{\rightarrow\bullet}{x}$ for all $t' > t$. Given some dynamic stability property of the equilibrium, one may expect that $\vec{x}(t')$ will be near $\overset{\rightarrow\bullet}{x}$ for all $t' > t$, if $\vec{x}(t)$ is close enough to $\overset{\rightarrow\bullet}{x}$. This behavior may be inherited by the stochastic dynamics defined by (3). Indeed, lowering the maximal possible physical capital, $\max_{l=1,2,...,L; j=1,2,...,J} b^{l,j}$, of entrants, the pure noise term, $\vec{I}(t, \vec{y}) - \vec{r}(\vec{y})$, may be made arbitrarily small. Then, regarding (3) as a perturbation of (4), one may expect these dynamics to have similar asymptotic behaviors.

When $x_s^{\bullet} = 0$, the corresponding efficiency class vanishes at the equilibrium. If $x_s^{\bullet} > 0$, the respective efficiency class is represented at the equilibrium. The productive capacity of every active firm present at the equilibrium declines when $W_s\left(\sum_{p=1}^{L\times J} x_p^{\bullet}\right) < d$. In fact, its investment schedule for substituting the outflow of physical capital turns out to be insufficient even to maintain a constant output level. However, unlike in a textbook treatment of perfect competition, these firms may earn positive profits. However, the profits are not sufficient to compensate the depreciation and, consequently, the firms decline. This effect is due to the dynamic nature of the model. At the level of a whole efficiency class, the decline of every active firm is compensated by the entrants. As a result, the total productive capacity of the class remains constant. The inflow persists because the probability to enter, $f_{l,j}\left(\max\left[h\left(\sum_{p=1}^{L\times J}x_p^*\right)-M_j-c^{l,j}vA_l,0\right]\right)$, remains positive for this class at the equilibrium. Indeed, $V_s\left(\sum_{p=1}^{L\times J}x_p^*\right)>0$, by positiveness of the corresponding $E\theta^{l,j}$, implies that $f_{l,j}\left(\max\left[h\left(\sum_{p=1}^{L\times J}x_p^*\right)-M_j-c^{l,j}vA_l,0\right]\right)>0$. Moreover, when $f_{l,j}(x)>0$ if and only if $x>0$, the anticipated profit is positive. In fact, a potential entrant to this class regards it as high enough, with respect to 'setup costs', to start a business. When $W_s\left(\sum_{p=1}^{L\times J}x_p^*\right)=d$, the productive capacity of every active firm remains constant at the equilibrium. They earn positive profits which, given the corresponding investment schedule, turn out to be sufficient just to compensate the outflow of physical capital due to depreciation. This situation is sustained because $V_s\left(\sum_{p=1}^{L\times J}x_p^*\right)=0$ and, consequently, there is no inflow of productive capacity in this class at the equilibrium. In other words, a potential entrant to this class regards the anticipated profit as insufficiently high, with respect to 'setup costs', to start a business.

The above analysis holds true as long as not all V_s identically equal zero. Indeed, with no firm ever entering the industry, the dynamic system (4) will be forever at its (conceptually trivial) singleton equilibrium $\vec{0}$.

Unfortunately, the study based on the analysis of a deterministic counterpart captures only some basic long-run balance relations, ignoring many important peculiarities of the stochastic industrial dynamics. Here are two examples of them.

First, even if no entry takes place for an efficiency class with $W_s\left(\sum_{p=1}^{L\times J}x_p^*\right)=d$ at the equilibrium, arguing about its positive total output, one has to be sure that there is at least one active firm delivering this quantity. The argument given above does not guarantee that such a firm exists. However, this situation does not seem to represent a conceptual problem. In fact, if an efficiency class is empty, why should it be considered?

Second, in spite of the general tendency to decline, there may be periods of time when active firms grow. In particular, when no entry takes place. Such situations may not be captured by the concept of a deterministic long-run equilibrium described above.

When the total equilibrium output, X^*, of the industry is known, the characterization of a singleton equilibrium given above imply that the total outputs, x_p^*, of efficiency classes present at the equilibrium read

$$x_s^* = V(X^*)/[d - W_s(X^*)] \text{ when both}$$
$$V_s(X^*) > 0 \text{ and } W_s(X^*) < d, \tag{6}$$

or

$$x_q^* = X^* - \sum_{s;V_s(X^*)>0} x_s^* \text{ when both}$$
$$V_s(X^*) = 0 \text{ and } W_q(X^*) = q. \tag{7}$$

Note that the inequality $d < W_s(X^*)$ is not possible at the equilibrium. Indeed, it would imply that every active firm from the corresponding efficiency class keeps growing. (Because it purchases more new physical capital than it loses due to depreciation.)

4. EXISTENCE OF AN INDUSTRY EQUILIBRIUM AND ITS CHARACTERIZATION

To identify the total equilibrium supply of the industry, consider the function

$$F(X) = X - \sum_{s=1}^{L \times J} V_s(X)/[d - W_s(X)].$$

Let us assume that all $\lambda^{i,j}$ and $f_{i,j}$ are continuous functions. Then all W_s and V_s are continuous functions as well. Set

$$\overline{Q}_s = \begin{cases} \max X \geq 0 & : W_s(X) = d, \quad \text{when } W_s(0) \geq d; \\ 0 & \text{if } W_s(0) < d. \end{cases}$$

Assume that $\overline{Q} > 0$, where $\overline{Q} = \max_{s=1,2,...,L \times J} \overline{Q}_s$. This condition means that there is a possibility for a firm to sustain its initial size, rather that to start declining immediately upon entry.

The function F is defined for $X > \overline{Q}$. Note that all W_s and V_s are non-increasing functions due to the earlier assumptions concerning monotonicity of $\lambda^{i,j}, f_{i,j}$ and h. Since $d < W_s(X)$ for all s when $X > \overline{Q}$, one concludes that every addend $V_s(X)/[d-W_s(X)]$ is a non-increasing continuous function in this domain. Then F is an increasing continuous function for $X > \overline{Q}$. Indeed, F is a sum of a linear increasing function and $L \times J$ non-decreasing functions.

Let us analyze the behavior of F when the argument approaches $\overline{Q}$ from the right. There are two possibilities:

1) $F(X) < 0$ for some $X > \overline{Q}$;
2) $F(X) > 0$ for all $X > \overline{Q}$.

Note that $F(X) = 0$ would imply, by monotonicity of F, that $F(X') < 0$ for some X', $\overline{Q} < X' < X$. Hence, the above two cases represent all possibilities.

Consider the second case. Since F is bounded from below and increases, $F(X)$ has a limit as $X \downarrow \overline{Q}$. Denote this limit by A. Then $A \geq 0$ and one may set, by continuity, $F(\overline{Q}) = A$.

In the *first case*, by the Intermediate Value Theorem, there exists a root, $X^* > \overline{Q}$, of F. It is unique, because F is an increasing function in this domain. At this equilibrium, the productive capacity of every active firm shrinks, but the inflow of new firms offsets this decline. The efficiency class corresponding to an index s is represented at the equilibrium if and only if $V_s(X^*) > 0$. Its total long-run output equals $V_s(X^*)/[d - W_s(X^*)]$.

In the *second case*, $V_s(\overline{Q}) = 0$ $\overline{Q}_s = \overline{Q}$ for every s for which $\overline{Q}_s = \overline{Q}$. Indeed, if for some s' one had $V_{s'}(\overline{Q}) > 0$ and $\overline{Q}_{s'} = \overline{Q}$, then

$$V_{s'}(X)/[d - W_{s'}(X)] \uparrow \infty \text{ as } X \downarrow \overline{Q}.$$

Hence, F would become negative for an $X' > \overline{Q}$. But this is the case already considered. Since V_s is a non-increasing function, $V_s(\overline{Q}) = 0$ implies that $V_s(X) = 0$ for all $X > \overline{Q}$. Consequently, when $X > \overline{Q}$, the formula for F does not contain terms corresponding to indexes s for which $W_s(\overline{Q}) = d$. In sum, F turns out to be a right continuous function at $\overline{Q}$ with $F(\overline{Q}) = A$. This equilibrium may contain two types of active firms: those that keep declining and those whose productive capacities remain constant. The total productive capacities of an efficiency class s containing firms of the first type reads $V_s(\overline{Q})/[d - W_s(\overline{Q})]$ with $V_s(\overline{Q}) > 0$. The total productive capacity of the efficiency class with firms of the second type is

$$\overline{Q} - \sum_{s;V_s(\overline{Q})>0} V_s(\overline{Q})/[d - W_s(\overline{Q})].$$

(Remember that this value is $F(\overline{Q}) \geq 0$.)

Let us summarize the argument and findings given above as a statement.

Proposition. *Assume that the inverse demand function h and all functions* $\lambda^{l,j}$ *and* $f_{l,j}$ *are continuous and non-decreasing. Set*

$$\overline{Q}_s = \begin{cases} \max X \geq 0 & : W_s(X) = d, \quad \text{when } W_s(0) \geq d; \\ 0 & \text{if } W_s(0) < d. \end{cases}$$

Let $\overline{Q} > 0$, *where* $\overline{Q} = \max_{s=1,2,\dots,L\times J} \overline{Q}_s$. *Then there is a singleton rest point of dynamics* (4). *All its coordinates are non-negative. The structure of the corresponding long-run equilibrium of the industry depend upon the behavior of the function* $F(X) = X - \sum_{s=1}^{L\times J} V_s(X)/[d - W_s(X)]$, *when* X *approaches* $\overline{Q}$ *from the right. There are two possibilities:* $F(X) < 0$ *for some* $X > \overline{Q}$ *or* $\lim_{X \downarrow \overline{Q}} F(X) = A \geq 0$.

In the first case, the total output of the industry, X^*, *obtains as a unique root of F belonging to* $(\overline{Q}, \infty)$. *Productive capacities of all active firms present at this equilibrium decline. The efficiency class corresponding to an index s is present at the equilibrium or not depending on whether its probability to enter is positive or not at* X^*. *If it is present, the respective long-run output equals* $V_s(X^*)/[d - W_s(X^*)]$. *Thus, the constancy of productive capacity in this class is maintained by entry of new firms. In the* second case, *the total equilibrium output of the industry is* $\overline{Q}$. *Two types of firms may be present at this equilibrium: with declining outputs and with outputs remaining constant. An efficiency class with declining firms is represented at the equilibrium if and only if the corresponding probability to enter is positive at* $\overline{Q}$. *Then its long-run output equals* $V_s(\overline{Q})/[d - W_s(\overline{Q})]$, *where s denotes the corresponding index. The balance of productive capacity in such class is maintained by persistent entry of new firms. When* $A > 0$, *the equilibrium structure contains firms whose productive capacities remain constant. (Given that in the course of industrial evolution at least one*

of them entered to the industry.) Their total output equals
$\overline{Q} - \sum_{s;V_s(Q)>0} V_s(\overline{Q})/[d - W_s(\overline{Q})]$. *There is no inflow of such firms at the equilibrium.*

A natural question is how an equilibrium with the above two types of firms may sustain. Indeed, any influx of productive capacity of 'shrinking firm' would lead to a decline of the output of every 'non-shrinking' firm, if the influx moves the total supply of the industry above $\overline{Q}$. By the Borel - Cantelli lemma, see, for example, Doob (1953), p. 104, positiveness of the probability to enter when the total industry output is $\overline{Q}$, would imply with certainty infinitely many of such influxes. Thus, given that no entry of 'non-shrinking' firms is possible at the levels of total supply $\overline{Q}$ and more, such firms would have died out with probability one. The only plausible explanation of why this extinction does not take place would be the following. Such increase of the total supply above $\overline{Q}$ causes a decline of the probability to enter of 'shrinking' firms. As a consequence, the total supply of the industry reduces to a level where the probability to enter for a 'non-shrinking' firm becomes positive. Then a 'non-shrinking' firms enters the industry and the process recurs.

In sum, an equilibrium with the above two types of firms is dynamic and stochastic in its nature, as well as an equilibrium where every firm decline. The former may take place only when the probability to enter for 'non-shrinking' firms is positive at levels of total supply below $\overline{Q}$. (This is exactly what constitutes a fundamental distinction of the stochastic industrial dynamics in question from deterministic ones.) With certainty, such levels are attained infinitely many times in the course of industrial evolution.

A useful insight in the nature of this equilibrium obtains by the sensitivity analysis given next.

LONG-RUN EQUILIBRIUM STRUCTURES FOR DIFFERENT INTENSITIES OF INFLOW OF PRODUCTIVE CAPACITY. Let us assume that $b^{l,j} = \overline{b}^{l,j}\kappa$ and $a^{l,j} = \overline{a}^{l,j}\kappa$ for a scaling parameter $\kappa > 0$. Then the expected value of the stochastic term in (3) changes according to the formulae $r_s^\kappa(\vec{y}) = r_s(\vec{y})\kappa$, $s = 1,2,...,L \times J$. When κ is large, one deals with an intensive inflow of physical capital due to entry of new firms. Indeed, given that all other parameters of the model are fixed, every time instant the total productive capacity ($\equiv$physical capital) of newcomers in this case is larger than in the basic situation with $\kappa = 1$. When κ is small, there is a weaker inflow of new productive capacity than in the basic case. In the limit situation of κ approaching 0, one may expect a picture similar to an industry without entry.

The function that defines the structure of the equilibrium now reads

$$F_\kappa(X) = X - \kappa \sum_{s=1}^{L \times J} V_s(X)/[d - W_s(X)], X > \overline{Q}.$$

Observe that $F_\kappa(X) \le F_{\kappa'}(X)$ if $\kappa' < \kappa$. This inequality is strict as long as $V_s(X)/[d - W_s(X)]$ is positive for at least one s. Denoting by X_κ^* the corresponding long-run total industry output, one sees that, as $\kappa \downarrow 0$,

1) $X_\kappa^* \downarrow \overline{Q}$ when $X_\kappa^* > \overline{Q}$, moreover, since the total output of every efficiency class s, for which $W_s(\overline{Q}) < d$, vanishes, the total supply of the efficiency class, where $W_s(\overline{Q}) = d$, approaches $\overline{Q}$;

2) the total production of firms, that do not shrink at the equilibrium, increases approaching $\overline{Q}$, if $X_\kappa^* = \overline{Q}$.

In sum, if the inflow of new firms vanishes uniformly for all efficiency classes, the long-run equilibrium structure becomes, in fact, like for a deterministic industrial dynamics (that is, without entry), where the industry supply is produced by the most efficient class.

Note that $X_\kappa^* > \overline{Q}$ for all sufficiently small $\kappa > 0$ implies that the most efficient firms are present at the corresponding equilibria. Moreover, one can prove that $V_s(\overline{Q}) > 0$, where s denotes the index of the most efficient firms. Then, by continuity of V_s, $V_s(X) > 0$ for all X sufficiently close to $\overline{Q}, X > \overline{Q}$. In particular, $V_s(X_\kappa^*) > 0$. In other words, the most efficient firms keep entering at this equilibrium. Indeed, the contrary, $V_s(\overline{Q}) = 0$, would imply, by monotonicity of the function V_s, that $V_s(X) = 0$ for $X \ge \overline{Q}$. Then the part of F_κ, that depend on κ, would vanish as $\kappa \downarrow 0$. Hence, when $X > \overline{Q}$, the inequality $F_\kappa(X) < 0$ would become impossible for all sufficiently small κ. Consequently, the corresponding equilibrium, X_κ^*, would cease to exist.

Remark that the notion 'most efficient' here refers to the technological factors, as captured by the corresponding capital ratio and variable costs, as well as to the managerial ones, represented by the respective investment schedules.

If $\kappa \to \infty$, that is, when the inflow of productive capacity may increase without bound, the analysis is complicated by the fact that V_s, being non-increasing functions, may become zero for large enough levels of total supply. However, if for an efficiency class the probability to enter remains positive for arbitrarily high levels of industry output, the total equilibrium supply increases without bound. This situation does not look plausible conceptually. In particular, the supply may grow so big that, given the output decision adopted by the model, no firm will produce at this equilibrium.

DYNAMIC STABILITY OF THE EQUILIBRIUM. Considering the differential

equation $\dfrac{d}{dt}\vec{y}(t) = \vec{R}(\vec{y}(t)) + \vec{r}(\vec{y}(t))$, $\vec{y}(0) = \vec{0}$ one obtains a *continuous*

time deterministic counterpart of (3). It has the same rest-points as (4). Using the stability theory for time-homogeneous ordinary differential equations, one may characterize the dynamic stability properties of a rest point and, consequently, of the corresponding long-run equilibrium of the industry. Applying the criterion of stability of a real matrix given in Marcus and Minc (1964) on p. 160, one can prove that, when the all functions involved are differentiable, the rest point is locally asymptotically stable for all sufficiently large κ. On the other hand, when $\kappa = 0$, the rest point attracts all trajectories corresponding to an initial industry structure with at least one most efficient firm. Indeed, $\kappa = 0$ implies a deterministic dynamics without entry. Thus, to argue about an equilibrium output delivered by the most efficient firms, one has to be sure that at least one of them is present initially in the industry. Intermediate values of κ may imply dynamics local asymptotic stability as well as its lack.

5. CONCLUSIONS

A comparative static analysis of the obtained above equilibrium may reveal the effect of each of the numerical parameters of the model on the long-run structure of the industry. Equivalently, the equilibrium may be represented and studied in market shares of the corresponding efficiency classes, rather than in total supplies like above. Unfortunately, this deterministic equilibrium has come to exist as a result of substitution the original stochastic industrial dynamics by a deterministic equivalent. This approach may look like a satisfactory, for an applied study, approximation to the reality, but the problem of a more rigorous analysis of the long-run behavior of the stochastic industrial dynamics defined by (3) remains open. Like in Winter, Dosi and Kaniovski (2003), it should be based on the *ergodic properties* of the industry. A key step in studying of the asymptotic behavior of a time homogeneous Markov process is to establish the existence of an *invariant probability measure*. The corresponding argument may be based on the stability results for time homogeneous Markov processes with discrete time given in Meyn and Tweedie (1993). But in this case no close form expression for the equilibrium may be found.

In sum, the approach suggested here seems to be useful for studying the stochastic model of perfect competition introduced in Winter, Dosi and Kaniovski (2003) by means of the traditional static equilibrium analysis.

REFERENCES

Aghion P. and P. Howitt (1992), "A Model of Growth Through Creative Destruction", *Econometrica*, 60(2), 323-351.

Arthur W. B. (1989), "Competing Technologies, Increasing Returns, and Lock-In by Historical Events", *Economic Journal*, 99(394), 116-131.

Arthur W. B., Y. M. Ermoliev and Y. M. Kaniovski (1987), "Path-dependent Processes and the Emergence of Macro-Structure", *European Journal of Operational Research*, 30(3), 294-303.

Bottazzi G., G. Dosi and G. Rocchetti (2001), "Models of Knowledge Accumulation, Entry Regimes and Patterns of Industrial Evolution", *Industrial and Corporate Change*, 10(3), 609-638.

Carlton D. W. and J. M. Perloff (1999), *Modern Industrial Organization*, 3rd ed., Reading, Addison-Wesley.

Carroll, G. R. and M. T. Hannan (2000), *The Demography of Corporations and Industries*, Princeton (NJ), Princeton University Press.

David, P. (1985), "Clio and the Econometrics of QWERTY", *American Economic Review*, 75(2), 332-337.

Doob, J. L. (1953), *Stochastic Processes*, New York, Chapman & Hall.

Ericson, R. and A. Pakes (1995), "Markov-Perfect Industry Dynamics: A Framework for Empirical Work", *Review of Economic Studies*, 62(1), 53-82.

Hashemi F. (2000), "An Evolutionary Model of the Size Distribution of Firms", *Journal of Evolutionary Economics*, 10(5), 507-521.

Hopenhayn, H. A. (1982), "Entry, Exit and Firm Dynamics in Long Run Equilibrium", *Econometrica*, 60(5), 1127-1150.

Jovanovic, B. (1982), "Selection and Evolution of Industry", *Econometrica*, 50(3), 649-670.

Kahneman, D. and A. Tversky (1979), "Prospect Theory: An Analysis of Decision under Risk", *Econometrica*, 47(2), 263-291.

Luo, G. Y. (1995), "Evolution and Market Competition", *Journal of Economic Theory*, 67(1), 223-250.

Lux, T. (1995) "Herd Behavior, Bubbles and Crashes", *Economic Journal*, 105(431), 881-896.

Marcus, M. and M. Minc (1964), *A Survey of Matrix Theory and Matrix Inequalities*, Boston, Allyn and Bacon.

Meyn, S. P. and R. L. Tweedie (1993), *Markov Chains and Stochastic Stability*, Berlin, Springer-Verlag.

Neveu, J. (1965), *Mathematical Foundations of the Calculus of Probability*, San Francisco, Holden-Day.

Nelson, R. R. and S. G. Winter (1982), *An Evolutionary Theory of Economic Change*, Cambridge (MA), The Belknap Press of Harvard University Press.

Sutton, J. (1991), *Sunk Costs and Market Structure (Price Competition, Advertising, and the Evolution of Concentration)*, Cambridge (MA), The MIT Press.

Winter, S. G., G. Dosi and Y. M. Kaniovski (2000), "Modelling Industrial Dynamics with Innovative Entrants", *Structural Change and Economic Dynamics*, 11(3), 255-293.

Winter, S. G., G. Dosi and Y. M. Kaniovski (2003), "A Baseline Model of Industry Evolution", *Journal of Evolutionary Economics*, 13(4), 355-383.

Chapter 2
INDUSTRY DYNAMICS *Á LA* STACKELBERG WITH STOCHASTIC CAPITAL ACCUMULATION

Luca Lambertini
University of Bologna

1. INTRODUCTION

Firms' entry and growth in an industry have attracted a great deal of attention within both industrial and applied economics for several decades. Ever since Gibrat's seminal contribution (Gibrat, 1931), the established wisdom has maintained that expected firm growth rates are independent of firm size, a property known as *Gibrat's Law*. Both theoretical and empirical research have been extensively carried out along this line.[1] So far, the existing literature provides heterogeneous answers to the question as the way we shall expect market dynamics to unravel, given some degree of initial asymmetry among firms.

Two relevant contributions by Lucas and Prescott (1971) and Lucas (1978) investigate entry and exit decisions in long-run competitive equilibrium models where prices, outputs and investments are driven by stochastic processes. In a pioneering paper, Jovanovic (1982) proposes a theory of noisy selection where firms enter over time and learn about their productive efficiency as they operate in the market. Those that are relatively more efficient grow and survive, while those who relatively less efficient decline and ultimately exit the industry. Hopenhayn (1992) analyzes the case of individual productivity shocks and their effects on entry, exit and market dynamics in the long-run. He finds that the steady state equilibrium implies a size distribution of firms by age cohorts, and proves that the size distribution is stochastically increasing in the age of the cohorts. Jovanovic's model is extended by Ericson and Pakes (1995) who consider two models of firm behaviour, allowing for heterogeneity among firms, idiosyncratic (or firm-specific) sources of uncertainty, and discrete outcomes (exit and/or entry).[2]

Broadly speaking, an overview of this literature leads one to think that 'older firms are bigger than younger firms'. An important question to this regard is the following: is moving first a prerequisite (i.e., a necessary condition) for a firm to become larger than its rivals, or is it a sufficient condition?

Here I propose a dynamic oligopoly model under uncertainty generalising some of the aspects treated in Lambertini (2005). Firms enter simultaneously and then compete hierarchically à la Stackelberg, at each instant over an infinite horizon. They accumulate capacity through costly investment, as in Solow's (1956) and Swan's (1956) growth model. At every instant, first the investment levels are chosen, then shocks realize and finally productive capacities are determined as a function of the shocks. Due to the formal properties of the model, the game possesses a unique and time consistent open-loop equilibrium.

The main results are as follows. The relative performance of firms depends on several factors, including the relative size of shocks as well as the relative number of leaders and followers. In particular, if investment costs are negligible, or the variance of the shock affecting the leaders is low, or again firms are subject to a common shock, then the expected profits of the representative leader exceed those of the representative follower. These results tend to confirm the acquired wisdom according to which leading entails a 'first mover advantage', when choice variables directly pertain to the size of the firm, as it also happens in static Cournot games (see Dowrick, 1986; Hamilton and Slutsky, 1990, *inter alia*). More interestingly, the opposite result is also admissible, namely, that the followers may ultimately overtake the leaders in the steady state (this can happen, for instance, when shocks are idiosyncratic, or when the variance of the shock affecting the leader is sufficiently large).

The model investigated in the present paper allows me to propose a few considerations as to the debate concerning the intertemporal growth of firms. First, the Stackelberg model described here shows that an industry equilibrium that is characterized by an uneven size distribution of firms may not necessarily be the outcome of the entry process, but may be rather the consequence of (*i*) a strategic advantage of some firms over the others, or (*ii*) an asymmetric distribution of shocks across firms that are otherwise fully symmetric and have played simultaneously along the entire history of the industry. Second, whether leaders grows more or less than followers is independent of initial conditions, which may or may not differ across firms. Consequently, in general, the present analysis does not confirm *Gibrat's Law*, since sequential play induces an asymmetry in growth rates for any admissible distribution of initial capacities across firms. Likewise, the indications provided by the Nash game are in contrast with *Gibrat's Law*, as the expected equilibrium size and performance of firms are symmetric irrespective of initial conditions, so that any asymmetric vector of initial capacities involves asymmetric growth rates in order to reach a symmetric steady state allocation (in expected value).

The remainder of the paper is structured as follows. Section 2 presents the general features of the model. The open-loop Stackelberg equilibrium is derived in section 3, while section 4 contains some comparative statics. Concluding remarks are in section 4.

2. THE SETUP

N firms operate over continuous time $t \in [0,\infty)$ in a market for differentiated goods, the demand function for variety v at any t being:

$$p_v(t) = a - q_v(t) - s\sum_{z \neq v} q_z(t),\qquad (1)$$

where $s \in [0,1]$ is the constant degree of substitutability between any two varieties. If $s = 0$ then each firm is a monopolist in a separate market, while on the contrary if $s = 1$ then firms supply homogeneous goods.

The game unravels following a sequential play framework. Out of the population of N firms, $f \equiv \{1,2,3,...F\}$ of them are followers while $l \equiv \{F+1, F+2, F+3,...N\}$ of them are leaders, with $F \geq 1$ and $N \geq F+1$. Each firm keeps playing the same role over the whole horizon of the game.

In order to supply the final good, firms must build up capacity (i.e., physical capital) $k_v(t)$ through intertemporal investment:

$$\frac{dk_v(t)}{dt} \equiv k_v = I_v(t) - \delta k_v(t) + \varepsilon_v(t), \quad v = 1,2,3,...,F, F+1,...,N,\qquad (2)$$

where $\delta \in [0,1]$ is the depreciation rate, constant and equal across firms; $\varepsilon_v(t)$ is the shock affecting firm v, and it is assumed to be i.i.d. across periods. Furthermore, for the sake of simplicity I will assume throughout the paper that

$$\varepsilon_v(t) = \varepsilon_F(t) \qquad \forall \ v = 1,2,3,...,F\qquad (3)$$

$$\varepsilon_v(t) = \varepsilon_L(t) \qquad \forall \ v = F+1, F+2, F+3,...,N\qquad (4)$$

$$E(\varepsilon_i) = 0; \quad E(\varepsilon_i^2) = \sigma_i^2, \quad i = F, L$$
$$\text{and } E(\varepsilon_F \varepsilon_L) = E(\varepsilon_L \varepsilon_F)\sigma_{FL}^2.$$

At any instant t, the sequence of events is taken to be as follows:
• firms sequentially choose investment efforts $I_v(t)$, then
• shocks realize, and finally
• the interaction between investments, depreciation and the firm-specific shock determines capacity through (2) and the dynamics of control, $dI_v(t)/dt$, for each firm.[3]

For the sake of simplicity, in the remainder I assume that $q_v(t) = k_v(t)$, i.e., all firms operate at full capacity at any instant. At any t, firm v bears the following total costs:

$$C_v(t) = b[I_v(t)]^2, \quad b \geq 0, \tag{5}$$

where marginal production cost is constant and normalised to zero in order to shrink to a minimum the set of parameters. The instantaneous profit of firm v is:

$$\pi_v(t) = p(t) - b[I_v(t)]^2. \tag{6}$$

For each firm v, the instantaneous investment effort $I_v(t)$ is the control variable, while capacity $k_v(t)$ is the state variable. The value of the state variables at $t = 0$ is given by the vector $k(0) = k_0$. The aim of firm v consists in:

$$\max_{I_v(t)} J_v \equiv \int_0^\infty \pi_{vv}(t) e^{-\rho t} dt \tag{7}$$

subject to the relevant dynamic constraints. The factor $e^{-\rho t}$ discounts future gains, and the discount rate $\rho > 0$ is assumed to be constant and common to all players. In order to solve the optimization problem, each firm defines a strategy $I_v(t)$ at each t, for any admissible $I_j(t)$, $j \neq v$. If, when choosing $I_v(t)$, firm v explicitly takes into account the stock of state variables $k(t)$ at time t (or their evolution up to that time), the game is solved in closed-loop strategies. Otherwise, if controls are chosen only upon calendar time, the game is solved in open-loop strategies. On the one hand, a closed-loop solution is clearly preferable in that it accounts for feedback effects at all times during the game; however, on the other hand, it is worth stressing that the choice of the solution concept may be taken depending upon the nature of the problem at hand. Indeed, the main difference between open-loop and closed-loop approaches is that in the former, players decide by looking at the clock (i.e., calendar time), while in the latter, they decide by looking at the stock (i.e., the past history of the game). Whether the second perspective is more realistic than the first has to be evaluated within the specific framework being used, in relation with the kind of story the model itself tries to account for (Clemhout and Wan, 1994, p. 812). If controls describe something like investment plans, these can in fact be sticky enough to justify the adoption of an open-loop solution. The next question is whether open-loop rules can produce subgame perfect equilibria or not. Briefly, an equilibrium is (at least weakly) time consistent if, at any intermediate time $\tau \in [0,\infty)$, no player has an incentive to deviate from the plan initially designed at time zero (at least in view of the stocks of state variables at time τ).[4]

3. THE GAME

The Stackelberg game is taken to be solved by firms in open-loop strategies. Consider first the optimum problem for the followers, i.e., firms belonging to the set $f \equiv \{1,2,3,...,F\}$. Given that all of them are a priori symmetric and face the same problem, I will confine my attention to a single representative follower, say, firm F. Its expected value Hamiltonian is:

$$E[H_F(k(t),I(t))] = E\left\{ \left[a - k_F(t) - s\left(\sum_{i=1}^{F-1} k_i(t) + \sum_{j=F+1}^{N} k_i(t) \right) \right] k_F(t) - b[I_F(t)]^2 + \right.$$
$$+ \mu_{FF}(t)[I_F(t) - \delta k_F(t) + \varepsilon_F(t)] + \sum_{i=1}^{F-1} \mu_{Fi}(t)[I_i(t) - \delta k_i(t) + \varepsilon_F(t)] +$$
$$\left. + \sum_{j=F+1}^{N} \mu_{Fj}(t)[I_j(t) - \delta k_j(t) + \varepsilon_L(t)] \right\}, \tag{8}$$

where $\mu_{Fj}(t)$ is the co-state variable associated with state variable $k_j(t)$. The first order conditions are (exponential discounting is omitted for brevity):

$$\frac{\partial E[H_F(k(t),I(t))]}{\partial I_F(t)} = -2bI_F(t) + \mu_{FF}(t) = 0; \tag{9}$$

$$-\frac{\partial[\mathrm{H}_F(\mathrm{k}(t),\mathrm{I}(t))]}{\partial k_F(t)} = \frac{\partial \mu_{FF}(t)}{\partial t} \Rightarrow \tag{10}$$

$$\frac{\partial \mu_{FF}(t)}{\partial t} = \mu_{FF}(t)\delta - a + s\left(\sum_{i=1}^{F-1}k_i(t) + \sum_{j=F+1}^{N}k_j(t)\right) + 2k_F(t); \tag{11}$$

$$-\frac{\partial[\mathrm{H}_F(\mathrm{k}(t),\mathrm{I}(t))]}{\partial k_h(t)} = \frac{\partial \mu_{Fh}(t)}{\partial t} \Rightarrow \frac{\partial \mu_{Fh}(t)}{\partial t} = \mu_{Fh}(t)\delta + sk_h(t), \quad \forall\, h \neq F. \tag{12}$$

Equations (9-12) must be considered together with the initial conditions $k(0) = k_0$ and the transversality condition:

$$\lim_{t\to\infty} \mu_{Fv}(t) \cdot k_v(t) = 0, \quad v = F+1, F+2, F+3,..., N. \tag{13}$$

From (9), one obtains:

$$\mu_{FF}(t) = 2bI_F(t); \quad \frac{\partial I_F(t)}{\partial t} = \frac{1}{2b}\frac{\partial \mu_{FF}(t)}{\partial t}. \tag{14}$$

Moreover, from co-state equations(11-12), one can check that the expressions of co-state variables:

$$\mu_{FF}(t) = \int \frac{\partial \mu_{FF}(t)}{\partial t}; \quad \mu_{Fh}(t) = \int \frac{\partial \mu_{Fh}(t)}{\partial t}, \quad \forall\, h \neq F \tag{15}$$

are independent of any rivals' controls, in particular the followers' controls. This fact proves the following result (see Xie, 1997):[5]

Lemma 1 *The Stackelberg game is uncontrollable by the leaders. Therefore, the open-loop Stackelberg equilibrium is time consistent.*

Before approaching the leader's problem, it is worth observing, again from (14), that the evolution of firm F's investment does not depend on any $\mu_{Fh}(t)$. This redundancy of the dynamics of the other firms' co-state variables as to the follower's decisions is going to become useful in order to characterise the equilibrium.

Now I can characterize the leader's problem. As with the follower, again in view of the ex ante symmetry characterising the population of leaders, I may focus upon a single firm that will be taken as a representative leader, say, firm N. Its Hamiltonian function (in expected value) is:

$$E[\mathrm{H}_N(\mathrm{k}(t), I_N(t))] = E\left\{\left[a - k_N(t) - s\left(\sum_{i=1}^{F} k_i(t) + \sum_{j=F+1}^{N-1} k_j(t)\right)\right]k_N(t) + \right.$$

$$- b[I_N(t)]^2 + \mu_{NN}(t)[I_N(t) - \delta k_N(t) + \varepsilon_L(t)] +$$

$$+ \sum_{j=F+1}^{N-1} \mu_{Nj}(t)[I_j(t) - \delta k_j(t) + \varepsilon_L(t)] + \sum_{i=1}^{F} \mu_{Ni}(t)\left[\frac{\mu_{ii}(t)}{2b} - \delta k_i(t) + \varepsilon_F(t)\right] +$$

$$+ \sum_{i=1}^{F} \theta_{Ni}(t)\left[\frac{\partial \mu_{ii}(t)}{\partial t}\right] + \sum_{i=1}^{F}\sum_{j=1}^{N-1} \phi_{Nj}(t)\left[\frac{\partial \mu_{ij}(t)}{\partial t}\right]\right\} \qquad (16)$$

where $\theta_{Ni}(t)$ and $\phi_{Nj}(t)$ are the additional co-state variables attached by the leader to the followers' co-state equations, and the expressions $\partial \mu_{ii}(t)/\partial t$ and $\partial \mu_{ij}(t)/\partial t$ are given by (11-12). Solving the leader's problem, one obtains (superscripts 1 and f stand for *leader* and *follower*, respectively):

Lemma 2 At *the steady state of the Stackelberg open-loop game, optimal capacities are:*

$$k^l = \frac{2(1 + b\delta^2)(a + 2b\delta\varepsilon_L) - s[a + 2b\delta(\varepsilon_L + F(\varepsilon_F - \varepsilon_L))]}{4(1 + b\delta^2)^2 + 2s(1 + b\delta^2)(N - 2) - s^2(N + F - 1)},$$

$$k^f = \frac{4(1 + b\delta^2)^2 (a + 2b\delta\varepsilon_F) + 2s(1 + b\delta^2)\Gamma - s^2\Psi}{8(1 + g\delta^2)^3 + 4s(1 + b\delta^2)^2 (N + F - 3) + s^2\Omega - s^3\Lambda},$$

$$\Gamma \equiv a(F - 2) + 2b\delta[\varepsilon_F(N - 2) - \varepsilon_L(N - F)];$$
$$\Psi \equiv a(2F - 1) + 2b\delta[\varepsilon_F(N + F - 1 - F(N - F)) - \varepsilon_L(N - F)(F - 1)];$$
$$\Omega \equiv 2(1 + b\delta^2)[3 - 2(N - F) + F(N - 5)];$$
$$\Lambda \equiv (F - 1)(N + F - 1).$$

Proof. The first order conditions for the representative leader are:

$$\frac{\partial E[H_N(\cdot)]}{\partial I_N(t)} = -2bI_N(t) + \mu_{NN}(t) = 0; \qquad (17)$$

$$-\frac{\partial E[H_N(\cdot)]}{\partial k_N(t)} = \frac{\partial \mu_{NN}(t)}{\partial t} \quad \Rightarrow \qquad (18)$$

$$\frac{\partial \mu_{NN}(t)}{\partial t} = \mu_{NN}(t)\delta - a + 2k_N(t) + s\left(\sum_{i=1}^{F} k_i(t) + \sum_{j=F+1}^{N-1} k_j(t)\right) - s\sum_{i=1}^{F}\theta_{Ni}(t);$$

(19)

$$-\frac{\partial E[H_N(\cdot)]}{\partial k_j(t)} = \frac{\partial \mu_{Nj}(t)}{\partial t} \quad\Rightarrow$$

(20)

$$\frac{\partial \mu_{Nj}(t)}{\partial t} = \mu_{Nj}(t)\delta + sk_N(t) - s\sum_{i=1}^{F}\theta_{Ni}(t);$$

(21)

$$-\frac{\partial E[H_N(\cdot)]}{\partial k_i(t)} = \frac{\partial \mu_{Ni}(t)}{\partial t} \quad\Rightarrow$$

(22)

$$\frac{\partial \mu_{Ni}(t)}{\partial t} = \mu_{Ni}(t)\delta + sk_N(t) - 2\theta_{Ni}(t) - s\left(\sum_{h\neq i}\theta_{Nh}(t) + \sum_{j=1}^{N-1}\phi_{Nj}(t)\right);$$

(23)

$$-\frac{\partial E[H_N(\cdot)]}{\partial h_{ih}(t)} = \frac{\partial \phi_{hj}(t)}{\partial t} \quad\Rightarrow\quad \frac{\partial \phi_{hj}(t)}{\partial t} = -\delta\phi_{Nh}(t);$$

(24)

$$-\frac{\partial E[H_1(\cdot)]}{\partial \mu_{ii}(t)} = \frac{\partial \theta_{Ni}(t)}{\partial t} \quad\Rightarrow\quad \frac{\partial \theta_{Ni}(t)}{\partial t} = -\frac{\mu_{Ni}(t)}{2b} - \delta\theta_{Li}(t).$$

(25)

The above conditions are accompanied by the initial conditions $k(0) = k_0$ as well as the transversality condition:

$$\lim_{t\to\infty}\mu_{Nj}(t)\cdot kj(t) = 0$$
$$\lim_{t\to\infty}\theta_{Ni}(t)\cdot \mu_{Ni}(t) = 0$$
$$\lim_{t\to\infty}\phi_{Nh}(t)\cdot \mu_{Nh}(t) = 0$$

(26)

for all i, j, h.

From (17) one immediately gets:

$$\mu_{NN}(t) = b + 2bI_N(t); \quad \frac{\partial I_N(t)}{\partial t} = \frac{1}{2b}\frac{\partial \mu_{NN}(t)}{\partial t} \quad\Rightarrow$$

(27)

$$\frac{\partial I_N(t)}{\partial t} = \frac{1}{2g}\left[\mu_{NN}(t)\delta - a + 2k_N(t) + s\left(\sum_{i=1}^{F} k_i(t) + \sum_{j=F+1}^{N-1} k_j(t)\right) - s\sum_{i=1}^{F}\theta_{Ni}(t)\right].$$

(28)

Additionally, from (24), we observe that $\frac{\partial \phi_{Nh}}{\partial t} = 0$ if and only if $\phi_{Nh} = 0$.

Proceeding likewise, note that from (25), we have:

$$\frac{\partial \theta_{Ni}(t)}{\partial t} = 0 \quad \Leftrightarrow \quad \theta_{Ni}(t) = -\frac{\mu_{Ni}(t)}{2b\delta}.$$

(29)

Now, having taken all the relevant first order conditions, I may impose symmetry across (i) leaders and (ii) follower, by setting

- $k_i(t) = k_F(t)$ for all i, $k_j(t) = k_N(t)$ for all j,
- $I_i(t) = I_F(t)$ for all i, $I_j(t) = I_N(t)$ for all j,

Accordingly, (19), (21) and (23) rewrite, respectively, as follows:

$$\frac{\partial \mu_{NN}(t)}{\partial t} = \mu_{NN}(t)\delta - a + 2k_N(t) + +s[k_F(t)F + k_N(t)(N - F - 11)] - sF\theta_{Ni}(t);$$

(30)

$$\frac{\partial \mu_{Nj}(t)}{\partial t} = \mu_{Nj}(t)\delta + sk_N(t) - sF\theta_{Ni}(t);$$

(31)

$$\frac{\partial \mu_{Ni}(t)}{\partial t} = \mu_{Ni}(t)\delta + sk_N(t) - 2\theta_{Ni}(t) - s[(F - 1)\theta_{Nh}(t) + (N - 1)\phi_{Nj}(t)].$$ (32)

Since I'm looking for the characterization of the steady state equilibrium, I may use (29) and impose stationarity upon equations (32), to obtain:

$$\mu_{Ni}(t) = -\frac{2bs\delta k_N(t)}{2(1 + b\delta^2) + s(F - 1)}.$$

(33)

Then, plugging (29) and (33) into (28), one obtains the following dynamic equation for the representative leader's investment (henceforth, I omit the indication of time for the sake of brevity):

$$\frac{\partial I_N}{\partial t} \propto (a - 2b\delta I_N - sFk_F)[2(1 + b\delta^2) + s(F - 1)] +$$
$$+ k_N[s^2F - (2(1 + b\delta^2) + s(F - 1))(s(N - F - 1) + 2)] \qquad (34)$$

which is nil at

$$I_N^* = \frac{(a - sFk_F)[2(1 + b\delta^2) + s(F - 1)]}{2b\delta[2(1 + b\delta^2) + s(F - 1)]} +$$
$$= + \frac{k_N[s^2F - (2(1 + b\delta^2) + s(F - 1))(s(N - F - 1) + 2)]}{2b\delta[2(1 + b\delta^2) + s(F - 1)]}. \qquad (35)$$

The representative follower's optimal investment is:

$$I_F^* = \frac{\mu_{FF}^*}{2b} = \frac{a - 2k_F - s[k_F(F - 1) + k_N(N - F)]}{2b\delta}. \qquad (36)$$

Obviously the sign of $I_N^* - I_F^*$ depends, amongst other things, upon the relative number of leaders and followers, for any given $\{k_F, k_N\}$:

$$I_N^* - I_F^* \propto k_F(2 - s)[2(1 + b\delta^2) + s(F - 1)] +$$
$$+ k_N[s(4 - s - 2F(1 - s)) - 2(2 + b\delta^2(2 - s))]. \qquad (37)$$

Of course the sign of the above expression can be determined on the basis of the relative size of capacities, the steady state levels of which can be determined imposing stationarity on the kinematic equations of state variables (2):

$$k^l = \frac{2(1 + b\delta^2)(a + 2b\delta\varepsilon_L) - s[a + 2b\delta(\varepsilon_L + F(\varepsilon_F - \varepsilon_L))]}{4(1 + b\delta^2)^2 + 2s(1 + b\delta^2)(N - 2) - s^2(N + F - 1)}; \qquad (38)$$

$$k^f = \frac{4(1 + b\delta^2)^2(a + 2b\delta\varepsilon_F) + 2s(1 + b\delta^2)\Gamma - s^2\Psi}{8(1 + g\delta^2)^3 + 4s(1 + b\delta^2)^2(N + F - 3) + s^2\Omega - s^3\Lambda}, \qquad (39)$$

where

$$\Gamma \equiv a(F - 2) + 2b\delta[\varepsilon_F(N - 2) - \varepsilon_L(N - F)];$$
$$\Psi \equiv a(2F - 1) + 2b\delta[\varepsilon_F(N + F - 1 - F(N - F)) - \varepsilon_L(N - F)(F - 1)]; \qquad (40)$$
$$\Omega \equiv 2(1 + b\delta^2)[3 - 2(N - F) + F(N - 5)];$$

$$\Lambda \equiv (F-1)(N+F-1).$$

Expressions (38-39) can be used to write the corresponding equilibrium expressions of $\{I^i = \delta I^i + \varepsilon_L, I^f = \delta I^f + \varepsilon_F\}$.

Before assessing the properties of steady state capacities, let me go briefly back to (37). The sign of this expression is difficult to determine, however there is a special case where it can be easily done. Assume $s = 1$, i.e., goods are homogeneous. If so, then

$$I_N^* - I_F^* \propto (1+2b\delta^2+F)k_F - (1+2b\delta^2)k_N > 0$$
$$\forall F > \frac{(1+2b\delta^2)(k_F-k_N)}{k_F} \equiv \hat{F} \qquad (41)$$

This allows me to prove the following result:

Lemma 3 *Suppose firms supplies perfect substitute goods. In such a case*:

- *if $k_N > k_F$, then $I_N^* > I_F^*$ for all $F > \hat{F}$;*
- *if $k_N > k_F$, then $I_N^* < I_F^*$ for all $F \in [1, \hat{F})$;*
- *if $k_N < k_F$, then $I_N^* > I_F^*$ for all $F \geq 1$.*

Proof. The first two claims in the above Lemma can be shown to hold by quickly observing that, provided $k_N > k_F$, then $\hat{F} > 1$ if $k_N/k_F > (1+b\delta^2)/(1+2b\delta^2)$, which is smaller than one for all admissible values of b and δ. Therefore $k_N > k_F$ suffices to ensure that $\hat{F} > 1$. If instead $k_N < k_F$, then $\hat{F} < 0$. Hence, $F > \hat{F}$ holds trivially.

The interesting feature of Lemma 3 lies in the fact that it highlights the existence of an admissible case where the representative leader is *bigger* than the representative follower in terms of installed capacity, but nonetheless the follower invests more than the leader. This happens if the number of the followers is low enough, and seems to suggest that decreasing the intensity of competition among followers (by shrinking their number) ultimately produces an incentive for them to outperform the leaders as far as the instantaneous optimal investment effort is concerned.

Assessing the difference between steady state capital endowments and investment levels, one finds that the sign of both $k^i - k^f$ and $I^i - I^f$ may change depending upon the relative size of shocks, ε_F and ε_L. However, if $\varepsilon_F = \varepsilon_L = \varepsilon$, we have:

$$k^l - k^f \propto I^l - I^f \propto (a + 2b\delta\varepsilon)/[8(1+b\delta^2)^3 + 4(1+b\delta^2)^2(N+F-3)s +$$
$$+ 2(1+b\delta^2)(3 - 2(N-F) + F(N-5))s^2 - (F-1)(N+F-1)], \qquad (42)$$

where the sign of the numerator depends on the size of the shock ε, while the sign of the denominator depends on F. In particular, the following holds:

Lemma 4 *Suppose* $\varepsilon_F = \varepsilon_L = \varepsilon$. *In such a case:*

- *if* $\varepsilon > -a/(2b\delta)$, *then* $k^l - k^f$ *and* $I^l - I^f$ *are:*

  (i) positive for all $F \in \left[1, \dfrac{[2(1+b\delta^2)-s][2(1+b\delta^2)+s(N-1)]}{s^2}\right)$;

  (ii) negative for all $F > \dfrac{[2(1+b\delta^2)-s][2(1+b\delta^2)+s(N-1)]}{s^2}$.

- *if* $\varepsilon < -a/(2b\delta)$, *then* $k^l - k^f$ *and* $I^l - I^f$ *are:*

  (i) positive for all $F > \dfrac{[2(1+b\delta^2)-s][2(1+b\delta^2)+s(N-1)]}{s^2}$;

  (ii) negative for all $F \in \left[1, \dfrac{[2(1+b\delta^2)-s][2(1+b\delta^2)+s(N-1)]}{s^2}\right)$.

Proof. The numerator of (42) is positive (resp., negative) for all ε larger (resp., smaller) than $-a/(2b\delta)$. The sign of the denominator changes in correspondence of

$$F = \frac{s - 2(1+b\delta^2)}{s} < 0; \qquad (43)$$

$$F = \frac{[2(1+b\delta^2)-s][2(1+b\delta^2)+s(N-1)]}{s^2} > 1.$$

Moreover, the polynomial at the denominator is positive inside the interval defined by the above roots. This suffices to prove the claim.

Using (35-36) and (38-39) together with (4), one can write the steady state Stackelberg expected equilibrium profits for a generic pair of leader and follower, $E(\pi^l)$ and $E(\pi^f)$, respectively.[6] The relative performance of the two representative firms in steady state is summarized by:

Proposition 5 *At the Stackelberg open-loop equilibrium:*

(i) for all $\sigma_L^2 \in \left(0, \overline{\sigma}_L^2\right)$, then any leader's expected profits are larger than any follower's;

(ii) if $\sigma_F^2 = \sigma_L^2 = \sigma_{FL}^2$, then any leader's expected profits are larger than any follower's, for all admissible values of F and N;

(iii) if $b \to 0$, then any leader's expected profits are larger than any follower's for all admissible values of $\sigma_F^2, \sigma_L^2, \sigma_{FL}^2, F$ and N.

Proof. Claim (i) of the Proposition requires simple albeit tedious algebra, the resulting threshold level $\overline{\sigma}_L^2$ being a cumbersome expression containing all the relevant parameters of the model. However, $\overline{\sigma}_L^2$ can be explicitly written in the duopoly case with $F=1$ and $N=2$,[7] where $E(\pi^l) > E(\pi^f)$ if

$$\sigma_L^2 < \frac{\{a^2(1+4b\delta^2)+16g^2\delta^2\sigma_{FL}^2 + 4b[4+b\sigma^2(29+4b\delta^2(18+b\delta^2(15+4b\delta^2))))]\sigma_F^2\}}{\varpi} \quad (44)$$

where

$$\varpi \equiv 16b(1+b\delta^2)(1+b\delta^2(1+b\delta^2)(7+4b\delta^2)). \quad (45)$$

As to claim (ii), observe that if $\sigma_F^2 = \sigma_L^2 = \sigma_{FL}^2$, then

$$E(\pi_1^l) - E(\pi_2^f) \propto [2(1+b\delta^2)-s]^2 + sF(1+b\delta^2 - s) \quad (46)$$

To prove claim (iii), it suffices to observe that

$$\lim_{b\to 0}[E(\pi^l) - E(\pi^{fl})] = (4+sF)(1-s)+s^2 > 0. \quad (47)$$

This concludes the proof.

Claim (i) in the above Proposition simply states the intuitive result that, if the degree of uncertainty borne by the representative leader is high enough, then, all else equal, following may be preferable to leading in terms of expected profits. Claim (ii) illustrates the special case in which all firms face the same shock. If so, then all that matters is having the first mover advantage at any point in time. Finally, claim (iii) deals with the limit case where investment costs are negligible. In this circumstance the leader is better off irrespective of the values of all other relevant parameters, the intuitive reason being that under this condition the role of uncertainty becomes immaterial.

The stability analysis of the Stackelberg open-loop game is rather cumbersome, yet it can be carried out (without resorting to numerical calculations) to verify that the steady state open-loop Stackelberg equilibrium (k^f, k^l, I^f, I^l) is a saddle point.[8]

I am now in a position to make a crucial remark concerning the growth rates exhibited by leaders and followers, respectively. Evaluating the sign of $\dot{k}_L - \dot{k}_F$ is a difficult task even in special cases. However, as a quick inspection of the proof of Lemma 2 reveals, growth rates surely differ because, in general, $\dot{I}_L$ and $\dot{I}_F$ differ at all $t \in [0,\infty)$. In addition to this, firms' saddle paths to the steady state are independent of initial conditions k_0; hence, there follows that growth rates are determined by the distribution of roles across firms in the games (i.e., the timing of moves) but not their initial respective sizes (or installed capacities), and the cases in which $k_L(0) < k_F(0)$ while $k^l > k^f$, are both admissible. This brief discussion ultimately entails that the present setup does not yield theoretical support to *Gibrat's Law*.

4. COMPARATIVE STATICS

First, I evaluate firms' profits under perfect certainty, i.e., at $\sigma_1 = \sigma_2 = \sigma_{12} = 0$:

$$\pi^l = \frac{a^2[2(1+b\delta^2)+s]^2[(1+b\delta^2)(2(1+b\delta^2)+s(F-1))-s^{2F}]}{(2(1+b\delta^2)+s(F-1))[2(1+b\delta^2)(s(N-2)+2(1+b\delta^2))-s^2(N+F-1)]^2}$$

(48)

$$\pi^f = a^2(1+b\delta^2)[2(1+b\delta^2)(s(F-2)+2(1+b\delta^2))-s^2(2F-1)]^2 / $$
$$\{2(1+b\delta^2)[(3-2(N-F)+(N-5)s^2)+$$
$$+2(1+b\delta^2)(s(N+F-3)+2(1+b\delta^2))]-(F-1)(N+F-1)s^2\}^2,$$

(49)

with
$$\pi^l - \pi^f \propto s^2 + [4(1+b\delta^2)+sF](1+b\delta^2-s) > 0$$

(50)

for all admissible values of parameters. The deterministic case yields the well known profit ranking usually associated with games in which controls are strategic substitutes (i.e., best replies are downward sloping), as is well known from previous literature (Dowrick, 1986; and Hamilton and Slutsky, 1990, *inter alia*). However, the ranking of firms' profits may drastically change due to uncertainty. For the sake of simplicity, relabel

$\sigma_L^2 = \zeta_L, \sigma_F^2 = \zeta_F$ and $\sigma_{FL}^2 = \zeta_{FL}$. The following properties can be ascertained:

$$\frac{\partial E(\pi^l)}{\partial \zeta_L} < 0; \quad \frac{\partial E(\pi^l)}{\partial \zeta_F} > 0; \quad \frac{\partial E(\pi^l)}{\partial \zeta_{FL}} < 0 \quad \forall \, b, s, \delta, N, F; \tag{51}$$

$$\frac{\partial E(\pi^f)}{\partial \zeta_L} > 0; \quad \frac{\partial E(\pi^f)}{\partial \zeta_F} < 0; \quad \frac{\partial E(\pi^f)}{\partial \zeta_{FL}} < 0 \quad \forall \, b, s, \delta, N, F. \tag{52}$$

Moreover:

$$\left| \frac{\partial E(\pi^l)}{\partial \zeta_L} \right| > \frac{\partial E(\pi^f)}{\partial \zeta_L}; \quad \left| \frac{\partial E(\pi^f)}{\partial \zeta_F} \right| > \frac{\partial E(\pi^l)}{\partial \zeta_F}; \quad \forall \, b, s, \delta, N, F. \tag{53}$$

The above list of partial derivatives reveals a few facts:
- increasing the variance of the shock affecting the leaders (resp., follower) generates a positive spillover for the followers (leaders), while obviously damaging the leaders (followers) themselves;
- moreover, the former effect is smaller than the latter in absolute value;
- increasing the correlation between shocks negatively affects the performance of both leaders and followers alike.[9]

5. CONCLUSIONS

I have described a stochastic differential game in which firms invest to increase productive capacity, following time-consistent open-loop Stackelberg strategies. The equilibrium of the model highlights different growth rates along the saddle path. Accordingly, the analysis carried out in this paper is clearly in contrast with *Gibrat's Law*. Moreover, it appears that there are admissible cases where the followers's growth rates are larger than the leaders', e.g. when the representative leader is indeed bigger than the representative follower in terms of installed capacity. This may ultimately lead to situations where equilibrium profits are larger for followers than for leaders.

NOTES

[1] For early empirical studies confirming *Gibrat's Law*, see Hart and Prais (1956), Simon and Bonini (1958) and Hymer and Pashigian (1962). An exhaustive overview of empirical findings is in Audretsch, Santarelli and Vivarelli (1999). For a thorough appraisal of Gibrat's contribution, see Sutton (1997).

[2] In a subsequent paper, Pakes and Ericson (1998) evaluate the empirical implications of Jovanovic's model and their model of industry dynamics.

[3] The deterministic version of the present model has been investigated, under simultaneous play only, in the previous literature (Fudenberg and Tirole, 1983; Fershtman and Muller, 1984; Reynolds, 1987) and can be ultimately traced back to Solow (1956) and Swan (1956).

[4] A more detailed illustration of these issues can be found in Dockner, Jørgensen, Van Long and Sorger (2000, section 4.3, pp. 98-107; and Ch. 5).

[5] See also Dockner, Jørgensen, Van Long and Sorger (2000, Ch. 5) and Cellini, Lambertini and Leitmann (2005).

[6] These expressions are omitted for brevity.

[7] See Proposition 10 in Lambertini (2005, p. 455).

[8] The detailed stability properties of the Jacobian matrix are fully illustrated in Lambertini (2005, Proposition 11, p. 455) for the duopoly case.

[9] It is worth noting that this result has interesting macroeconomic implications, suggesting that integration or globalization may favour the diffusion of shocks across markets/ countries, so that firms located in markets previously separated by significantly high trade barriers are no longer protected from shocks taking place abroad.

REFERENCES

Audretsch, D. B., E. Santarelli and M. Vivarelli (1999), "Does Start-Up Size Influence the Likelihood of Survival?", in D. B. Audretsch and A. R. Thurik (eds.), *Innovation, Industry Evolution and Employment*, Cambridge, Cambridge University Press, 280-296.

Cellini, R., L. Lambertini and G. Leitmann (2005), "Degenerate Feedback and Time Consistency in Differential Games", in E. P. Hofer and E. Reithmeier (eds), *Modeling and Control of Autonomous Decision Support Based Systems*. Proceedings of the 13th International Workshop on Dynamics and Control, Aachen, Shaker Verlag, 185-192.

Clemhout, S. and H. Y. Wan, Jr. (1994), "Differential Games. Economic Applications", in R. J. Aumann and S. Hart (eds), *Handbook of Game Theory*, Amsterdam, North-Holland, vol. 2, ch. 23, 801-825.

Dockner, E. J, S. Jørgensen, N. Van Long and G. Sorger (2000), *Differential Games in Economics and Management Science*, Cambridge, Cambridge University Press.

Dowrick, S. (1986), "von Stackelberg and Cournot Duopoly: Choosing Roles", *RAND Journal of Economics*, 17(2), 251-260.

Ericson, R. and A. Pakes (1995), "Markov-Perfect Industry Dynamics: A Framework for Empirical Work", *Review of Economic Studies*, 62(1), 53-82.

Fershtman, C. and E. Muller (1984), "Capital Accumulation Games of Infinite Duration", *Journal of Economic Theory*, 33(3), 322-339.

Fudenberg, D. and J. Tirole (1983), "Capital as a Commitment: Strategic Investment to Deter Mobility", *Journal of Economic Theory*, 31(2), 227-250.

Gibrat, R. (1931), *Les Inegalites Economiques*, Paris, Librairie du Recueil Sirey.

Hamilton, J. H. and S. M. Slutsky (1990), "Endogenous Timing in Duopoly Games: Stackelberg or Cournot Equilibria", *Games and Economic Behavior*, 2(1), 29-46.

Hart, P. E. and S. J. Prais (1956), "The Analysis of Business Concentration: A Statistical Approach", *Journal of the Royal Statistical Society*, 119(A), 150-191.

Hopenhayn, H. A. (1992), "Entry, Exit, and Firm Dynamics in Long Run Equilibrium", *Econometrica*, 60(5), 1127-1150.

Hymer, S. and P. Pashigian (1962), "Firm Size and the Rate of Growth", *Journal of Political Economy*, 70(4), 556-569.

Jovanovic, B. (1982), "Selection and the Evolution of Industry", *Econometrica*, 50(3), 649-670.

Lambertini, L. (2005), "Stackelberg Leadership in a Dynamic Duopoly with Stochastic Capital Accumulation", *Journal of Evolutionary Economics*, 15(4), 443-465.

Lucas, R. E. Jr. (1978), "On the Size Distribution of Business Firms", *Bell Journal of Economics*, 9(2), 508-523.

Lucas, R. E. Jr. and E. Prescott (1971), "Investment under Uncertainty", *Econometrica*, 39(4), 659-681.

Pakes, A, and R. Ericson (1998), "Empirical Implications of Alternative Models of Firm Dynamics", *Journal of Economic Theory*, 79(1), 1-45.

Reynolds, S. S. (1987), "Capacity Investment, Preemption and Commitment in an Infinite Horizon Model", *International Economic Review*, 28(1), 69-88.

Simon, H.A. and C. P. Bonini (1958), "The Size Distribution of Business Firms", *American Economic Review*, 48(5), 607-617.

Solow, R. (1956), "A Contribution to the Theory of Economic Growth", *Quarterly Journal of Economics*, 70(1), 65-94.

Sutton, J. (1997), "Gibrat's Legacy", *Journal of Economic Literature*, 35(1), 40-59.

Swan, T. W. (1956), "Economic Growth and Capital Accumulation", *Economic Record*, 32(3), 334-361.

Xie, D. (1997), "On Time Consistency: A Technical Issue in Stackelberg Differential Games", *Journal of Economic Theory*, 76(5), 412-430.

Chapter 3
GIBRAT'S LAW: AN OVERVIEW OF THE EMPIRICAL LITERATURE

Enrico Santarelli
University of Bologna, and Max Planck Institute of Economics, Jena

Luuk Klomp
Ministry of Economic Affairs, The Hague

A. Roy Thurik
Erasmus University Rotterdam, EIM Business and Policy Research, Zoetermeer, and Max Planck Institute of Economics, Jena

1. INTRODUCTION

In two recent studies (Audretsch, Klomp, Santarelli and Thurik, 2004 and Piergovanni, Santarelli, Klomp and Thurik, 2003) we tried to test the validity of *Gibrat's Law*, i.e., growth rates are independent of size, for small scale service industries in the Netherlands and Italy. While generally the results seem to be to inconclusive, there is a tendency that *Gibrat's Law* holds in the case of the Dutch industries while it does not for the Italian ones. Our findings do not contradict those of Geroski (1995), Sutton (1997) and Caves (1998). These influential surveys on intraindustry dynamics of firms conclude independently that the empirical evidence does not support *Gibrat's Law*. The fact that growth rates of surviving firms tend to systematically decrease with increasing firm size led Geroski (1995) to classify this as a Stylised Result in his survey of "What do we know about entry?"

Gibrat's Law (Gibrat, 1931) is the first attempt to explain in stochastic terms the systematically skewed pattern of the distributions of firms' size within an industry (Aitchison and Brown, 1957). As shown by Armatte (1995, 1998), this version of *Gibrat's Law* has to do with a Galton-McAllister's or a Kapteyn's distribution, and it predicts, when applying Laplace's central limit theorem, that the empirical distribution of firms' sizes converges towards a lognormal distribution, under the hypothesis that this represents the limit distribution. As a consequence, it cannot be rejected that the resulting distributions of firms' sizes are approximately lognormal McCloughan, 1995). Nevertheless, when identifying distributions of firms' sizes skewed to the right, one cannot a priori exclude that this skewness is the result of turbulence, i.e., the presence of new entrants in the right tail of the distribution. *Gibrat's Law* is sometimes referred to as the *Law of Proportionate Effect* because the basic tenet underlying *Gibrat's Law* is that the growth rate of a given firm is independent of its size at the beginning of the examined period. In other words, "the probability of a given proportionate change in size during a specified period is the same for all firms in a given industry - regardless of their size at the beginning of the period" (Mansfield, 1962, p. 1031).

This simplicity of *Gibrat's Law* has led to waves of studies. Unfortunately they are difficult to compare because the samples used and the methodologies applied differ widely. In the context of our recent studies we tried to set up a new survey of empirical studies. In Audretsch, Klomp, Santarelli and Thurik (2004) a concise version of this survey is provided. Below we give an updated version of this survey with detailed description of the data material, method and findings. We do so because readers of Audretsch, Klomp, Santarelli and Thurik (2004) have often approached us with the question to make this detailed material available.

2. THIS SURVEY

The comparison of empirical studies testing *Gibrat's Law* is not always possible in a straightforward manner, since they differ in both the samples used and the methodologies applied. Therefore, we build this survey chapter by dividing the studies into groups of which the results can be compared. We take two characteristics into account.

Firstly, in several studies, like Mansfield (1962), a static analysis is carried out, while other studies, like Chesher (1979), deal with the persistence of growth.

Secondly, we follow Mansfield (1962) who shows that *Gibrat's Law* can be empirically tested in at least three different ways.

a) One can assume that it holds for all firms in a given industry, including those which have exited the industry during the period examined (setting the proportional growth rate of disappearing firms equal to minus one).

b) One can postulate that it holds only for firms that survive over the entire time period. If survival is not independent of firm's initial size - that is, if smaller firms are more likely to exit than their larger counterparts - this empirical test can be affected by a sample selection bias and estimates must take account of this possibility. This observation applies in particular to new and small firms, for which the hazard rate is generally high.

c) One can state that *Gibrat's Law* only applies to firms large enough to have overcome the minimum efficient scale (MES) of a given industry (for instance, Simon and Bonini (1958) found that the *Law* was confirmed for the 500 largest U.S. industrial corporations).

Both static and temporal analysis of the three versions would lead to six types of empirical growth studies. However, the first version of *Gibrat's Law* cannot be studied in the case of persistence of growth: it is not possible to analyze the persistence of growth for firms that leave the industry during the observation period. Recently, some attention has been paid to the post-entry growth of new firms. We add such studies as the sixth group to our review. In each of the Tables 1 through 6 one of the six groups is reviewed. It should be noted that different versions of *Gibrat's Law* are tested in some studies. Such studies appear more than once in the tables. Finally, a concise version of the contents of all six tables is given in Table 7. This table is an update of the table in Audretsch, Klomp, Santarelli and Thurik (2004).

From the about 60 papers taken into account in this survey, one cannot conclude that the *Law* is generally valid nor that it is systematically rejected. In effect, only in relation to certain sectors (in particular in the service industries) and size classes (the largest ones) the probability of a given proportionate change in size during the relevant period turns out to be the same for all firms. This implies that *Gibrat's Law* cannot be regarded as a Law in the strict sense, given that heterogeneous patterns of behavior do emerge across industries and size classes.

Table 1 - Static analysis and version 1

Authors (year of publication)	Model and version
Mansfield (1962)	A - *Static analysis and version 1*

DATA CHARACTERISTICS - Almost all firms in three U.S. manufacturing industries (Steel, Petroleum refining and Rubber tire) are observed; In each industry several periods of some 10 years between 1916 and 1957 are considered.
RESEARCH METHODS - The distributions of growth rates for several size classes are compared.
MAJOR FINDINGS - *Gibrat's Law* is rejected in 7 out of 10 cases; Smaller firms are more likely to leave the industry.

Acs and Audretsch (1990)	A - *Static analysis and version 1*

DATA CHARACTERISTICS - Acs and Audretsch used the Small Business Data Base like Evans (1987a and 1987b) did; They aggregated the data into 408 4-digit U.S. manufacturing industries; Firm growth is considered for the period 1976-1980.
RESEARCH METHODS - Based on 1,976 firm size each 4-digit industry is divided in 4 size classes; Mean (employment) firm growth rates are calculated for every size class in

every industry; The hypothesis to be tested is that the mean growth rates in the 4 firm size classes are equal.

MAJOR FINDINGS - In 60% of the 408 industries mean growth rates in the size classes are not significantly different; *Gibrat's Law* holds in 60% of the industries, this finding is different from Evans (1987b), incorporating the impact of exits tends to produce more support for *Gibrat's Law* than otherwise would be found.

Fariñas and Moreno (2000)   *A - Static analysis and version 1*

DATA CHARACTERISTICS - Fariñas and Moreno used a sample of 1,971 manufacturing firms drawn from the Encuesta sobre Estrategieas Empresariales (ESEE) carried by the Ministry of Industry in Spain; Average annual growth rates are considered over the period 1990-1995, for a total number of 7,265 observations; Size is measured in terms of employment.

RESEARCH METHODS - The empirical model examines how the mean growth rate and the exit rate vary across size and age of firms, controlling for industry and year categories; The offsetting effect predicted by the selection model is that the probability of failure diminishes with size and age; Fariñas and Moreno correct for sample selection bias and heteroscedasticity; They follow the method proposed by Dunne, Roberts and Samuelson (1988) to distinguish between potential and observed growth rates in order to account for sample selection due to exit.

MAJOR FINDINGS - Application of Wald statistics using robust variance estimates shows that the size pattern is not uniform at all, and the differences in growth rates across the size of firms are not statistically significant; This pattern of no relationship between expected growth and size appears because the reduction in the failure rate with increased size and the reduction in the growth rate of non-failing firms with increased size compensate each other; Besides, the net effect of age on firm growth is similar to the effects of size.

Piergiovanni, Santarelli, Klomp and Thurik (2003)   *A - Static analysis and version 1*

DATA CHARACTERISTICS – 9,051 newborn firms in five 4-digit Italian hospitality industries (Restaurants, Cafeterias, Cafes, Hotels and Camping sites) between 1989 and 1994; Annual observations for firm size are available from INPS (National Institute for Social Security) data files; Size is measured in terms of employment.

RESEARCH METHODS - Divide the observed firm sizes into several size classes and then examines whether firm growth rates are equally distributed across these classes; To construct these size classes firms were ranked in order of size and divided into quartiles in each sub-sector in the hospitality sector; Similarly, firm growth rates were also divided into quartiles; If the observed frequencies of the resulting 16 cells in the cross tables of firm size and growth rates are equal, *Gibrat's Law* would be supported; Whether or not growth rates and firm size are independent is tested using the χ^2 statistic.

MAJOR FINDINGS - *Gibrat's Law* is rejected in 3 of the 5 sub-sectors for the sample including all firms; Only for the Cafeterias and the Camping sites are size and growth found to be statistically independent.

Audretsch, Klomp, Santarelli and Thurik (2004)   *A - Static analysis and version 1*

DATA CHARACTERISTICS – 1,170 firms in five 4-digit Dutch hospitality industries (Restaurants, Cafeterias, Cafes, Hotels and Camping sites) between 1987 and 1991; Annual observations for firm size are available from CBS (Statistics Netherlands) data files; While a firm can consist of more than one establishment, 94% of all firms in Dutch hospitality are single-establishment enterprises, reflecting a sector of independent and family-owned businesses; Size is measured in terms of sales.

RESEARCH METHODS - Divide the observed firm sizes into several size classes and then examines whether firm growth rates are equally distributed across these classes; To construct these size classes firms were ranked in order of size and divided into quartiles in each sub-sector in the hospitality sector; Similarly, firm growth rates were also divided into quartiles; If the observed frequencies of the resulting 16 cells in the cross tables of firm size and growth rates are equal, *Gibrat's Law* would be supported; Whether or not growth rates and firm size are independent is tested using the χ^2 statistic.

MAJOR FINDINGS - *Gibrat's Law* is rejected in 4 of the 5 sub-sectors for the sample including all firms; Only for the Camping sites are size and growth found to be statistically independent.

Table 2 - Static analysis and version 2

Authors (year of publication)	Model and version
Mansfield (1962)	B - *Static analysis and version 2*

DATA CHARACTERISTICS - Almost all firms in three U.S. manufacturing industries (Steel, Petroleum refining and Rubber tire) are observed; In each industry several periods of some 10 years between 1916 and 1957 are considered.

RESEARCH METHODS - The distributions of growth rates for several size classes are compared; The regression of the logarithm of size at the end of the period on the logarithm of size in the beginning of the period is also carried out.

MAJOR FINDINGS - *Gibrat's Law* is rejected in 4 out of 10 cases when distributions of growth rates for different size classes are compared and in 3 out of 10 cases when the regression estimates are used.

Evans (1987a)	B - *Static analysis and version 2*

DATA CHARACTERISTICS - Data for approximately 20,000 U.S. manufacturing firms are used; Firm growth is analysed between 1976 and 1982; Data are pooled across industries; Very small firms are under-represented.

RESEARCH METHODS - Regression analysis is carried out for (employment) growth rates on firm size, firm age, and quadratic terms and the cross product of size and age; Evans corrects for sample selection bias and heteroscedasticity and reports for young and old firms separately.

MAJOR FINDINGS - Firm growth decreases with size; Departures from *Gibrat's Law* tend to decrease with firm size; For young firms growth decreases with age when size is held constant; This result supports Jovanovic's (1982) theory; Young firm survival increases with size and age.

Evans (1987b)	B - *Static analysis and version 2*

DATA CHARACTERISTICS - A sample of 100 U.S. 4-digit manufacturing industries was selected randomly from the population of 450 4-digit industries; Data for 42,339 firms operating in 1976 were divided in 13,735 young and 28,604 old firms; Firm growth is considered for the period 1976-1980; During this period about 33% of the young firms and about 15% of the old firms are dissolved.

RESEARCH METHODS - Regression analysis is carried out for (employment) growth rates on size, age, the number of plants, quadratic terms and cross products of these variables; Evans controls for sample selection bias and heteroscedasticity and reports for young and old firms separately.

MAJOR FINDINGS - Firm growth decreases at a diminishing rate with firm size even after controlling for sample selection bias; *Gibrat's Law* fails and the departures from the *Law* are more severe for small firms; For young as well as for old firms growth decreases with age; Firm growth decreases with size in 89% of the industries and with age in 76% of the industries.

Contini and Revelli (1989)   B - *Static analysis and version 2*

DATA CHARACTERISTICS - Data for Italian manufacturing firms are used for the period 1980-1986; The period is divided in two sub-periods, a recession period (1980-1983) and an expansion period (1983-1986); In both sub-periods data for over 1,000 firms are available.

RESEARCH METHODS - Regression results for (3 year employment) growth rates on firm size and age are obtained; Due to multicollinearity squared terms and the cross product are not included; Also lagged growth rates are added to the regressions; Problems of heteroscedasticity and sample selection bias are mentioned.

MAJOR FINDINGS - In all regressions the firm growth rate declines significantly with size; The coefficient changes only slightly when different periods of time or when only large firms are used or when lagged growth rates is added as an explanatory variable; Departures from *Gibrat's Law* are modest; In the recession period there is hardly association between growth rates and age; In the expansion period the growth rates decline with age.

FitzRoy and Kraft (1991)   B - *Static analysis and version 2*

DATA CHARACTERISTICS - A sample of 51 West German firms in the metalworking sector is used; Data are available for the years 1977 and 1979.

RESEARCH METHODS - Regression results for growth rates on size and several other explanatory variables, like age (measured by a dummy variable) are obtained; The growth rate is defined as the difference of the 1979 sales and the 1977 sales divided by the (initial) sales in 1977; The results are corrected for heteroscedasticity.

MAJOR FINDINGS - In the German metalworking sector larger firms display significantly lower growth than the smaller ones; *Gibrat's Law* seems to fail; The age dummy variable is positive, so younger firms do grow faster, controlling for employment; More innovative and more profitable firms grow faster, also firms with a higher education workforce do.

Variyam and Kraybill (1992)   B - *Static analysis and version 2*

DATA CHARACTERISTICS - Only small and medium sized firms, defined as businesses employing less than 500 employees, are included; A sample of 422 firms in Georgia (U.S.) is conducted; The firms belong to various sectors, including retailing as well as manufacturing.

RESEARCH METHODS - Regression analysis is carried out for 5 year (employment) growth rates on size, age and quadratic terms and the cross product of these two variables; Also some dummy variables are included; The results are controlled for heteroscedasticity.

MAJOR FINDINGS - Firm growth rates decreases significantly with firm size and age; *Gibrat's Law* is rejected; Holding other firm characteristics constant, the growth rate is significantly smaller for independent, single establishment firms compared to multiple establishment firms; The overall results come close to those reported by Evans (1987a).

Bianco and Sestito (1993)   B - *Static analysis and version 2*

DATA CHARACTERISTICS - A sample of 288,000 firms covering the entire private sector in Italy for the period 1985-1990 is used; For computational feasibility a sub-sample of 1 over 10 firms is used in the estimation procedures.

RESEARCH METHODS - The Authors use (almost) the same growth and survival equations like Evans (1987b) did; They discuss econometric issues like the functional form to be chosen, sample selection, heteroscedasticity and measurement error.

MAJOR FINDINGS - *Gibrat's Law* is rejected in favour of Jovanovic's theory of learning; Negative relationships between growth and size and growth and age are found; The correction for sample selection hardly changes the estimates; *Gibrat's Law* is accepted for firms employing more than 45 people.

Dunne and Hughes (1994)   *B - Static analysis and version 2*

DATA CHARACTERISTICS - Data for over 2,000 U.K. companies covering the entire private sector are available; Growth is available for the periods 1975-1980 and 1980-1985, while survival is observed only for the most recent period; Small firms are underrepresented.

RESEARCH METHODS - A probit model for survival on (asset) growth is estimated; The logarithm of size at the end of the period is regressed on the logarithm of size at the beginning of the period; The effects of age on growth and survival are only considered for quoted companies; The Authors estimate a sample selection model and correct for heteroscedasticity.

MAJOR FINDINGS - Smaller companies grow faster than larger ones, *Gibrat's Law* does not hold amongst smaller firms and age is negatively related to growth; The results are not an artefact of sample selection bias; The smallest companies face the highest exit rates, but together with the largest firms they are least vulnerable to take-over.

Acs and Armington (2001)   *B - Static analysis and version 2*

DATA CHARACTERISTICS - Data for the entire population of U.S. businesses with employees included in the LEEM file (approximately 6 million establishments) over the 1994-1995 period are used to analyse the relationship of their growth rates to their firm size, establishment age and establishment size.

RESEARCH METHODS - Observations on individual establishments are grouped into cells with other establishments that had similar characteristics (as in Dunne, Roberts and Samuelson, 1989); Then average gross and net job flows are calculated for each cell, based on the aggregate over all the establishments in each cell; These constructed cells are the observations on which the regression analysis is based; Finally, variations in gross and net job growth rates are estimated as log-linear functions of the age of establishments, the size of firms, and additionally, by the establishment size in multi-unit firms.

MAJOR FINDINGS - *Gibrat's Law* holds broadly only for existing firms with multiple establishments, after taking into consideration the effects of establishment size and age on their growth rates; The employment growth rates are negatively related to the size of establishments (individual business locations), whether they were single establishments/firms or units of multi-establishment firms; However, they are not significantly related to the size of the firms that own these establishments.

Delmar, Davidsson and Gartner (2003)   *B - Static analysis and version 2*

DATA CHARACTERISTICS - Using data for 11,748 Swedish manufacturing and service firms in existence in 1996, the Authors analyse their growth for each year during the previous 10 years (1987 to 1996); From this population of firms a sample of 1,501 high-growth firms is extracted according to multiple criteria; Growth is measured using 19 different indicators, including relative and absolute sales growth, relative and absolute employee growth, organic growth *vs.* acquisition growth, the regularity and volatility of growth rates over the 10-year period.

RESEARCH METHODS - A four-step approach to cluster analysis is utilised for developing a taxonomy of growth patterns; The first step is the selection of 19 growth variables as a base for clustering; Then, the population of firms is divided into a try-out sample and a hold-out sample, with the latter used to validate the results from the former; The number of clusters is determined using hierarchical clustering with Ward's method and Euclidean distances; The third step is aimed at validating the most stable solution; For this purpose, the hold-out sample is used and a K-means clustering is performed using the centroids from the try-out sample as a base; A second cluster using hierarchical clustering with Ward's method is then performed; By using the lambda statistics in comparing the first clustering to the second one, it is found that the highest stability is achieved with a seven-cluster solution, which is taken as optimal from both theoretical and empirical viewpoint; In the fourth step, the seven-cluster solution is extracted on the complete high-growth population of firms, and this in order to find a stable cluster solution and thereby securing its internal validity.

MAJOR FINDINGS - Seven growth patterns are identified, leading to contrasting results as far as *Gibrat's Law* is concerned; The most interesting results are found for the following clusters: *Super absolute growers*: SMEs in knowledge intensive manufacturing industries exhibit high absolute growth both in sales and employment; *Steady sales growers*: large firms in traditional manufacturing industries exhibit rapid growth in sales and negative employment growth; *Super relative growers*: SMEs in knowledge-intensive service industries are found to have a somewhat erratic development of both sales and employment; *Erratic one-shot growers*: SMEs in low-technology services exhibit on average negative size development, with exception of one single very strong-growth year.

Piergiovanni, Santarelli, Klomp and Thurik (2003)   B - *Static analysis and version 2*

DATA CHARACTERISTICS – 9,051 newborn firms in five 4-digit Italian hospitality industries (Restaurants, Cafeterias, Cafes, Hotels and camping sites) between 1989 and 1994; Annual observations for firm size are available from INPS (National Institite for Social Security) data files; Size is measured in terms of employment.

RESEARCH METHODS - Divide the observed firm sizes into several size classes and then examines whether firm growth rates are equally distributed across these classes; To construct these size classes firms were ranked in order of size and divided into quartiles in each sub-sector in the hospitality sector; Similarly, firm growth rates were also divided into quartiles. If the observed frequencies of the resulting 16 cells in the cross tables of firm size and growth rates are equal, *Gibrat's Law* would be supported. Whether or not growth rates and firm size are independent is tested using the χ^2 statistic.

MAJOR FINDINGS - For the sample containing only surviving firms *Gibrat's Law* is rejected in 4 of the 5 sub-sectors; Only for the Camping sites are size and growth found to be statistically independent.

Audretsch, Klomp, Santarelli and Thurik (2004)   B - *Static analysis and version 2*

DATA CHARACTERISTICS – 1,170 firm in five 4-digit Dutch hospitality industries (Restaurants, Cafeterias, Cafes, Hotels and Camping sites) between 1987 and 1991; Annual observations for firm size are available from CBS (Statistics Netherlands) data files; While a firm can consist of more than one establishment, 94% of all firms in Dutch hospitality are single-establishment enterprises, reflecting a sector of independent and family-owned businesses; Size is measured in terms of sales.

RESEARCH METHODS - Divide the observed firm sizes into several size classes and then examines whether firm growth rates are equally distributed across these classes; To construct these size classes firms were ranked in order of size and divided into quartiles in each sub-sector in the hospitality sector; Similarly, firm growth rates were also divided into quartiles; If the observed frequencies of the resulting 16 cells in the cross tables of firm size and growth rates are equal, *Gibrat's Law* would be supported; Whether or not growth rates and firm size are independent is tested using the χ^2 statistic.

MAJOR FINDINGS - For the sample containing only surviving firms the *Law* is accepted for the Cafes, Hotels and Camping sites, but is rejected for the Restaurants and Cafeterias.

Johansson (2004)	*B - Static analysis and version 2*

DATA CHARACTERISTICS – Annual data for firms in the Swedish IT industry, covering manufacturing and services, compiled by Statistics Sweden are available for the 1993-1998 period; Size is measured in terms of employment.

RESEARCH METHODS - Conclusions are drawn based on regression results using OLS and fixed and random effects; A panel data approach is applied.

MAJOR FINDINGS - *Gibrat's Law* is rejected: firm growth decreases with firm size as well as with firm age; The research method does not influence the findings: *Gibrat's Law* is rejected regardless of the estimation technique that has been applied.

Lensink, van Steen and Sterken (2005)	*B - Static analysis and version 2*

DATA CHARACTERISTICS – This paper used data from an annual survey among a panel of Dutch firms; Data on 811 firms for years 1995 and 1999 are used for the estimates dealing with *Gibrat's Law*.

RESEARCH METHODS - Separate multinomial logit regressions for investment, labour demand, and expected maturity are estimated for small firms with less than 50 employees and large firms with more than 50 employees in 1995; Lensink, van Steen and Sterken check whether firm growth (measured as the difference between the number of employees in 1999 and 1995) has a different shape for small and large firms.

MAJOR FINDINGS - In general, it is argued that there is no complete clear picture that emerges from the analysis of firm size; This finding is in line with *Gibrat's Law*: firm growth is independent of firm size.

Table 3 - Static analysis and version 3

Authors (year of publication)	*Model and version*
Hart and Prais (1956)	*C - Static analysis and version 3*

DATA CHARACTERISTICS - Quoted companies in the U.K. at 6 years between 1885 and 1950; Companies listed in the categories (Breweries and Distilleries, Commercial and Industrial and Iron, Coal and Steel) are added up.

RESEARCH METHODS - Firms have been grouped into 3 approximately numerical equal classes, called small, medium and large; The distribution of growth rates (defined as final size divided by original size) of small, medium and large firms are compared for a 16-year period.

MAJOR FINDINGS - The distributions of growth rates for the three size classes are quite equal; *Gibrat's Law* tends to hold.

Simon and Bonini (1958)	*C - Static analysis and version 3*

DATA CHARACTERISTICS - 500 largest U.S. industrial corporations from 1954 to 1956; The sample of Hart and Prais (1956) is also used.

RESEARCH METHODS - Firms have been grouped into 3 size classes, called small, medium and large; The distribution of growth rates are compared for the three groups; Also a plot on a logarithmic scale of firm size at the beginning and the end of the time interval is drawn.

MAJOR FINDINGS - The distributions of growth rates for the 3 size classes are quite equal; The regression line in the plot has a slope of approximately 450 and the plot is homoscedastic; *Gibrat's Law* tends to hold.

Hymer and Pashigian (1962)   *C - Static analysis and version 3*

DATA CHARACTERISTICS – 1,000 largest U.S. manufacturing firms of December 1946; Growth rate is measured by the percentage change in the assets between 1946 and 1955.

RESEARCH METHODS - In ten 2-digit industries the firms were ranked by size into quartiles; The mean and standard deviation for the size classes are compared.

MAJOR FINDINGS - The mean growth rate is not related to the size of the firm while the standard deviation of the distribution of growth rates is inversely related to the size of the firm; *Gibrat's Law* tends to fail.

Mansfield (1962)   *C - Static analysis and version 3*

DATA CHARACTERISTICS – Almost all firms in three U.S. manufacturing industries (Steel, Petroleum refining and Rubber tire) are observed; In each industry several periods of some 10 years between 1916 and 1957 are considered.

RESEARCH METHODS - *Gibrat's Law* is tested in two ways; Firstly by regressing the logarithm of size at the end of the period on the logarithm of size at the beginning of the period and secondly by testing the ratio of variances of growth rates of the largest firms and the smallest firms.

MAJOR FINDINGS - The regression analyses show that the results are quite consistent with *Gibrat's Law* in all 10 cases; The variances of growth rates are significantly lower for the largest firms than for the smallest firms in 6 out of 10 cases; This last result conflicts with *Gibrat's Law*.

Singh and Whittington (1975)   *C - Static analysis and version 3*

DATA CHARACTERISTICS – All quoted U.K. companies in some industries (Manufacturing, Construction, Distribution and Miscellaneous Services) which survived over the period 1948-1960 (1,955 companies); The period 1948-1960 is divided into the sub-periods 1948-1954 and 1954-1960.

RESEARCH METHODS - *Gibrat's Law* is tested for all industries together and for 21 industries separately; The mean and the standard deviation of the growth rates are related to the size classes of the firms; For every industry a regression is carried out for the logarithms of size in 1960 on the logarithm of size in 1948.

MAJOR FINDINGS - The average growth rate of firms shows a weak positive relationship with size, while the standard deviation of growth rates declines with an increase in firm size; *Gibrat's Law* fails; Regression results show that in 19 out of 21 industries the large firms grow faster; However the results are significant in only three industries.

Droucopoulos (1983)   *C - Static analysis and version 3*

DATA CHARACTERISTICS – Data for the world's largest industrial firms are collected for 4 time periods, 1957-1977, 1967-1972, 1972-1977 and 1967-1977; The numbers of observations are 152, 420, 551 and 396 for the periods of time respectively.

RESEARCH METHODS - Growth rates are regressed on size and industry and country dummies; Second- and third-order results for the size variables are also given.

MAJOR FINDINGS - A weak negative relationship between growth and size is found for the bulk of the firms, although the period 1972-1977 suggests that growth is positively related to size; It seems that *Gibrat's Law* does not hold, but departures of the *Law* are modest and vary over time.

Buckley, Dunning and Pearce (1984)   *C - Static analysis and version 3*

DATA CHARACTERISTICS – Data for the world's largest firms, classified by 19 industry groups and nationality, in 1972 and 1977 are obtained; The sample consists of 636 and 866 firms in 1972 and 1977 respectively.

RESEARCH METHODS - Growth rates and profitability are regressed on size, the degree of multinationality, quadratic terms of size and multinationality and industry and nationality dummies.

MAJOR FINDINGS - The relationship between firm growth and size is not (often) significant; *Gibrat's Law* tends to hold; However, growth rates differ significantly between nationalities and industry groups.

Hall (1987)   *C - Static analysis and version 3*

DATA CHARACTERISTICS – A sample of 1,778 publicly traded manufacturing firms in the U.S. is used; The period considered is 1972-1983; The firms cover 90% of the employment in the manufacturing sector in 1976 but only 1% of the firms; Two sub-periods 1973-1979 and 1976-1983 are considered.

RESEARCH METHODS - Regression analysis is carried out for (employment) growth rates on size (measured by the logarithm of employment); Hall corrects for sample selection, measurement errors and heteroscedasticity and also tests for nonlinearity.

MAJOR FINDINGS - A negative relation between size and growth rates is found; The relation is almost the same for the smallest and the largest firms in the sample; *Gibrat's Law* fails; The variance of growth rates declines with size.

Bourlakis (1990)   *C - Static analysis and version 3*

DATA CHARACTERISTICS – Data on 633 corporations in the Greek manufacturing industries between 1966 and 1986 are used; 305 corporations survived over the twenty years; All limited liability and public limited corporations into twenty 2-digit industries are registered.

RESEARCH METHODS - Regression results for growth rates on size, age and other explanatory variables are obtained; The results are controlled for sample selection bias and heteroscedasticity; Results are also reported separately for non-durable and durable consumers' goods and for capital goods markets.

MAJOR FINDINGS - Firm growth rates decline with age and size; *Gibrat's Law* is rejected; The effects of size and age on the growth equations are quite similar for three different types of markets.

Konings and Faggio (2003)   *C - Static analysis and version 3*

DATA CHARACTERISTICS – Firm level data from the Amadeus CD-ROM, a pan European financial database provided by Bureau van Dijk Electronic Publishing SA are available; The unbalanced panel data set contains information on 834 firms in Poland, 233 firms in Estonia, 511 firms in Slovenia and 1,548 firms in Bulgaria over the period 1993-1997, and for 3776 firms in Romania between 1994 and 1997; Data on firm employment size are retrieved from company accounts published by Polish InfoCredit, Estonian Krediidiinfo AS, Intercredit Ljubljana, Creditreform Bulgaria and the Romanian Chamber of Commerce and Industry.

RESEARCH METHODS - Konings and Faggio estimate 5 (one for each country) nested specifications of an employment growth model where the dependent variable is the firm annual employment growth at time t and the independent variable is the log firm size at time t–2; They further include a trade orientation dummy, two ownership dummies (foreign and state, the benchmark being "domestic private"), interactions variables between lagged firm size and ownership dummies, regional and time dummies; They follow Hamilton (1998) in using robust regression analysis to estimate the firm growth equation.

MAJOR FINDINGS - The underlying assumption is that a negative relationship between firm size and growth (implying that *Gibrat's Law* does not hold) might be interpreted as a test of initial restructuring of large enterprises, since transition requires the downsizing of large and inefficient state-owned enterprises; Negative relationship between size and growth is found for all five countries, leading to a rejection of *Gibrat's Law*.

Audretsch, Klomp, Santarelli and Thurik (2004)   C - *Static analysis and version 3*

DATA CHARACTERISTICS – 1,170 firm in five 4-digit Dutch hospitality industries (Restaurants, Cafeterias, Cafes, Hotels and Camping sites) between 1987 and 1991; Annual observations for firm size are available from CBS (Statistics Netherlands) data files; While a firm can consist of more than one establishment, 94% of all firms in Dutch hospitality are single-establishment enterprises, reflecting a sector of independent and family-owned businesses; Size is measured in terms of sales.

RESEARCH METHODS - Divide the observed firm sizes into several size classes and then examines whether firm growth rates are equally distributed across these classes; To construct these size classes firms were ranked in order of size and divided into quartiles in each sub-sector in the hospitality sector; Similarly, firm growth rates were also divided into quartiles; If the observed frequencies of the resulting 16 cells in the cross tables of firm size and growth rates are equal, *Gibrat's Law* would be supported; Whether or not growth rates and firm size are independent is tested using the χ^2 statistic.

MAJOR FINDINGS - For the sample of large firms *Gibrat's Law* is accepted for 4 sub-sectors, the only exception being represented by the restaurants sub-sector.

Table 4 - Temporal analysis and version 2

Authors (year of publication)	Model and version
Mansfield (1962)	D - *Temporal analysis and version 2*

DATA CHARACTERISTICS - Almost all firms in three U.S. manufacturing industries (Steel, Petroleum refining and Rubber tire) are observed; In each industry several periods of some 10 years between 1916 and 1957 are considered.

RESEARCH METHODS - Mansfield analyses the amount of mobility in an industry i.e. the extent to which firms change their relative positions in the size distribution.

MAJOR FINDINGS - Tentative findings, based on only 10 observations, are reported; It is suggested however, that the amount of mobility in an industry depends significantly on its size and its market structure; *Gibrat's Law* seems to fail.

Contini and Revelli (1989)   D - *Temporal analysis and version 2*

DATA CHARACTERISTICS - Data for Italian manufacturing firms are used for the period 1980-1986; The period is divided in two sub-periods, a recession period (1980-1983) and an expansion period (1983-1986); In both sub-periods data for over 1,000 firms are available.

RESEARCH METHODS - Regression results for (3 year employment) growth rates on (3 year) lagged growth rates, on firm size and on firm age are obtained; For the period 1983-1986 also estimates for only large firms (more than 10 employees) are given; The problems of heteroscedasticity and sample selection bias are mentioned.

MAJOR FINDINGS - The Authors argue that small firms (which form the largest part of the data) often have expansions and contractions, measured over periods of 3-4 years, in alternating sequence; This explains the negative relation between growth and lagged growth; When only larger firms are selected the lagged growth changes sign and becomes significantly larger than zero; Overall the departures from *Gibrat's Law* are modest.

Wagner (1992)   D - *Temporal analysis and version 2*

DATA CHARACTERISTICS - Data for 7,000 firms which formed the manufacturing sector of the German federal state Lower Saxony between 1978 and 1989 are used; In most industries only firms in which at least 20 persons are employed are included; Results are given for various sub-periods.

RESEARCH METHODS - Chesher's (1979) method, regressing the deviation of the logarithm of the firm size from the mean of the logarithms of the firm sizes at year t (z_t) on the similar deviations one and two years before, is applied; Like Chesher a first order auto-regressive process is assumed; Results are reported for different periods of time and a distinction is made between firms producing basic products and firms producing consumer goods.

MAJOR FINDINGS - In 18 out of 20 regressions where no distinction in firm size has been made *Gibrat's Law* is rejected, although the (consistent) estimates for the coefficient in the regression of z_t on z_{t-1} is close to one in each of the 20 regressions; In general positive autocorrelation between growth rates is found; Neither in the case of firms producing basic products nor in the case of firms producing consumer goods small firms grow systematically faster or slower compared to large firms, or *vice versa*.

Tschoegl (1996)   D - *Temporal analysis and version 2*

DATA CHARACTERISTICS - Data (employment size) on 66 Japanese regional banks over the 1954-1993 period are available.

RESEARCH METHODS - A logarithmic model and a percentage growth model are estimated, each of which incorporates the possibility of serial correlation of growth rates in the equation.

MAJOR FINDINGS - The results suggest that *Gibrat's Law* does not hold, since larger Japanese regional banks tend to grow more slowly than smaller ones; Nevertheless, the magnitude of the deviation from one in the logarithmic specification is not large: the minimum estimate is 0.940 and the maximum 1.016; Controlling for sample selection was not necessary in this particular study because no Japanese regional bank has failed during the period of observation.

Harhoff, Stahl and Woywode (1998)   D - *Temporal analysis and version 2*

DATA CHARACTERISTICS - Data for 10,902 German manufacturing firms extracted from the Creditreform Database are used for the 1989-1994 period; Size is measured in terms of employment.

RESEARCH METHODS - Chesher's (1979) method, regressing the deviation of the logarithm of the firm size from the mean of the logarithms of the firm sizes at year t (z_t) on the similar deviations in the initial year and one year before is applied; Like Chesher a first order autoregressive process is assumed; Log of size in the last year for which data are available is regressed on log of initial size for the entire period; The problems of sample selection bias (Heckman's (1979) method), heteroscedasticity and the persistence of growth are analysed.

MAJOR FINDINGS - Evidence against *Gibrat's Law* is found, and the marginal effect of firm size is negative for 93.8% of all observations in the sample; The effect of firm age is less pronounced: it is negative for 86.4% of the observations and only weakly significant for the majority of cases.

Hart and Oulton (1999)   D - *Temporal analysis and version 2*

DATA CHARACTERISTICS - Data for 29,000 U.K. independent firms divided into 12 size
(employment) classes over the period 1989-1993.

RESEARCH METHODS - Estimation of a Galton regression model in which Galtonian
regression towards the geometric mean occurs when $\beta<1$; A first group of
estimations is run disaggregating the model to size classes, a second one
disaggregating the model to ten SIC (1980) divisions.

MAJOR FINDINGS - Small companies grow more quickly than larger companies with more
than eight employees, therefore leading to rejection of *Gibrat's Law*; The within
size regressions show that the smallest size classes have the largest Galtonian
regression towards the mean, which implies that the smaller companies created
proportionately more jobs; Disaggregation of the Galton regression model to SIC
divisions shows that in each SIC divisions (including "Distribution and Hotels") the
regression slope is below unity.

Fariñas and Moreno (2000)   D - *Temporal analysis and version 2*

DATA CHARACTERISTICS - Fariñas and Moreno used a sample of 1,971 manufacturing
firms drawn from the Encuesta sobre Estrategieas Empresariales (ESEE) carried by
the Ministry of Industry in Spain; Average annual growth rates are considered over
the period 1990-1995, for a total number of 6,861 observations on non-failing firms;
Size is measured in terms of employment.

RESEARCH METHODS - The empirical model examines how the mean growth rate varies
across size and age of firms, controlling for industry and year categories.

MAJOR FINDINGS - Application of Wald statistics using robust variance estimates shows
that size and age have significant effects on growth patterns, with the mean growth
rates of non-failing firms which decrease with firm size and firm age; When
coefficients are examined for a given size category, mean growth rates are
decreasing with age although this relationship is less pronounced for the largest
category of firms with more than 500 employees.

Machado and Mata (2000)   D - *Temporal analysis and version 2*

DATA CHARACTERISTICS - The data set includes all firms operating in 155 industries in
Portuguese manufacturing in 1983 (18,552 firms) and 1991 (26,515 firms);
Information comes from an inquiry conducted by the Portuguese Ministry of
Employment and covers the whole range of firm sizes.

RESEARCH METHODS - Machado and Mata use the Box-Cox quantile regression model to
analyse the firm size distribution (FSD); In particular, the effect of selected industry
attributes is estimated on the location, scale, skewness, and kurtosis of the
conditional FSD; The model is estimated by Generalised Least Squares and a
normality test is performed on the standardized estimated residuals.

MAJOR FINDINGS - Industry attributes are found to affect the size of firms in the same
direction across the distribution, but their effects are much greater at the largest
quintiles; Over time, the FSD shifts toward smaller firms, due to the way the
economy responds to industry characteristics; Accordingly, the prediction of
lognormality, implied by *Gibrat's Law*, is rejected by the observed distribution of
firm sizes.

Heshmati (2001)   D - *Temporal analysis and version 2*

DATA CHARACTERISTICS - A sample of Swedish firms (5,913) with a taxable turnover
exceeding SEK 10,000 over the period 1993-1998 is considered; Size is measured
in terms of employment, total assets and total sales.

RESEARCH METHODS - Three distinct panel models are estimated for employment growth, assets growth and sales growth respectively; In estimation of each model; The estimation methods account for heterogeneity among firms not reflected in their age and size differences; In the estimation of the growth rate Heshmati controls for various factors characterizing the sample firms, their performance, human capital and local labour market conditions.

MAJOR FINDINGS - The relationship between firm size and firm growth is found to be negative in the employment model, while it is positive in the sales model, which implies the presence of scale effects when sales are considered; The size effect is instead not statistically significant in the assets model.

Vander Vennet (2001)   D - *Temporal analysis and version 2*

DATA CHARACTERISTICS - Data on the size of the aggregate banking sectors in 23 OECD countries over the 1985-1994 period are available; Two measures of size are employed: *1*) the total asset volume of the aggregated banking sector, calculated for the broadest possible sample of credit institutions; *2*) a measure of adjusted total asset (ATA) incorporating an estimate of off-balance-sheet activities.

RESEARCH METHODS - Panel data estimates for the entire 1985-1994 period and the 1985-1989 and 1990-1994 sub-periods are conducted for each of the two measures of size; Chesher's (1979) method, regressing the deviation of the logarithm of the size of market from the mean of the logarithms of market sizes at year t (z_t) on the similar deviations in the previous year is applied; Like Chesher a first order autoregressive process is assumed.

MAJOR FINDINGS - It is found that the 1985-1989 period was characterized by size convergence, implying that smaller bank sectors were expanding more rapidly; However, in the 1990-1994 period the pattern reversed to proportionate growth; From this evidence, Vander Vennet argues that the shift in the growth pattern of the bank markets is related to other determinants of their expansion, including the macroeconomic growth performance of the economy and the degree of operational efficiency of the banking sector.

Becchetti and Trovato (2002)   D - *Temporal analysis and version 2*

DATA CHARACTERISTICS - A sample of Italian small and medium sized firm (included in the Mediocredito Centrale database) over the period 1995-1997 is considered: 1,144 with less than 50 employees, 1,427 with less than 100 employees. A control sample of 462 firms with more than 100 employees is also analysed.

RESEARCH METHODS - Estimation of a multivariate model in which the dependent variable represents changes in size and each regressor represents a different factor that is expected to affect firm growth. Controls are included for age, size, the availability of external finance, market rents and access to foreign market.

MAJOR FINDINGS - *Gibrat's Law* is not rejected for large firms, whereas it is rejected for small and medium sized firms under financial constraints.

Hardwick and Adams (2002)   D - *Temporal analysis and version 2*

DATA CHARACTERISTICS - Annual data for 176 firms in the life insurance industry in the U.K. that have been in operation in 1987 and survived until at least until the end of 1996 under the same corporate name have been collected. Size is measured as annual total net assets in the 1987-1996 period. Growth is measured as "organic" growth in firm size.

RESEARCH METHODS - Serial correlation is measured applying method introduced by Chesher (1979). Moreover, a multivariate model in which the dependent variable is the logarithm of size is regressed on a variety of different factors that is expected to affect firm growth. Controls are included for the input cost ratio, for profitability,

for the output mix and for some dummy variables. Estimation results are corrected
for sample attrition bias and the WLS procedure is applied.

MAJOR FINDINGS - *Gibrat's Law* is accepted for the entire period of 1987-1996. The firm
size-growth relation of life insurers varies, however, over time. Smaller firms grew
faster than larger ones in the booming years 1987-1990, while the larger firms grew
faster during the recession of 1990-1993 and continued to do so during the recovery
years of 1993-1996. When firm-specific determinants of asset growth are analysed,
no evidence is found that the growth of life insurance companies is inversely related
to profitability.

Del Monte and Papagni (2003)   D - *Temporal analysis and version 2*

DATA CHARACTERISTICS - A sample of 659 Italian manufacturing firms over the period
1989-1997 is considered; Size is measured in terms of total sales (deflated with the
industry deflator of value added) and employment.

RESEARCH METHODS - Distinct panel models are estimated for firms classified by sectors
in Pavitt's sense and employment size class; A unit root test is employed based on
the estimates carried out on the time series of each firm; The null hypothesis of unit
root is H_0: $\beta_i = 0$ for all i; A test based on individual Lagrange multiplier
(introduced by Im, Pesaran and Shin, 2003) is employed on a sub-sample of firms
relative to sales.

MAJOR FINDINGS - Test of *Gibrat's Law* performed by applying a panel unit root test
confirms the hypothesis put forward by Gibrat on the stochastic features of the rate
of growth of firms.

Chen and Lu (2003)   D - *Temporal analysis and version 2*

DATA CHARACTERISTICS - *Taiwan Economic Journal* (TAJ) database from 1988 to 1999,
containing 48 seasons of data of publicly-traded companies; Total number of firms
in the sample is 258; Size is measured in terms of fixed assets.

RESEARCH METHODS - Panel unit root test to study the relationship between the
logarithms of firm sizes at the beginning of the period and at the end of the period:
a) under the independent and identical distribution assumption (iid); *b*) by
considering the cross-sectional correlations.

MAJOR FINDINGS - Under the iid assumption, *Gibrat's Law* does not hold in the case of 4
(including Food, Textiles, Electronics) out 18 industries alone; When the cross-
sectional correlations are taken into account, the *Law* cannot be rejected for 6
(including Pulp, Automobile and Tourism) out of 18 industries; Thus, the
conclusion is not the same when using different estimation procedures.

Piergiovanni, Santarelli, Klomp and Thurik (2003)   D - *Temporal analysis and version 2*

DATA CHARACTERISTICS – 9,051 newborn firms in five 4-digit Italian hospitality
industries (Restaurants, Cafeterias, Cafes, Hotels and Camping sites) between 1989
and 1994; Annual observations for firm size are available from INPS (National
Institute for Social Security) data files; Size is measured in terms of employment.

RESEARCH METHODS - Use the non-linear regression procedure by Marquardt (1963) to
obtain (asymptotic) standard errors for β and ρ. *Gibrat's Law* is considered to be
valid if the joint hypotheses $(\beta\ \rho) = (1\ 0)$ is accepted. Assuming that the estimators
of β and ρ are asymptotically normally distributed, the test-statistic for the joint
hypothesis is (asymptotically) chi-squared distributed with two degrees of freedom.

MAJOR FINDINGS - Only in 1 of the 15 cases *Gibrat's Law* is accepted in a
straightforward manner; However, application of a probability plot test of the "droit
de Henry" type to the logarithm of the differences in size between final (1994) and
initial (1989) year, suggests that also for the cafeterias business group does the
empirical distribution of firm sizes converge towards a lognormal distribution.

Fotopoulos and Louri (2004)   D - *Temporal analysis and version 2*

DATA CHARACTERISTICS – Data on 2,640 Greek manufacturing firms operating in both 1992 and 1997 are used; Information on employment, age and share of foreign ownership is available.

RESEARCH METHODS - A non parametric kernel density estimation is performed; The data on the logarithm of firm size in 1997 are taken in deviation from their mean, so that the resulting variable has a zero mean; Besides, quantile regressions are performed at various quantiles.

MAJOR FINDINGS - Firm growth is not quite random, since both firm size and age have a definitely negative effect on growth, which is more important for the faster growing firms.

Audretsch, Klomp, Santarelli and Thurik (2004)   D - *Temporal analysis and version 2*

DATA CHARACTERISTICS – 1,170 firm in five 4-digit Dutch hospitality industries (Restaurants, Cafeterias, Cafes, Hotels and Camping sites) between 1987 and 1991; Annual observations for firm size are available from CBS (Statistics Netherlands) data files; While a firm can consist of more than one establishment, 94% of all firms in Dutch hospitality are single-establishment enterprises, reflecting a sector of independent and family-owned businesses; Size is measured in terms of sales.

RESEARCH METHODS - Use the non-linear regression procedure by Marquardt (1963) to obtain (asymptotic) standard errors for β and ρ. *Gibrat's Law* is considered to be valid if the joint hypotheses $(\beta\ \rho) = (1\ 0)$ is accepted. Assuming that the estimators of β and ρ are asymptotically normally distributed, the test-statistic for the joint hypothesis is (asymptotically) chi-squared distributed with two degrees of freedom.

MAJOR FINDINGS - In 11 of the 15 cases *Gibrat's Law* is accepted; This is a sharp contrast to the findings for manufacturing by, among others, Singh and Whittington (1975), Chesher (1979), Kumar (1985) and Wagner (1992) where the *Law* is generally rejected; In all of these studies the autoregressive coefficients (ρ) are positive and statistically different from zero, while β is close to unity; Only negligible or very modest autocorrelation coefficients are found in this exercise.

Harris and Trainor (2005)   D - *Temporal analysis and version 2*

DATA CHARACTERISTICS – Data from the Annual Respondents Database (ARD) for a subset of 26 4-digit industries in U.K. manufacturing covering the period 1973-1998. The sample accounts for one-third of total manufacturing real gross output during the relevant period; Size is measured as real gross output, employment and real gross value added.

RESEARCH METHODS - Four panel unit root tests to study the relationship between growth and size. The tests were applied to unbalanced plant-level panel data; Testing procedure based on the Levin, Lin and Chu (2002) tests and Im, Pesaran and Shin (2003) test as implemented by Pedroni (1999) when using unbalanced data.

MAJOR FINDINGS - *Gibrat's Law* is rejected in virtually all cases; The results of applying panel unit root tests to plant-level real gross output data for various industry samples, broken down into plant size and sub-periods shows that there is strong evidence to reject *Gibrat's Law* that firm growth is a random process in favour of the alternative proposition of mean reversion; Results are presented for real gross output only; However, results using employment or value added growth show the same pattern.

Table 5 - Temporal analysis and version 3

Authors (year of publication)	Model and version

Hart and Prais (1956)   E - *Temporal analysis and version 3*

DATA CHARACTERISTICS - Quoted companies in the U.K. at 6 years between 1885 and 1950; Companies listed in the categories (Breweries and Distilleries, Commercial and Industrial and Iron, Coal and Steel) are added up.

RESEARCH METHODS - The mobility of firms is considered for 5 periods of time; For the firms the consecutive ranks in the distributions and the deviations of the firm size from the mean size in the period are analysed; The birth of new firms, the exits of firms and the changes in size distributions of incumbents are looked after separately.

MAJOR FINDINGS - In any period of time business units that cease to exist are smaller, by about a half than the average size of units alive at the beginning of the period; *Gibrat's Law* holds for the period from 1885 till 1939; In the period from 1939 till 1950 the smaller companies grow much faster than the larger ones; *Gibrat's Law* fails for the last period.

Singh and Whittington (1975)   E - *Temporal analysis and version 3*

DATA CHARACTERISTICS - All quoted U.K. companies in some industries (Manufacturing, Construction, Distribution and Miscellaneous Services) which survived over the period 1948-1960 (1955 companies); The period 1948-1960 is divided into the sub-periods 1948-1954 and 1954-1960.

RESEARCH METHODS - The growth rates in the period 1954-1960 are regressed on the growth rates in the period 1948-1954; The "opening" size is also added as an explanatory variable to the regression analysis.

MAJOR FINDINGS - There is a significant tendency that firms which have an above (or below) average growth rate over the first 6-year period also have an above (or below) average growth rate in the subsequent 6-year period; So *Gibrat's Law* fails; The values of R^2 are uniformly low (about 0.05) for the different industries.

Chesher (1979)   E - *Temporal analysis and version 3*

DATA CHARACTERISTICS - A sample of 183 quoted companies in the U.K. that are classified as "Commercial and Industrial" is used; Only companies that are in existence in 1960 and in 1969 are included; In each year of the period 1960-1969 data are available.

RESEARCH METHODS - Regression analysis is proposed for the deviation of the logarithm of the firm size from the mean of the logarithms of the firm sizes at year t on the similar deviation one year before; Chesher assumes a first order autoregressive process in the disturbances to get consistent estimates for the regression coefficient.

MAJOR FINDINGS - The estimation of the regression coefficient is close to unity (which is consistent with *Gibrat's Law*), but the first order autoregressive correlation coefficient is quite large and positive; For the various years the hypothesis that the regression coefficient is equal to one *and* the first order autoregressive coefficient is equal to zero is rejected; *Gibrat's Law* is not valid.

Kumar (1985)   E - *Temporal analysis and version 3*

DATA CHARACTERISTICS - Over 2,000 quoted companies for the U.K. over the period 1960-1976 are used; 5 sub-samples for different periods are available; Internal growth rates and acquisition growth rates are distinguished; 5 different size measures are used.

RESEARCH METHODS - Five year growth rates are regressed on growth rates in the period five years before and on the (initial) firm size; 3 different assets growth rates are used; Negligible heteroscedasticity was found, so no correction was made;

Regression results for acquisition growth rates on past acquisition growth rates and (initial) size are also obtained.

MAJOR FINDINGS - There was some persistency in firm growth rates over time, but is was weaker than in Singh and Whittington (1975); R^2_{adj} is about 0.02; There was a mild tendency for firm growth to be negatively related to size; *Gibrat's Law* is not valid; The results are quite robust for the use of different growth measures and time periods.

Amirkhalkhali and Mukhopadhyay (1993)   E - *Temporal analysis and version 3*

DATA CHARACTERISTICS - The data set consists of 231 firms, chosen from the Fortune list of the largest firms in the U.S., who maintain their identity over the 1965-1987 period; The sample is broken down into 4 sub-periods.

RESEARCH METHODS - Growth rates are regressed on growth rates in the preceding period and on the (initial) firm size; A dummy variable for (76) R&D-intensive and (155) non-R&D-intensive firms is used; The Authors mention the problem of sample selection.

MAJOR FINDINGS - The results suggest that *Gibrat's Law* does not hold; The autocorrelation between growth rates appears to be positive; Moreover a weak negative relationship between firm size and growth is found.

Amaral, Buldyrev, Havlin, Leschhorn, Maass, Salinger, Stanley and Stanley (1997)
                                                     E - *Temporal analysis and version 3*

DATA CHARACTERISTICS - The Compustat database is used for analysis of all U.S. manufacturing publicly-traded firms (with SIC code from 2000 to 3999) during the 1974-1993 period.

RESEARCH METHODS - Standard and separate panel tests of *Gibrat's Law* are conducted, based on regression of log growth on initial log firm size; Tests include a set of time dummy variables, to control for macro-economic or other influences on growth common to all firms and specific to each time period, and a full set of interaction dummies between sectors and time periods, to control for sector-specific shocks in each time-period; Monte Carlo methods are used to investigate the sampling distributions and power functions of the tests.

MAJOR FINDINGS - The results, besides pointing to a limitation of the cross-sectional test - which suffers of a loss of power and therefore has difficulty in rejecting *Gibrat's Law* - support the hypothesis that log firm size are mean-reverting (with the tendency towards mean-reversion that is stronger during periods of sluggish economic growth than when growth is high), possibly towards heterogeneous individual firm effects; Accordingly, *Gibrat's Law* is rejected.

Bottazzi, Dosi, Lippi, Pammolli and Riccaboni (2001) E - *Temporal analysis and version 3*

DATA CHARACTERISTICS - Sales figures and market shares for 150 large firms in the pharmaceutical industry are used; The data set covers the seven largest Western markets (U.S., U.K., France, Germany, Spain, Italy and Canada) over the 1987-1997 period.

RESEARCH METHODS - Departure from *Gibrat's Law* is analysed by checking for possible "reversion to the mean" in the data; A growth model - $g_i(t+1)=\beta g_i(t) + \varepsilon(t)$ - is estimated cross-sectionally for all the years.

MAJOR FINDINGS - Values for β statistically equal to one are found, leading to rejection of the "reversion to the mean" hypothesis; According to the Authors, the autocorrelation in firm growth, increasing with the scale of observation, hints at some significant firm-specific structure in the growth process, related with firm-specific organizational competences in the search and introduction of products in different markets.

Goddard, Wilson and Blandon (2002)   E - *Temporal analysis and version 3*

> DATA CHARACTERISTICS - The data set consists of 443 manufacturing firms quoted on the First or Second Divisions of the Japanese Stock Exchange, for which continuous annual data on total assets are available for the period 1980-1996; The firms are classified in 13 broad industrial sectors.
>
> RESEARCH METHODS - Standard and separate panel tests of *Gibrat's Law* are conducted, based on regression of log growth on initial log firm size; Tests include a set of time dummy variables, to control for macro-economic or other influences on growth common to all firms and specific to each time period, and a full set of interaction dummies between sectors and time periods, to control for sector-specific shocks in each time-period; Monte Carlo methods are used to investigate the sampling distributions and power functions of the tests.
>
> MAJOR FINDINGS - The results, besides pointing to a limitation of the cross-sectional test - which suffers of a loss of power and therefore has difficulty in rejecting *Gibrat's Law* - support the hypothesis that log firm size are mean-reverting (with the tendency towards mean-reversion that is stronger during periods of sluggish economic growth than when growth is high), possibly towards heterogeneous individual firm effects; Accordingly, *Gibrat's Law* is rejected.

Pfaffermayr and Bellak (2002)   E - *Temporal analysis and version 3*

> DATA CHARACTERISTICS - Corporate level data for 700 large, both domestic and foreign-owned firms in Austrian manufacturing over the period 1996-1999 are available.
>
> RESEARCH METHODS - Standard estimate of *Gibrat's Law* is conducted, based on regression of log growth on initial log firm size; Accordingly, *Gibrat's Law* cannot be rejected.
>
> MAJOR FINDINGS - Firms' growth turns out to be mainly randomly determined and idiosyncratic with systematic influence being of minor importance.

Geroski, Lazarova, Urga and Walters (2003)   E - *Temporal analysis and version 3*

> DATA CHARACTERISTICS - Data on real total net assets for a sample of 147 large, quoted U.K. firms over the 1955-1985 period are used; These firms represent a balanced sub-sample of the DTI-Meeks-Whittington data set.
>
> RESEARCH METHODS – This paper tests the hypothesis that firms converge towards a common long run size by applying the standard logarithmic model to each firm taken in turn; To check whether the individual time series are integrated, they examine the null hypothesis of non-stationarity by using Dickey-Fuller (DF) tests augmented with one lagged dependent variable, with and without deterministic trends; Since the DF tests are likely to suffer from small sample problems, the Authors then use the tests proposed by Im, Pesaran and Shin (2003) and by Maddala and Wu (1999) to overcome this problem.
>
> MAJOR FINDINGS - The results suggest that the growth rates of firms who survive long enough to record 30 years of history are random; Besides, firm size displays no tendency to converge to either a common, steady state optimum firm size or to a set of stable size differences between firms.

Bothner (2005)   E - *Temporal analysis and version 3*

> DATA CHARACTERISTICS - The data set from International Data Corporation (IDC) consists of 1,140 market segments in 43 countries in which more than 400 vendors sale PCs for the period 1995-1999; Relative size of firms is measured as a function of the level of structural equivalence between firms having market contacts; After defining market contact as a binary outcome, the author weights by the degree of structural equivalence between firms i and k; Consequently, after collecting k firms with which i firm has contact in at least one national market, the level of structural equivalence between i and k is computed on the basis of their similarity in patterns

of shipping computers across segments defined by geography, channel, and technology.

RESEARCH METHODS - Three standard panel tests of *Gibrat's Law* are conducted, based on regression of log growth on initial log firm size; Tests include a set of additional variables, to control for acquisitions, national market size, changes in firm strategy; Firm scope, and size-localized competition.

MAJOR FINDINGS - Proportional growth declines only moderately with size, showing a small departure from *Gibrat's Law*, according to which the estimate on lagged sales would equal unity; Adding fixed effects for firms and for time periods, it is apparent that the coefficient on lagged sales drops substantially below one; Adding covariates identified as important in previous studies of firm growth, the adjustment for acquisitions is significant in light of the added physical, human and marketing related resources a firm has in its possession after such events; The measure of strategic change is instead insignificant; Finally, the effects of scope and of size-localized competition are significant, while that of market size is not.

Table 6 - The post-entry performance of new firms

Authors (year of publication)	Model and version

Dunne, Roberts and Samuelson (1988)   F - *The post-entry performance of new firms*

DATA CHARACTERISTICS The data set covers firms producing in each 4-digit manufacturing industry in the U.S. in the years 1963, 1967, 1972, 1977 and 1982; There are approximately 265,000 firms present in each of the first three years and 295,000 in the last two years; Information is available on different types of entrants, the entry and exits over time and the post entry performance of the entrants.

RESEARCH METHODS - Results for market shares, relative average size of surviving firms and cumulative failure rates for each entry cohort in each year are presented; Means and standard deviations across 387 4-digit industries are given; The results are also disaggregated for 3 types of entrants, *1*) new firms, new plant; *2*) diversifying firm, new plant and *3*) diversifying firm, product mix.

MAJOR FINDINGS - The market share of each cohort declines, on average in each census year following entry; The relative size of each cohort's surviving firms increases as the cohort ages; The cumulative failure rates increases at diminishing rates over time for each cohort; Diversifying firms entering with new plants have the largest relative size of the 3 types of entrants, and the lowest exit rates.

Dunne, Roberts and Samuelson (1989)   F - *The post-entry performance of new firms*

DATA CHARACTERISTICS - The sample of data contains U.S. manufacturing plants that entered in 1967, 1972 or 1977; In order to minimize the effects of potential measurement error only firms that have at least five employees in at least one year are included; This results in a total of 219,754 different plants and in a total of 326,936 plant/year observations because of the multiple time periods.

RESEARCH METHODS - Plant (employment) growth rates and failure rates are regressed on dummies for age categories and size classes; Regressions for mean growth rates and variance of growth rates are carried out for successful plants and for all plants; Separate results are given for single-unit and multi-unit plants.

MAJOR FINDINGS - Failure rates are lower for older plants, regardless of ownership type, and for larger plants, particularly those owned by multi-plant firms; Mean growth rates of successful plants and variance of growth rate of successful plants decline with firm size and age for both single unit and multi-unit plants; For single-plant and multi-plant firms *Gibrat's Law* is rejected in the case of including only successful plants as well as in the case of including all plants.

Phillips and Kirchhoff (1989)   *F - The post-entry performance of new firms*

DATA CHARACTERISTICS - The database covers approximately 93% of full time business activity in the U.S. for the period 1976-1986; The new firms, defined as single, new establishment firms with 500 or fewer employees, are selected.

RESEARCH METHODS - Survival rates and growth rates are reported for different periods of time; Results are differentiated for 9 sectors such as manufacturing and retail trade; Survival and growth are also differentiated by age.

MAJOR FINDINGS - On average 39.8% of new firms survive 6 or more years; The survival rates however more than double for firms that grow; The proportion of firms that grow increases with age; The opportunities for growth varies substantially from industry to industry.

Audretsch and Mahmood (1994)   *F - The post-entry performance of new firms*

DATA CHARACTERISTICS - The post-entry performances of approximately 11,300 manufacturing new firms started in the U.S. in 1976 are observed bi-annually throughout the subsequent 10-year period; It is known if a start-up is a single-plant firm or a multi-plant firm.

RESEARCH METHODS - The mean firm growth rates and failure rates are given over time; The results are also presented for 19 manufacturing sectors; Regression of new firm (employment) growth and survival rates are carried out for different time periods; The explanatory variables used are: firm size, innovative activity, scale economies, capital intensity, industry growth and a dummy for multi-plant firms.

MAJOR FINDINGS - Firm growth is found to be (significantly) negatively influenced by firm size over all periods of time; Firm growth is found to be positively related to the innovative activity, the extent of scale economies, the capital intensity, the industry growth and the multi-plant dummy; The survival rates are positively affected by firm size, industry growth, capital intensity and negatively affected by the extent of scale economies and the multi-plant dummy.

Mata (1994)   *F - The post-entry performance of new firms*

DATA CHARACTERISTICS - Data for 3,308 Portuguese manufacturing firms that entered in 1983 are available; Firms are followed during 5 consecutive years.

RESEARCH METHODS - For each of the years in the period 1984-1987 a growth and survival equation is estimated; (employment) growth rates and firm survival are assumed to depend on (employment) size in the preceding year; Mata discusses both the problems of sample selection and heteroscedasticity.

MAJOR FINDINGS - Survival increases with (start-up) firm size, but a great proportion of new firms disappear in the first years subsequent to their birth; Survivors, however, grow quite fast and small firms grow faster than their larger counterparts; *Gibrat's Law* fails.

Wagner (1994)   *F - The post-entry performance of new firms*

DATA CHARACTERISTICS - Data for 10,743 manufacturing firms established in Lower Saxony, the second largest of the 'old' federal states of Germany, are used for the period 1978-1990; Single establishment new firms with a start-up size of less than 50 employees are focused.

RESEARCH METHODS - Survival and growth of new firms is analysed; A probit model is used to explain firm survival; Exogenous variables are start-up size and 4 industry variables, like concentration, capital intensity, R&D-intensity and the average rate of (employment) growth; For surviving entrants the heterogeneity of growth patterns and the persistence of growth are analysed.

MAJOR FINDINGS - Entrants face a high risk of failure, hazard rates tend to increase during the first years and to decrease afterwards; Firm survival is neither clearly related to start-up size nor to any of the industry variables; Moreover, the actual annual growth of each new small firm seems to be determined by random sampling from the same distribution of growth possibilities; *Gibrat's Law* tends to hold.

Reid (1995)   F - *The post-entry performance of new firms*

DATA CHARACTERISTICS Data for 73 less than 3-year old micro-firms (with fewer than 10 employees) in Scotland for the period 1985-1988 are available; The sample comprises private companies (50%), partnerships (20%), and sole proprietorships (30%).

RESEARCH METHODS - A simultaneous equations model of growth and profitability is estimated.

MAJOR FINDINGS - *Gibrat's Law* is rejected, with smaller among new Small Business Enterprises (SBEs) growing faster than larger new SBEs; *Gibrat's Law* is rejected in favour of an alternative (managerial) hypothesis put forward in the paper which implies a growth/profitability trade-off.

Santarelli (1997)   F - *The post-entry performance of new firms*

DATA CHARACTERISTICS - Data for 11,660 Italian start-ups in the hospitality sector for the period 1989-1994 are available.

RESEARCH METHODS - Chesher's (1979) method, regressing the deviation of the logarithm of the firm size from the mean of the logarithms of the firm sizes at year t (z_t) on the similar deviations in the initial year is applied; Like Chesher a first order auto-regressive process is assumed; 20 groups of region-level equations are estimated.

MAJOR FINDINGS - *Gibrat's Law* cannot be rejected in the case of 14 out of 20 Italian regions, with the estimated parameters not significantly different from one.

Audretsch, Santarelli and Vivarelli (1999)   F - *The post-entry performance of new firms*

DATA CHARACTERISTICS - Data for 1,570 Italian manufacturing (13 industries) firms that entered in 1987 are available; Firms are followed during 6 consecutive years.

RESEARCH METHODS - Survival rates and growth rates are reported; Logit and tobit equations are estimated, in which firm survival is assumed to depend on (employment) size in the initial year; Chesher's (1979) method, regressing the deviation of the logarithm of the firm size from the mean of the logarithms of the firm sizes at year t (z_t) on the similar deviations in the initial year is applied; Like Chesher a first order auto-regressive process is assumed; For the entire 1987-1993 period 2 groups of industry level equations are estimated: one for all firms and one for surviving firms only.

MAJOR FINDINGS - The likelihood of survival does not increase with (start-up) firm size; *Gibrat's Law* is rejected in 9 out of 13 cases in the estimations carried out for all firms, whereas in 11 out of 12 in those for surviving firms only.

Almus and Nerlinger (2000)   F - *The post-entry performance of new firms*

DATA CHARACTERISTICS - Data for West German start-ups in manufacturing (both non-technology and technology intensive branches) for the period 1989-96 (divided into 5 sub-periods: 1990-92: 784 firms; 1991-93: 1, 420; 1992-94: 2, 831; 1993-95: 3, 495; 1994-96: 4, 278) and 3 size classes (less than 5 employers, between 6 and 19, more than 19).

RESEARCH METHODS - Kernel density estimations (with bandwidth parameter 2, so that to calculate the density all employment observations within the interval of the size of 2 employees around the number of employees chosen are included) to test whether the approx. log-normal distribution of firm size holds also for young firms.

MAJOR FINDINGS - Almus and Nerlinger find that *Gibrat's Law* is rejected in all cases with the estimated parameters smaller than one; In addition, the deviation from *Gibrat's Law* is found to decrease with increasing firm size.

Lotti, Santarelli and Vivarelli (2001)   F - *The post-entry performance of new firms*

DATA CHARACTERISTICS - Data for 214 Italian instruments industry firms that entered in 1987 are available; Firms are followed during 6 consecutive years.

RESEARCH METHODS - Chesher's (1979) method, regressing the deviation of the logarithm of the firm size from the mean of the logarithms of the firm sizes at year t (z_t) on the similar deviations in the initial year and one year before is applied; Like Chesher a first order auto-regressive process is assumed; Log of size in the last year for which data are available is regressed on log of initial size for the entire period; Besides, log of size in each year is regressed on log of size in previous year; Each estimate is conducted for all firms, firms with an initial size comprised between 1 and 5 employees, firms with an initial size above 5 employees; The problems of sample selection bias - Heckman's (1979) method - heteroscedasticity and the persistence of growth are analyzed.

MAJOR FINDINGS - *Gibrat's Law* fails to hold during the first year following start-up - when smaller entrants grow faster than their larger counterparts - whereas it becomes valid once a minimum threshold in terms of size and age has been reached; Thus, smaller ones among new-born firms, having entered with a marked sub-optimal scale, adjust their size towards the mean size exhibited by larger entrants.

Lotti, Santarelli and Vivarelli (2003)   F - *The post-entry performance of new firms*

DATA CHARACTERISTICS - Italian National Institute for Social Security (INPS) data set; This data set identifies 855 new firms (with at least one paid employee) in 6 (Electrical and electronic engineering, Instruments, Food, Footwear and clothing, Wood and furniture, Rubber and plastics) manufacturing industries born in January 1987 and tracks their post-entry employment performance at monthly intervals until January 1993; No information on firms with zero paid employees is obtainable from the INPS file; Size is measured in terms of employment.

RESEARCH METHODS - The Authors use the quantile regression as a suitable methodology to deal with *conditional objects* by hypothesizing the existence of an *unobserved* behavioral model; Normally, this leads to a deviation of the distribution of the error terms from the canonical hypotheses of normality and homoskedasticity; In such a framework, the quantile regression (QR) represents a robust alternative to the least squares estimation: it consists in a Least Absolute Deviation estimator (LAD) that fits the median to a linear function of the covariates; In this way, the estimates are robust for all the deviations from the normality of the error terms and especially for the presence of outliers; This methodology defines the conditional quantiles as a minimization problem of a non differentiable function in β that can be easily solved by linear programming (Buchinsky, 1995). It is studied, for the overall period and year by year, the effects of firm size on growth at different quantiles ($\theta[0.10]$, $\theta[0.25]$, $\theta[0.50]$, $\theta[0.75]$, $\theta[0.90]$).

MAJOR FINDINGS - The Authors first consider the results for the 6-year period (1987-1993): In 5 out of 6 industries (with the exception of food) and in the aggregate estimate, the QR estimates of β_1, although significantly different from zero, are significantly less than one; This confirms that, in general, smaller firms grow faster than their larger counterparts over the entire period. Even more interesting results are yielded by the separate estimations carried out for each year and each industry: In five industries out of six, *Gibrat's Law* fails to hold in the year immediately following start-up, whereas it holds, or fails less severely, when firms approach maturity; In all sectors (apart from food) only in the first year following start-up do the QR estimates yield a β_1 significantly less than one, while an almost monotonic convergence of β_1 towards one occurs in the subsequent years, with the Wald test never rejecting *Gibrat's Law*.

Mata and Portugal (2004)   F - *The post-entry performance of new firms*

DATA CHARACTERISTICS - Annual data for over 100,000 firms are obtained from the Portuguese Ministry of Employment for the period 1982-1992; Due to data characteristics analysis is applied for the period 1983-1989 only; Firms are divided in domestic and foreign firms; The latter group is split in greenfield and acquisition entrants; Size is measured as employment.

RESEARCH METHODS - Survival rates have been estimated for domestic and foreign firms. A logit model is applied to estimate differences in survival rates between domestic entrants and the two types of entrants from abroad: greenfield and acquisition; Growth rates are estimated for the 3 types of entrants and the significance of differences in growth rates is tested.

MAJOR FINDINGS - There are important differences in the post-entry performance of the different types of entrants; Domestic entrants are much more likely to exit than foreign ones, both greenfield and acquisition; With respect to post-entry growth, however a mixed pattern emerges; Foreign acquisition entrants grow very little, foreign greenfields grow very quickly, and domestic entrants are in between.

Table 7 – Empirical Studies on Firm Growth Rates

Study	Type	Country	Period	Ind	GL	Size	Age	Lag Grow	EcIss
Mansfield (1962)	A	U.S.	1916-1957	M	M	na	na	na	...
Acs and Audretsch (1990)	A	U.S.	1976-1980	M	M	na	na	na	...
Fariñas and Moreno (2000)	A	Spain	1990-1995	M	A	0	0	na	ss;het
Piergiovanni, Santarelli, Klomp and Thurik (2003)	A	Italy	1989-1994	S	M	-/0	na	na	het
Audretsch, Klomp, Santarelli and Thurik (2004)	A	Netherlands	1981-1991	S	M	–	–	+/0	het
Mansfield (1962)	B	U.S.	1916-1957	M	M	na	na	na	...
Evans (1987a)	B	U.S.	1976-1982	M	R	–	–	na	ss;het
Evans (1987b)	B	U.S.	1976-1980	M	R	–	–	na	ss;het
Contini and Revelli (1989)	B	Italy	1980-1986	M	R	–	–/0	na	het
FitzRoy and Kraft (1991)	B	Germany	1977-1979	M	R	–	–	na	het
Variyam and Kraybill (1992)	B	U.S.	1985-1990	M/S	R	–	–	na	het

Study	Type	Country	Period	Ind	GL	Size	Age	Lag Grow	EcIss
Bianco and Sestito (1993)	B	Italy	1985-1990	M/S	R	–	–	na	ss;het;mea
Dunne and Hughes (1994)	B	U.K.	1975-1985	M/S	R	–	–	na	ss;het
Acs and Armington (2001)	B	U.S.	1994-1995	M/S	M	-/0	–	na	...
Delmar, Davidsson and Gartner (2003)	B	Sweden	1987-1996	M/S	M	0	na	na	...
Piergiovanni, Santarelli, Klomp and Thurik (2003)	B	Italy	1989-1991	S	M	-/0	na	na	het
Audretsch, Klomp, Santarelli and Thurik (2004)	B	Netherlands	1987-1991	S	M	–	–	+/0	het
Johansson (2004)	B	Sweden	1993-1998	M/S	R	–	–	na	...
Lensink, van Steen and Sterken (2005)	B	Netherlands	1995,1999	M/S	A	0	–	na	...
Hart and Prais (1956)	C	U.K.	1885-1950	M	A	na	na	na	...
Simon and Bonini (1958)	C	U.S.	1954-1956	M	A	na	na	na	...
Hymer and Pashigian (1962)	C	U.S.	1946-1955	M	M	na	na	na	...
Mansfield (1962)	C	U.S.	1916-1957	M	M	na	na	na	...
Singh and Whittington (1975)	C	U.K.	1948-1960	M/S	M	+	na	na	...
Droucopoulos (1983)	C	World	1957-1977	M	M	–	na	na	...
Buckley, Dunning and Pearce (1984)	C	World	1972-1977	M	A	0	na	na	...
Hall (1987)	C	U.S.	1972-1983	M	R	–	na	na	ss;het;mea
Bourlakis (1990)	C	Greece	1966-1986	M	R	–	–	na	ss;het

Study	Type	Country	Period	Ind	GL	Size	Age	Lag Grow	EcIss
Konings and Faggio (2003)	C	5 transition countries	1993-1994	M/S	R	-	na	na	...
Audretsch, Klomp, Santarelli and Thurik (2004)	C	Netherlands	1987-1991	S	M	–	–	+/0	het
Mansfield (1962)	D	U.S.	1916-1957	M	R	na	na	na	...
Contini and Revelli (1989)	D	Italy	1980-1986	M	R	-	–	+/–	ss;het
Wagner (1992)	D	Germany	1978-1989	M	R	na	na	+	...
Tschoegl (1996)	D	Japan	1954-1993	S	R	–	na	+	het
Harhoff, Stahl and Woywode (1998)	D	Germany	1989-1994	M	R	–	–/0	na	ss;het
Hardwick and Adams (2002)	D	U.K.	1987-1996	S	M	–/0/+	na	na	ss;het;mea
Hart and Oulton (1999)	D	U.K.	1989-1993	M/S	R	–	na	na	het
Fariñas and Moreno (2000)	D	Spain	1990-1995	M	R	–	–	na	ss;het
Machado and Mata (2000)	D	Portugal	1983, 1991	M	R	–	na	na	het
Heshmati (2001)	D	Sweden	1993-1998	M/S	M	–	–	na	het;mea
Van der Vennet (2001)	D	OECD area	1985-1994	S	M	–/0	...	...	...
Becchetti and Trovato (2002)	D	Italy	1989-1997	...	...	...	...	...	...
Del Monte and Papagni (2003)	D	Italy	1989-1997	M	A	0	–	+	purt
Chen and Lu (2003)	D	Taiwan	1988-1999	...	...	...	...	...	...
Fotopoulos and Louri (2004)	D	Greece	1992-1997	M	R	–	–	na	het
Piergiovanni, Santarelli, Klomp and Thurik (2003)	D	Italy	1989-1994	S	M	–/0	na	na	het

Study	Type	Country	Period	Ind	GL	Size	Age	Lag Grow	EcIss
Audretsch, Klomp, Santarelli and Thurik (2004)	D	Netherlands	1987-1991	S	M	–	–	+/0	het
Harris and Trainor (2005)	D	U.K.	1973-1998	M	R	–	na	na	purt
Hart and Prais (1956)	E	U.K.	1885-1950	M	M	na	na	na	...
Singh and Whittington (1975)	E	U.K.	1948-1960	M/S	R	0	na	+	...
Chesher (1979)	E	U.K.	1960-1969	M	R	0	na	+	...
Kumar (1985)	E	U.K.	1960-1976	M/S	R	–	na	+	...
Amirkhalkhali and Mukhopadhyay (1993)	E	U.S.	1965-1987	M	R	–	na	+	...
Amaral *et al.* (1997)	E	U.S.	1974-1993	M	R	–	na	na	...
Geroski, Lazarova, Urga Walters (2003)	E	U.K.	1955-1985	M/S	A	0	na	na	purt
Pfaffermayr and Bellak (2002)	E	Austria	1996-1999	M/S	A	0	na	na	...
Bottazzi *et al.* (2001)	E	World	1987-1997	M	A	0	na	+	ss;het
Goddard, Wilson and Blandon (2002)	E	Japan	1980-1996	M	R	–	na	na	purt
Bothner (2005)	E	World	1995-1999	M	R	–	na	na	purt
Dunne, Roberts and Samuelson (1988)	F	U.S.	1963-1982	M	na	na	na	na	...
Dunne, Roberts and Samuelson (1989)	F	U.S.	1967-1982	M	R	–	–	na	...
Phillips and Kirchhoff (1989)	F	U.S.	1976-1986	M/S	na	na	na	na	...

Study	Type	Country	Period	Ind	GL	Size	Age	Lag Grow	EcIss
Audretsch and Mahmood (1994)	F	U.S.	1976-1986	M	R	–	na	na	...
Mata (1994)	F	Portugal	1983-1987	M	R	–	na	na	...
Wagner (1994)	F	Germany	1978-1990	M	A	0	na	na	...
Reid (1995)	F	U.K.	1985-1988	M	R	–	–	na	het
Santarelli (1997)	F	Italy	1989-1994	S	M	0/-	na	na	het
Audretsch, Santarelli and Vivarelli (1999)	F	Italy	1987-1993	M	M	-/0	na	na	het
Almus and Nerlinger (2000)	F	West Germany	1989-1996	M	R	–	na	na	het
Lotti, Santarelli and Vivarelli (2001)	F	Italy	1987-1993	M	M	-/0	0	na	ss;het
Lotti, Santarelli and Vivarelli (2003)	F	Italy	1987-1993	M	M	–	na	na	ss;qua
Mata and Portugal (2004)	F	Portugal	1983-1989	M/S	M	-/0/+	na	na	...

Type (of empirical growth study)
A : Static analysis and version 1
B : Static analysis and version 2
C : Static analysis and version 3
D : Temporal analysis and version 2
E : Temporal analysis and version 3
F : The post-entry performance of new firms

Size, Age and Lag(ged) Grow(th)
– : negative effect on growth
0 : no effect on growth
+ : positive effect on growth
na : not available
...

Ind(ustry)
M : Manufacturing;
S : Services

G(ibrat's)L(aw)
A : Accepted
R : Rejected
M : Mixed Results

Ec(onometric)Iss(ues)
ss : corrected for sample selection
het : corrected for heteroscedasticity
mea : corrected for measurement error
purt : panel unit root tests
qua: quantile regression

Acknowledgement: The current chapter builds on previous work by Audretsch, Klomp, Santarelli and Thurik (2004). It benefited from a visit of Enrico Santarelli to the Tinbergen Institute in Rotterdam. The contribution by Luuk Klomp does not necessarily reflect the policies of the Ministry of Economic Affairs.

REFERENCES

Acs, Z. J. and D. B. Audretsch (1990), *Innovation and Small Firms*, Cambridge (MA), The MIT Press.

Acs, Z. J. and C. Armington (2001), "Gibrat's Law Reconsidered: The Relationship Between Firm Growth, Establishment Age, Establishment Size and Firm Size", Working Paper of the Regional Entrepreneurship Catalyst Kauffman Center for Entrepreneurial Leadership, Kansas City, MO.

Aitchison, J. and J. A. C. Brown (1957), *The Lognormal Distribution*, Cambridge, Cambridge University Press.

Almus, M. and E. A. Nerlinger (2000), "Testing Gibrat's Law for Young Firms - Empirical Results for West Germany", *Small Business Economics*, 15(1), 1-12.

Amaral, L. A. N, S. W. Buldyrev, S. Havlin, H. Leschhorn, P. Maass, M. A. Salinger, H. E. Stanley and M. H. R. Stanley (1997), "Scaling Behavior in Economics: Empirical Results for Company Growth", *Journal de Physique I*, 7, 621-633

Amirkhalkhali, S. and A. K. Mukhopadhyay (1993), "The Influence of Size and R&D on the Growth of Firms in the U.S.", *Eastern Economic Journal*, 19(2), 223-233.

Armatte, M. (1995), "Robert Gibrat et la Loi de l'Effet Proportionnel", *Mathematiques Informatiques et Science Humaines*, 129(1), 5-55.

Armatte, M. (1998), "Robert Gibrat and the Law of Proportional Effect", in W. J. Samuels (ed.), *European Economists of the Early 20th Century: Studies of Neglected Thinkers of Belgium, France, the Netherlands and Scandinavia*, Cheltenham, Edward Elgar, Vol. 1.

Audretsch D. B. and T. Mahmood (1994), "Firm Selection and Industry Evolution: The Post-Entry Performance of New Firms", *Journal of Evolutionary Economics*, 4(2), 243-260.

Audretsch, D. B., E. Santarelli and M. Vivarelli (1999), "Start-up Size and Industrial Dynamics: Some Evidence from Italian Manufacturing", *International Journal of Industrial Organization*, 17(7), 965-983.

Audretsch, D. B., L. Klomp, E. Santarelli and A. R. Thurik (2004), "Gibrat's Law: Are the Services Different?", *Review of Industrial Organization*, 24(3), 301-324.

Becchetti, L. and G. Trovato (2002), "The Determinants of Growth for Small and Medium Sized Firms", *Small Business Economics*, 19(3), 291-306.

Bianco, M. and P. Sestito (1993), "Entry and Growth of Firms: Evidence for the Italian Case", Unpublished manuscript, Banca d'Italia, Rome.

Bottazzi, G., G. Dosi, M. Lippi, F. Pammolli and M. Riccaboni (2001), "Innovation and Corporate Growth in the Evolution of the Drug Industry", *International Journal of Industrial Organization*, 19(7), 1161-1187.

Bothner, M. S. (2005), "Relative Size and Firm Growth in the Global Computer Industry", *Industrial and Corporate Change*, 14(4), 617-638.

Bourlakis, C. A. (1990), "Probability of Survival and Firm Growth in Greek Manufacturing Industries", Paper presented at the 17th Annual Conference of the European Association for Research in Industrial Economics (EARIE), mimeo, University of Leeds.

Buchinsky, M. (1995), "Estimating the Asymptotic Covariance Matrix for Quantile Regression Models: A Monte Carlo Study", *Journal of Econometrics*, 68(2), 303-338.

Buckley, P. J., J. H. Dunning and R. D. Pearce (1984), "An Analysis of the Growth and Profitability of the World's Largest Firms 1972 1977", *Kyklos*, 37(1), 3-26.

Caves, R. E. (1998), "Industrial Organization and New Findings on the Turnover and Mobility of Firms", *Journal of Economic Literature*, 36(4), 1947-1983.

Chen, J.-R. and W.-C. Lu (2003), "Panel Unit Root Test of Firm Size and its Growth", *Applied Economics Letters*, 10(4), 343-345.

Chesher, A. (1979), "Testing the Law of Proportionate Effect", *Journal of Industrial Economics*, 27(4), 403-411.

Contini, B. and R. Revelli (1989), "The Relationship between Firm Growth and Labor Demand", *Small Business Economics*, 1(3), 309-314.

Delmar, F., P. Davidsson and W. B. Gartner (2003), "Arriving at the High-growth Firm", *Journal of Business Venturing*, 18(2), 189-216.

Del Monte A. and E. Papagni (2003), "R&D and the Growth of Firms. An Empirical Analysis of a Panel of Italian Firms", *Research Policy*, 32(8), 1003-1014.

Droucopoulos, V. (1983), "International Big Business Revisited: On the Size and Growth of the World's Largest Firms", *Managerial and Decision Economics*, 4(3), 244-252.

Dunne, P. and A. Hughes (1994), "Age, Size, Growth and Survival: U.K. Companies in the 1980s", *Journal of Industrial Economics*, 42(2), 115-140.

Dunne, T., M. J. Roberts and L. Samuelson (1988), "Patterns of Firm Entry and Exit in U.S. Manufacturing Industries", *Rand Journal of Economics*, 19(4), 495-515.

Dunne, T., M. J. Roberts and L. Samuelson (1989), "The Growth and Failure of U.S. Manufacturing Plants", *Quarterly Journal of Economics*, 104(4), 671-698.

Evans, D. S. (1987a), "The Relationship between Firm Growth, Size, and Age: Estimates for 100 Manufacturing Industries", *Journal of Industrial Economics*, 35(4), 567-581.

Evans, D. S. (1987b), "Tests of Alternative Theories of Firm Growth", *Journal of Political Economy*, 95(4), 657-674.

Fariñas, J. C. and L. Moreno (2000), "Firms' Growth, Size and Age: A Nonparametric Approach", *Review of Industrial Organization*, 17(3), 249-265.

FitzRoy, F. R. and K. Kraft (1991), "Firm Size, Growth and Innovation: Some Evidence from West Germany", in Z. J. Acs and D. B. Audretsch (eds.), *Innovation and Technological Change: An International Comparison*, London, Harvester Wheatsheaf, 152-159.

Fotopoulos, G. and H. Louri (2004), "Corporate Growth and FDI: Are Multinationals Stimulating Local Industrial Development?", *Journal of Industry, Competition and Trade*, 4(2), 163-189.

Geroski, P. A., S. Lazarova, G. Urga and C. F. Walters (2003), "Are Differences in Firm Size Transitory or Permanent?", *Journal of Applied Econometrics*, 18(1), 47-59.

Gibrat, R. (1931), *Les Inégalités Économiques*, Paris, Librairie du Recueil Sirey.

Goddard, J., J. Wilson and P. Blandon (2002), "Panel Tests of Gibrat's Law for Japanese Manufacturing", *International Journal of Industrial Organization*, 20(4), 415-433.

Hall, B. H. (1987), "The Relationship between Firm Size and Firm Growth in the U.S. Manufacturing Sector", *Journal of Industrial Economics*, 35(4), 583-606.

Hamilton, L. (1998), *Statistics with Stata 5*, Pacific Grove (CA), Duxbury Press, Brooks/Cole Publishing.

Hardwick, P. and M. Adams (2002), "Firm Size and Growth in the United Kingdom Life Insurance Industry", *Journal of Risk and Insurance*, 69(5), 577-593.

Harhoff, D., K. Stahl and M. Woywode (1998), "Legal Form, Growth and Exit of West German Firms. Empirical Results for Manufacturing, Construction, Trade and Service Industries", *Journal of Industrial Economics*, 46(4), 453-488.

Harris, R. and M. Trainor (2005), "Plant-level Analysis using the ARD: Another Look at Gibrat's Law", *Scottish Journal of Political Economy*, 52(3), 492-518.

Hart, P. E. and S. J. Prais (1956), "The Analysis of Business Concentration: A Statistical Approach", *Journal of the Royal Statistical Society*, 119 (part 2, series A), 150-191.

Hart, P. E. and N. Oulton (1999), "Gibrat, Galton and Job Generation", *International Journal of the Economics of Business*, 6(2), 149-164.

Heckman, J. J. (1979), "Sample Selection Bias as a Specification Error", *Econometrica*, 47(2), 153-161.

Heshmati, A. (2001), "On the Growth of Micro and Small Firms: Evidence from Sweden", *Small Business Economics*, 17(3), 213-228.

Hymer, S. and P. Pashigian (1962), "Firm Size and Rate of Growth", *Journal of Political Economy*, 70(4), 556-569.

Im, K. S., M. H. Pesaran and Y. Shin (2003), "Testing for Unit Roots in Heterogeneous Panels", *Journal of Econometrics*, 11(1), 53-74.

Johansson, D. (2004), "Is Small Beautiful? The Case of the Swedish IT Industry", *Entrepreneurship & Regional Development*, 16(3), 271-287.

Jovanovic, B. (1982), "Selection and Evolution of Industry", *Econometrica*, 50(5), 649-670.

Konings, J. and G. Faggio (2003), "Job Creation, Job Destruction and Employment Growth in Emerging Market Economies", *Economic Systems*, 27(2), 129-154.

Kumar, M. S. (1985), "Growth, Acquisition Activity and Firm Size: Evidence from the United Kingdom", *Journal of Industrial Economics*, 33(3), 327-338.

Lensink, R., P. van Steen and E. Sterken (2005), "Uncertainty and Growth of the Firm", *Small Business Economics*, 24(4), 381-391.

Levin, A., C. F. Lin and C. S. Chu (2002), "Unit Root Test in Panel Data: Asymptotic and Finite-Sample Properties", *Journal of Econometrics*, 68(1), 53-78.

Lotti F., E. Santarelli and M. Vivarelli (2001), "The Relationship between Size and Growth: The Case of Italian New-born Firms", *Applied Economics Letters*, 8(7), 451-454.

Lotti, F., E. Santarelli and M. Vivarelli (2003), "Does Gibrat's Law Hold among Young, Small Firms?", *Journal of Evolutionary Economics*, 14(3), 213-235.

Machado, J. A. F. and J. Mata (2000), "Box-Cox Quantile Regression and the Distribution of Firm Sizes", *Journal of Applied Econometrics*, 15(3), 253-274.

Maddala, G. and S. Wu (1999), "A Comparative Study of Unit Root Tests with Panel Data and a New Simple Test", *Oxford Bulletin of Economics and Statistics*, 61(8), 1399-1416.

Mansfield, E. (1962), "Entry, Gibrat's Law, Innovation, and the Growth of Firms", *American Economic Review*, 52(5), 1023-1051.

Marquardt, D. W. (1963), "An Algorithm for Least Squares Estimation of Non-linear Parameters", *Journal of the Society for Industrial and Applied Mathematics*, 11(5), 431-441.

Mata, J. (1994), "Firm Growth During Infancy", *Small Business Economics*, 6(1), 27-39.

Mata, J. and P. Portugal (2004), "Patterns of Entry, Post-Entry Growth and Survival", *Small Business Economics*, 22(3), 283-298.

McCloughan, P. (1995), "Simulation of Concentration Development from Modified Gibrat Growth-Entry-Exit Processes", *Journal of Industrial Economics*, 43(4), 405-433.

Pedroni, P. (1999), "Critical Values for Cointegration Tests in Heterogeneous Panels with Multiple Regressors", *Oxford Bulletin of Economics and Statistics*, 61(4), 653-678.

Pfaffermayr, M. and Ch. Bellak (2002), "Why Foreign-owned Firms are Different: A Conceptual Framework and Empirical Evidence for Austria", in R. Jungnickel (ed.), *Foreign-owned Firms – Are They Different?*, Houndmills, Palgrave Macmillan, 13-57.

Phillips, B. D. and B. A. Kirchhoff (1989), "Formation, Growth and Survival; Small Firm Dynamics in the U.S. Economy", *Small Business Economics*, 1(1), 65-74.

Piergiovanni, R., E. Santarelli, L. Klomp and A. R. Thurik (2003), "Gibrat's Law and the Firm Size/Firm Growth Relationship in Italian Services", *Revue d'Economie Industrielle*, 102, 69-82.

Reid G. (1995), "Early Life-cycle Behaviour of Micro-Firms in Scotland", *Small Business Economics*, 7(1), 89-95.

Santarelli E. (1997), "La relazione tra dimensione iniziale, sopravvivenza e crescita delle imprese nel settore turistico in Italia", *Statistica*, 57(2), 125-138.

Simon, H. A. and Ch. P. Bonini (1958), "The Size Distribution of Business Firms", *American Economic Review*, 48(4), 607-617.

Singh A. and G. Whittington (1975), "The Size and Growth of Firms", *Review of Economic Studies*, 42(1), 15-26.

Sutton J. (1997), "Gibrat's Legacy", *Journal of Economic Literature*, 35(1), 40-59.

Tschoegl, A. (1996), "Managerial Dis(economies) of Scale: The Case of Regional Banks in Japan", Reginald H. Jones Center for Management and Policy, Strategy and

Organization, The Wharton School of the University of Pennsylvania, Working Paper No. 96-04.

Vander Vennet, R. (2001), "The Law of Proportionate Effect and OECD Bank Sectors", *Applied Economics*, 33(4), 539-546.

Variyam J. N. and D. S. Kraybill (1992), "Empirical Evidence on Determinants of Firm Growth", *Economics Letters*, 38(1), 31-36.

Wagner J. (1992), "Firm Size, Firm Growth, and Persistence of Chance: Testing Gibrat's Law with Establishment Data from Lower Saxony, 1978-1989", *Small Business Economics*, 4(2), 125-131.

Wagner J. (1994), "The Post-Entry Performance of New Small Firms in German Manufacturing Industries", *Journal of Industrial Economics*, 42(2), 141-154.

Chapter 4
ENTREPRENEURSHIP IN THE OLD AND NEW EUROPE

Isabel Grilo
European Commission, Brussels, Université de Lille 3, and CORE - Université Catholique de Louvain

A. Roy Thurik
Erasmus University Rotterdam, EIM Business and Policy Research, and Max Planck Institute of Economics, Jena

1. INTRODUCTION

Developing an SME (small and medium-sized enterprises) sector is essential for countries transforming their centrally planned economy into a market oriented one. New firm formation is the major driver of this transition. Obviously, entrepreneurial energy is a necessary condition for new firm formation. The centrally planned economies of Central and Eastern Europe and the Baltics were particularly hostile toward entrepreneurial activities. Large state run enterprises in an economy dominated by heavy industries were considered the prime driver of economic progress and hence the symbol of the communist ideology (Earle and Sakova, 2000). The ensuing misallocation of resources led to the obvious gaps and shortages on the output side. Privatization of the existing large enterprises ruined by years of communist governance was generally considered inadequate to transform the centrally planned economies. A wider process of social and economic restructuring was needed (Blanchard, 1997) in which an entirely new private sector had to be put in place. A major challenge then becomes to develop an SME sector by means of stimulating entry. There are many roles of SMEs in the process of transformation (Smallbone and Welter, 2001b), the most important of which is channeling entrepreneurial energy. The present paper attempts to explain country differences in entrepreneurial energy. This energy is captured as latent and actual entrepreneurship. Level and determinants of both latent and actual entrepreneurship are investigated with specific attention to differences between transition and non-transition E.U. member states.

The main goal of the present paper is to establish whether entrepreneurial activity differs between the new and old member states of the European Union.[1] Particular attention will be paid to the eight former communist countries. In this sense the terms 'old' and 'new' Europe will be used in a loose fashion reflecting a direct interest in the role of transition versus market economies in shaping entrepreneurial energy. Our investigation uses 2004 survey data of 7,914 participants of the 25 European member states, including the U.S. The survey assesses both latent (declared preference, i.e., drive) and actual entrepreneurship. Moreover, several demographic, attitudinal and preference characteristics of the surveyed population are measured. This allows establishing whether the influence of these characteristics differs between new and old member states, in particular, between the eight former communist transition countries and the remaining 17 countries.

The transition phase with its dramatic institutional and economic shocks may have led to different entrepreneurial aspiration and activity levels when compared to long standing market economies which did not experience abrupt changes.[2] For instance, it is well-known that entrepreneurial opportunities are not just the result of the push effect of (the threat of) unemployment but also of the pull effect produced by a thriving economy as well as by past entrepreneurial activities.[3] This mix may be entirely different in transition countries than in existing market economies. The flood of new opportunities brought forward by the liberalization aspect goes hand in hand with the dramatic fall of the demand for labor due to the demise of the state run large enterprises. The present paper is a first step toward systematic investigation of entrepreneurial differences between transition and non-transition member states. It reports on the differences of the levels of latent and actual entrepreneurship, on the characteristics of those involved and on the determinants of these involvements.

Insight in the determinants of entrepreneurship is crucial for shaping public policies and the assessment of their merits. This is not only the case in the relatively robust environment of existing market economies (Verheul, Wennekers, Audretsch and Thurik, 2002; Storey, 2003; and Hart, 2003) but holds true in particular in the framework of the complex and sensitive transition process of the former communist economies (Smallbone and Weltcr, 2001b; and Worldbank, 2005). Policy-makers' awareness that individuals may be discouraged to become entrepreneurs due to administrative hurdles, lack of information on how to start, an unfavorable economic climate and the absence of financial and human capital requires a sound knowledge of (dis)incentives. The present paper deals with these and other factors and their influence on latent and actual entrepreneurship, particularly in a setting were differences between transition and non-transition E.U. member states can be established.

The present paper follows the setup of Grilo and Irigoyen (2005) where 2000 survey data are used from the 15 E.U. member states and the U.S. to establish the effect of demographic and other variables on latent and actual entrepreneurship. In Grilo and Thurik (2005a) a similar analysis is done using 2004 data. They show that in terms of unweighted averages actual entrepreneurship remained about the same in the period 2000 to 2004. Latent entrepreneurship dropped while this drop seems to have occurred evenly in the U.S. and the old E.U. member states. Latent entrepreneurship is measured by the probability of a declared preference for self-employment over employment. Other than demographic variables such as gender, age and education level, the set of explanatory variables includes country specific effects, the perception by respondents of administrative complexities and of availability of financial support and a rough measure of risk tolerance. The contribution of Grilo and Irigoyen (2005) and Grilo and Thurik (2005a) is that both the preference and the actual status of entrepreneurship are investigated in a multi-country setting using a structural two-equation model.[4] Grilo and Irigoyen (2005) find that concerning administrative and financial obstacles, both perceptions play a significant negative role in self-employment status, in addition to its indirect effect through preferences. They conclude that these results, combined with the ones obtained for latent entrepreneurship, indicate that administrative complexities hinder both the willingness to become self-employed and its materialization in actual status. Administrative complexities have both a direct and an indirect effect (through preferences) on actual entrepreneurship; while lack of financial support has only a direct effect on the fact of being self-employed but no significant impact on preferences.[5] Grilo and Thurik (2005a) report that, while a majority of the surveyed population identifies lack of financial support as an obstacle to starting a new business, the role of this variable in both latent and actual entrepreneurship appears to be even more counterintuitive in 2004 than in 2000: it has no impact on actual entrepreneurship and is positively related to latent entrepreneurship.

The results of Grilo and Irigoyen (2005) and Grilo and Thurik (2005a) reinforce the message that the degree of entrepreneurship varies widely across countries. They show that country-specific effects are significant both for entrepreneurial drive and for entrepreneurial activity even after the effects on entrepreneurship of demographic and perception variables have been accounted for. The results show that no old E.U. country scores better than the U.S., confirming the widespread belief of a more developed entrepreneurial spirit across the Atlantic. In our present paper – covering 7,914 respondents surveyed in 2004 - we will make a comparison of the determinants of the entrepreneurial drive and activity between the 15 old member states of the E.U. and the ten new ones - in particular the eight former communist ones. Also – when compared to Grilo and Thurik (2005a) – we will introduce several new covariates such as whether parents are self-employed, internal and external locus of control and the perception by respondents of accessibility of information for start-up and whether the current economic climate is favorable.

The contribution of the present paper is that a precise account is given of the differences of the levels of latent and actual entrepreneurship between the eight former communist member states of the European Union on the one hand and the remaining 17 countries on the other. Moreover, differences in the characteristics of the individuals surveyed are described. Finally and most importantly, differences in the determinants between the two groups of countries are established in a multi-country setting using a structural two-equation probit model explaining the probability of the preference to become self-employed and of actually being self-employed.

The most striking results of the present paper is that risk tolerance has a significantly higher influence on both latent and actual entrepreneurship in transition economies than in market economies. This opens the discussion on the importance for these countries of policy measures directed at the risks and consequences of business failure. Another important result concerns the impact of 'belonging to these economies' on latent and actual entrepreneurship once the available explanatory variables are accounted for. The results show that once these other variables are controlled for there is a significantly higher probability of being self-employed for a resident of a transition economy than for someone living in an E.U. market economy.

The present paper is organized as follows: Section 2 highlights some literature and results concerning determinants of entrepreneurship. In Section 3 the variables are discussed. In Sections 4 and 5 the results of latent and actual entrepreneurship using the 2004 survey are presented. Section 6 concludes.

2. DETERMINANTS OF ENTREPRENEURSHIP

Entrepreneurial activities differ largely between countries (Acs, Audretsch, Evans, 1994; Blanchflower, 2000 and 2004; Acs, Arenius, Hay and Minniti, 2005; van Stel, 2005; Observatory of European SMEs, 2005a; Grilo and Irigoyen, 2005; and Grilo and Thurik, 2005b). This holds true for various measures of entrepreneurship such as start-up activity, business ownership, small business share, nascent entrepreneurship and the preference for entrepreneurship. Many determinants have been brought forward (Blanchflower, 2000; Parker, 2004; Verheul, Wennekers, Audretsch and Thurik, 2002; and Wennekers, Uhlaner and Thurik, 2002). Next to many individual characteristics the level of economic development (Reynolds, Bygrave, Autio, Cox and Hay, 2002; and Audretsch, Carree, Thurik and van Stel, 2005) and cultural aspects (Noorderhaven, Wennekers, Thurik and van Stel, 2004, and Uhlaner and Thurik, 2005) are often mentioned as the principal drivers of entrepreneurial activity.

At the individual level, the tools of neo-classical microeconomics have provided a framework for studying self-employment decisions known as the theory of income choice. This field has proved useful in describing some of the factors influencing this occupational decision.[6]

This field has basically four dimensions. Some authors stress the role of entrepreneurial ability in the decision to become an entrepreneur. They postulate differences across potential entrepreneurs (or firms) in terms of some form of entrepreneurial efficiency (Jovanovic, 1982 and 1994; Lucas, 1978; Murphy, Shleifer and Vishny, 1991; Holmes and Schmitz, 1990 and Lazear, 2004). The second dimension emphasizes the role of risk and underlines the importance of risk attitudes in the occupational choice. In Kihlstrom and Laffont (1979) and Parker (1996 and 1997) the degree of risk aversion and the differences in risk of the two occupational alternatives determine the occupational choice. A third dimension that has been emphasized in explaining different occupational choices is the existence of liquidity constraints. Evans and Jovanovic (1989) building upon Lucas (1978) and Jovanovic (1982) show that under certain conditions, due to capital constraints, there is a positive relationship between the probability of becoming self-employed and the assets of the entrepreneur. This influential paper led to many follow up investigations of both conceptual and empirical nature. The empirical establishments of whether wealthier individuals have a higher probability of becoming entrepreneur is widely researched. See Holtz-Eakin, Joulfaian and Rosen (1994) and Taylor (2001). Hurst and Lusardi (2004) show that the relationship between household wealth and the propensity to start a business is highly non-linear.[7] The fourth dimension involves a more eclectic approach and uses a multitude of variables to describe the factors influencing the (relative) returns to self-employment such as the preferences, abilities and resources of the individuals. Most studies in this area use longitudinal data for a given country and have as dependent variable the transition into self-employment and sometimes the business longevity and the exit from self-employment. Typical explanatory variables include age, gender, race, education, earnings, capital assets, previous professional experience, marital status, professional status of the parents, and scores from psychological tests. Examples of empirical work following this approach can be found in Bates (1990), Blanchflower (2004), Blanchflower and Meyer (1994), Blanchflower and Oswald (1998), Blau (1987), Douglas and Shepherd (2002), Evans and Leighton (1989 and 1990), Grilo and Irigoyen (2005), Grilo and Thurik (2005a and 2005b), Lin, Picot and Compton (2000), Rees and Shah (1986), Reynolds (1997), Wagner (2003) and Wit and van Winden (1989).

In analyzing the determinants of entrepreneurship, Verheul, Wennekers, Audretsch and Thurik (2002) present an Eclectic Framework of the determinants of entrepreneurship bringing together elements from different fields and levels of analysis. In particular, they combine the supply effect of the above mentioned fourth dimension (preferences, abilities and resources of the individuals) with the demand effect of market opportunities.[8] Our approach is loosely inspired by the Eclectic Framework.[9]

Below we will list some earlier findings in the empirical literature of the determinants of entrepreneurship. We limit ourselves to variables available in the Flash Eurobarometer Survey 2004. For an extensive account of the literature on the determinants of entrepreneurship we refer to Grilo and Thurik (2005a and 2005c) and the references therein.

Being (or becoming) self-employed received ample attention as a variable to be explained.

- Most studies find that men have a higher probability of engaging in entrepreneurship than women.[10]
- The likelihood of becoming self-employed varies with age. Many business owners are within the age category of 25 to 45 years old.[11]
- The level of education is a variable for which contrasting results have been obtained. The results vary regarding the existence of a significant impact and the nature of this impact. Among the studies finding that education has a significant impact, the nature of the impact varies from study to study – some find a positive relation others a negative one and still others a negative up to some level of education and positive thereafter.[12]
- The conventional wisdom that "breeding entrepreneurs starts at home" is confirmed by results in the literature. There are many results showing the positive intergenerational correlation often with some mediator like race, parents' occupation or sex.[13]
- Financial constrains, often evaluated through the role of capital assets in the probability of being self-employed[14], are generally found to have a negative impact on the decision to become an entrepreneur. Grilo and Irigoyen (2005) report a negative effect of the perception of lack of financial on the probability of being self-employed using European data of 2000 whereas Grilo and Thurik (2005a) report no effect for 2004.
- Both Grilo and Irigoyen (2005) and Grilo and Thurik (2005a) report a negative effect of the perception of administrative complexities on the probability of being self-employed using European data of 2000 and 2004, respectively.
- Grilo and Thurik (2005b) do not find a negative effect of the difficulty to obtain sufficient information nor of the perception of an unfavorable

economic climate using their multinomial logit model of entrepreneurial engagement levels.

- Both Grilo and Irigoyen (2005) and Grilo and Thurik (2005a) report that, not surprisingly, having a preference for self-employment increases the probability of actually being self-employed.
- Risk tolerance is found to increase the probability of being self-employed.[15]
- The perception of internal and external success factors is closely related to the concept of locus of control. This refers to the perceived control over events. In his social learning theory Rotter (1966) differentiated between internal and external locus of control. Individuals with an internal locus of control believe themselves to be in control of their destiny. Individuals with an external locus of control believe that outside forces determine their future. The obvious expectation is that self-employed have a high internal locus of control and a low external one.[16]
- In cross country comparisons, and for the role of country specific effects, the few studies addressing this issue indicate that entrepreneurship is stronger in the U.S. than in European countries. Below we will discuss some findings concerning former communist transition economies.

Preferences for self-employment, which can be seen as a measure of latent or potential entrepreneurship, have been less often analyzed.[17] Some influences generally found in other studies are listed below.

- Being a male has a positive significant impact on the decision to start a new firm, while this decision is negatively affected by age.[18]
- Nascent entrepreneurship rates are highest in the age category of 25 to 34 years old, although some studies suggest that people increasingly start businesses at a younger age.[19]
- The level of education does not have a significant impact on preferences for self-employment.[20]
- Grilo and Thurik (2005b) using their multinomial logit model of entrepreneurial engagement levels report that having self-employed parents increases the odds of all engagement levels, potentially leading to an effective entrepreneurial activity relative to not considering such activities. Moreover, the odds of having a young business relative to any low involvement category are boosted by having self-employed parents. Also, having had the example of self-employed parents makes giving up on starting a business less likely. More precisely, the odds of giving up relative to any category from taking steps onwards are negatively affected by this variable.
- Grilo and Irigoyen (2005) have studied the role of perceptions of administrative complexities and financial constraints on latent entrepreneurship. The results indicate that perceived administrative

complexities have a negative impact while perceived financial
constraints do not seem to play a role.

- Tolerance of risk – a key factor for entrepreneurship – has, as could be
  expected, a positive impact on the preference for self-employment.[21]
- Concerning cross country comparisons and the role of country specific
  effects, the results of Grilo and Irigoyen (2005) indicate that for most old
  E.U. countries entrepreneurial drive is lower than in the U.S.[22]

Some viewpoints on the role of economic transition, being the specific
theme of the present paper, will be discussed in the remainder of this section.
There are three questions to be discussed. First, whether the preference to be
self-employed and the incidence of self-employment differ between former
communist countries and countries with a longer capitalist history. Second,
whether the characteristics of those involved differ between the two country
groups. Third, whether the influence of the above mentioned factors on the
probability of preferring to be self-employed and of actually being self-
employed differs between these two categories of countries. We will abstain
from making precise assumptions about the answers to these three questions
because the existing literature provides only few hints and because this
would result in a plethora of statements given our set-up with two equations
and many variables. Rather, we concentrate on a posteriori interpretation of
the outcomes of our analyses. Nevertheless, some connection to the existing
literature will be given.

Obviously, the transformation process is intervening profoundly in
economic and social life through elements like the shift from public to
private ownership, the liberalization of markets and the creation of
accompanying institutions like financial and service intermediaries. The
effects on level and characteristics of entrepreneurial activities may be
immense. It is straightforward to expect these effects to depend upon the
phase and the speed of the transition (Mugler, 2000), the relative starting
point (countries like Hungary and Poland experimented with mild forms of
entrepreneurship in the last phase of the communist regime) and whether
there is any tradition of private enterprise (like in 19th century
Czechoslovakia). Smallbone and Welter (2001a) give many examples of
these dependencies and provide some evidence that different forms of
entrepreneurship emerge with distinct characteristics of entrepreneurs.

During the transformation process the eight former communist countries
entered the E.U. in 2004. We will not discuss the nature of the integration in
terms of the important inflows of foreign direct investments as well as
financial aid; the implementation of the 'acquis communautaire'
(adjustments of legal and regulatory frameworks) and its consequences for
the business environment; and the labor market with its consequences for
entrepreneurial activities and opportunities (Observatory of European SMEs,
2005b). We cannot discriminate between former communist countries which

entered the E.U. in 2004 and similar countries like Rumania, Bulgaria, etc which didn't. Our data set does not cover these non-E.U. countries. Below we will concentrate on the fact that these countries are formerly centrally planned.

The economic structure of former communist (or transition) countries differs from that of non-transition countries. In centrally planned economies entrepreneurial activity was restricted (or absent) as the emphasis was on economies of scale and the business culture did not support innovation and entrepreneurship (Roman, 1990; Mugler, 2000). During the transition process new, small firms start replacing the larger incumbent industrial enterprises and there is a shift away from unskilled, labor-intensive production towards capital-, technology- and skill-intensive production (Brunner, 1993). However, the development of entrepreneurship in most transition countries still lags behind that of non-transition countries.[23] This is because the business environment in transition countries is less favorable than in most non-transition economies. Transition economies tend to be characterized by a relatively unstable economic environment, a low domestic purchasing power and uncertainty with respect to property rights (Smallbone and Welter, 2001b). Probably, this instability is compensated by other positive aspects such as new opportunities in those former communist countries which accessed the E.U. in 2004. Other impediments to entrepreneurship in transition economies as described by Mugler (2000) include a shortage of entrepreneurial and management skills, underdevelopment of the regulatory system, bureaucratic and time-consuming registration, need for modernization of infrastructure and communication network, limited access to capital and limited knowledge and organization of market services. Furthermore, it is well-known that entrepreneurial opportunities are not just the result of the push effect of (the threat of) unemployment but also of the pull effect produced by a thriving economy as well as by past entrepreneurial activities. This mix may be entirely different in transition countries than in existing market economies. The flood of new opportunities brought forward by the liberalization wave go hand in hand with the dramatic fall of the demand for labor due to the demise of the state run large enterprises. Finally, it should be noted that the transition effect on entrepreneurship is likely to differ between transition countries, depending upon the phase and pace of the reforms (Smallbone and Welter, 2001a; Mugler, 2000). However, when comparing transition and non-transition countries we will not take into account the diversity within each group of countries when explaining the influence of determinants (socio-demographic and perceptions) on latent and actual self-employment. Summing up, it is expected that there is a negative effect of economic transition on both latent and actual entrepreneurship.[24]

3. DATA

Data used are from the Flash Eurobarometer survey on Entrepreneurship conducted during April 2004 on a random sample from the 25 Member States and the U.S., covering 19,550 respondents[25]. The survey provides information on demographic variables such as gender, age, education level and whether parents are self-employed, four perceptions of 'obstacles' as well as information allowing the construction of loose measures of risk tolerance and of internal and external locus of control. The 'obstacle' variables include the perception by respondents of administrative complexities, of availability of financial support, of accessibility of information for start-up and whether the current economic climate is favorable. Two different indicators of entrepreneurship are used.

The first indicator of entrepreneurship aims at capturing the population's entrepreneurial drive (latent entrepreneurship). The following question provides the basis for the measure of entrepreneurial drive: suppose you could choose between different kinds of jobs. Which one would you prefer: being an employee or being self-employed? This is admittedly a simplified concept of latent entrepreneurship but has the advantage of consistency across our 26 countries.[26]

The second indicator, used to measure actual entrepreneurship - those effectively in self-employment - has been widely used in the empirical literature on entrepreneurship due to its generally good statistical availability and the ease in international comparisons.

In the next sections estimation results are presented of two probit equations relating the probability of revealing a preference for self-employment and the probability of actually being self-employed to various explanatory variables:

$$\Pr(y_1 = 1 | X) = F(Xb_1),$$

where $y_1 = 1$ if the individual prefers self-employment and $= 0$ if the individual prefers employment and where $X = (1$, male, age, low education, high education, self-employed parent, lack of financial support, presence of administrative complexities, lack of start-up information, economic climate, risk tolerance, internal and external locus of control, country dummies);

$$\Pr(y_2 = 1 | X, y_1) = F(Xb_2 + y_1 a),$$

where $y_2 = 1$ if the individual is self-employment and $= 0$ if the individual is employed.[27]

We did an equation-by-equation probit estimation using 7,914 observations of the original 19,550 interviews.[28] The sample used in the estimation contains the observations of the active surveyed population (in the sense of being either employed or self-employed) and for which respondents have answered all the questions used to construct the explanatory variables. The explanatory variables used in the present study can be divided into three types.

Socio-demographic variables: gender, self-employed parents, age and level of education. "Age when finished full education" is used to construct three education levels: The first encompasses those with no education or having left school before the age of 15; the second refers to those who left school between the age of 15 and 21; and the third to those having left school past the age of 21.[29] A dummy variable is used for the lower level and another for the higher level so that the intermediary level works as the base. Male and self-employed parents are the obvious dummy variables.

Perception and preference variables: the perception of lack of available financial support, the perception of complexity of administrative procedures, lack of sufficient information, economic climate and risk tolerance are captured, respectively, by the following questions:

"Do you strongly agree, agree, disagree or strongly disagree with the following statements?"
"It is difficult to start one's own business due to a lack of available financial support."
"It is difficult to start one's own business due to the complex administrative procedures."
"It is difficult to obtain sufficient information on how to start a business."
"The current economic climate is not favorable to start one's own business."
"One should not start a business if there is a risk it might fail."

For each statement a dummy variable was constructed. The dummy variables take the value "1" in the case of "strongly agree" or "agree" for the first four statements.[30] For the fifth statement the risk tolerance dummy takes value "1" if "disagree" or "strongly disagree".[31]

The perception of internal and external success factors (internal versus external locus of control) is captured by the following questions:

When one runs a business, what do you think most determine its success (max two answers)?

a. The director's personality.
b. The general management of the business.
c. The overall economy.
d. The political context.
e. Outside entities.
f. Other.

Two dummy variables are constructed. Internal locus of control equals "1" if a and/or b are mentioned whereas c, d or e are not mentioned and external locus of control equals "1" if c, d and/or e are mentioned whereas a or b are not mentioned.

Country dummies: country-specific effects are evaluated using country dummy variables with the U.S. as the base. Therefore the coefficients associated with these variables are to be interpreted as the impact of being in the corresponding country rather than being in the U.S. A country group dummy variable taking value one for observations from transition economies was also used in regressions discussed but not reported in this paper.

A very clear regularity reported in Table 1 is that in all 26 countries the proportion of the respondents with a declared preference for self-employment is higher than that actually involved in entrepreneurial activities.[32] The unweighted average of actual entrepreneurship is 19 percent whereas that of declared preference is 49 percent. This discrepancy between latent and actual entrepreneurship ranges from 49 percent in Lithuania to 8 percent in Finland. It is higher in the former communist Europe (32%) than in the remaining member states (28%) but still small when compared to the discrepancy in the U.S. (47%). A high proportion of respondents perceiving a lack of financial support, complex administrative procedures or an unfavorable economic climate may explain this untapped entrepreneurial potential.[33] Average unweighted actual entrepreneurship in the non-communist Europe, the former communist Europe and the U.S. is about the same (20, 18 and 21%, respectively). Average unweighted latent entrepreneurship in the former communist Europe is roughly the same as in the other E.U. member states, while that in the U.S. is considerably higher (49, 48 and 68% respectively).

Clearly, all obstacles seem relevant in all countries. Noteworthy exceptions are start-up information in the Netherlands and Finland which is mentioned by only 17 percent and 22 percent respectively as difficult to obtain. Apart from start-up information the former communist Europe generally feels the obstacles more deeply than the non-communist Europe: 87 percent versus 72 percent for lack of financial support, 78 percent versus 69 percent for complex administrative procedures and 75 perecent versus 65 percent for unfavorable economic climate. On the whole, start-up information is perceived as the least frustrating of the four obstacles: 46 percent and 43 percent in the former communist countries and the other countries, respectively. All four obstacles play a lesser role in the U.S. when compared to the unweighted European average. In particular, the differences for complex administrative procedures and unfavorable economic climate are salient: the U.S. reports 13 percent lower than Europe for both obstacles.

Table 1 - Distribution of variables by country (2004)

	Actual entrepreneurship	Latent entrepreneurship	Low education	High education	Self-employed parents	Financial support	Administrative complexities	Sufficient information	Econmic climate	Risk toleance	Intern success factors	Extern success factors	Obs.
Belgium	20	37	7	44	29	76	75	52	69	46	52	23	428
Denmark	14	39	3	70	29	52	81	31	50	51	35	18	195
Germany	19	46	8	45	24	74	69	40	76	46	28	19	490
Greece	42	57	18	44	54	88	71	60	80	62	41	12	451
Spain	18	59	22	40	31	80	76	56	62	59	60	14	312
France	10	42	8	44	29	82	75	56	71	62	55	14	472
Ireland	24	62	12	32	44	68	70	34	41	69	63	14	214
Italy	21	51	29	22	35	85	74	54	85	55	59	14	444
Luxembourg	10	52	10	42	26	79	65	47	62	47	37	20	219
Netherlands	20	36	6	43	32	47	60	17	61	59	39	21	471
Austria	21	48	24	19	32	70	59	35	61	36	40	24	168
Portugal	19	63	37	28	35	86	84	72	88	42	35	39	381
Finland	25	33	4	68	35	40	57	22	43	61	48	21	195
Sweden	14	39	5	46	28	74	70	45	67	52	27	41	222
U.K.	19	47	16	25	29	59	64	37	45	60	33	15	420
Cyprus	26	60	21	35	32	79	58	49	68	44	53	15	219
Malta	14	49	13	17	25	80	60	29	77	31	37	18	146
Czech Republic	20	38	7	14	9	78	73	37	82	37	10	29	435
Estonia	17	58	7	23	4	77	68	34	63	37	31	18	163
Latvia	9	48	5	28	6	95	78	34	69	44	18	43	197
Lithuania	12	61	3	30	3	85	88	48	76	29	7	37	161
Hungary	21	49	7	31	8	90	80	54	72	17	5	5	368
Poland	28	59	3	36	31	90	70	55	78	38	28	46	302
Slovenia	11	38	17	27	21	90	87	53	79	28	28	12	149
Slovakia	23	43	4	17	6	94	77	50	79	40	18	47	191
U.S.	21	68	2	57	29	70	59	36	55	75	69	23	501

Source: Eurobarometer 160.

Table 2 – Correlation matrix (2004)

	1	2	3	4	5	6	7	8	9	10	11	12	13	14	15
1. Actual self-employment	1.000														
2. Pref. for self-empl.	0.301**	1.000													
3. Male	0.127**	0.148**	1.000												
4. Age	0.153**	-0.024**	0.042**	1.000											
5. Age/100 (squared)	0.157**	-0.014	0.049**	0.986**	1.000										
6. Low education	0.069**	0.017	0.016	0.185**	0.196**	1.000									
7. High education	-0.012	0.001	-0.024*	0.003	-0.004	-0.279**	1.000								
8. Self-empl. parents	0.181**	0.099**	0.019	0.030**	0.040**	0.050**	0.060**	1.000							
9. Financial support	-0.009	0.026*	-0.054**	-0.024*	-0.020	0.053**	-0.084**	-0.007	1.000						
10. Admin. complexities.	-0.057**	-0.046**	-0.026*	0.042**	0.043**	0.054**	-0.070**	-0.017	0.202**	1.000					
11. Sufficient information	0.022*	0.016	-0.001	0.032**	0.034**	0.102**	-0.073**	0.009	0.215**	0.270**	1.000				
12. Economic climate	-0.013	-0.055**	-0.041**	-0.014	-0.014	0.069**	-0.100**	-0.008	0.264**	0.171**	0.179**	1.000			
13. Risk tolerance	0.047**	0.117**	0.032**	-0.083**	-0.080**	-0.081**	0.169**	0.065**	-0.136**	-0.139**	-0.151**	-0.183**	1.000		
14. Internal succ. factors	0.040**	0.076**	0.029*	-0.003	0.004	0.033**	0.050**	0.062**	-0.076**	-0.045**	-0.012	-0.117**	0.146**	1.000	
15. External succ. factors	0.001	-0.038**	0.019	0.019	0.020	0.013	-0.068**	-0.013	0.065**	0.036**	0.060**	0.100**	-0.090**	-0.422**	1.000

*indicates significance at the 5% level; ** indicates significance at the 1% level.
Source: Eurobarometer 160.

Defining the General Obstacle Perception (GOP) as the average over the four obstacles per country we observe that the unweighted average of GOP for the non-communist Europe is 62 percent, whereas that for the former communist Europe is 71 percent and for the U.S. 55 percent. Particularly interesting is the spread of GOP across countries: in the non-communist Europe it varies from Finland with 41 percent to Portugal with 83 percent. In the former communist Europe this variation is much lower: from Estonia with 61 percent to Slovenia with 77 percent.

The unweighted percentage of those having left school past the age of 21 ("high education") is higher in the non-communist member states than in the former communist one (39% versus 26%) but the European average is considerably lower than the U.S. (36% versus 57%). Concerning risk tolerance, the population of the non-communist European countries reveals a more positive attitude (52%) than that in the former communist countries (34%) but the U.S. ranks the highest (75%) followed by Ireland (69%) whereas the lowest level appears to occur in Hungary (17%). In terms of internal versus external success factors there are marked differences between the non-communist E.U. member states, the former communist ones and the U.S. In the U.S. internal success factors dominate external ones (69% versus 23%). This is also the case in the non-communist Europe but to a lower degree (44% versus 20%). The reverse is observed in the former communist countries (18% versus 30%). This result reinforces the prejudice that despite the regime switch the population of former communist countries still believes strongly in the role of external factors.

From Table 2 we see that there are only five coefficients in excess of |0.25|. Obviously, those between actual self-employment and preference for self-employment and between age and age (squared); but also between low and high education and between internal and external success factors. It is not surprising that the correlation coefficient between perception of administrative complexities and insufficient information is also in excess of 0.25.

4. ANALYSIS OF LATENT ENTREPRENEURSHIP

This section uses the information concerning the revealed preference for self-employment versus employment and establishes, by means of a probit regression, the impact of gender, age, education level, self-employed parent, perception of availability of financial support, perception of complexity of administrative procedures, perception of accessibility of information for start-up and whether the current economic climate is favorable, risk tolerance, internal and external success factors and country effects on the probability of wanting to be self-employed. Table 3 presents the effects of each explanatory variable on the probability of preferring self-employment using probit estimation.

To establish differences between the former communist member states and the remaining 17 ones we constructed a dummy variable which has value "1" in case an observation belongs to one of the eight former communist countries and "0" otherwise. Using this dummy variable we investigated whether the influence of any of the 13 variables depends on the region of origin. We constructed 13 new variables equal to original variable times the former communist dummy[34]. Using a cut-off point represented by a t-value of the coefficient of this new interaction variable of 1.5 we left out those variables having a t-value below 1.5. The results of this second regression using a multiplicative dummy on self-employed parents, risk tolerance, internal and external success factors is given in Table 3.

Table 3 - Effects of the probability of preferring to be self-employed and on the probability of being self-employed (2004)

	Preference for self-empl.			Actual self-employment		
	Coeff.	Std. Err.	dF/dx	Coeff.	Std. Err.	dF/dx
Constant	0.453*	0.174	0.168*	-2.987*	0.218	-0.681*
Male	0.374*	0.029	0.138*	0.251*	0.037	0.057*
Age	-0.021*	0.008	-0.008*	0.030*	0.009	0.007*
Age/100 (squared)	2.236*	0.880	0.827*	-0.110	1.023	-0.252
Low education	0.008	0.050	0.003	0.134*	0.058	0.031*
High education	-0.036	0.033	-0.013	-0.049	0.041	-0.011
Self-employed parents	0.250*	0.036	0.092*	0.475*	0.039	0.108*
Self-employed parents former comm.	0.189	0.103	0.070	-	-	-
Perc. lack of financial support	0.112*	0.038	0.042*	-0.019	0.045	-0.004
Perc. administrative complexity	-0.106*	0.034	-0.039*	-0.139*	0.046	-0.032*
Perc. adm. complexity former comm.	-	-	-	-0.159	0.093	-0.036
Perc. insufficient info	0.063*	0.032	0.023*	0.099*	0.039	0.023*
Perc. unfavorable economic climate	-0.119*	0.034	-0.044*	0.026	0.042	0.006
Preference for self-employment	-	-	-	0.941*	0.039	0.215*
Risk tolerance	0.213*	0.035	0.079*	0.022	0.044	0.005
Risk tolerance former comm.	0.254*	0.072	0.094*	0.218*	0.087	0.050*
Internal success factors	0.135*	0.039	0.050*	0.114*	0.044	0.026*
Internal success factors former comm.	0.134	0.088	0.050	-	-	-
External success factors	-0.038	0.048	-0.014	0.114*	0.050	0.026*
External success factors former comm.	0.174	0.096	0.064	-	-	-
Belgium	-0.734*	0.088	-0.272*	0.232*	0.104	0.053*
Denmark	-0.618*	0.111	-0.229*	0.004	0.143	0.001
Germany	-0.411*	0.085	-0.152*	0.198	0.102	0.045

	Preference for self-empl.			Actual self-employment		
	Coeff.	Std. Err.	dF/dx	Coeff.	Std. Err.	dF/dx
Greece	-0.310*	0.088	-0.115*	0.730*	0.097	0.166*
Spain	-0.200*	0.095	-0.074*	0.000	0.115	0.001
France	-0.622*	0.085	-0.230*	-0.235*	0.111	-0.054*
Ireland	-0.209	0.108	-0.077	0.128	0.125	0.029
Italy	-0.406*	0.087	-0.150*	0.121	0.103	0.028
Luxembourg	-0.331*	0.106	-0.123*	-0.389*	0.148	-0.089*
Netherlands	-0.747*	0.087	-0.276*	0.313*	0.102	0.071*
Austria	-0.436*	0.117	-0.161*	0.199	0.142	0.045
Portugal	-0.047	0.093	-0.017	-0.053	0.110	-0.012
Finland	-0.830*	0.113	-0.307*	0.480*	0.131	0.109*
Sweden	-0.636*	0.106	-0.235*	0.002	0.135	0.000
United Kingdom	-0.494*	0.089	-0.183*	0.165	0.106	0.038
Cyprus	-0.164	0.106	-0.061	0.280*	0.121	0.064*
Malta	-0.407*	0.123	-0.151*	-0.020	0.158	-0.005
Czech Republic	-0.917*	0.151	-0.339*	0.503*	0.134	0.115*
Estonia	-0.362*	0.164	-0.134*	0.208	0.163	0.047
Latvia	-0.643*	0.156	-0.238*	-0.081	0.176	-0.019
Lithuania	-0.251	0.168	-0.093	0.032	0.177	0.007
Hungary	-0.583*	0.162	-0.216*	0.501*	0.137	0.114*
Poland	-0.442*	0.143	-0.164*	0.459*	0.134	0.105*
Slovenia	-0.951*	0.172	-0.352*	-0.055	0.190	-0.013
Slovakia	-0.787*	0.157	-0.291*	0.539*	0.158	0.123*
Observations	7,914			7,914		
LR χ^2 / Degrees of freedom	734.42		42	1,458.826		41
Prob>χ^2			0			0
LogLikelihood			-5,117.674			-3,226.887
Pseudo R^2			0.067			0.184

*indicates significance at the 5% level.
Source: Eurobarometer 160.

Since the prime goal of this paper is to assess whether transition economies display differences relative to countries with a longer history of market economy, the first result noteworthy is the fact that in terms of possible difference in the influence of determinants of latent entrepreneurship only risk tolerance appears as having a significantly different impact on preference for self-employment in former communist countries compared to 'old' Europe and the U.S.[35] More precisely, these results suggest that in former communist countries the fact of being risk tolerant increases the probability of preferring self-employment more than in 'old' Europe[36]. The possible policy implications of this result are linked to the aspects that determine this risk tolerance. Recalling that this variable takes value one for those who do not think that one should not start a business if there is a risk it may fail, there are at least two avenues for action. One is by acting upon the consequences of a business failure for entrepreneurs (this may change the attitudes of some into more risk tolerance) for instance through bankruptcy law or efficient transfer or closing down procedures. The second policy avenue is to directly address the risks of failure rather than its consequences. Every measure that enhances management competencies and specific skills needed to successfully run a business fall in this strand. This covers a wide array of policy measures, from education and training in entrepreneurship/management to support services to SMEs to help them survive and strive in the market. Recalling from the discussion of Table 1 in section 3 that former communist countries display lower rates of risk tolerance than the remaining E.U. member states, measures addressing the risk of failure and/or its consequences appear as particularly useful in fostering entrepreneurship in these countries.

Another interesting question when discussing possible differences between transition and market economy countries is whether, once all personal determinants (socio-demographic and perceptions) are accounted for, there remain significant differences in latent entrepreneurship between these two groups of countries. Table 3 reports the individual country dummies' coefficients. It shows that, relative to the U.S., belonging to any E.U. country decreases the probability of preferring self-employment, with the exception of Ireland, Portugal, Cyprus and Lithuania. Clearly, this information is not sufficient to assess whether the two groups can be said to be significantly different. To this end a regression where the individual country dummies are replaced by the U.S. and former communist country dummies (leaving 'old' Europe as the base) shows that there is no significant difference between the E.U. transition economies and E.U. market economies once all determinants are accounted for. This regression also shows that the U.S. displays higher preference for self-employment than E.U. market economies even after other explanatory variables are controlled for. This unreported regression where individual country dummies are replaced by the U.S. and former communist dummies presents the same qualitative results as those in Table 3 for all other explanatory variables.

We will not comment upon the results of Table 3 in detail and refer to Grilo and Thurik (2005a) for a deeper analysis of this type of results and its policy implications. We nevertheless signal the lack of significant impact of perceived lack of financial support on actual entrepreneurship and its counterintuitive positive effect on preference for self-employment. These results are in agreement with those in Grilo and Irigoyen (2005) and in Grilo and Thurik (2005a) and have been discussed at length there. The same applies to the positive effect of perceived insufficient information on both latent and actual entrepreneurship.

5. ANALYSIS OF ACTUAL ENTREPRENEURSHIP

This section uses the information concerning gender, age, education level, self-employed parent, preference for self-employment, perception of availability of financial support, perception of complexity of administrative procedures, perception of accessibility of information for start-up and whether the current economic climate is favorable, risk tolerance, internal and external success factors and country effects. This is done to establish their impact on the probability of actually being self-employed. Table 3 presents the effects of each explanatory variable on the actual employment status using probit estimation.

We attempted to establish the differences between the former communist member states and the remaining 17 ones similarly to the procedure explaining preference for self-employment. Using the former communist country dummy variable we investigated whether the influence of any of the 14 variables depends on the region of origin. We constructed 14 new variables equal to the original variable times the former communist dummy. Using a cut-off point represented by a *t*-value of the coefficient of this new variable of 1.5 we left out those variables having a t-value below 1.5. This second regression using a multiplicative dummy on perception of administrative complexities and risk tolerance is given in Table 3[37].

Following the same line of reasoning as in the previous section and concentrating on the differences between transition and market economies in terms of actual entrepreneurship, the last columns of Table 3 suggests that, again, only risk tolerance plays a more important stimulating role in entrepreneurship in transition economies relative to market economies. In particular, these results indicate that for market economies risk tolerance magnifies the willingness to become self-employed, and therefore indirectly increases the probability of actually being self-employed through the positive effect of preferences, but does not directly affect actual entrepreneurship. On the contrary, for transition economies risk tolerance positively affects actual entrepreneurship both indirectly, through preferences, and directly since the dummy 'risk tolerance/former communist' displays a significant positive coefficient. This result reinforces the importance of policy measures addressing this factor for transition economies.

Concerning the possible differences in actual entrepreneurship between transition and market economies once all personal determinants (socio-demographic and perceptions) are accounted for, the results suggest significant differences between these two groups of countries. Table 3 reports the individual country dummies' coefficients showing that, relative to the U.S., belonging to any E.U. country decreases the probability of being self-employed only for France and Luxembourg while for all other countries it either has no effect or it increases this probability. As discussed in the previous section this information is not sufficient to assess whether the two groups can be said to be significantly different and a regression where the individual country dummies are replaced by the U.S. and former communist country dummies (leaving 'old' Europe as the base) shows that belonging to an E.U. transition country rather than to an E.U. market economy increases the probability of being self-employed once all determinants are accounted for. This regression also shows that the U.S. displays lower self-employment than E.U. market economies after other explanatory variables are controlled for. This unreported regression where individual country dummies are replaced by the U.S. and former communist dummies presents the same qualitative results as those in Table 3 for all other explanatory variables.

The higher 'intrinsic' actual entrepreneurship, i.e. after controlling for other variables, in transition economies combined with the fact that this group of countries does not display a significant difference in actual entrepreneurship rates relative to E.U. market economies (see Table 1) suggests that the obstacles and other socio-demographic characteristics identified in this study go a long way in holding back the entrepreneurial potential of these economies.

6. CONCLUSIONS

In the last decade research concentrated on macro-economic, labor market and trade and investment effects of the enlargement process of the E.U. for both the incumbent countries and the candidate countries (Observatory of European SMEs, 2005b). The present paper is an attempt to disclose differences at the micro level in the year the eight former communist countries joined the E.U. and some fifteen years after the transition process from a centrally planned regime to a market oriented one started. E.U. membership represents a major challenge for countries where less than fifteen years ago entrepreneurship hardly existed or not at all (Smallbone and Rogut, 2005). In this transition process the complete reorganization of the business sector plays a key role. The development of an SME sector with its new entrants plays a key role in this reorganization phase.[38] The present paper addresses the issue of latent and actual entrepreneurial energy behind this phase. In the next three paragraphs some remarks will be made concerning the three goals of the present paper: the investigation of the differences of the levels of latent and actual entrepreneurship, of the characteristics of those involved and of the determinants of these involvements between old and new member states.

A very clear regularity found in these data is the much higher proportion of the respondents with a declared preference for self-employment than of those actually involved in entrepreneurial activities in every country. This discrepancy between latent and actual entrepreneurship is higher in the former communist Europe than in the remaining E.U. member states.

This stronger discrepancy in transition economies may be the result of more deeply felt obstacles to entrepreneurial ventures. Data show that, with the exception of start-up information, the former communist Europe generally identifies the remaining three obstacles (lack of financial support, complex administrative procedures and unfavorable economic climate) more often than the non-communist Europe.[39] In terms of internal versus external success factors there is a very clear difference between transition economies and market economies: while in the U.S. and in 'old' Europe internal success factors dominate external ones, in transition countries the opposite is observed. This suggests that despite the regime switch, the population of former communist countries still believes strongly in the role of external factors in determining the success of a business. Concerning risk tolerance, the population in transition economies reveals a more cautious attitude than that of the 'old' Europe or the U.S.

Once the various socio-demographic and perception variables are allowed to play their role in explaining entrepreneurship rates and their influence is allowed to differ between transition and market economies, we find that risk tolerance has a significantly higher influence on both latent and actual entrepreneurship in transition economies than in market economies. This result opens the discussion of the importance for these countries of policy measures directed at the risks and consequences of business failure. Another important result is that, once socio-demographic and perception variables are controlled for, there is a significantly higher probability of being self-employed for a resident of a transition economy than for someone living in an E.U. market economy while such difference is not found for latent entrepreneurship.

Despite the policy implications of these results a word of caution is in order. Even if entrepreneurship is conceivably linked to an enhanced economic performance this is no automatic justification for public policy intervention. The economic rationale for public intervention relies on the existence of distortions and market failures. In particular, the presence of externalities is an important element leading to market failures in the context of entrepreneurship. A first step in guiding policy action is to identify possible factors behind lower entrepreneurial energy or its materialization. This paper is an attempt in this direction. In designing policy measures a further effort has to be made to gauge whether the factors behind lower entrepreneurship result indeed from distortions or market failures.[40] The concept of a "level playing field" for businesses addresses a possible source of distortions in the treatment of different types of enterprises (according to their age, size, sector or origin). The establishment of a "level playing field" is therefore an aim of enterprise policy. Access to finance, taxation rules, labor and market regulations as well as administrative burdens fall within these preoccupations.

NOTES

[1] In May 2004 ten new countries joined the European Union. Of these ten countries the Czech Republic, Estonia, Latvia, Lithuania, Hungary, Poland, Slovenia and Slovakia are former communist ones. There has been considerable variety in the way central planning was maintained in these countries before the Berlin wall fell. For instance, central planning in Yugoslavia – hence in Slovenia – was already abolished in 1952. There has also been considerable variety is the policy approaches of these countries since the fall of the Berlin wall. See Earle and Sakova (2000) and Petrin (2005). Cyprus and Malta have no communist past.

[2] Earle and Sakova (2000), Smallbone and Welter (2001a and 2001b) and Verheul, van Stel and Thurik (2006).

[3] Wennekers and Thurik (1999) and Audretsch, Carree, Thurik and van Stel (2005).

[4] Blanchflower, Oswald and Stutzer (2001) use a similar approach though their model has more of a reduced form flavour whereas no perception variables are taken into account. Also van Stel, Storey, Thurik and Wennekers (2006) apply a two-equation model explaining the nascent entrepreneurship rate and the young business entrepreneurship rate using a sample of countries participating in the Global Entrepreneurship Monitor between 2002 and 2004.

[5] Using an entirely different model explaining various entrepreneurial engagement levels Grilo and Thurik (2005b) conclude that, relative to never having considered setting up a business, the odds of thinking about it or having thought and given up are not significantly affected by the perception of administrative complexities. However, the odds of other more active entrepreneurial positions such as being in the process of starting a business or actually having started one (whether active for less or longer than three years) are significantly negatively affected by a perception of administrative complexity. However, they establish that the perception of lack of financial support has almost no discriminative effect across the various levels of entrepreneurial engagement.

[6] This approach views agents as (expected)-utility maximisers taking an occupational choice decision – to become employees or entrepreneurs (self-employed) – on the grounds of the utility associated with the returns accruing from the two types of activity. Though the specification and the working assumptions used in this strand of literature vary according to the factor being emphasized as playing the key role in explaining self-employment decisions, most of this constrained optimization approach can be traced back to the vision of the role of an entrepreneur found in the work of Knight (1921).

[7] Using American income data Hurst and Lusardi (2004) show that a positive relation can be found only for households in the top 5 percent of the wealth distribution.

[8] The *Eclectic Framework* also distinguishes between actual and 'natural' rates of entrepreneurship. The concept of 'natural' rate is relevant for analyzing government opportunities for and modalities of intervention. Clearly, there is room for the government

to act when the actual rate of entrepreneurship deviates from the 'natural' rate. Verheul, Wennekers, Audretsch and Thurik (2002) discriminate between five types of interventon.

[9] See Grilo and Thurik (2005b) were the same set a variables is used in the context of a multinomial logit model.

[10] There are many sources. See Minniti, Arenius and Langowitz (2005) and Verheul, van Stel and Thurik (2006).

[11] See Storey (1994) and Reynolds, Hay and Camp (1999).

[12] Robinson and Sexton (1994) and Cooper and Dunkelberg (1987) show that the self-employment decision is influenced by educational attainment. However, a study at the macro level by Uhlaner and Thurik (2005) shows that a higher level of education in a country is accompanied by a lower self-employment rate. See also Wit and van Winden (1989). Blanchflower (2004) reports that education is positively correlated with self-employment in the U.S. but negatively so in Europe.

[13] See Matthews and Moser (1996), Dunn and Holtz-Eakin (2000) and Hout and Rosen (2000).

[14] The argument behind the use and interpretation of capital assets to proxy financial constrains is the so-called equivalence theorem in Evans and Jovanovic (1989). See Cressy (1999) for a discussion of the limitations of this theorem.

[15] See Grilo and Irigoyen (2005).

[16] In their literature review Rauch and Frese (2000) find mild empirical evidence for a relationship between internal locus of control and business success. See also Beugelsdijk and Noorderhaven (2005).

[17] See Blanchflower, Oswald and Stutzer (2001) for some first results.

[18] According to Reynolds, Bygrave, Autio, Cox and Hay (2002) men are about twice as likely involved in entrepreneurial activity than women. See also Minniti, Arenius and Langowitz (2005). See also Blanchflower, Oswald and Stutzer (2001), Grilo and Irigoyen (2005) and Grilo and Thurik (2005a).

[19] See Delmar and Davidsson (2000).

[20] The results of Delmar and Davidsson (2000) and Davidsson and Honig (2003) show a clear education effect in the case of nascent entrepreneurs.

[21] See Grilo and Irigoyen (2005) and Grilo and Thurik (2005a) for European data of 200 and 2004, respectively.

[22] After controlling for other factors influencing self-employment preferences, Greece Ireland, Italy and Portugal are exceptions to this result. Blanchflower, Oswald and Stutzer (2001) also perform cross-country comparisons and find results compatible with these.

[23] Grilo and Thurik (2005b) report on the differences of the entrepreneurial engagement levels between old and new member countries of the European Union. Wennekers, van Stel, Thurik and Reynolds (2005) show that a 'former communist' dummy plays a role regressing global entrepreneurship (GEM) 2002 data for nascent entrepreneurship in 36 countries on the level of economic development. Using the same data set Stel, Carree and Thurik (2005) show some weak evidence that Hungary, Poland and Russia belong to a group of countries for which the positive influence of entrepreneurship on economic growth is relatively low.

[24] The transition effect may be stronger for women who are twice as less likely to become entrepreneurs than men (UNECE, 2002). Although self-employment in the form of cross-border trade, street trade or subcontracting work at home is a much pursued avenue of employment for women in transition countries, at the same time they experience gender-related barriers with respect to access to information, networks and collateral (Ruminska-Zimny, 2002). Verheul, van Stel and Thurik (2006) do not find clear differences between men and women in former communist countries.

[25] This survey was conducted on behalf of the European Commission's Enterprise Directorate-General, and the key findings are presented in *Flash Eurobarometer 160*

"Entrepreneurship",   European   Commission   2004,   available   at "http://europa.eu.int/comm/public_opinion/flash/fl160_en.pdf".

[26] As already remarked in Blanchflower, Oswald and Stutzer (2001) and Grilo and Irigoyen (2005), the answer to this type of questions can be misleading. In fact, a value judgement about attractive attributes associated with self-employment – independence, higher income, opportunity of tax evasion – may provoke a bias towards a preference for entrepreneurship.

[27] Grilo and Irigoyen (2005) and Grilo and Thurik (2005a) estimate a similar set of equations but there X= (1, men, age, low education, high education, lack of financial support, presence of administrative complexities, risk tolerance, country dummies).

[28] Given the recursive nature of the model this procedure provides consistent estimators provided the error terms are uncorrelated across equations. To investigate the assumption of across-equation independent errors we estimated each equation by least squares using a linear probability setting and then performed a seemingly unrelated regression on the two-equation model. The results show that: first, equation-by-equation estimation using probit or linear probability gives similar results; second, we performed a Breusch-Pagan test and concluded that there is no evidence that the error terms are correlated across equations.

[29] We chose not to treat this information as a continuous variable due to the discontinuity associated with the group "never having attended full time school".

[30] These two dummy variables capture, at best, the perception individuals have of the existence of financial or administrative barriers not their actual existence. Perceptions of these barriers are probably more influential in determining an individual's willingness to become self-employed than the actual existence of such barriers. The importance of perceptions over actual existence is probably less obvious when discussing the influence on actually being self-employed. Most likely, in the process of becoming self-employed, one's perceptions of barriers are confronted with reality and revised accordingly if relevant.

[31] Clearly, this is a crude indicator of risk attitudes and calling this dummy "risk tolerance" may be abusive. Nevertheless, in the absence of a better measure we believe it provides some information on how taking risks is perceived by the respondent.

[32] This result was also reported and discussed in Blanchflower, Oswald and Stutzer (2001) and in Grilo and Irigoyen (2005) using the Eurobarometer 2000 survey.

[33] Alternative explanations may be that in the area of socio-demografic and personality characteristics there are principle differences between the self-employed and the salaried or unemployed or that there are simply not enough business opportunities (Verheul, Wennekers, Audretsch and Thurik, 2002). In the present data set, for instance, 43 percent of those being self-employed report self-employed parents, whereas of those not being self-employed only 23 percent have self-employed parents.

[34] A likelihood ratio test showed that there is a significant difference between former communist countries and the other ones where in the restricted model all 13 multiplicative dummies are left out and in the unrestricted model they are all included. A second likelihood ratio test showed that there is also a significant difference between the restricted model and one where the four multiplicative dummies mentioned above are used. This finding is not surprising since the influence of risk tolerance differs significantly between former communist countries and other countries.

[35] Note that the group of countries against which the transition economies are being contrasted here includes the 15 'old' E.U. member states, Cyprus, Malta and the U.S.

[36] This can be seen by the fact that the only interaction variable with a significant, and positive, coefficient is risk tolerance.

[37] A likelihood ratio test showed that there is no significant difference between former communist countries and the other ones where in the restricted model all 14 multiplicative dummies are left out and in the unrestricted model they are all included. Since only the influence of risk tolerance differs significantly between former communist countries and other countries this test suggests that this aspect is not sufficient to create an overall

statistically significant difference between the two specifications. A second likelihood ratio test showed that there is a significant difference between the restricted model and one where the two multiplicative dummies mentioned above are used. The latter finding is not surprising since the influence of risk tolerance differs significantly between former communist countries and other countries.

[38] Long before any anticipation of former communist countries joining the E.U. d'Andrea Tyson, Petrin and Rogers (1994) already suggested a list of policy directives promoting entrepreneurship in Eastern Europe.

[39] All four obstacles play a lesser role in the U.S. when compared to Europe.

[40] Note however that even if such failures exist it still needs to be discussed whether public intervention does not create further distortions when addressing the original ones.

REFERENCES

Acs, Z. J., P. Arenius, M. Hay, and M. Minniti (2005), *Global Entrepreneurship Monitor: 2004 Executive Report*, Babson Park (MA), Babson College and London, London Business School.

Acs, Z. J., D. B. Audretsch, and D. S. Evans (1994), "The Determinants of Variations in Self-Employment Rates across Countries and over Time", Discussion Paper 871, Centre for Economic Policy Research (CEPR), London.

Andrea Tyson, L. d', T. Petrin and H. Rogers (1994), "Promoting Entrepreneurship in Eastern Europe", *Small Business Economics*, 6(3), 165-184.

Audretsch, D. B., M. A. Carree, A. R. Thurik, and A. J. van Stel (2005), "Does Self-employment Reduce Unemployment?", Discussion Paper 5057, Centre for Economic Policy Research (CEPR), London.

Bates, T. (1990), "Entrepreneur Human Capital Inputs and Small Business Longevity", *The Review of Economics and Statistics*, 72(4), 551-559.

Beugelsdijk, S. and N. Noorderhaven (2005), "Personality Characteristics of Self-employed; an Empirical Study", *Small Business Economics*, 24(2), 159-167.

Blanchard, O. (1997), *The Economics of Post-Communist Transition*, Oxford, Oxford University Press.

Blanchflower, D. G. (2000), "Self-employment in OECD Countries", *Labor Economics*, 7(2), 471-505.

Blanchflower, D. G. (2004), "Self-employment: More May Not Be Better", National Bureau of Economic Research (NBER), Working Paper 10286 Cambridge (MA).

Blanchflower, D. G. and B. D. Meyer (1994), "A Longitudinal Analysis of the Young Self-employed in Australia and the United States", *Small Business Economics*, 6(1), 1-19.

Blanchflower, D. G. and A. J. Oswald (1998), "What Makes an Entrepreneur?", *Journal of Labor Economics*, 16(1), 26-60.

Blanchflower, D. G., A. Oswald and A. Stutzer (2001), "Latent Entrepreneurship Across Nations", *European Economic Review*, 45(5), 680-691.

Blau, D. (1987), "A Time-series Analysis of Self-employment in the U.S.", *Journal of Political Economy*, 95(3), 445-467.

Brunner, H. -P. (1993), "The Development Experience and Government Policies in South-East Asia with Respect to Small Firms: Lessons for Eastern Europe?", in Acs, Z. J. and D. B. Audretsch (eds), *Small Firms and Entrepreneurship – An East-West Perspective*, Cambridge, Cambridge University Press.

Cooper, A. C. and W. C. Dunkelberg (1987), "Entrepreneurial Research: Old Questions, New Answers and Methodological Issues", *American Journal of Small Business*, 1(1), 11-23.

Cressy, R. (1999), "The Evans and Jovanovic Equivalence Theorem and Credit Rationing: Another Look", *Small Business Economics*, 12(4), 295-297.

Davidsson, P. and B. Honig (2003), "The Role of Social and Human Capital Among Nascent Entrepreneurs", *Journal of Business Venturing*, 18(3), 301-331.

Delmar, F. and P. Davidsson (2000), "Where Do They Come From? Prevalence and Characteristics of Nascent Entrepreneurs", *Entrepreneurship and Regional Development*, 12(1), 1-23.

Douglas, E. J. and D. A. Shepherd (2002), "Self-employment as a Career Choice: Attitudes, Entrepreneurial Intentions, and Utility Maximization", *Entrepreneurship Theory and Practice*, 26(3), 81-90.

Dunn, T. and D. Holtz-Eakin (2000), "Financial Capital, Human Capital, and the Transition to Self-employment: Evidence from Intergenerational Links", *Journal of Labor Economics*, 18(2), 282-305.

Earle, J. S. and Z. Sakova (2000), "Business Start-ups or Disguised Unemployment? Evidence on the Character of Self-employment from Transition Economies", *Labour Economics*, 7(5), 575-601.

Evans, D. S. and B. Jovanovic (1989), "An Estimated Model of Entrepreneurial Choice under Liquidity Constraints", *Journal of Political Economy*, 97(4), 808-827.

Evans, D. S. and L. S. Leighton (1989), "Some Empirical Aspects of Entrepreneurship", *American Economic Review*, 79(3), 519-535.

Evans, D. S. and L. S. Leighton (1990), "Small Business Formation by Unemployed and Employed Workers", *Small Business Economics*, 2(3), 319-330.

Grilo, I. and J. M. Irigoyen (2005), "Entrepreneurship in the E.U.: to Wish and Not to Be", *Small Business Economics*, forthcoming.

Grilo, I. and A. R. Thurik (2005a), "Latent and Actual Entrepreneurship in Europe and the U.S.", *International Entrepreneurship and Management Journal*, 1(4), forthcoming.

Grilo, I. and A. R. Thurik (2005b), "Entrepreneurial Engagement Levels in the European Union", *International Journal of Entrepreneurship Education*, 3(2), forthcoming.

Grilo, I. and A. R. Thurik (2005c), "Determinants of Entrepreneurial Engagement Levels in Europe and the U.S.", Papers on Entrepreneurship, Growth and Public Policy No. 05-2005, Max Planck Institute of Economics, Jena, Germany.

Hart, D. M. (ed) (2003), *The Emergence of Entrepreneurship Policy: Governance, Start-ups, and Growth in the U.S. Knowledge Economy*, Cambridge, Cambridge University Press.

Holmes, Th. J. and J. A. Schmitz Jr. (1990), "A Theory of Entrepreneurship and its Application to the Study of Business Transfers", *Journal of Political Economy*, 98(2), 265-294.

Holtz-Eakin, D., D. Joulfaian and H. S. Rosen (1994), "Entrepreneurial Decisions and Liquidity Constraints", *Rand Journal of Economics*, 25(2), 334-347.

Hout, M. and H. Rosen (2000), "Self-employment, Family Background and Race", *Journal of Human Resources*, 35(4), 670-692.

Hurst, E. and A. Lusardi (2004), "Liquidity Constraints, Household Wealth and Entrepreneurship", *Journal of Political Economy*, 112(2), 319-347.

Jovanovic, B. (1982), "Selection and the Evolution of Industry", *Econometrica*, 50(3), 649-670.

Jovanovic, B. (1994), "Firm Formation with Heterogeneous Management and Labor Skills", *Small Business Economics*, 6(2), 185-191.

Kihlstrom, R. E. and J. -J. Laffont (1979), "A General Equilibrium Entrepreneurial Theory of the Firm Based on Risk Aversion", *Journal of Political Economy*, 87(4), 719-748.

Knight, F. H. (1921), *Risk, Uncertainty and Profit*, New York, Houghton Mifflin.

Lazear, E. P. (2004), "Balanced Skills and Entrepreneurship", *American Economic Review*, 94(2), 208-211.

Lin, Z., G. Picot and J. Compton (2000), "The Entry and Exit Dynamics of Self-employment in Canada", *Small Business Economics*, 15(2), 105-125.

Lucas, R. E., Jr. (1978), "On the Size Distribution of Business Firms", *Bell Journal of Economics*, 9(3), 508-523.

Matthews, Ch. H. and S. B. Moser (1996), "A Longitudinal Investigation of the Impact of Family Background and Gender in Small Firm Ownership", *Journal of Small Business Management*, 34(2), 29-44.

Minniti, M., P. Arenius and N. Langowitz (2005), "GEM 2004 Report on Women and Entrepreneurship", Centre for Women's Leadership at Babson College/London Business School.

Mugler, J. (2000), "The Climate for Entrepreneurship in European Countries in Transition", in Sexton, D. L. and H. Landström (eds.), *The Blackwell Handbook of Entrepreneurship*, Oxford / Malden, Basil Blackwell, 150-175.

Murphy, K. M., A. Shleifer and R. W. Vishny (1991), "The Allocation of Talent: Implications for Growth", *Quarterly Journal of Economics*, 106(2), 503-530.

Noorderhaven, N. G., A. R. M. Wennekers, A. R. Thurik and A. J. van Stel (2004), "Self-employment Across 15 European Countries: the Role of Dissatisfaction", *Entrepreneurship: Theory and Practice*, 29(1), 447-466.

Observatory of European SMEs (2005a), *SMEs in Europe 2003, 2003/7*, Brussels, European Commission (KPMG Special services and EIM Business and policy research in the Netherlands).

Observatory of European SMEs (2005b), *The Impact of EU Enlargement on European SMEs, 2003/6*, Brussels, European Commission (KPMG Special services and EIM Business and policy research in the Netherlands).

Parker, S. C. (1996), "A Time-series Model of Self-employment under Uncertainty", *Economica*, 63(3), 459-475.

Parker, S. C. (1997), "The Effects of Risk on Self-employment", *Small Business Economics*, 9(4), 515-522.

Parker, S. C. (2004), The *Economics of Self-Employment and Entrepreneurship*, Cambridge: Cambridge University Press.

Petrin, T. (2005), "Industrial Policy to Foster Medium-sized Firms in Slovenia", in J. Prašnikar (ed.), *Medium-Sized Firms and Economic Growth*, New York, Nova Science Publishers, 169-180.

Rauch, A. and M. Frese (2000), "Psychological Approaches to Entrepreneurial Success: a general Model and an Overview of Findings", in C. L. Cooper and I. T. Robinson (eds), *International Review of Industrial and Organizational Psychology*, Chichester, Wiley, 101-142.

Rees, H. and A. Shah (1986), "An Empirical Analysis of Self-employment in the U.K.", *Journal of Applied Econometrics*, 1(1), 95-108.

Reynolds, P. D. (1997), "Who Starts New Firms? – Preliminary Explorations of Firms-in-Gestation", *Small Business Economics*, 9(5), 449-462.

Reynolds, P. D., M. Hay, and S. M. Camp (1999), *Global Entrepreneurship Monitor: 1999 Executive Report*, Babson College, London Business School and the Kauffman Center for Entrepreneurial Leadership.

Reynolds, P. D., W. D. Bygrave, E. Autio, L. W. Cox, and M. Hay (2002), *Global Entrepreneurship Monitor, 2002 Executive Report*, Babson College, London Business School and Kauffman Foundation.

Robinson, P. B. and E. A. Sexton (1994), "The Effect of Education and Experience on Self-employment Success", *Journal of Business Venturing*, 9(2), 141-156.

Roman, Z. (1990), "Strengthening Small and Medium-sized Enterprises in Eastern European Economies", paper presented at the UNDP/UNIDO workshop, Trieste, Italy.

Rotter, J. B. (1966), "Generalized Expectancies for Internal versus External Control of Reinforcement", *Psychological Monographs: General and Applied*, 80(1).

Ruminska-Zimny, E. (2002), "Women's Entrepreneurship and Labor Market Trends in Transition Countries", in *Women's Entrepreneurship in Eastern Europe and CIS Countries*, UNECE, Geneva, United Nations.

Smallbone, D. and A. Rogut (2005), "The Challenge Facing SMEs in the E.U.'s New Member States", *International Entrepreneurship and Management Journal*, 1(2), 219-240.

Smallbone, D. and F. Welter (2001a), "The Distinctiveness of Entrepreneurship in Transition Economies", *Small Business Economics*, 16(4), 249-262.

Smallbone, D. and F. Welter (2001b), "The Role of Government in SME Development in Transition Countries", *International Small Business Journal*, 19(4), 63-77.

Stel, A. J. van (2005), "COMPENDIA: Harmonizing Business Ownership Data across Countries and over Time", *International Entrepreneurship and Management Journal*, 1(1), 105-123.

Stel, A. J. van, M. A. Carree and A. R. Thurik (2005), "The Effect of Entrepreneurial Activity on National Economic Growth", *Small Business Economics*, 24(3), 311-321.

Stel, A. J. van, D. Storey, A. R. Thurik and S. Wennekers (2006), "From Nascent to Actual Entrepreneurship: the Effect of Entry Barriers", Papers on Entrepreneurship, Growth and Public Policy, Max Planck Institute of Economics, Jena, Germany, forthcoming.

Storey, D. J. (1994), *Understanding the Small Business Sector*, London/New York, Routledge.

Storey, D. J. (2003), "Entrepreneurship, Small and Medium Sized Enterprises and Public Policies", in D. B. Audretsch and Z. J. Acs (eds), *Handbook of Entrepreneurship Research*, Boston/Dordrecht, Kluwer Academic Publishers, 473-511.

Taylor, M. P. (2001), "Self-employment and Windfall Gains in Britain: Evidence from Panel Data", *Economica*, 68(272), 539-565.

Uhlaner, L. and A. R. Thurik (2005), "Post-materialism: a Cultural Factor Influencing Total Entrepreneurial Activity Across Nations", Papers on Entrepreneurship, Growth and Public Policy no 20-2005, Max Planck Institute of Economics, Jena, Germany.

UNECE (United Nations Economic Commission for Europe) (2002), *Women's Entrepreneurship in Eastern Europe and CIS Countries* (Entrepreneurship and SMEs series), Geneva, United Nations.

Verheul, I., A. J. van Stel and A. R. Thurik (2006), "Explaining Female and Male Entrepreneurship across 29 Countries", *Entrepreneurship and Regional Development*, forthcoming.

Verheul, I., S. Wennekers, D. B. Audretsch and A. R. Thurik (2002), "An Eclectic Theory of Entrepreneurship: Policies, Institutions and Culture", in D. B. Audretsch, A. R. Thurik, I. Verheul and A. R. M. Wennekers (eds), *Entrepreneurship: Determinants and Policy in a European-U.S. Comparison*, Boston/Dordrecht, Kluwer Academic Publishers, 11-81.

Wagner, J. (2003), "Testing Lazear's Jack-of-all-trades View of Entrepreneurship with German Micro Data", *Applied Economics Letters*, 10(11), 687-689.

Wennekers, S., A. J. van Stel, A. R. Thurik and P. D. Reynolds (2005), "Nascent Entrepreneurship and the Level of Economic Development", *Small Business Economics*, 24(3), 293-309.

Wennekers, A. R. M. and A. R. Thurik (1999), "Linking Entrepreneurship and Economic Growth", *Small Business Economics*, 13(1), 27-55.

Wennekers, A. R. M., L. Uhlaner and A. R. Thurik (2002), "Entrepreneurship and its Conditions: a Macro Perspective", *International Journal of Entrepreneurship Education*, 1(1), 25-64.

Wit, G. de and F. A. A. M. van Winden (1989), "An Empirical Analysis of Self-employment in the Netherlands", *Small Business Economics*, 1(4), 263-272.

Worldbank (2005), *Beyond Transition: Newsletter about Transforming Economies*, 16(1), (see http://www.worldbank.org/transitionnewsletter).

Chapter 5
NEW FIRM FORMATION AND THE REGION: EMPIRICAL RESULTS FROM THE UNITED STATES

Zoltan J. Acs
University of Baltimore, and U.S. Bureau of the Census

1. INTRODUCTION

This paper examines regional variation in entrepreneurial activity in light of theoretical developments in economic geography (Krugman, 1991) and new growth theory (Romer, 1990). The ability to transform new knowledge into economic knowledge requires a set of skills, aptitudes, insights and circumstances that is neither uniformly nor widely distributed in the population. Thus a closer connection between endogenous growth models and models of entrepreneurship seems necessary (Acs and Armington, 2006).

We use firm formation data annually from 1991 to 1998: these microdata facilitate research on the dynamics of American Businesses, especially on their patterns of formation, employment change and mergers. In order to test hypotheses about how and why regions differ in their rates of firm formation one needs a database that represents all industries, distinguishes between establishments and firms, identifies start-ups and specifies the location and changing employment of each establishment through time. We find considerable variation in the new firm formation rate across regions, but little variation over time. Variation in firm formation rates is substantially explained by regional differences in industry specialization, human capital, firm size and local population and income growth rates.

To test the hypotheses that the new firm formation rates are positively related to the level of human capital we estimate a model where the dependent variable is the annual service firm formation rate. The results suggest that the regional differences in service firm formation rates depend to a large degree on the educational requirements and the market served by the newly formed firms. The local levels of educational attainment impact primarily the firm formation rates of the types of firms that are normally founded by better-educated entrepreneurs, and do not affect start-up rates for those normally founded by individuals with less than a college degree. However, we also find that regions that have higher levels of both the best educated, and the worst educated, are the most innovative, with armies of unskilled supplying low level services to the most educated and creative (Florida, 2005).

The next Section examines the data including the description of the data and the importance of longitudinal microdata to evaluate theories of industry dynamics. Section 3 discusses the use of longitudinal data to explore entrepreneurship, geography and growth. The empirical model and results are in Section 4. In Section 5 some conclusions are drawn.

2. THE BUSINESS INFORMATION TRACKING SYSTEM (BITS)

2.1. Brief Description of the Database

The current Business Information Tracking Series (BITS) file facilitates tracking employment, payroll, and firm affiliation and (employment) size for the more than thirteen million establishments that existed at some time during 1989 through 2001. This database was constructed from the Census Bureau's Statistics of U.S. Business (SUSB) files, which were developed from the microdata underlying the aggregate data published in Census' County Business Patterns. These annual data describing establishments were linked together using the SUSB Longitudinal Pointer File, which facilitates tracking establishments over time, even when they change ownership and identification numbers. The SUSB data beginning in 1988, their Longitudinal Pointer File, and the BITS files were constructed by Census with substantial support from the Office of Advocacy of the U.S. Small Business Administration.[1] The basic unit of the BITS data is a business establishment (location or plant). The microdata describe each establishment for each year of its existence in terms of its employment, annual payroll, location (state, county, and metropolitan area), primary industry, and start year. The recorded start year is the year that establishment entered the Census register, which would normally be the year it first hired any paid employees. Additional data for each establishment and year identify the firm (or enterprise) to which the establishment belongs, and the total employment of that firm.

As with most microdata at the Census Bureau, the BITS data are confidential, so the microdata can only be used at the Census Bureau by

Census employees, or by approved outside researchers working at one of the Census Centers for Economic Research. These microdata are referred to there as LEEM data (for Longitudinal Establishment and Enterprise Microdata) files. However, many tabulations of these data have been prepared for use by the SBA for other research projects, and these aggregated data are available for further research use.

2.2. Longitudinal Microdata Required to Evaluate Dynamic Theories

In order to test hypotheses about how and why regions differ in their rates of formation of new firms and growth of employment, one needs a database representing all industry sectors, that distinguishes business establishments from firms, identifies start-ups of new firms, and specifies the location and changing employment of each establishment through time. The studies reported here depend crucially on use of the BITS database that the Bureau of the Census has constructed for the Office of Advocacy of the U.S. Small Business Administration for study of entry, survival, and growth in different types of businesses.

This database is a unique by-product of the complex register that Census maintains with information on all businesses in the United States. This Standard Statistical Establishment List (SSEL) is updated continuously with data from many other sources, but its underlying coverage is based on new business names and addresses from the Master Business File of the Internal Revenue Service. Therefore, every business in the United States that files any tax return is covered by the SSEL, and IRS data from quarterly payroll tax filings (including employment only for the March 12 payroll period) are used to provide comprehensive coverage of all U.S. employment. However, some of the employment numbers are estimated from the payroll numbers, which provide good estimates for establishments that are themselves single-location firms (tax-filing units), but are less reliable for the tax-filing units that represent multiple establishments owned by a single firm.

The data in the SSEL on the individual locations of multi-unit businesses are therefore somewhat less consistent and comprehensive than those for independent, or single-location, firms. All large (over 250 employees reported) multi-unit firms are surveyed annually (Company Organization Survey, except in Economic Census years) to determine the location, industry, and employment (and predecessor or successor owners) of the individual establishments that are or were owned or controlled by each. A sample of the smaller multi-unit firms is also covered each year, on a rotating basis, so that all but the smallest (with less than 10 employees) are surveyed at least once between each Economic Census, in addition to their coverage in the quinquenial Economic Census (in each year ending with 2 or 7). The resulting lags in the reporting of the formation, closure, or change in ownership of some locations of smaller multi-unit firms (as well as formerly single-unit firms that have become multi-unit) causes false jumps in some of their establishment employment data, as the temporarily aggregated employment of the covered locations is subsequently correctly distributed to the updated list of actual locations.[2]

Census' annual County Business Patterns (CBP) publication provides aggregations of data on establishments selected from the SSEL and extensively edited at both the establishment level (relative to the previous year's data) and the aggregate level. This CBP subset of the SSEL population represents all active (with positive annual payroll) private sector establishments except those in agricultural production, railroads, large pension, health and welfare funds, and private households. The numbers of establishments, employment, and payroll are classified by state, industry, and employment-size class and then processed to avoid disclosure of confidential data, and published annually as CBP.

The microdata behind the CBP provide the starting point for each annual SUSB file. These are further processed to calculate Metropolitan Statistical Area (MSA) codes, and to improve industry code reporting using the industry codes from the subsequent year SSEL whenever they are more precise. Then firm-level data are constructed by aggregating data from all establishments belonging to each enterprise (industry-wide and country-wide), and these firm-level data are attached to each of the component establishment records. These firm-level data include employment, payroll, and receipts (unedited), with the primary state, primary industry division, and primary (3-digit SIC) industry within the primary division, based on the largest share of annual payroll. These SUSB data are tabulated and processed for disclosure for a number of standardized tables by firm size for the Office of Advocacy of the SBA, and for the aggregate SUSB (public) database of the Census Bureau.

A Longitudinal Pointer File is then constructed to link each year's establishment record to the prior year's record for the same establishment, allowing for a change in identity or ownership of continuing establishments. The CFN is the basic Census identification number, which is assigned to each new establishment, and is generally retained consistently over time. However, a change in ownership or legal form, or a change in status between single-unit and multi-unit, will cause a change in CFN. A complex system of computerized matching of records for establishments that might have changed CFN's is used to identify continuing establishments in the SUSB and to update the Longitudinal Pointer File each year. This system examines a wide variety of information, including Permanent Plant Numbers (PPN's), Employer Identification Numbers (EIN's), and statistical matching of records for single units, based on such attributes as name, address, zip code, and industry codes. Matches are sought both between years, and within years (mid-year reorganizations).[3] The records that remain unmatched are assumed to represent new establishment formations or closures of existing establishments.

The BITS files are constructed by merging annual SUSB files using the Longitudinal Pointer Files to create a single longitudinal record for each establishment that appears in any of the annual files. Where there has been a mid-year reorganization the data from the two records representing the same establishment are combined for that year, and both CFN's are retained in the BITS file. Because some establishments with mid-year reorganizations report March employment in both of their records, the aggregate employment from the BITS is slightly lower that that from the SUSB file for each year, since only the employment from the second record for an establishment identified as a midyear reorganization was used if that employment was non-zero.

The Company Statistics Division of the Census Bureau prepares for the SBA Office of Advocacy an extensive set of tables of aggregated BITS data on annual gross flows (establishment and firm start-ups and closures, employment gains from start-ups and expansions of establishments, and employment losses from closures and contractions) for multi-unit and single-unit firms, by firm size, industry, and location. They also prepare custom tabulations on a contract basis for specific research projects. However, many research needs cannot be met by these tabular data designed for public use because they are limited to predefined cells representing some minimum number of firms, and do not allow exploration of the data, nor refinement of the specification of variables. Access to the microdata is also necessary to avoid biasing analyses as a result of the necessary suppression of any small cell values and their complementary cells during the disclosure processing for tabular data. These small cells may contribute crucial information to statistical analyses performed within a Census Center for Economic Studies, while avoiding any disclosure problems in the empirical results.

3. USING CENSUS' BITS TO EXPLORE ENTREPRENEURSHIP, GEOGRAPHY AND ECONOMIC GROWTH

3.1. The Theoretical Framework

The knowledge-based growth models have three cornerstones: spatially constrained externalities, increasing returns in the production of goods, and decreasing returns in the production of knowledge (Romer, 1986, 1990; Lucas, 1988). New knowledge – in the form of products, processes or organizations – leads to opportunities that agents exploit commercially. Such opportunities are then a function of the distribution of knowledge within and between societies. But opportunities rarely present themselves in neat packages - they have to be discovered and packaged. Precisely for that reason, the nexus of opportunity and enterprising individuals is crucial in understanding economic growth (Shane and Eckhardt, 2003).

However, the ability to transform new knowledge into what Arrow (1962) designated 'economic knowledge' (leading to commercial opportunity) requires a set of skills, aptitudes, insights and circumstances that is neither uniformly nor widely distributed in the population. Moreover, empirical findings support the proposition that entry and entrepreneurship provide important links between knowledge creation and the commercialization of such knowledge, particularly at the early stage when knowledge is still fluid (Audretsch and Keilbach, 2004).

The basic shortcoming of the endogenous growth model is that it fails to recognize that only some of the aggregate stock of knowledge (often associated with R&D costs or products) is economically useful, and that even economically relevant knowledge may not be successfully exploited if the transmission links are missing. Furthermore, much of the general stock of knowledge is not in the public domain, and it may not spill over easily from one carrier to another. Most knowledge, regardless of whether it is in the public or private domain, requires a certain absorptive capacity on the part of the recipients in order for successful transmission to occur. This suggests that there is a filter between the stock of knowledge and the more limited economically useful knowledge. Not only does the level of knowledge vary among countries and regions; the transmission capacity of the filter also varies.

Consequently, despite the gains in terms of transparency and technical ease obtained by imposing strong assumptions in the endogenous growth models, these advantages have to be measured in relation to the drawbacks of deviations from real world behavior. Hayek (1945) pointed out that the central feature of a market economy is the partitioning of knowledge or information about the economy. The endogenous model fails to incorporate one of the most crucial elements in the growth process; transmission of knowledge through entrepreneurship – new firm formation - and the resulting spatial dimension of growth.

Thus, a closer connection between the endogenous growth models and the models of entrepreneurship seems necessary. The fact that knowledge-producing inputs are not evenly distributed across space implies that regions may not grow at the same rate, not only because they have different levels of investment in knowledge but also because they exploit knowledge at different rates. Even if the stock of knowledge were freely available, including the tacit and non-tacit parts, the ability to transform that knowledge into economic knowledge, or commercialized products, would not be. Moreover, most knowledge is not a free good at everyone's disposal. Often only a few individuals know about a particular scarcity, or a new invention, or a particular resource lying fallow or not being put to best use. This knowledge is both idiosyncratic and local, because it is acquired through each individual's own networks, depending on their occupation, on-the-job routines, social relationships, and daily life. It is frequently this particular knowledge, obtained through a local knowledge network, which leads to profit-making insight (Michelacci, 2003).

The dispersion of information among different agents who do not have access to the same observations, interpretations or experiences, has implications for growth. Since this is not recognized in the endogenous growth model, we need to extend it with some additional assumptions and outline an alternative structure to improve the model. In order to remedy the limitations of the endogenous growth model and to specify the nature of the transmission mechanism that diffuse knowledge and converts it, via entrepreneurship, to growth, we propose the following assumptions.

1. New firms are assumed to be the primary mechanism to commercialize new knowledge, regardless of whether it is drawn from the stock of existing knowledge, or is newly discovered, and whether it is scientific knowledge or other. This transformation into economically relevant knowledge often occurs via spillovers that are exploited in new ventures, evidenced in firm formations. When existing firms acquire new economic knowledge, they may create new establishments within the firm, but the majority of such secondary new establishments are replications of other establishments owned by multi-location firms. Thus new firm formations are seen as the primary indicator of knowledge spillovers leading to economic growth.

2. Each new firm embodies a new idea, or innovation, expecting to provide a new, or improved, or more competitive product or service to customers. Schumpeter (1911)[4] suggests that a new idea (innovation) represents any kind of new combination of new or existing knowledge. These new firms are extremely heterogeneous, not only in the size, but also in terms of characteristics such as absorptive capacity, strategy, technology, product range, and performance (profitability, productivity, etc.). Because new entrants often make mistakes and fail, a very high formation (or gross entry) rate is necessary to sustain long-term growth.

3. Knowledge spillovers are primarily local events; there are few important interregional spillovers. Success in converting available public or private knowledge into economically useful firm-specific knowledge depends on the initiative and skills of the local potential entrepreneurs, and these

entrepreneurial conditions vary across regions. Local policy and previous history (path-dependence) determines the local entrepreneurial climate, which may be embedded in the local infrastructure, regulation, attitudes, educational policies, networks, technology transfer mechanisms, etc.

The combined result of these assumptions, when added to the endogenous growth model, can be characterized as a filter (here defined in terms of entrepreneurship) that determines the proportion of local knowledge that is converted into economically useful firm-specific knowledge (Acs, Audretsch, Braunerhjelm and Carlsson, 2004). This suggests that an increasing stock of knowledge (through R&D and education) will lead to higher economic growth only if the knowledge is economically useful and if the economy is endowed with factors of production that can select, evaluate and transform knowledge into commercial use, i.e., entrepreneurs. If these conditions are not fulfilled, an increase in the knowledge stock may have no impact on growth. Similarly, highly entrepreneurial regions with smaller knowledge stocks may experience higher growth than regions more abundantly endowed with knowledge.

The basic structure of the model accommodates both incumbent firms and new firms. Incumbent firms accumulate knowledge over their lifetime, and this accumulated firm-specific knowledge influences their ability to exploit new knowledge spillovers - the degree of firm specificity of their existing knowledge constrains their future absorption of knowledge spillovers. Hence, the incumbent firms' ability to exploit spillovers is determined by path-dependence. Furthermore, new establishments that are created by incumbent firms may be located in other regions, since their location decisions are likely to be based on cost-minimizing decisions.

New firms differ from incumbents, in that their economic knowledge is not governed by path-dependence to the same extent, but is built on the local entrepreneurs' ability to exploit opportunities arising from aggregate spillovers. Start-ups entering the market thus provide direct evidence of the conversion of knowledge to growth. They produce genuinely new products and services, or compete using new processes or filling under-served niches.

Both types of firms exploit knowledge spillovers, albeit in different ways. Together their performance determines the share of knowledge spillovers that are commercialized. We can think of θ as the absorptive capacity of incumbent firms and λ as a proxy for entrepreneurship within an economy. Then, in accordance with assumptions 1 and 2, the standard production function has to be modified to account also for entrepreneurship:

$$F(k_i, x, (\lambda + \theta)K)$$

where k_i is new knowledge produced by firm i, x is a vector representing all other inputs, and since each individual firm cannot appropriate all the knowledge they create. Thus, if entrepreneurship is non-existent in an economy (so λ is zero) and θ is constant, then knowledge spillovers will not provide the same solution as in the endogenous growth model with automatic and all encompassing spillovers. In fact, the model will then reduce to the neoclassical growth model.

It is obvious that it is not only the size of K and the absorptive capacity of incumbent firms that matter, but also the presence of entrepreneurs as captured by λ. Our empirical work was driven by the effort to estimate the size of λ. In Romer's work (1990), λ equals unity, which implies that all knowledge (K) is accessible and convertible into economic knowledge (Acs and Varga, 2002), a very strong and unlikely assumption (Acs and Varga, 2004).

The total amount of entrepreneurial activity (E) in a particular region $_L$– given broader institutional constraints (B) – is a function of the profit (π^*) in excess of wages (w) accruing to the exploitation of new knowledge from (K) the stock of knowledge and the portion of knowledge not commercialized by large firms (θ) and the entrepreneurial culture in a region (C). Thus, the knowledge spillover model of entrepreneurship estimated here is as follows:

$$E_L = \gamma(\pi^* (K_L, \theta_L, C_L) - w)1/\beta \qquad (1)$$

where we expect K_L to be > 0, θ_L to be < 0 and C_L to be >0.

A rich literature exists in regional economics that sheds some light on how to capture the extent to which pooled labor markets, non-pecuniary transactions, and information spillovers exist. One approach suggests that the infrastructure of services is more developed in regions that are more densely populated. According to Krugman (1991, p. 484), "The concentration of several firms in a single location offers a pooled market for workers with industry-specific skills, ensuring both a lower probability of unemployment and a lower probability of labor shortage." Thus the start-up rate for each industry sector should increase with the existing density of establishments in each sector. Another view is that localized industries tend to support the production of non-tradable specialized inputs. Thirdly, informational spillovers give clustered firms a better production function than isolated producers have. The high level of human capital embodied in their general and specific skills is another mechanism by which new firm start-ups are supported. Thus regions that are rich in this resource should have more start-up activity. University graduates – especially engineers – provide a supply of labor to local firms. New firm start-ups should be positively related to higher average levels of education, and negatively related to the levels of unskilled and semi-skilled workers in the region.

Also associated with studies of new firm formation from the 1980s was the role of industrial restructuring. Industrial restructuring has been associated with *1*) the shift from manufacturing employment to services, *2*) a reduction in both firm and plant size, and *3*) a shift to higher levels of technology. The shift from manufacturing to services, which are usually less capital intensive than manufacturing, could increase the rate of new firm formation. Regions that are dominated by large branch plants or firms will have less new firm formation, in part because such areas have relatively fewer people with the managerial or skilled labor backgrounds that are the source of most firm founders.[5,6]

4. THE CONSTRUCTION OF VARIABLES FOR EMPIRICAL EXAMINATIONS

4.1. The Unit of Observation for these Studies

Although the BITS data support analysis at the firm level, these studies focus on the analysis of regional variations within the United States, and seek understanding of why various levels of economic activity vary across regions. Therefore, after considerable preliminary analysis of the data at the firm level, the scope and definitions of the relevant regional data were carefully defined and the firm-level data were aggregated to create regional data.

The geographic unit of analysis chosen for this study, the Labor Market Areas (LMAs) defined by Tolbert and Sizer (1996), is ideal for our purposes because it identifies economic areas broad enough to contain most of the labor supply and the local market for their business population, while being small enough to substantially avoid the worst of the aggregation problems of larger geographic units. These LMAs are aggregations of the 3,141 U.S. counties into 394 geographical regions based on the predominant commuting patterns (journey-to-work) between them in 1990. Each LMA contains at least one central city, along with the surrounding counties that constitute both its labor supply and its local consumer and business market. Many of the 394 LMA's cut across state boundaries, to better define regionally integrated areas of local economic activity.

Tolbert and Sizer specified these LMA's for the Department of Agriculture, using the Journey-to-Work data from the 1990 U.S. Census of Population. The LMA's are named according to the largest place within them in 1990. Some LMA's incorporate more than one MSA, while others separate some of the larger MSA's into more than one LMA, depending on the commuter patterns. A few smaller independent (usually rural) Commuting Zones have been appended to adjacent LMA's so that each

LMA had a minimum of 100,000 population in 1990, which is necessary to avoid possible disclosure of confidential Census data that have been aggregated for LMA's. Alaska and Hawaii each are treated as a single integrated LMA, although they clearly have little mobility across their entire areas. See Reynolds (1994) for further discussion of why LMAs are the most suitble unit for this type of analysis.

The LMA unit of observation has the advantage of including both the employment location and the residence location of the population and labor force within the same area. Being based on counties, a wide variety of data collected at the county or Zip-code level can be aggregated to construct LMA-level data. Finally, the 394 LMAs together cover the whole country, so that their data can be aggregated to U.S. totals, and all areas are represented.

4.2. Measurement of Formation and Growth Rates

In the research reported here we are investigating regional differences in gross new firm formation rates, not the net change in numbers of firms or establishments in an area. The factors we are focusing on to account for differences in rates of new firm formation include local differences in educational attainments, entrepreneurship, innovation, and industrial evolution. The factors contributing to explanations of local differences in firm deaths, plant entry and exit, all of which affect the net numbers of establishments, are far beyond the scope of this paper, and generally not strongly related to local human capital.

Firm formation rates are calculated for each of the 394 LMAs, based on new firm formations during the period under study.[7] Single unit firm formations in year t are identified on the BITS as non-affiliated establishments that reported a Census start-year of t or t-1, that had no employment in March of year t-1, and had positive employment below 500 in March of year t. (The Census start-year is the year that the establishment first reported any payroll and therefore entered the Census business register.) This avoids inclusion of either new firms that have not yet actually hired an employee, or firms recovering from temporary inactivity. About 400,000 new firms generally appear in the business register (with some positive annual payroll) the year before they have any March employment, and we postpone their 'birth' until their first year of reported employment. An average of 90,000 older firms each year have no employees in March, but recover some employees the following year. Those new firms that had 500 or more employees in their first year of activity appear to be primarily offshoots of existing companies.[8]

New firm formations include most of the primary locations of the relatively few multi-unit firms (1,500 to 6,000 per year) that appeared to start up with less than 500 employees (firm wide) in multiple locations in their first year. We limited multi-unit firm formations to those whose employment in their new primary location constituted at least a third of their total employment in the first year.[9] This rule effectively eliminated the 600 to 1,000 new firms each year which were apparently set up to manage existing locations - relatively small new headquarters supervising large numbers of employees in mainly older branch locations which were newly acquired, or perhaps contributed by joint venture partners.

Because the Labor Market Areas vary greatly in size, the absolute numbers of new firm formations must be standardized by some measure of the LMA size before it is meaningful to compare them across areas. When dealing with the whole service sector, firm formation rates are calculated as the number of new firms per thousand members of the labor force in the LMA in the prior year. This labor force approach has a particular theoretical appeal, in that it is based on the theory of entrepreneurial choice proposed by Evans and Jovanovic (1989). Each worker in the LMA chooses whether to be an employee of an existing business, or to become an entrepreneur and form a new firm. This approach implicitly assumes that the entrepreneur starts the new business in the same labor market where he or she previously worked or sought employment. It also has the added property that there is a clear lower bound of 0.00 (for no new businesses), and a theoretical upper bound of 1.00, which would represent the extreme case where every worker within a region started a new business during a year.

However, when comparing firm formation rates for different industries, or across sub-sectors of the service industry, we need to standardize for the differences in sizes of both areas and sub-sectors. For this purpose we calculate formation rates in terms of the number of new formations per thousand establishments already in existence in that industry or sub-sector in each LMA. This could be termed the ecological approach, because it considers the amount of start-up activity relative to the size of the existing population of businesses in that sector.

Two considerations of the timing of the firm birth rate data should be noted. While new firms enter the business register underlying the BITS file on a nearly continuous basis, their employment data are reported only for a pay period in March of each year. Since we require positive employment before recognizing a new firm, if a firm begins hiring after March, we do not count its formation until the following year. Therefore, each specified year's firm formation counts actually represent firms that hired their first employees sometime between April of the prior year and March of the specified year, for an average of nine months lagged reporting. Further, Reynolds, Miller and Maki (1995) and others have shown that the time between an individual's decision to create a new firm and the start of the resulting economic activity averages about two years, and is often longer. With such lags in the initialization and reporting of new firm formations, we would not expect to be able to identify a lag structure between differences in their annual rates and the regional factors associated with these differences, even though we have nine years of annual data on new firm formations.

4.3. Industry Sectors

We distinguish six broad industry sectors for the analysis of growth, to facilitate analysis of different industries' sensitivities to factors affecting their growth, and to better control for aggregation effects in regions with different shares of weak industries - manufacturing, agriculture, and mining sectors. This expands both the scope and the industrial detail beyond that of previous studies, most of which were limited to manufacturing. Industry codes are based on the most recently reported 4-digit SIC code for each establishment, because the precision and accuracy of the codes tends to increase over time.[10]

Sector	Standard Industrial Classifications
Distributive	4000-5199 (transportation, communication, public utilities, and wholesale trade)
Manufacturing	2000-3999
Business services	7300-7399 and 8700-8799 (including engineering, accounting, research, and management services)
Extractive	0700-1499 (agricultural services and mining)
Retail trade	5200-5999
Local market	1500-1799 and 6000-8999 excluding business services (construction, consumer and financial services)

These six broad sectors distinguish industries that might differ in their sensitivity to local market conditions. For instance, local consumer services and construction are more dependent on local regional demand than manufacturing and distributive services are, while manufacturing and distributive services may have greater dependence on the supply of semi- and unskilled labor. Growth in extractive industries is limited by the local supply of natural resources and arable land.

4.4. Variability in Formation in the 1990s

During the period from 1991 to 1996 U.S. private employment increased over 10 percent, while the employment gains from new establishments during that period contributed over 26 percent. Looking at the comparable growth rates for the six industry sectors we distinguished, in Table 1, it is apparent that the greatest growth was in business services (28.7% net increase, with 43.6% gross increase from employment in new establishments), followed by other local market services and construction (12.2%, with 25.8% in new establishments). Employment in manufacturing and extractive industries was virtually constant, although both showed substantial gains in new establishments, indicating that those sectors were continuing to evolve new products and processes to replace those that were discontinued or shrinking.

Table 1 – Establishment employment, gross change in births, and firm formation rates 1991-1996, by firm type, and by industry sector

Establ. class	Employment		91-96 Empl. change		LMA Employment growth ratios annualized			LMA Firm formation rate per 1000 labor force		
	1991	1996	net %	birth %	Mean	Min.	Max.	Mean	Min.	Max.
All establ.	92,265,576	102,149,281	10.2	26.3	1.03	0.99	1.08	3.67	2.05	10.00
FIRM TYPE										
Single unit	38,532,294	44,811,609	15.1	31.3						
Multi-unit	53,731,429	57,324,994	6.5	22.6						
INDUSTRY SECTOR										
Bus. services	7,780,445	10,385,762	28.7	43.6	1.07	0.94	1.39	0.35	0.11	1.14
Distribution	11,887,375	12,719,155	6.8	23.4	1.02	0.95	1.10	0.41	0.20	1.72
Extractive	1,269,551	1,237,600	-2.5	24.5	1.01	0.79	1.27	0.09	0.01	0.51
Local market	33,434,183	37,773,144	12.2	25.8	1.04	0.98	1.11	1.75	0.94	5.20
Manufactures	18,450,502	18,556,546	0.6	13.3	1.01	0.92	1.13	0.19	0.06	0.50
Retail trade	19,443,520	21,477,074	9.9	33.3	1.03	0.99	1.09	0.88	0.52	2.61

When we shift from the national totals to looking at the (unweighted) averages of our regional data for the 394 LMAs the mean growth and formation rates are less striking, but the variation across regions is remarkable. Average annual employment growth varies from a small loss to annual growth of 8 percent, while firm formation rates vary from 2 new firms per thousand labor force to a high of 10 new firms per thousand labor force. The local market sector mean firm formation rate accounts for nearly half of the total, although that sector accounted for just over a third of the employment. Similarly, business services, retail trade, and even the extractive industries accounted for somewhat more of the firm formations than their shares of employment. Firm formations in the manufacturing and distributive industries both lagged their employment shares.

The considerable variation in firm formation rates is shown in Table 2, although it is limited to the two-year average formation rates for 1994 to 1996, but there is little change in the two-year average formation rate rankings throughout the 1990s. Most of the highest-ranking areas were in Florida, the Southwest and Northwest. Miami and West Palm Beach were the only LMA's with large cities included among these. The lowest-ranking areas were predominately found in Pennsylvania, New York, Ohio, and Indiana. These included the fairly large cities of Dayton OH, Harrisburg PA, and Syracuse NY.

Table 2 - Establishments and 1994-1996 firm formations and formation rates selected labor market areas, sorted by decreasing 1994-1996 formations per 1,000 labor force

LMA	Biggest Place	State	Formations /1,000 LF	1994 Establ.	Avg. ann. Formations
	United States		3.85	5,770,090	504,939
HIGHEST 20 LMA's					
287	Laramie	WY	10.18	5,898	887
72	Cape Coral	FL	7.20	14,543	1,782
352	Grand Junction	CO	6.95	4,319	613
71	West Palm Beach	FL	6.84	32,743	4,161
392	Bend	OR	6.61	4,608	625
393	Bellingham	WA	6.60	6,509	735
359	St. George	UT	6.54	3,187	536
70	Miami	FL	6.49	90,179	11,644
345	Missoula	MT	6.47	6,520	817
354	Flagstaff	AZ	6.44	6,037	835
69	Sarasota	FL	6.23	15,683	1,746
344	Bozeman	MT	6.03	5,696	682
353	Farmington	NM	5.92	3,157	417
88	Savannah	GA	5.67	8,734	986
15	Wilmington	NC	5.59	6,805	866
387	Longview	WA	5.57	5,025	514
298	Monett	MO	5.55	2,442	373
348	Santa Fe	NM	5.51	6,801	824
376	Reno	NV	5.38	11,736	1,356
78	Ocala	FL	5.34	6,079	661
LOWEST 20 LMA's					
134	Lima	OH	2.54	5,312	333
182	Olean	NY	2.54	4,677	282
213	Mankato	MN	2.53	5,430	353
139	Kokomo	IN	2.52	3,585	235
125	Dayton	OH	2.52	24,505	1,613
237	Galesburg	IL	2.51	2,861	180
165	Erie	PA	2.51	13,602	790
192	Harrisburg	PA	2.50	20,484	1,323
208	Springfield	MA	2.49	13,904	819
224	Sheboygan	WI	2.49	3,717	258
140	Muncie	IN	2.48	7,760	527
133	Findlay	OH	2.47	4,938	313
177	Syracuse	NY	2.46	22,325	1,317
126	Richmond	IN	2.31	2,127	130
178	Oneonta	NY	2.31	3,281	176
187	Sunbury	PA	2.28	3,509	206
183	Watertown	NY	2.28	4,342	246
219	Marshalltown	IA	2.18	2,360	129
179	Binghamton	NY	2.11	5,557	309
181	Elmira	NY	2.06	6,501	346

Source: 1989-1996 LEEM file tabulations at Census' Center for Economic Studies.

Table 3 - Regional Variation in Service Firm Formation Rates, 1996-1998 ranked by average service firm formations per thousand 1995 labor force

LMA	Largest Place	State	Avg. 1996-98 ann. Formation Rate	Service Firms 1995	1995 Labor Force
TOP 20 LMA's					
287	Laramie	WY	3.28	2,250	90,242
71	West Palm Beach	FL	2.79	12,791	602,263
72	Cape Coral	FL	2.60	4,845	251,563
70	Miami	FL	2.52	36,811	1,794,995
393	Bellingham	WA	2.36	2,244	114,745
69	Sarasota	FL	2.32	5,704	280,316
344	Bozeman	MT	2.28	2,255	113,581
376	Reno	NV	2.26	4,421	254,723
345	Missoula	MT	2.21	2,398	126,036
91	Atlanta	GA	2.19	26,826	1,746,367
352	Grand Junction	CO	2.14	1,628	92,686
289	Denver	CO	2.13	20,972	1,241,321
359	St. George	UT	2.11	1,037	82,660
353	Farmington	NM	2.08	1,137	73,850
354	Flagstaff	AZ	2.07	2,173	139,112
379	Las Vegas	NV	2.06	7,083	613,097
75	Daytona Beach	FL	2.03	3,614	217,087
74	Orlando	FL	2.01	11,732	763,432
67	Tampa	FL	2.01	18,150	1,090,154
392	Bend	OR	1.99	1,492	95,114
BOTTOM 20 LMA's					
151	Lorain	OH	0.80	2,505	211,001
139	Kokomo	IN	0.80	1,153	95,821
133	Findlay	OH	0.79	1,553	128,032
225	Appleton	WI	0.79	3,497	316,960
224	Sheboygan	WI	0.79	1,147	106,522
183	Watertown	NY	0.78	1,248	105,549
227	Wausau	WI	0.77	2,178	195,815
187	Sunbury	PA	0.77	1,135	89,741
181	Elmira	NY	0.77	2,149	167,177
128	Greensburg	IN	0.77	658	69,562
182	Olean	NY	0.77	1,378	112,608
134	Lima	OH	0.76	1,679	132,715
6	North Wilkesboro	NC	0.76	766	74,383
185	Amsterdam	NY	0.76	652	53,750
154	Zanesville	OH	0.76	1,033	85,927
237	Galesburg	IL	0.73	878	70,347
219	Marshalltown	IA	0.71	725	59,299
178	Oneonta	NY	0.67	996	75,827
218	Mason City	IA	0.67	1,156	81,392
126	Richmond	IN	0.66	713	55,891

When we focus on new firm formations in the service sector (SIC 70-89), for a slightly later period (1996-1998), we see in Table 3 that the areas with the highest formation rates are still concentrated in Florida and the West, but many more areas with large cities are included in the top 20, in addition to

Miami and West Palm Beach: Atlanta, Denver, Las Vegas, Orlando, and Tampa. The locus of the areas with very low rates of service firm formation is the North Central, with the addition of several small LMA's in New York. None of these bottom 20 areas have large or medium-sized cities in them. Our analysis seeks to identify some of the important factors that explain these regional variations.

5. EMPIRICAL RESULTS

5.1. Regional Variation in Entrepreneurship[11]

5.1.1. Central Hypotheses and Model Estimated

A growing literature has sought the determinants of variation in new firm formation on a regional basis (Reynolds 1994; Keeble and Walker, 1994; Audretsch and Fritsch, 1994; Reynolds, Miller and Maki, 1995). We focus primarily on four determinants of regional variation in the firm birth rate: *1*) higher birth rates are promoted by regional spillovers, especially of relevant knowledge; *2*) higher unemployment may deter start-ups in some sectors and increase them in others; *3*) industrial restructuring should promote new firm formation; and *4*) the existence of an entrepreneurial culture should promote start-up activity.

To test these hypotheses, we estimate a regression model where the dependent variable is the average annual firm birth rate in year t divided by the labor force in year t (in thousands). This is analogous to the method used by Keeble and Walker (1994).

5.2. The Explanatory (Exogenous) Variables

Establishment size is a proxy for the structure of industry in the region. It is measured as employment in year *t* divided by the number of establishments in year *t* in the region. It should be negatively related to regional birth rate since larger average establishment size indicates greater dominance by large firms or branch plants.

In order to assess the potential for positive effects from spillovers, many studies have measured density using the square root of the regional population, or population per square mile. Such measures, however, do not indicate the extent of pooled labor markets very well, since they tell us nothing about the density of similar establishments in the region. Therefore, we introduce a new measure that captures both population density and the number of establishments in a region. *Sector specialization* is the number of establishments in the industry and region in year *t* divided by the region's population in year *t*. The greater the number of establishments relative to the population, the more spillovers should be facilitated (Ciccone and Hall, 1996).

Population growth is the average annual rate of increase in the region in a previous period (calculating the two-year change from the ratio of the population in year *t* divided by population in *t*-2, and taking the square root of that two-year change ratio to calculate the annual change ratio). *Income growth* is the average annual rate of increase of personal income in the region similarly calculated. Both of these growth factors from the period preceding our start-up measurement period are expected to promote new firm start-ups in the subsequent period.

The *unemployment rate* is the traditional calculation for the first year of our start-up measurement period - the average number of unemployed in year *t* divided by the labor force in year *t*. It is expected to be negatively related to start-ups overall, but probably positively related to new firm start up rates in industries with low capital requirements, and negatively related to those with high capital requirements. The simple correlation between the unemployment rate and the firm birth rate is close to zero, and is not statistically significant.

The *share of proprietors* in the economy is measured as the number of proprietors in year *t* divided by the labor force in year *t*. Proprietors are members of the labor force who are also business owners. It includes both the self-employed who have no employees, and the owners of unincorporated businesses that have employees. The simple correlation between the regional birth rate and the share of proprietors is 0.30, indication of a moderately strong positive relationship between these variables.

To measure the level of human capital in the economy we include two measures of educational attainment in each region. The first is the share of adults with *no high school degree*, defined as the number of adults without a high school degree in 1990 divided by the number of adults (population 25 years or older). The lack of a high school degree should be a good proxy for the proportion of unskilled and semi-skilled labor, and should be negatively related to the birth rate. The mean percent of the population without a high school degree is 27 percent. In fact, the simple correlation between the percentage of the population without a high school degree and the birth rate is -0.19.

Finally, share of *college graduates* is defined as the number of adults with college degrees in 1990 divided by the total number of adults. This is a proxy measure of both technical skills needed in the economy, for example engineers and scientists, and skills needed to start and build a business, like finance and marketing and complex reasoning. In 1990 an average of 15.9 percent of the adult population had a college degree. Its simple correlation with the regional birth rates is positive.

5.3. Summary of Results

As summarized in Table 4, sector specialization and population growth are both strongly positive and statistically significant, as predicted by the theory of regional spillovers. In fact, these coefficients are nearly three times as large as the coefficient on income growth, which is also positive and significant. When analyzed separately for each of the industry sectors, we find that both industry specialization and population growth are positive and significant for each of the six industry sectors. However, the parameters on income growth are very small, and are only significant for business services and local market.

Table 4 - Summary of impacts of regional variables on entrepreneurial activity in LMAs in the mid-nineties

Independent variables	Firm formation rates	Sub-sector Formation
Establishment size	-	-
Sector specialization	+	+
Business specialization	+	0
High school degree*	-	-
College degree	+	+
Population growth	+	+
Income growth	+	+
Share of proprietors	0	NA
Unemployment rate	0	0

* The coefficient on high-school degree is the negative of that on high-school dropout share.

The coefficient for large firm presence, measured as establishment size, is negative for all industries, and for all sectors by business services and extractive industries, indicating that regions with predominately smaller establishments have a higher start-up rate than regions with more large establishments. This supports the thesis that regions that have already restructured away from large manufacturing dominance have a higher start-up rate than regions that have not.

The coefficient for the unemployment rate is positive, although it is tiny and not statistically significant at the all-industry level. This result is surprising, given that previous cross-sectional studies have generally found a consistently negative result (Storey, 1991). Furthermore, the coefficients on unemployment were positive for all of the six sectors, and significantly so for all but the extractive industries. Perhaps the exceptionally low levels of unemployment and even shortages of labor in the United States in the 1990s account for the prevailingly positive relationship between unemployment and new firm births in this period. The implication here is that as workers shift from being employed to unemployed, the overall entry rate in the region tends to go up slightly, although there is no evidence that it is necessarily the unemployed who are starting the new firms.

The coefficient on the culture variable, measured as the share of proprietors in the region, is negative and statistically insignificant for the all-industry equation, perhaps because the share of proprietors is strongly negatively correlated with establishment size, -0.63. As the average establishment size in a region increases there are fewer opportunities for self-employment, and a smaller proportion of the labor force is made up of owners. When we drop establishment size from the estimated regression, the coefficient on self-employment becomes positive and statistically significant, while the other variables remain virtually unchanged. Within several of the industry sectors – local market, manufacturing, and retail – the share of proprietors is significantly positively related to firm formation rates.

Finally, the coefficient for human capital, as measured by share of college graduates, is positive and statistically significant, suggesting that regions that have higher levels of education will have higher firm formation rates. This is consistent with Anselin, Varga and Acs (1997), who found that in technologically advanced industries individuals with greater skills, knowledge and expertise are more likely to start businesses. However, for both business services and manufacturing this coefficient is only barely positive, and not statistically significant. Reynolds (1994) found a negative and statistically significant relationship between college education and the new firm birth rate in manufacturing. The results do suggest that manufacturing firms may behave differently than other sectors of the economy.

The positive and statistically significant coefficient for the percentage of the population without a high school degree is at first surprising, but can be easily explained. The correlation between the share with no high school degree and the new firm start up rate is negative, -0.19, as expected. However, it is much more strongly negatively correlated with college education, with a coefficient of -0.70. After controlling for the proportion of adults with college degrees, the additional effect of a greater share of less educated workers is to facilitate the start-up process by providing cheap labor for the educated and creative classes. This positive impact of 'no high school degree' after controlling for 'college degree' is consistent across most of the industry sectors, except for business services, with the strongest positive relationship appearing in the distributive industries.

In summary, using annual data on firm births for 384 labor market areas, in six industry sectors, between 1991-1998, we find considerable variation in the new firm formation rate across regions, but little variation over time. Variations in the firm birth rates are substantially explained by the lack of large firms, the presence of human capital, regional differences in sector specialization and population growth and income growth, as suggested by the new economic geography.

6. HUMAN CAPITAL AND ENTREPRENEURSHIP[12]

6.1. Central Hypotheses and Model Estimated

It is clear from the data shown earlier in Table 4 that the service firm formation rates vary greatly across local economic areas, and we will seek the determinants of this local variation in the same factors that contributed earlier to the explanation of the differences in formation rates for all industries. The agglomeration effects that contribute to new service firm formation can come both from demand effects associated with increased local population, income, and business activity, and from supply factors related to the quality of the local labor market and business climate.

Among areas with broadly similar regional demand and business climate characteristics, there are further differences in rates of new firm formation and economic growth that are associated with the specific qualities of their human capital, and the propensity of locally available knowledge to spillover and stimulate innovative activity which culminates in new firm formations. Highly educated populations provide the human capital embodied in their general and specific skills for implementing new ideas for creating new businesses. They also create an environment rich in local knowledge spillovers, which support another mechanism by which new firm start-ups are initiated and sustained. Thus, regions that are richer in educated people should have more start-up activity, and local new firm formation rates should be positively related to local educational attainment rates. Furthermore, areas that already have relatively intense development of service businesses are likely to have higher levels of service firm formations, resulting in large part from spillovers of relevant specialized knowledge. We would expect that areas with relatively high shares of high-school dropouts would have lower rates of new firm formation.

To test the basic hypotheses that the new firm formation rates are positively related to the level of human capital in a region, we estimate a regression model where the dependent variable is the average annual new service firm formation rate (dividing births by the labor force in thousands) for 1996-1998.[13]

6.2. The Explanatory (Exogenous) Variables

The primary explanatory variables are the same measures of the level of human capital and knowledge spillover conditions that were used earlier. Formal education itself does not usually provide either the skills or the inspiration to start a new business. But higher education trains individuals to rationally assess information, and to seek new ideas. Therefore more educated people are more likely to acquire useful local knowledge spillovers from others who are involved in research or in managing some service business. The quantity of potentially useful knowledge spillovers is expected to be a function of the number of similar business establishments, relative to the population of the economic area. *Service-industry intensity* is defined as the number of service establishments in the region divided by the region's population in thousands. The greater the number of establishments relative to the population, the more spillovers should be facilitated due to density of establishments (Ciccone and Hall, 1996).

6.3 Summary of Results

Only two of the three human capital variables showed the hypothesized relationships. First, for human capital measured by share of college graduates, are positive and statistically significant for all except the 1993-1995 periods, confirming that regions with higher shares of college-educated adults have higher firm formation rates. This positive result on human capital is consistent with previous research (Storey, 1994).

The positive coefficient for high-school dropouts as a share of the non-college adult population is at first surprising - however it is consistent with earlier results for the whole economy (Armington and Acs, 2002). There it was suggested that after controlling for the proportion of adults with college degrees,[14] the additional effect of a greater share of less educated workers is to facilitate the start-up process by providing cheap labor for the new firms. Even the most sophisticated businesses need some workers who are less educated to do the manual labor. Thus, the relationship between educational attainment and new firm start-ups at the regional level may be U-shaped, with both low levels and high levels of education conducive to firm formation and growth.

Thirdly, the coefficient on intensity of service establishments is positive and statistically significant, suggesting that regions that already have a relatively strong supply of service establishments will have higher rates of new service firm formation, as predicted by the theory of regional spillovers (Jovanovic and Rob, 1989). Indeed, this factor has the strongest relationship of any of our independent variables. The 0.60 value estimated for the standardized coefficient indicates that a locality with a service establishment intensity that is one standard deviation more intense than the mean will be likely to have firm start-up rates that are 0.6 standard deviation higher than the mean.

The unemployment rate is positive and statistically significant for 1990-1992, when the economy was undergoing a small recession. However, it is negative and barely significant during 1993-1995 and insignificant during

1996-1998, suggesting that this positive effect disappears as the economy improves, or as mean unemployment falls.

Hoping to better distinguish the impacts of our independent variables on the start-up rates of various types of service activities, but limited by data disclosure constraints, we defined 9 service sub-sectors, using two dimensions that should be relevant to our analysis of variation in start-up rates. The dimensions chosen were the market segment served and the customary education requirement for founder of new firms in each class of service activity. Each of these dimensions was broken into just three categories, so that applying both dimensions resulted in the classification of all services into nine sub-sectors, within which the service activities were fairly homogeneous with respect to these two dimensions.

We distinguish activities that are most frequently started by people who do not have college degrees (called 'high school' level for simplicity), from those generally requiring an 'advanced' (graduate, post-graduate, or professional) degree, and assigned the remainder to 'college.' These allocations were based on subjective judgment, using our general knowledge of service industries, supplemented by detailed descriptions of the 4-digit SIC classes in the 1987 Standard Industrial Classification Manual.[15,16]

For the nine sub-sectors defined by the education requirement and the market segment together, the firm formation rate was highest, at 14.78, for businesses in non-local markets with founders normally having advanced degrees. The sub-sector requiring the same advanced degree for founders, but serving the local consumer market, had only 5.31 new firms for each hundred existing establishments in that sub-sector. For businesses that normally require a college degree for their founder, the birth rate is quite similar across all three of the market segments. Businesses requiring less educated founders (high school degree) also showed great variation across market segments, with high formation rates for non-local market, and low ones for the local consumer market.

Service firm birth rates were calculated as before for all firms for each of the 394 LMAs, based on new firm formations during each of three recent time periods - 1990 through 1992, 1993 through 1995, and 1996 through 1998, and standardizing across different sizes of LMA's by dividing by the size of the labor force (in thousands) in the LMA in the prior year. However, for comparing new firm formation rates for different sub-sectors of the service industry we need to standardize for the differences in size of both areas and sub-sectors. For this purpose we express new firm formation rates in terms of the number of new firms relative to the number of establishments already in existence in that sub-sector and LMA. his could be termed the ecological approach, because it considers the amount of start-up activity relative to the size of the existing population of businesses.

In order to allow for variation in the estimated coefficients of variables that should be sensitive to our sub-sector dimensions, while controlling consistently for other regional characteristics, we expand the independent variables to be sub-sector-specific for the dimensions we want to test. Naturally, we expected the educational attainment variables to be sensitive to the Education requirement dimension

Using the previous notation, this more detailed pooled estimation model has the following form:

$$\text{Birth rate}_{LEM} = f\big(\text{Coll}_{LE}, \text{High Sch drop}_{LE}, \text{Subsector estab intensity}_{LEM},$$
$$\text{Pop gro}_{LM}, \text{Income gro}_{LE}, \text{Pop log}_{LEM}, \text{Unempl}_{LE}, \qquad (2)$$
$$\text{Estab Size}_{LM}, \text{All ind estab intensity}_{LM}\big)$$

In order to estimate this model, we first standardized all of the exogenous and endogenous variables to have a mean of zero and a standard deviation of one, within each of the nine sub-sectors. Therefore, each represents a relative measure for the LMA, within the sub-sector. Then we created dummy variables for each of the three values for each of the sub-sector dimensions – market and education. Finally, we multiplied each exogenous variable times the appropriate dummies to create specialized exogenous variables that distinguished among the dimensions we wanted to test for differences in estimated coefficients. The results of the estimation of this model are shown in the last six columns of Table 9.

Looking first at the human capital variables in these estimated models for sub-sectors, we see that the share of adults with college degrees is not significant for the formation rate of service businesses requiring only a high school education for the founder. For services businesses requiring a college education, the variation in the local formation rates is much more sensitive than was indicated by either the all-service regression or the pooled sub-sector regression. here is also a significant positive relationship between the share of adults with college degrees and the formation rates of service businesses normally requiring an advanced degree for the founder. This results from the high correlation of the distribution of college degrees with that of advanced degrees.

The positive and statistically significant coefficient for the relationship of shares of high-school dropouts to formation of new service firms that require advanced degrees suggests that such businesses may be more dependent on having a large pool of unskilled labor. The statistically insignificant coefficients for the impact of the share of high school dropouts on formation rates in the sub-sectors of services that require only high school or college degrees suggests that such businesses are not as sensitive to the supply of unskilled labor. They may find that the unskilled labor supply in most areas is adequate for their needs.

The relative intensity of establishments in the same sub-sector of services is a significant explanatory variable for all market segments, but the formation of new firms serving non-local markets is particularly sensitive to the prior existence of similar businesses. This corroborates the many prior case study analyses that addressed the spillover effects of certain rapidly growing local industry clusters, and suggests that these spillover effects are particularly important for businesses that are not focusing on local markets.

Most of the estimated coefficients for regional characteristics crossed with education or market dummies were similar to those estimated without such distinctions. However, the differences that appeared are quite illuminating. The log of population was crossed with all six dummies, and the tiny and insignificant variables crossed with College degree and with Non-local markets were later omitted, to strengthen the remaining estimates. These show that, unlike services to local markets, those to non-local markets are not sensitive to the size of the local economic area. Perhaps the high coefficient on sub-sector intensity for non-local services has captured all of the relevant agglomeration effects for that sub-sector. Distinguishing by the education dimension, larger population contributes a bit to the formation rate of services firms requiring founders with advanced degrees, but it reduces the formation rate of firms normally started by high school dropouts.

The coefficient on unemployment is positive and statistically significant only for service firms normally started by college graduates. This provides some clarification of the conflicting results found in previous studies of the effects of unemployment levels on new firm formation rates. Apparently, after controlling for regional differences in income growth rates, an increase in unemployment tends to lead to an increase in new firm formation by those with college degrees, but not by high school dropouts or those with advanced degrees.

Finally, the negative coefficient on average size of local businesses is strongest for formation of new firms serving local consumer markets, while that on the intensity of all establishments is significant only for formation of new firms serving non-local markets.

In summary, these results suggest that the regional differences in new firm formation rates do indeed depend to a large degree on the educational requirements and the market served by the newly formed firms. In particular, the local levels of educational attainment impact primarily the firm formation rates of the types of firms that are normally founded by better-educated entrepreneurs, and do not affect start-up rates for those normally founded by individuals with less than a college degree. While formation rates of all service businesses are higher in areas with higher intensities of similar service establishments, new formations of firms serving non-local markets are three times more sensitive to this than those serving local consumer markets, and those serving local business markets are twice as sensitive as those serving local consumers.

7. CONCLUSIONS

The BITS database constructed for the Office of Advocacy of the U.S. Small Business Administration is uniquely suitable for testing new approaches to explaining regional differences in economic growth rates. Recent theories of economic growth view local externalities, as opposed to scale economies, as the primary engine in generating growth in cities with their closely integrated surrounding counties (Labor Market Areas). While scale economies operate at the plant level, externalities operate at the level of the firm, primarily through entrepreneurial activity.

Using the BITS data we examined the impact of these externalities on regional employment growth from an entrepreneurial perspective by examining the relationship of local economic growth to local entrepreneurial activity. Since higher rates of entrepreneurial activity in an industry sector and region imply lower barriers to birth and greater local competition, this analysis can also be interpreted as an investigation of the impact of local competition on local economic growth. We found that higher rates of entrepreneurial activity were strongly associated with faster growth of local economies.

NOTES

[1] For documentation of the SUSB files, see U.S. Small Business Administration (1999).

[2] For example, if a single-unit retail firm/establishment with 10 employees opens 2 additional branch stores with another 10 employees in each, the original establishment would appear to have 30 employees until it was surveyed. The more accurate reporting resulting from the survey would lead to its employment being reduced from 30 to 10, and the 2 new establishments being listed as new formations with 10 employees each.

[3] Taking the match of 1993 to 1992 as a typical example, 5.56 million records matched on CFN, another 32 thousand on PPN, and 3 thousand on EIN. The remaining unmatched single-unit records were then grouped by zip code, and another 19 thousand between years and 24 thousand within 1993 were matched on business name, and another 11 thousand across years and 13 thousand within 1993 were matched on industry (3-digit SIC) and street number.

[4] See also Knight (1921), Hannan and Freeman (1989), Acs and Audretsch (1990), Winter (1984), and Williamson (1985).

[5] For example, if a single-unit retail firm/establishment with 10 employees opens 2 additional branch stores with another 10 employees in each, the original establishment would appear

to have 30 employees until it was surveyed. The more accurate reporting resulting from the survey would lead to its employment being reduced from 30 to 10, and the 2 new establishments being listed as new formations with 10 employees each.

[6] Taking the match of 1993 to 1992 as a typical example, 5.56 million records matched on CFN, another 32 thousand on PPN, and 3 thousand on EIN. The remaining unmatched single-unit records were then grouped by zip code, and another 19 thousand between years and 24 thousand within 1993 were matched on business name, and another 11 thousand across years and 13 thousand within 1993 were matched on industry (3-digit SIC) and street number.

[7] In fact, birth rates were calculated for each annual period from 1990 through 1998, but these were found to be quite consistent in their rank ordering across LMA's, so the averages of several recent years was used for most of this analysis. Using period averages serves both to smooth out irregularities and to minimize the possibility of disclosure problems with very small numbers of annual births for the smaller LMAs and sub-sectors.

[8] Annually, there were less than 150 such large apparent births of single-unit firms, with an average of about 1,500 employees each. About a third of these larger single unit firms were employee-leasing firms or employment agencies, while the remainder were widely distributed across industries. However, examination of the new firms with 100-499 employees in their first year showed that most seemed to be credible start-ups, frequently in industries that are associated with large business units, such as hotels and hospitals. Since this study is not concerned with the employment impact of start-ups, there is no danger of the bulk of the data on smaller start-ups being swamped by that of a few larger start-ups that might actually be offshoots of existing businesses, herefore, the start-ups with 100 to 499 employees were included, if they qualified otherwise.

[9] We tested a similar rule using one-half, and found that the primary difference was in quite small multi-unit firms, where the smaller share was more credible for the first year.

[10] There is a small number (10,000 to 16,000) of new firms each year for which no industry code is ever available. Most of these are small and short-lived. These have been added to the Local market category, which is, by far, the largest of our sectors.

[11] Summary of research reported more fully in Armington and Acs (2002).

[12] Summary of research reported more fully in Acs and Armington (2003a).

[13] Although we have annual firm formation data for 1990 through 1999, we have chosen not to use pooled cross-section time series regressions, because most of the independent variables describing the characteristics of the LMAs change very little over time, and the errors from omitted variables will be nearly identical for each LMA from year to year, so the diagnostic statistics from such an analysis would be very misleading.

[14] Note that when estimated in separate equations for 1996-1998 the coefficient for College degree falls to 0.10 and that for high school dropout falls to 0.12, while other coefficients remain substantially the same.

[15] We originally hoped to base this classification on the BLS occupational distribution data for each (3-digit) industry, but we found that many activities requiring academic skills or advanced training for leadership positions, in fact had occupational distributions very heavily weighted toward semi-skilled and unskilled workers. Hospitals and hotels were extreme examples of this contrast between educational requirements for workers and those for the individual responsible for starting the business.

[16] The sub-sector classifications for each 4-digit SIC can be found in the Appendix of Acs and Armington (2002), where they are ordered by SIC code within each sub-sector. Data on the number of establishments and employees in each 4-digit SIC in 1995, and their net changes to 1998, as well as the total number of new firm formations during 1996 through 1998 per hundred (1995) establishments, are provided for each entry in this table.

132   *New Firm Formation and the Region. Empirical Results from the United States*

REFERENCES

Acs, Z. J. and C. Armington (2003a), "The Geographic Concentration of New Firm Formation and Human Capital", CES-WP- 03-05.

Acs, Z. J. and C. Armington (2003b), "Endogenous Growth and Entrepreneurial Activity in Cities", CES-WP- 03-02.

Acs, Z. J. and C. Armington (2006), *Entrepreneurship, Geography and American Economic Growth*, Cambridge, Cambridge University Press.

Acs, Z. J. and D. B. Audretsch (1990), *Innovation and Small Firms*, Cambridge (MA), The MIT Press.

Acs, Z. J., D. B. Audretsch, P. Braunerhjelm and B. Carlsson (2004), "The Missing Link: The Knowledge Filter, Entrepreneurship and Endogenous Growth", Center for Economic Policy Research, London Working Paper # 4783.

Acs, Z. J. and A. Varga (2002), "Geography, Endogenous Growth and Innovation", *International Regional Science Review*, 25(1), 132-148.

Acs, Z. J and A. Varga (2004), "Entrepreneurship, Agglomeration and Technological Change", *Small Business Economics*, 38(8), 911-928.

Anselin, L., A. Varga and Z. J. Acs (1997), "Local Geographic Spillovers between University Research and High Technology Innovation", *Journal of Urban Economics*, 42(3), 422-448.

Armington, C. and Z. J. Acs (2002), "The Determinants of Regional Variation in New Firm Formation", *Regional Studies*, 35(1), 33-45.

Audretsch, D. B. and M. Fritsch (1994), "The Geography of Firm Births in Germany", *Regional Studies*, 28(4), 359-365.

Audretsch, D. B. and M. Keilbach (2004), "Entrepreneurship and Regional Growth - An Evolutionary Perspective", *Journal of Evolutionary Economics*, 14(5), 605-616

Arrow, K. E. (1962), "Economic Welfare and the Allocation of Resources for Invention", in R. R. Nelson (ed.), *The Rate and Direction of Inventive Activity*, Princeton, Princeton University Press.

Ciccone, A. and R. Hall (1996) "Productivity and the Density of Economic Activity", *American Economic Review*, 86(1), 54-70.

Eckhardt, J. T. and S. A. Shane (2003), "Opportunities and Entrepreneurship", *Journal of Management*, 2003, 29(3), 333-349.

Florida, R. (2005), "The World is Spiky", *The Atlantic Monthly*, 296(3), 49-51.

Evans, D. and B. Jovanovic (1989), "An Estimated Model of Entrepreneurial Choice Under Liquidity Constraints", *Journal of Political Economy*, 97(4), 807-827.

Hannan M. T. and J. Freeman (1989), *Organizational Ecology*, Cambridge (MA), Harvard University Press.

Hayek, J. (1945), "The Use of Knowledge in Society", *American Economic Review*, 35(4), 519-530.

Keeble, D. and S. Walker (1994), "New Firms, Small Firms and Dead Firms: Spatial Patterns and Determinants in the United Kingdom", *Regional Studies*, 28(4), 411-427.

Jovanovic, B. and R. Rob (1989), "The Growth and Diffusion of Knowledge", *Review of Economic Studies*, 56(4), 569-582.

Knight, F. H. (1921), *Risk, Uncertainty and Profit*, Boston, Houghton Mifflin.

Krugman, P. (1991), "Increasing Returns and Economic Geography", *Journal of Political Economy*, 99(3), 483-99.

Lucas, R. E., Jr. (1988), "On the Mechanisms of Economic Development", *Journal of Monetary Economics*, 22(1), 3-39.

Michelacci, C. (2003), "Low Returns in R&D due to the Lack of Entrepreneurial Skills", *Economic Journal*, 113 (484), 207-225.

Reynolds, P. D. (1994), "Autonomous Firm Dynamics and Economic Growth in the United States, 1986-1990", *Regional Studies*, 28(4), 429-442.

Reynolds, P. D., B. Miller and W. R. Maki (1995), "Explaining Regional Variation in Business Births and Deaths: U.S. 1976-88", *Small Business Economics*, 7(4), 387-407.

Romer, P. (1986), "Increasing Returns and Long Run Growth", *Journal of Political Economy*, 94(5), 1003-1037.

Romer, P. (1990), "Endogenous Technological Change", *Journal of Political Economy*, 98(5, part 2), S71-S102.

Schumpeter, J. A. (1911) (1934), *The Theory of Economic Development*, Cambridge (MA), Harvard University Press.

Stel, A. J. van and D. J. Storey (2004), "The Link Between Firm Births and Job Creation: Is there a Upas Tree Effect?", *Regional Studies*, 38(8), 893-909.

Storey, D. J. (1991). "The Birth of New Firms - Does Unemployment Matter? A Review of the Evidence", *Small Business Economics*, 3(3), 167-178.

Storey, D. J. (1994), *Understanding the Small Business Sector*, London/New York, Routledge.

Tolbert, C. M. and M. Sizer (1996), "U.S. Commuting Zones and Labor Market Areas: a 1990 Update", Rural Economy Division, Economic Research Service, U.S. Department of Agriculture, Staff Paper No. AGES-9614.

U.S. Small Business Administration (1988a), *Uses and Limitations of USEEM/USELM Data*, Washington (DC), Office of Advocacy.

U.S. Small Business Administration (1988b), *Handbook of Small Business Data*, Washington (DC), Office of Advocacy.

U.S. Small Business Administration (1999), *Statistics of U.S. Business – Microdata and Tables of SBA/Census Data*, Washington (DC), Office of Advocacy.

Williamson, O. (1985), *The Economic Institutions of Capitalism*, New York, The Free Press.

Winter, S. G. (1984), "Schumpeterian Competition in Alternative Technological Regimes", *Journal of Economic Behavior and Organization*, 5(3-4), 287-320.

Chapter 6
R&D INTENSITY AND THE RELATIONSHIP BETWEEN FIRM SIZE AND GROWTH IN GERMANY

David B. Audretsch
Indiana University, and Max Planck Institute of Economics, Jena

Julie Ann Elston
Oregon State University, and Max Planck Institute of Economics, Jena

1. INTRODUCTION

Interest in establishing or refuting the empirical validity of the *Law of Proportional Effect*, or what has become known as *Gibrat's Law*, has exploded in recent years. In his comprehensive survey on "Gibrat's Legacy", Sutton (1997, p. 40) interprets the *Law* as an "expected value of the increment firm's size in each period is proportional to the current size of the firm." The plethora of empirical studies has produced such a body of evidence, that it has taken three major surveys (Caves, 1998; Sutton, 1997; and Geroski, 1995), two of which are published in the *Journal of Economic Literature*, to interpret and digest the wealth of empirical results.

The fundamental question addressed by these studies, as articulated by Mansfield (1962, pp. 1030-1031), is whether "the probability of a given proportionate change in size during a specified period is the same for all firms regardless of their size at the beginning of the period." As Sutton (1997) points out, research testing *Gibrat's Law* produces an answer that is either "yes" or "no". While the earlier studies (Hart, 1962; Mansfield, 1962) provided compelling evidence that the answer is "yes", that is *Gibrat's Law* seemed to hold, more recent studies (Evans, 1987; Hall, 1987; Dunne, Roberts and Samuelson, 1989; Audretsch, 1995) suggested exactly the opposite answer - "no", *Gibrat's Law* did not seem to hold. As Sutton (1997) points out, resolution to these seemingly contradictory results lies in systematic differences in the samples selected. The earlier studies included only large firms, but the more recent studies included a broader spectrum of firm sizes, including small enterprises as well as large firms. However, one thing both the earlier and more recent studies have in common is their formulation of the hypothesis, which, once subjected to an empirical test would be either confirmed or refuted.

The purpose of this paper is to suggest that perhaps the literature testing *Gibrat's Law* has focused on the wrong question. Rather than asking whether the *Law* holds or not, we argue that the more relevant question may be "Under what contexts is the empirical evidence compatible with *Gibrat's Law* and under what contexts is it not?" In particular, in this paper we suggest that the relationship between firm size and growth is shaped by the context, which reflects the country, time period and particular industry. We test for the validity of *Gibrat's Law* in Germany[1] in different time periods and across different industries and then compare these results with the findings summarized in Caves (1998), Geroski (1995) and Sutton (1997).

In the second section we explore why the validity of *Gibrat's Law* may vary according to context. The data base and measurement issues are explained in the third section. In the fourth section the empirical model to be estimated is introduced. Empirical results are provided in the fifth section. Finally, in the sixth section a summary and conclusions are provided. In particular, the empirical evidence suggests that whether or not *Gibrat's Law* holds very much depends upon the context, in terms of country-specific institutions, the industry, and the time period.

2. GIBRAT'S LAW: WHY CONTEXT MATTERS

2.1. The Country Context

There are many ways in which German institutions differ sharply from those in the United States. One institutional difference that may directly impact the relationship between firm size and growth involves the system of firm finance. The systematic differential ability of firms of different sizes to obtain finance may influence the relationship between firm size and growth. The different financial systems between the United States and Germany might then account for differences in the size-growth relationship between the two countries.

A series of recent papers based on the U.S. has found that liquidity constraints tend to have a greater impact on smaller enterprises than on their larger counterparts. In particular, small firms are more likely to be unable to obtain capital at market interest rates and therefore subject to credit rationing. Fazzari, Hubbard, and Petersen (1988) found that smaller publicly traded firms face liquidity constraints and that such smaller enterprises in particular experience difficulties obtaining capital during periods of macroeconomic downturns. That is, the likelihood of a firm experiencing a liquidity constraint decreases along with increasing firm size. According to Fazzari, Hubbard and Petersen (1988), smaller firms tend to be more dependent upon internal finance or bank loans than are their larger counterparts.[2] While the large firms in their study issued 99 percent of all new equity shares and 92 percent of all new corporate bonds, they accounted for only 74 percent of total manufacturing assets. Because smaller firms are more dependent upon loans from commercial banks, they are more prone to experiencing a credit crunch, especially during recessions. Fazzari, Hubbard and Petersen (1988) find evidence suggesting that the credit sources for smaller firms tend to dry up more rapidly during economic downturns than do the credit sources for larger enterprises.

There are two institutional features of the German financial system that sharply contrast to that practiced in the United States and the United Kingdom, both of which may impact the extent to which liquidity constraints occur. First, companies in Germany typically rely almost exclusively upon banks for external finance. The external capital market remains relatively undeveloped. Second, not only do the banks represent the major financial intermediary supplying capital to firms, but they are also extensively represented on the supervisory boards of companies. Cable (1985, p. 119) refers to this peculiarity of the German financial system which links finance to supervision as a "quasi-internal capital market".

Some studies such as Vitols (1998), have mentioned that the spread in lending rates between the largest and the smallest firms is lower in Germany than in the U.K. or the U.S. This is due in part to the effect of strong local and regional bank networks that target as customers the small and medium firms. It is still unclear however, how much this spread in rates affects German firm investment behavior between different sizes of firms.

While considerable attention has been placed on the role that the *Big Three* private banks play[3] in terms of financing the largest manufacturing corporations of Germany,[4] considerably less emphasis has been placed on the other institutions comprising the German financial system. Vitols (1998) points out that, in fact, the *Big Three* German banks only account for slightly less than one-tenth of all banking assets.[5] The bulk of credit from the *Big Three* private banks is channeled into the largest German firms. According to Vitols (1998), these banks have traditionally confined their industrial lending activities to larger corporate accounts. The largest financial institutions are the *Sparkassen*, which are essentially public savings banks, and the *Genossenschaftsbanken*, which essentially are co-operative banks. While the *Sparkassen* account for around 40 percent of all banking assets, the *Genossenschaftsbanken* account for about 15 percent of total banking assets (Deeg, 1992 and 1998). These financial institutions are generally oriented towards financing the *German Mittelstand*, or small- and medium-sized firms in Germany. While the economic and political power of the *Big Three* German banks, particularly in terms of providing finance and direction to the largest firms of Germany, has tended to pre-empt the attention from overseas, what must be one of the better kept secrets of Germany is the magnitude and role that these other institutions play in shaping the overall financial landscape of Germany - particularly in providing finance to smaller enterprises.

The existence of these financial intermediaries channeling funds into the German *Mittelstand* has resulted in the emergence mechanisms providing smaller banks access to long-term, fixed rate funds. As Vitols (1998, p. 12) points out, these mechanisms, which are less developed or less absent in the United States and United Kingdom, include: *1*) special credit institutes which among other things issue bonds on national bond markets to refinance long-term fixed-rate loans to small firms, *2*) refinancing and risk pooling mechanisms within both the savings bank and co-operative bank sectors, and *3*) mechanisms allowing for the channeling of a high proportion of long-term savings held at insurance companies to the banks through bank bonds. Roughly two-thirds of long-term bank lending to small companies is refinanced through these three mechanisms.

It is the existence of this infrastructure of financial institutions mandated with providing the German *Mittelstand*, or medium-sized enterprises, with finance that supposedly defuses the problem of liquidity constraints confronting smaller enterprises found by Evans and Jovanovic (1989) and Fazzari, Hubbard and Petersen (1988), among others, to exist for the United States. Whether, of course, the financial institutions under the German model are, in fact, able to avoid financial constraints imposed upon firms, and particularly smaller sized firms, is an empirical question which will be answered in the following sections. As Petersen and Rajan (1992, p. 1) point out, "One way to overcome frictions is for firms to build close relationships with the suppliers of capital. These relationships allow the lender to collect information about the borrower and their investments and to monitor the actions of the borrower."

If the degree to which different sized firms experience liquidity constraints differs systematically in Germany from the U.S., then the validity of *Gibrat's Law* might also be different in Germany than in the U.S. That is, significant differences in institutional factors across countries suggest differences in context that may lead to significant differences in performance.

2.2. The Industry Context

Why should the industry context make a difference? One important
dimension of heterogeneity across industries is the relative importance of
new ideas, or knowledge as an input. Stephan (1996) and Dasgupta and
David (1994) argue that firms engaging in knowledge-based activities are
typically associated with a greater degree of uncertainty, or *hyper-
uncertainty*, and *hyper-knowledge asymmetries*, about the potential
economic value of their investments. As Arrow (1962) emphasizes, more
than most other economic goods, the production of new economic
knowledge generally suffers from three sources constituting market failure –
indivisibilities and monopoly, uncertainty, and externalities. The first source
of market failure emanates from the propensity for knowledge to be a
discrete rather than a continuous commodity. As a result, both economies of
scale and scope are often associated with the production of knowledge
(Mueller and Tilton, 1969).

The second source of market failure involves the extraordinarily high
degree of uncertainty inherent in new economic knowledge. While virtually
every economic good is subject to uncertainty, almost none is exposed to the
degree of risk involved in knowledge-based new technologies. There are two
additional elements of uncertainty inherent in innovative activity that are not
present in other goods. The first is in the realm of production. How a new
good can be technically produced is typically shrouded in uncertainty. The
second involves marketing the product. Whether a demand for the new
product exists is not known. Even if the knowledge can result in a new
product, it is not at all clear that the product can be profitably sold.
Knowledge leading to a new economic good can be produced, but there is no
guarantee that the new knowledge is economic knowledge.

The third source of market failure stems from the public good nature and
non-exclusive externalities inherent in knowledge-based economic activity.
The production of knowledge does not preclude other economic agents from
applying that knowledge for economic gain. It is difficult to delineate and
enforce property rights to newly created knowledge. The externalities
associated with the production of new knowledge make it difficult for firms
undertaking such activities to appropriate the economic returns accruing
from their investment.

Since firms engaged in knowledge-based activity are subject to *hyper-
uncertainty*, *hyper-knowledge asymmetries*, as well as *non-exclusivity* it
might be expected that they experience a greater degree of liquidity
constraints imposed upon them by traditional lending institutions than do
non-knowledge based firms. Thus, firm size would be expected to be
positively related to growth in such knowledge-based industries.

Larger firms can finance capital expenditures from internal earnings, issuance of equity, or debt. By contrast, smaller firms are limited in the extent of their internal earnings and the potential for issuing equity.

2.3. The Time Period

The third dimension that may influence the context involves the time period. In the case of Germany, there are compelling reasons to think that the validity of *Gibrat's Law* may differ before and after the mid-1970s. In Germany in particular since 1974, firms have been obligated by law to retain pension funds for employees. These funds, which can run into billions of Deutsche marks, have become an important alternative source of firm financing, particularly for the larger firms. It is expected that this would loosen the impact of liquidity constraints across firms, but particularly for the largest firms. In terms of the study, any results indicating binding liquidity constraints after 1974 should be strengthened.

The evidence found by Audretsch and Elston (2002) shows a systematic difference in the impact of liquidity constraints on the investment behavior of smaller firms. Apparently smaller firms were not subject to significant liquidity constraints prior to the mid-1970s but became subject to liquidity constraints subsequent to 1970s. Consistent with these results were the changes in the West German discount lending rates which rose substantially from a mean rate of 4.7 percent between 1968 and 1973 to 5.1 percent between 1974 and 1980, then down slightly to 4.9 percent on the average between 1981 and 1992. It may be that the financial institutions of Germany did provide a system of finance that was different from the Anglo-Saxon model, in that liquidity constraints could be avoided - but only prior to the mid-1970s. Since then, there is no evidence suggesting that the German model of finance has managed to mitigate the impact of liquidity constraints.

3. DATA AND MEASUREMENT

3.1. Description of the Data

The firm level data for this study were taken from the Bonn Database. The Bonn Database is a relatively new data source tracking the financial performance of a comprehensive set of German firms, and was constructed from annual business reports of firms, the *Handbuch Der Aktiengesellschaften*, and the *Statistisches Jahrbuch*. It contains effectively all publicly traded German firms from 1970-1984 totaling 295 firms.

It is important to consider the possibility of bias in results due to entry and exit of firms during the sample period. We examined firm survival and hazard rates for this sample using the methodology outlined in Cox (1972) for a set of standard for 50-250 year time estimates and found no evidence of bias introduced from firm entry or exit in this data. In fact on the average, firm survival rate was rather high at 99 percent over the sample time period. We tested for and found heteroskedasticity in the data and subsequently corrected for it in all estimations.

FIRM GROWTH is calculated as the log of employment in the ending time period minus the log of employment in the initial time period over the log of employment in the initial time period.[6] The variable SIZE is the log of employment, and AGE is the log of the life span of the firm in the initial time period. In order to examine the potential importance of industry specific growth behavior, firms were grouped using 4-digit industry sector codes into four groups. Industry Group 1 contains all 61 firms from Metals, Minerals, Chemicals & Fiber industries, Group 2 has 77 firms from Mechanical Engineering, Electric & Precision instruments, and Motor vehicles. Group 3 has 67 Food, Tobacco & Texiles firms, and Group 4 contains all other firms in the sample, which totals 70 firms, including utility companies.

High technology firms were defined using criteria from Audretsch and Weigand (2005) on firm total expenditures for R&D and innovation as a percent of sales revenue in 1980. The 75 high technology firms, are in fact the larger firms in the sample in terms of net sales and number of employees. This is interesting because empirical studies on the U.S. have generally found that the smaller firms were doing more of the research. One reason for this may be that during the 1970s and 1980s in Germany larger firms supposedly had better access to capital markets for R&D funding, which was one justification for the new capital markets (eg. Neuer Markt was initiated in 1997) to channel investment capital for R&D to smaller high technology firms.

4. THE EMPIRICAL GROWTH MODELS AND REFUTABLE HYPOTHESES

The empirical growth equations which are well established in the growth literature, are derived from *Gibrat's Law* which suggests that the present size of firm i in period t may be decomposed into the product of a "proportional effect" and the initial firm size as:

$Size_{i,t} = (1 + \varepsilon)Size_{i,t-1}$ where $(1 + \varepsilon_t)$ denotes the proportional effect for firm i in period t. Here the random shock ε_t is assumed to be identically and independently distributed. Taking the natural log and using the fact that for small ε, $\ln(1 + \varepsilon) \approx \varepsilon_t$, we derive the following relationship:

$$\ln(\text{Size}_{i,t}) = \ln(\text{Size}_{i,0}) + \sum_{k=1}^{t} \varepsilon_{i,t} \tag{1}$$

which as $t \to \infty$ results is a distribution which is approximately log normal with properties that $\ln(\text{Size}_{i,t}) \approx N(t\mu_\varepsilon, t\sigma^2_\varepsilon)$.[7]

Annual percentage firm growth, can be then measured, using number of employees of the firm, as:

$$\text{Growth}_{it} = \ln(\text{Size}_{i,t}) - \ln(\text{Size}_{i,t-1}), \tag{2}$$

where Growth is calculated as the difference in the log of size for firm i between this period t and the initial period $(t-1)$ size, over log of the initial period size.

Based on Hall (1987) or Evans (1987) the traditional empirical growth equation (3) below can be used for testing the hypothesis that initial firm size impacts firm growth:

$$\text{Growth}_{it} = B_1 \ln(\text{Size}_{i,t-1}) + B_2 \ln(\text{Size}_{i,t-1})^2 + B_3 \text{Age}_{i,t-1} + B_4 D_{ind} + \varepsilon_I \tag{3}$$

where Growth is a function of Size, measured by the log of employment in the initial time period; Age, measured by the log of the life span of the firm in the initial time period; and ε_I, is a stochastic error term. Regressions control for D_{ind} industry and annual effects by using a vector of year and industry dummies - except when regressions are divided into industry groups. The former is important to control for recessions and oil shocks in the data.

To test for the importance of size on growth for different class of industries these equations are run on an all firm sample, as well as on sub-groups of firms sorted into high and low technology, the four industry groupings, and five year time periods from 1970 to 1984.

5. RESULTS

The results estimating the validity of *Gibrat's Law* for the entire sample of firms over the entire sample period, 1970-1984 are shown in Table 1. As the positive and statistically significant coefficients of both the size and size-squared terms suggest, for the most general sample *Gibrat's Law* does not hold. While this finding is compatible with results for North America, there is an important difference. In the North American context firm size is negatively related to growth. However, for the entire sample over the entire sample period for Germany, firm size is found to be positively related to growth.

Table 1 .- Industry fixed-effects growth model, 1970-1984

Growth	All Firms 1970 1984	Low R&D Intensity	High R&D Intensity	Ind. Group 1	Ind. Group 2	Ind. Group 3	Ind. Group 4
Size	0.343678*	0.48915*	1.010471	-0.16551*	-0.21328**	-0.04395	0.224059*
	(3.30)	(3.98)	(1.33)	(-2.34)	(-1.68)	(-0.70)	(2.39)
Size2	-0.04314*	-0.06817*	-0.1088	0.026946*	0.031195	0.012227	-0.02802
	(-2.75)	(-3.42)	(-1.18)	(2.20)	(1.63)	(0.85)	(-1.59)
Size3	0.001773*	0.003069*	0.003805	-0.00133*	-0.00134	-0.00092	0.001161
	(2.37)	(3.02)	(1.04)	(-2.01)	(-1.43)	(-0.93)	(1.16)
Age	-0.01731	-0.03854*	0.156247*	0.050805	0.07602	-0.00529	-0.13399*
	(-0.94)	(-2.22)	(2.13)	(1.62)	(1.16)	(-0.24)	(-4.12)
N	226	168	58	49	66	53	58
Adj. R^2	0.0777	0.1640	0.1674	0.0215	0.0046	0.0181	0.2984

Statistically significant at * 5% and ** 10% levels. Regressions include industry and annual dummies. Industry Groups: Group 1, Metal & chemicals; Group 2, Engineering & vehicles, Group 3, Food & textiles; Group 4, Utilities & other. R&D intensity is defined by Audretsch and Weigand (2005).

Table 1 also suggests that industry context matters. For the low R&D industries, a positive relationship emerges between firm size and growth. By contrast, for the knowledge-intensive industries, there is no statistically significant relationship observed between firm size and growth. That is, *Gibrat's Law* apparently holds in knowledge-based industries over this period.

The relationship between firm age and growth also varies systematically between industry contexts. As the negative and statistically significant coefficient of age in low-knowledge industries suggests, growth rates tend to decline systematically over the life-cycle of the firm. By contrast, in the high-knowledge industries, the positive and statistically significant coefficient of age indicates that growth rates tend to increase systematically over the life-cycle of the firm. Thus, different results emerge for both the firm size-growth relationship and the firm age-growth relationship between the low- and high-knowledge industry contexts.

Separate results from the four industry groups provide even further evidence that the industry context matters. *Gibrat's Law* is found to hold for Group 3, Engineering & vehicles. However, *Gibrat's Law* clearly does not hold for Group 1, Metal & chemicals, Group 2, Engineering & vehicles, or Group 4, Utilities & others. While a negative relationship exists between firm size and growth for Metals & chemicals, and for Engineering & vehicles, a positive relationship is found for Utilities & other industries.

Table 2 provides results for the early 1970s. Between 1970 and 1974 *Gibrat's Law* is found to hold for all firms. In fact, during this period, the industry context plays no significant role. *Gibrat's Law* is found to hold for low-knowledge industries, high-knowledge industries, and for all four of the industry groups.

Table 2 - Industry fixed-effects growth model, 1970-1974

Growth	All Firms 1970 1974	Low R&D Intensity	High R&D Intensity	Ind Group 1	Ind Group 2	Ind Group 3	Ind Group 4
Size	-0.00325	-0.01443	0.213387	-0.02005	-0.0031	0.01073	-0.00323
	(-0.10)	(-0.32)	(1.02)	(-0.91)	(-0.76)	(0.32)	(-0.10)
Size2	0.000512	0.002314	-0.02628	0.003945	-0.0021	-0.0022	0.000912
	(0.10)	(0.32)	(-1.04)	(1.02)	(0.43)	(-0.28)	(-0.19)
Size3	-0.00003	-0.00012	0.001037	-0.0002	-0.00006	0.000058	-0.00007
	(-0.11)	(-0.32)	(1.04)	(-0.97)	(-0.22)	(0.11)	(-0.19)
Age	0.00271	0.000901	0.014204	0.001799	0.019489	-0.00028	0.000795
	(0.45)	(0.14)	(0.75)	(0.19)	(1.04)	(-0.03)	(0.07)
N	259	190	69	58	73	62	66
Adj. R^2	0.0417	0.0263	0.0720	0.0337	0.0181	0.0038	0.0013

Statistically significant at * 5% and ** 10% levels. Regressions include industry and annual dummies. Industry Groups: Group 1, Metal & chemicals; Group 2, Engineering & vehicles, Group 3, Food & textiles; Group 4, Utilities & other. R&D intensity is defined by Audretsch and Weigand (2005).

Table 3 provides results for the late 1970s. Between 1975-1979 the evidence does not support *Gibrat's Law*. Rather, a positive relationship exists between firm size and growth. While these results hold for both of the industry contexts based on R&D intensity, there is support for *Gibrat's Law* in Metals & chemicals, Engineering & vehicles, and Utilities & other industries. *Gibrat's Law* apparently does not hold in Food & textiles.

Table 3 - Industry fixed-effects growth model, 1975-1979

Growth	All Firms 1975 1979	Low R&D Intensity	High R&D Intensity	Ind Group 1	Ind Group 2	Ind Group 3	Ind Group 4
Size	0.1603*	0.2432*	0.3983*	-0.0553	0.0023	-0.0471	0.02375
	(3.88)	(3.98)	(3.14)	(-0.95)	(0.11)	(-1.62)	(0.50)
Size2	-0.0230*	-0.0368*	-0.046*	0.0080	-0.00158	0.0123**	-0.0029
	(-3.71)	(-3.73)	(-2.94)	(0.98)	(-0.53)	(1.70)	(-0.32)
Size3	0.001*	0.0017*	0.0017*	-0.0004	0.0001	-0.0009**	0.0001
	(3.54)	(3.45)	(2.78)	(-0.91)	(0.83)	(-1.71)	(0.20)
Age	0.0087	0.0075	0.0110	0.0085	0.0028	0.0029	-0.0115
	(1.22)	(0.90)	(0.86)	(0.40)	(0.27)	(0.33)	(-0.69)
N	257	189	68	59	73	62	63
Adj. R^2	0.0715	0.098	0.1225	0.0177	0.0338	0.0377	0.0135

Legend: see endnote to Table 1.

The results for the 1980s are provided in Table 4. As for the late 1970s, *Gibrat's Law* is found not to hold. However, one difference in the 1980s is that the evidence does support the validity of *Gibrat's law* in high knowledge industries. Other differences are that the *Law* apparently does not hold in Metals & chemicals, Food & tobacco, and Utilities & others, while it does hold in Engineering & vehicles.

Table 4.- Industry fixed-effects growth model, 1980-1984

Growth	All Firms 1980 1984	Low R&D Intensity	High R&D Intensity	Ind Group 1	Ind Group 2	Ind Group 3	Ind Group 4
Size	0.20874*	0.3134*	-0.2752	-0.1104*	-0.1099	-0.0659*	0.2111*
	(3.39)	(5.08)	(-0.68)	(-2.11)	(-1.12)	(-1.67)	(3.64)
Size2	-0.02554*	-0.044*	0.0450	0.0154**	0.0195	0.0204*	-0.0291*
	(-2.64)	(-4.25)	(0.86)	(1.75)	(1.36)	(2.12)	(-2.63)
Size3	0.001029*	0.0020*	-0.0022	-0.0007	-0.0009	-0.0015*	0.0013*
	(2.16)	(3.68)	(-0.99)	(-1.53)	(-1.35)	(-2.16)	(2.12)
Age	- 0.02299**	-0.0361*	0.1076*	0.0505*	0.0182	-0.0056	-0.1174*
	(-1.69)	(-3.15)	(1.80)	(2.22)	(0.35)	(-0.45)	(-6.19)
N	230	171	59	49	67	55	59
Adj. R^2	0.1430	0.3134	0.1542	0.0697	0.0110	0.0471	0.4760

Legend: see endnote to Table 1.

6. CONCLUSIONS

A massive literature has been compiled that tests the validity of *Gibrat's Law*. In posing the question, "Is *Gibrat's Law* valid or not?" these studies have generally produced results that either confirm or refute the *Law*. The results of this study suggest that perhaps this literature has been asking the wrong question. Rather a slightly different question may be more relevant, "Under which context does *Gibrat's Law* hold and under which context does it not?"

In fact, the empirical evidence provided by this paper suggests that the validity of *Gibrat's Law* is shaped by context. In particular, the context of country-specific institutions, the industry, and the time period apparently make a difference in determining the validity of *Gibrat's Law*. Studies testing *Gibrat's Law* for North American have found that either the *Law* holds (earlier studies) or that a negative relationship exists between firm size and growth. For Germany a positive relationship emerges between firm size and growth. The different relationship between size and growth may reflect differences in institutions such as the system of finance. Just as the evidence suggests that the relationship between firm size and growth has been different in Germany than for North America, we also find that the results vary systematically across the industry context and the time period context.

The relationship between firm size and growth may be considerably different in Germany with the development of high-technology entrepreneurial start-ups in the last several years. The establishment of the Neuer Markt (New Market) has led to an explosion of such knowledge-based start-ups. Future research needs to identify how this new context influences the relationship between firm size and growth in Germany.

NOTES

[1] Wagner (1992) has tested *Gibrat's Law* for establishments (not firms) in Lower Saxony. Almus and Nerlinger (1999 and 2000) have tested *Gibrat's Law* for young firms in Germany.

[2] Not surprisingly, small enterprises more frequently turn to commercial banks for funding of capital projects. But, as Stoll (1984) notes, smaller firms typically face higher credit costs than do their larger counterparts. For example, a Federal Reserve Board study of loan rates charged by commercial banks on loans made between November 3 and November 7, 1986 found that short-term loans at a fixed rate had an average rate of 11.2 percent for loans of less than $24,000. However, the rate fell steadily to a mean of 6.8 percent for loans exceeding $1 million. For loans with a floating rate, the differential was not quite as great. The smallest loans had an average rate of 9.7 percent, while the largest loans were for 7.5 percent. Very similar patterns were identified for long-term loans at both fixed and floating rates (United States Small Business Administration, 1987, Table A2.7, p. 91). Thus, the evidence clearly indicates that the cost of capital tends to fall as the size of the loan increases.

[3] The Big Three German banks are the Deutsche Bank, Dresdner Bank and the Commerzbank.

[4] See for example Cable (1985).

[5] The Monthly Report of the Deutsche Bundesbank (April 1989, p. 15, Table 4.1) points out that the market share of the Big Three fell from 10.2 percent in 1970 to 10.6 percent in 1978 to 8.9 percent in 1988.

[6] All log variable transformations use the natural log.

[7] Almus and Nerlinger (2000) confirm this distributional assumption via kernel density estimates for German firms 1990-1996.

REFERENCES

Almus, M. and E. A. Nerlinger (1999), "Growth of New Technology-Based Firms: Which Factors Matter?", *Small Business Economics*, 13(2), 141-154.

Almus, M. and E. A. Nerlinger (2000), "Testing Gibrat's Law for Young Firms – Empirical Results for West Germany", *Small Business Economics*, 15(1), 1-12.

Arrow, K. E. (1962), "Economic Welfare and the Allocation of Resources for Invention", in R. R. Nelson (ed.), *The Rate and Direction of Inventive Activity*, Princeton, Princeton University Press.

Audretsch, D. B. (1995), *Innovation and Industry Evolution*, Cambridge (MA), The MIT Press.

Audretsch, D. B. and J. A. Elston (2002), "Does Firm Size Matter? Evidence on the Impact of Liquidity Constraints on Firm Investment Behavior in Germany", *International Journal of Industrial Organization*, 20(1), 1-17.

Audretsch, D. B. and J. Weigand (2005), "Do Knowledge Condition Make a Difference? Investment, Finance and Ownership in German Industries", *Research Policy*, 34(5), 595-613.

Cable, J. (1985), "Capital Market Information and Industrial Performance: The Role of West German Banks", *Economic Journal*, 95(377), 118-132.

Caves, R. E. (1998) "Industrial Organization and New Findings on the Turnover and Mobility of Firms", *Journal of Economic Literature*, 36(4), 1947-1982.

Cox, D. R. (1972) "Regression Models and Life Tables", *Journal of the Royal Statistical Society*, 34(2), 187-220.

Dasgupta, D and P. David (1994), "Toward a New Economics of Science", *Research Policy* 23(4), 487-521.

Deeg, R. (1992), "Banks and the State in Germany: The Critical Role of Subnational Institutions in Economic Governance", unpublished Ph.D. Dissertation, MIT.

Deeg, R. (1998), "What Makes German Banks Different?", *Small Business Economics*, 10(2), 93-101.

Dunne, T., J. M. Roberts and L. Samuelson, (1989), "The Growth and Failure of U.S. Manufacturing Plants", *Quarterly Journal of Economics*, 104(4), 671-698.

Evans, D. S. (1987), "Tests of Alternative Theories of Firm Growth", *Journal of Political Economy*, 95(4), 658-674.

Evans, D. S. and B. Jovanovic (1989), "An Estimated Model of Entrepreneurial Choice Under Liquidity Constraints", *Journal of Political Economy*, 97(4), 808-827.

Fazzari, S., R. G. Hubbard, and B. C. Petersen (1988), "Financing Constraints and Corporate Investment", *Brookings Papers on Economic Activity*, 0(1), 141-195.

Federal Republic of Germany, Federal Statistics Office (various years), *Statistisches Jahrbuch*, Wiesbaden.

Geroski, P. A. (1995) "What Do We Know About Entry?", *International Journal of Industrial Organization*, 13(4), 450-456.

Hall, B. H. (1987), "The Relationship Between Firm Size and Firm Growth in the U.S. Manufacturing Sector", *International Journal of Industrial Organization*, 35(4), 583-604.

Hart, P. E. (1962), "The Size and Growth of Firms", *Economica*, 29(113), 29-39.

Mansfield, E. (1962), "Entry, Gibrat's Law, Innovation, and the Growth of Firms", *American Economic Review*, 52(5), 1023-1051.

Mueller, D. C. and J. Tilton (1969), "Research and Develpoment Costs as a Barrier to Entry", *Canadian Journal of Economics*, 56(4), 570-579.

Petersen, M. A. and R. G. Rajan (1992), "The Benefits of Lending Relationships: Evidence from Small Business Data", *Journal of Finance*, 49(1), 3-37.

Stephan, P. E. (1996), "The Economics of Science", *Journal of Economic Literature*, 34(4), 1199-1235.

Stoll, H. R. (1984), "Small Firms' Access to Public Equity Financing", in Paul M. Horvitz and R. Richardson Pettit (eds.), *Small Business Finance: Problems in the Financing of Small Business*, Greenwich (Conn.), JAI Press, 187-238.

Sutton, J. (1997) "Gibrat's Legacy", *Journal of Economic Literature*, 35(1), 40-59.

Vitols, S. (1998), "Are German Banks Different?" *Small Business Economics*, 10(2), 79-91.

Wagner, J. (1992), "Firm Size, Firm Growth and Persistence of Chance: Testing Gibrat's Law with Establishment Data from Lower Saxony", 1978-1989, *Small Business Economics*, 4(2), 125-132.

Chapter 7
GIBRAT'S LAW IN A MEDIUM-TECHNOLOGY INDUSTRY: EMPIRICAL EVIDENCE FOR ITALY

Francesca Lotti
Bank of Italy, Roma

Enrico Santarelli
University of Bologna, and Max Planck Institute of Economics, Jena

Marco Vivarelli
Catholic University of Piacenza, and Max Planck Institute of Economics, Jena

1. INTRODUCTION

From an empirical viewpoint, *Gibrat's Law* (Gibrat, 1931) can be tested in two ways: either by using a sample of firms continuously active during a given period (balanced panel analysis), or by using a population of firms and testing the *Law* with sample attrition taken into account, since a portion of firms alive at the beginning of the period do not survive until the end of the same period (unbalanced panel analysis).[1] Both approaches have some shortcomings. Tracking only incumbent surviving firms is by definition equivalent to considering only a sub-sample of the firms' population and to neglecting important elements of industrial dynamics, i.e. entries and failures. Thus, this approach is correct only under the assumption that the equations' residuals are not correlated with unobservable characteristics concerning the decision to exit the market. Accordingly, if *Gibrat's Law* is not a feature of the best incumbent firms, but a general pattern of industrial dynamics, it should be tested over the entire population of firms in a given time span (with the inclusion of new entries and firms that may exit the market in the subsequent periods). It is probably for this reason that the most recent estimates of the *Law*[2] have used the second methodology. Yet, neither in this case do most studies specifically consider newborn firms and they deal with the survival/failure phenomenon by taking account only of sample attrition due to exit. Most of previous studies, in fact, pool large incumbents, newborn firms and small transient firms together, although estimates over a given time period are corrected for sample bias.

By contrast, this paper attempts to consider both the entry process and the role of selection mechanisms in reshaping a given population of firms over time. It consequently differs from the previous literature in that it tries *1*) to take joint account of both incumbents and newborn firms and *2*) to consider the selection process as it occurs both over the entire period and year by year[3]. Repeating the test of *Gibrat's Law* year by year enables one to consider what happens when the original heterogeneous population is gradually reshaped in favor of larger, most efficient and well-established firms. Indeed, whilst most of the previous literature has found that *Gibrat's Law* must be rejected in the case of manufacturing[4], since smaller firms tend to grow faster than their larger counterparts, no previous study has attempted to determine whether this result is robust once industrial dynamics are taken fully into account. More specifically, in this paper we deal with the Italian Radio, TV & Telecommunications equipment industry in January 1987 (including 122 newborn firms and 3,163 incumbents). The rationale behind the decision to choose this industry is that, during the period examined, it was a rather mature one in Italy and still lagging behind in the technological revolution brought about by the passage from analog to digital signals. Besides, according to industry insiders and experts, between the late 1980s and early 1990s it experienced a significant shakeout (as defined by Klepper and Miller, 1995) that, as the leading firms proved unable to cope with the technological revolution, eventually resulted in a contraction of the entire industry. In this connection, the Italian Radio, TV & Telecommunication industry can be regarded, in the period under examination, as an aging one (on the likely impact of ageing on entrepreneurship, cf. Peters, Cressy and Storey, 1999).

Many small firms in the industry operated in one of its three submarkets, whereas only a few large multi-product firms competed against each other in all of those submarkets. Consequently, this study is affected by a certain degree of arbitrariness in its definition of the industry's boundaries which, according to Sutton (1998), is likely to make it impossible to take account of the fact that each industry contains a number of submarkets *between* which rivalry is less intense than it is *within* each (cf. also Giorgetti, 2003; Roberts and Thompson, 2003). Nonetheless, it is less severely affected by this arbitrariness than are studies which focus on several different industries. *Gibrat's Law* is tested by using a sample selection procedure (augmented with age) for all firms, incumbent firms and newborn firms respectively, both over the entire period (1987-1994) and year by year. This set of estimates will enable us to answer the following questions:

a) Is *Gibrat's Law* valid in general (that is for all firms and over the entire period)?

b) Is *Gibrat's Law* less valid for new entries than for incumbent firms (smaller sub-optimal firms are relatively more common among new entries)?

c) Is there any convergence towards a Gibrat's like pattern of growth over time (due to market selection particularly adverse against smaller firms)?

The empirical findings support the following string of answers: NO/YES/YES.

Our interpretation is that previous results rejecting *Gibrat's Law* have been partially determined by incomplete consideration of the entry and selection processes. More specifically, *Gibrat's Law* fails to hold because a given population of firms is characterized by the presence of both newborn firms and 'fragile' firms (which will subsequently fail). Smaller firms are over-represented in both categories, but it is precisely the presence of smaller fast-growing firms that leads to the rejection of *Gibrat's Law*. As a result of market selection, surviving larger firms tend to behave in accordance with *Gibrat's Law* and this holds for both incumbents and newborn firms. Hence, if these results are correct, and if they are confirmed by other studies, *Gibrat's Law* and industrial dynamics are interrelated and it is incorrect either to assume or to deny *Gibrat's Law a priori*. Although the *Law* is not confirmed in general, it may be an accurate representation of the pattern of growth assumed by a mature population of well-established firms, that is, a population already selected by market forces (cf., for example, Lotti and Santarelli, 2004).

The paper is organized as follows. Section 2 presents the dataset and deals with some methodological issues related to the estimation of *Gibrat's Law*; Section 3 discusses the econometric results and Section 4 summarizes the main findings of the study.

2. DATA AND METHODOLOGY

We use a unique data set from the Italian National Institute for Social Security (INPS). This data set identifies all incumbents and newborn firms with at least one paid employee in the Radio, TV & Telecommunication equipment industry in Italy, and tracks their employment performance at yearly intervals from January 1987 to January 1994.[5] The original INPS file was checked in order to identify entry and failure times correctly and to detect inconsistencies in individual tracks due to administrative factors, and cancellations due to firm transfers, mergers and take-overs. This cleaning procedure reduced the total number of firms in the database to 3,285, of which 122 were new entries in January 1987. As far as the new entries are concerned, it is worth noting that no public policies supporting new firm formation were in operation in Italy at the beginning of 1997 (on the likely impact of public policies on new firm formation and SMEs in general, cf. Storey, 2003).

The central relationship tested in this study is the original logarithmic specification of the *Law*:

$$\log S_{i,t} = \beta_0 + \beta_1 \log S_{i,t-1} + \varepsilon_{i,t} \tag{1}$$

where $S_{i,t}$ is the size of firm i at time t, $S_{i,t-1}$ is the size of the same firm in the previous period and $\varepsilon_{i,t}$ is a random variable distributed independently of $S_{i,t-1}$. Following Chesher (1979, p.404), if both sides of equation (1) are exponentiated, it becomes clear that if β_1 is equal to unity, then growth rate and initial size are independently distributed[6] and *Gibrat's Law* is in operation. By contrast, if $\beta_1 < 1$ smaller firms grow at a systematically higher rate than do their larger counterparts, while the opposite is the case if $\beta_1 > 1$. If - as in the majority of previous studies - growth and exit are not treated as homogeneous phenomena (that is, on the disputable hypothesis that exit is equal to a minus one rate of growth), empirical estimates need only deal with surviving firms, obtaining results conditional on survival.

Let $\chi_{i,t}$ be an indicator function which takes value 1 if firm i is still alive at time t and 0 otherwise. Accordingly, observed data on firm size can give only the conditional expectation of $S_{i,t}$ given $S_{i,t-1}$ and $\chi_{i,t}=1$, i.e. according to our specification,

$$E\left(S_{i,t} \mid S_{i,t-1}, \chi_{i,t} = 1\right) = \beta_0 + \beta_1 \log S_{i,t-1} + E\left(\varepsilon_{i,t} \mid S_{i,t-1}, \chi_{i,t} = 1\right) \tag{2}$$

If the conditional expectation of ε_t is zero, the regression function for the selected sub-sample is the same as the population regression function, the only drawback being a loss of efficiency due to the smaller number of observations available. But if this is not true, the last term of equation (2) need to be included in the regression function. It is for this reason that a rule for χ_t is required, and the most natural way to deal with this kind of selection is to use a survival equation (i.e. a probit model), given that we can exactly identify when a firm exits the market. In a more general formulation, this is the same as saying that:

$$\begin{cases} \Pr ob(x_i = 1) = \phi\!\left(a'z_i\right) & \text{Probit } \textit{Selection Equation} \\ y_i = \beta'x_i + \varepsilon_i & \text{observe only if } x_i = 1 \end{cases} \tag{3a} \tag{3b}$$

If we denote the residual of equation (3a) with $\mu_{i,t}$ and if we assume that the error terms are normal, respectively $\varepsilon_i \sim N(0, \sigma_\varepsilon)$ and $\mu_i \sim N(0, \sigma_\mu)$ with $corr(\varepsilon_i, \mu_i) = \rho$, we can reformulate equation (2) as:

$$E\left(S_{i,t} \mid S_{i,t-1}, \chi_{i,t} = 1\right) = \beta_0 + \beta_1 \log S_{i,t-1} + \rho \sigma_\varepsilon \lambda_i \qquad (4)$$

where $\lambda_i = \dfrac{\phi(\alpha' z_i)}{\Phi(\alpha' z_i)}$ is the inverse of the Mills' ratio.[7] The two-step estimation procedure requires one to estimate the probit selection model first. Once λ_i has been obtained for each observation, the growth equation (4) is estimated, augmenting the observations with the Mills' ratio inverse, to obtain an additional parameter estimate $\beta_M = \hat{\rho}\hat{\sigma}_\varepsilon$ from which we can simply recover the two-step estimate of $\hat{\rho} = \dfrac{\beta_M}{\hat{\sigma}_\varepsilon}$. We used Maximum Likelihood estimation[8] with heteroscedasticity robust standard errors.

Consistently with most previous studies, both the main and the selection equations were augmented with the age variable (which is obviously only relevant to incumbent firms). Regressions were run separately for all firms, all firms with a dummy for newborn ones, only incumbent firms and only newborn firms. The same specifications were tested over the entire period (1987-1994) and year by year (7 separate estimates for each group of firms).[9] The descriptive statistics in Table 1 confirm the importance of market selection: only 59 percent of incumbents and 51 percent of newborn firms survive until the end of the 7 years period. This selection, as it is evident from the average sizes of surviving firms, is dramatically biased towards smaller firms (especially in the first years).

Table 1 – Number of active firms, average size and its standard deviation

Year	Number of active firms	Avg. size of surviv. firms	Stand. dev.	Number of active firms	Avg. size of surviv. firms	Stand. dev.	Number of active firms	Avg. size of surviv. firms	Stand. dev.
	ALL FIRMS			INCUMBENTS			NEWBORN FIRMS		
1987	3,285	35.99	285.14	3,163	36.94	290.43	122	11.38	41.61
1988	3,216	37.07	277.46	3,095	37.97	282.61	121	14.10	52.70
1989	2,893	44.34	343.17	2,786	45.36	349.46	107	17.55	61.11
1990	2,743	44.89	337.04	2,646	45.81	342.89	97	19.82	67.45
1991	2,564	46.10	336.10	2,476	47.00	341.73	88	20.74	70.39
1992	2,347	45.11	368.56	2,265	46.00	374.84	81	20.12	67.90
1993	2,149	46.31	346.37	2,078	47.18	352.00	71	20.83	65.76
1994	1,933	45.83	378.60	1,871	46.76	384.66	62	17.76	54.91

3. RESULTS

Tables 2 and following present the regressions results over the entire period examined (1987-1994) and year by year. The model specification is reported in the headline, while coefficients estimates are presented together with robust standard errors and level of statistical significance (*=90%; **=95%; ***=99%). Estimates of the Gibrat's coefficient $\beta 1$ are also coupled with a Wald test, whose null is $\beta 1=1$ (that is the *Law* is not rejected). After the coefficients estimates of the sample equation have been presented, some overall diagnostic tests are reported, among which the estimate of the correlation between the residuals of the two models (ρ) and the related significance level of the corresponding Likelihood Ratio test,[10] and a Wald test for the overall validity of the model. As can be seen from all tables, the need for the sample selection model has been confirmed, especially in the first years of the period examined. Finally, the reader can follow the market selection process by looking at the number of observations, the decrease of which marks the incidence of firms' failures.

Examination of Table 2 (all 3,285 firms operating in January 1987) prompts a number of considerations:

1. Consistently with previous studies (see Section 1), *Gibrat's Law* is rejected, with a $\beta_1=0.847$ significantly different from 1; smaller firms grow faster than their larger counterparts. Moreover, an initial larger size improves the likelihood of survival, although in a non-linear fashion;

2. $\beta 1$ is not only closer to 1 in the yearly estimates (this being simply a consequence of the expected close similarity in size in two adjacent years), but this coefficient is increasing over time and not statistically different from 1 in the last periods.[11] Overall, convergence to Gibrat-like behavior emerges. While these results remain unchanged when a dummy for newborn firms is included,[12] some further considerations arise when one looks at Table 3, which takes the age variable into account.

3. Consistently with previous studies, the inverse relationship between age and growth and the positive link between age and survival are both confirmed over the entire period. Yet age seems to lose its role in the second sub-period (1990-1994).

4. As in the previous estimates, *Gibrat's Law* is rejected in general, but some convergence towards the validity of the Law occurs over time. In this table the Wald test does not reject the hypothesis of $\beta 1=1$ from 1990-91: not surprisingly, the departure from *Gibrat's Law* is confined to the first three years, when the population of firms is still strongly characterized by the presence of small transient firms and when the sample selection is particularly significant (the null $\rho = 0$ is rejected). In

this case, too, the inclusion of a dummy for newborn firms does not change the results.

Before our sample is split into incumbent and newborn firms, a preliminary conclusion can be drawn. *Gibrat's Law* does not hold for the entire population of 3,285 firms and over the entire period, because smaller and younger firms exhibit a higher propensity to grow. Nevertheless, allowing for market selection through failures, the core of survivors display Gibrat-like behavior; that is, *within the sub-population of larger and more efficient firms, Gibrat's Law* seems to hold and relative size and age loose their roles. In other words, it is plausible to conclude that the 1,933 surviving firms exhibit (and will probably exhibit in the subsequent periods for which data are not available) growth patterns consistent with the *Law of Proportionate Effect*. This result is even more marked if attention is turned to newborn firms, where market selection through early failure is even more dramatic.

Table 4 prompts the following comments:

5. As in the previous tables, *Gibrat's Law* is rejected over the entire period. Here the departure from the Law is larger than in the previous cases, with a lower $\beta_1=0.725$. Yet, β_1 is increasing over time and becomes not significantly different from 1 from the fourth period on.

6. Unlike in the previous tables, initial size seems to play a minor role in determining the likelihood of survival (probably due to the fact that almost all the new entries enter the market at a sub-optimal scale).

Hence, *even within the particular population of newborn firms*, smaller firms grow faster in the years immediately after entry, but then the reshaped population of surviving firms tends to behave in a Gibrat-like way. In other words, a post-entry size adjustment occurs immediately after entry when the very sub-optimal firms try to converge to the average entry size; this process ends within the first 3 years after entry.

Turning to incumbent firms alone, not surprisingly we find further confirmation for the previous results (see Table 5 and Table 6 with the additional age variable).

7. *Within incumbent firms, Gibrat's Law* is again rejected in general, but it is confirmed once market selection has reshaped the original population in favor of the larger and more efficient firms.

8. Unlike in the case of newborn firms, initial size and age continue to be good predictors of incumbents' likelihood of survival.

Table 2 – Estimates for all firms, basic model

ALL FIRMS		Growth equation $\ln S_{i,t}=\beta_0+\beta_1\ln S_{i,t-1}+\varepsilon_{i,t}$				Selection equation $Pr(\delta_{i,t}=1)=F(\ln S_{i,t-1}, \ln S_{i,t-1}^2, const)$			
		1987-94	1987-88	1988-89	1989-90	1990-91	1991-92	1992-93	1993-94
GROWTH EQUATION	β_1	0.847***	0.959***	0.968***	0.973***	0.988***	0.986***	0.986***	0.982***
		(0.023)	(0.005)	(0.005)	(0.007)	(0.007)	(0.008)	(0.008)	(0.011)
	β_0	0.360**	0.183***	0.155***	0.091***	0.020	-0.006	-0.019	0.028
		(0.168)	(0.011)	(0.013)	(0.017)	(0.018)	(0.021)	(0.020)	(0.030)
Wald Test $\beta_1=1$		44.50***	78.44***	42.27***	13.69***	3.15*	3.07*	2.79*	2.58
SELECTION EQUATION	α_1	0.227***	0.298***	0.411***	0.334***	0.319***	0.332***	0.374***	0.240***
		(0.040)	(0.081)	(0.050)	(0.066)	(0.062)	(0.060)	(0.064)	(0.063)
	α_2	-0.025***	-0.029**	-0.041***	-0.027***	-0.035***	-0.040***	-0.035***	-0.031***
		(0.008)	(0.014)	(0.008)	(0.009)	(0.010)	(0.009)	(0.011)	(0.010)
	α_0	-0.066	1.690***	0.758***	1.140***	1.072***	0.928***	0.826***	0.965***
		(0.047)	(0.088)	(0.060)	(0.085)	(0.084)	(0.082)	(0.084)	(0.087)
ρ		0.467	0.054***	0.109***	0.049**	0.073	0.045	0.077	-0.012
λ		0.344	0.018	0.036	0.015	0.023	0.014	0.024	-0.004
Wald χ^2		1360.97***	42470.04***	38275.57***	17548.49***	19762.35***	15749.22***	14505.59***	7358.87***
log L		-4372.26	-1343.91	-1897.21	-1180.25	-1340.00	-1346.80	-1233.71	-1251.28
Number of observations		3,285	3,285	3,216	2,893	2,473	2,564	2,347	2,149
	Censored	1,352	69	323	150	179	217	198	216
	Uncensored	1,933	3,216	2,893	2,743	2,564	2,347	2,149	1,933

Table 3 – Estimates for all firms, basic model augmented with age

Growth equation $\ln S_{i,t} = \beta_0 + \beta_1 \ln S_{i,t-1} + \beta_2 Age_{i,t} + \varepsilon_{i,t}$, Selection equation $Pr(\delta_{i,t}=1) = F(\ln S_{i,t-1}, \ln S_{i,t-1}^2, Age_{i,t}, Age_{i,t}^2, const)$

ALL FIRMS		1987-94	1987-88	1988-89	1989-90	1990-91	1991-92	1992-93	1993-94
Growth Equation	β_1	0.893***	0.974***	0.978***	0.980***	0.990***	0.988***	0.988***	0.982***
		(0.019)	(0.005)	(0.005)	(0.007)	(0.007)	(0.008)	(0.008)	(0.011)
	β_2	-0.026***	-0.009***	-0.007***	-0.005***	-0.002	-0.001	-0.001	0.000
		(0.003)	(0.001)	(0.001)	(0.001)	(0.001)	(0.001)	(0.001)	(0.002)
	β_0	0.467***	0.219***	0.187***	0.123***	0.033	0.002	-0.008	0.033
		(0.116)	(0.012)	(0.014)	(0.019)	(0.024)	(0.025)	(0.028)	(0.039)
Wald Test $\beta_1=1$		31.64***	29.60***	18.04***	7.99***	2.17	2.57	2.56	2.61
Selection Equation	α_1	0.200***	0.274***	0.404***	0.337***	0.318***	0.326***	0.376***	0.236***
		(0.042)	(0.079)	(0.050)	(0.066)	(0.063)	(0.060)	(0.064)	(0.063)
	α_2	-0.022***	-0.027*	-0.041***	-0.028***	-0.037***	-0.038***	-0.035***	-0.031***
		(0.008)	(0.014)	(0.008)	(0.010)	(0.010)	(0.010)	(0.011)	(0.010)
	α_3	0.037***	0.032	0.021	-0.006	0.038	0.038	-0.010	0.026
		(0.013)	(0.027)	(0.018)	(0.027)	(0.026)	(0.026)	(0.030)	(0.030)
	α_4	-0.001**	-0.001	-0.001	0.000	-0.001	-0.001	0.000	-0.001
		(0.001)	(0.001)	(0.001)	(0.001)	(0.001)	(0.001)	(0.001)	(0.001)
	α_0	-0.174***	1.605***	0.671***	1.149***	0.842***	0.727***	0.890***	0.774***
		(0.058)	(0.117)	(0.087)	(0.144)	(0.146)	(0.167)	(0.209)	(0.223)
	ρ	0.450**	0.071***	0.124***	0.054**	0.092	0.055	0.081	-0.015
	λ	0.326	0.023	0.041	0.016	0.029	0.017	0.026	-0.005
Wald χ^2		2203.05***	42929.42***	38234.76***	19860.07	22145.77***	16578.43***	17287.31	8007.68
log L		-4331.79	-1309.29	-1879.30	-1167.77	-1336.34	-1345.34	-1223.25	-1250.80
Number of observations		3,285	3,285	3,216	2,893	2,473	2,564	2,347	2,149
	Censored	1,352	69	323	150	179	217	198	216
	Uncensored	1,933	3,216	2,893	2,743	2,564	2,347	2,149	1,933

Table 4 – Estimates for newborn firms, basic model

NEWBORN FIRMS		1987-94	1987-88	1988-89	1989-90	1990-91	1991-92	1992-93	1993-94
		Growth equation $\ln S_{i,t}=\beta_0+\beta_1 \ln S_{i,t-1}+\varepsilon_{i,t}$				Selection equation $Pr(\delta_{i,t}=1)=F(\ln S_{i,t-1}, \ln S_{i,t-1}^2, const)$			
Growth Equation	β_1	0.725***	0.929***	0.922***	0.951***	1.009***	0.979***	0.994***	0.982***
		(0.125)	(0.023)	(0.031)	(0.022)	(0.025)	(0.029)	(0.021)	(0.042)
	β_0	0.405	0.367***	0.263***	0.185***	0.038	0.027	-0.006	0.033
		(0.470)	(0.053)	(0.079)	(0.056)	(0.055)	(0.085)	(0.063)	(0.106)
Wald Test β_1=1		4.79**	9.85***	6.12**	4.92**	0.13	0.54	0.08	0.19
Selection Equation	α_1	0.228	7.249***	0.673**	0.670**	0.476*	0.317	0.512**	0.775**
		(0.248)	(0.674)	(0.312)	(0.341)	(0.287)	(0.351)	(0.226)	(0.357)
	α_2	-0.071	-1.092***	-0.077	-0.104**	-0.082*	-0.073	-0.081**	-0.142**
		(0.052)	(0.102)	(0.063)	(0.053)	(0.044)	(0.052)	(0.035)	(0.063)
	α_0	-0.034	2.010***	0.631**	0.714**	0.848**	1.203**	0.567**	0.482
		(0.198)	(0.417)	(0.249)	(0.335)	(0.381)	(0.487)	(0.274)	(0.404)
ρ		0.860*	0.001	0.246**	0.225	-0.585	0.145*	-0.928***	0.327
λ		0.994	0.001	0.109	0.067	-0.178	0.059	-0.281	0.111
Wald χ^2		33.40***	1667.57***	863.29***	1817.77***	1597.20	1175.47***	2287.17***	535.31***
log L		-160.39	-60.02	-105.56	-51.80	-44.92	-65.26	-31.94	-44.34
Number of observations		122	122	121	107	97	88	81	71
	Censored	60	1	14	10	9	7	10	9
	Uncensored	62	121	107	97	88	81	71	62

Table 5 – Estimates for incumbent firms, basic model

INCUMBENT FIRMS		Growth equation $\ln S_{i,t}=\beta_0+\beta_1\ln S_{i,t-1}+\varepsilon_{i,t}$				Selection equation $\Pr(\delta_{i,t}=1)=F(\ln S_{i,t-1},\ln S_{i,t-1}^2, const)$			
		1987-94	1987-88	1988-89	1989-90	1990-91	1991-92	1992-93	1993-94
Growth Equation	β_1	0.854***	0.962***	0.970***	0.974***	0.987***	0.987***	0.985***	0.982***
		(0.023)	(0.005)	(0.005)	(0.008)	(0.007)	(0.008)	(0.008)	(0.012)
	β_0	0.371**	0.171***	0.149***	0.086***	0.020	-0.008	-0.015	0.026
		(0.160)	(0.012)	(0.013)	(0.017)	(0.019)	(0.021)	(0.020)	(0.032)
Wald Test $\beta_1=1$		41.83***	64.20***	36.44***	11.88***	3.24*	2.77*	3.21*	2.38
Selection Equation	α_1	0.224***	0.307***	0.403***	0.315***	0.316***	0.338***	0.361***	0.222***
		(0.042)	(0.082)	(0.051)	(0.068)	(0.064)	(0.061)	(0.066)	(0.065)
	α_2	-0.023***	-0.030**	-0.040***	-0.023**	-0.034***	-0.040***	-0.033***	-0.028***
		(0.008)	(0.014)	(0.008)	(0.010)	(0.010)	(0.010)	(0.011)	(0.010)
	α_0	-0.063	1.664***	0.764***	1.170***	1.081***	0.913***	0.850***	0.987***
		(0.049)	(0.090)	(0.088)	(0.088)	(0.087)	(0.083)	(0.086)	(0.090)
ρ		0.390	0.050***	0.100***	0.047**	0.080	0.044	0.080	-0.018
λ		0.285	0.017	0.033	0.014	0.025	0.014	0.025	-0.006
Wald χ^2		1420.84***	41558.40***	38032.74***	16802.53***	18833.90***	15019.50***	13898.11***	6977.67***
log L		-4195.29	-1265.31	-1773.78	-1124.22	-1292.87	-1273.91	-1185.92	-1204.72
Number of observations		3,163	3,163	3,095	2,786	2,646	2,476	2,265	2,078
Censored		1,292	68	309	140	170	211	188	207
Uncensored		1,871	3,095	2,786	2,646	2,476	2,265	2,078	1,871

Table 6 – Estimates for incumbent firms, basic model augmented with age

INCUMBENT FIRMS — Growth equation $\ln S_{i,t}=\beta_0+\beta_1\ln S_{i,t-1}+\beta_2 Age_{i,t}+\varepsilon_{i,t}$ Selection equation $Pr(\delta_{i,t}=1)=F(\ln S_{i,t-1}, \ln S_{i,t-1}^2, Age_{i,t}, Age_{i,t}+Age_{i,t}^2, const)$

INCUMBENT FIRMS		1987-94	1987-88	1988-89	1989-90	1990-91	1991-92	1992-93	1993-94
Growth Equation	β_1	0.897***	0.976***	0.980***	0.981***	0.989***	0.988***	0.987***	0.982***
		(0.019)	(0.005)	(0.005)	(0.007)	(0.007)	(0.008)	(0.008)	(0.011)
	β_2	-0.024***	-0.009***	-0.007***	-0.005***	-0.002	-0.001	-0.001	0.000
		(0.003)	(0.001)	(0.001)	(0.001)	(0.001)	(0.001)	(0.001)	(0.002)
	β_0	0.469***	0.206***	0.183***	0.119***	0.032	0.000	-0.001	0.030
		(0.113)	(0.013)	(0.014)	(0.020)	(0.025)	(0.026)	(0.029)	(0.041)
Wald Test $\beta_1=1$		28.67***	24.34***	14.13***	6.95***	2.38	2.37	2.84*	2.45
Selection Equation	α_1	0.201***	0.273***	0.395***	0.321***	0.315***	0.331***	0.364***	0.219***
		(0.042)	(0.080)	(0.051)	(0.068)	(0.064)	(0.061)	(0.066)	(0.065)
	α_2	-0.022***	-0.027**	-0.040***	-0.025**	-0.036***	-0.038***	-0.033***	-0.028***
		(0.008)	(0.014)	(0.008)	(0.010)	(0.010)	(0.010)	(0.011)	(0.011)
	α_3	0.035***	0.050*	0.029	-0.022	0.037	0.045	-0.021	0.025
		(0.014)	(0.028)	(0.020)	(0.029)	(0.027)	(0.028)	(0.032)	(0.031)
	α_4	-0.001*	-0.002	-0.001	0.001	-0.001	-0.002*	0.001	-0.001
		(0.001)	(0.001)	(0.001)	(0.001)	(0.001)	(0.001)	(0.001)	(0.001)
	α_0	-0.174***	1.521***	0.642***	1.252***	0.849***	0.666***	0.992	0.805***
		(0.064)	(0.126)	(0.095)	(0.159)	(0.157)	(0.180)	(0.227)	(0.240)
ρ		0.392**	0.070***	0.123***	0.049**	0.097	0.055	0.085*	-0.024
λ		0.282	0.023	-1.130	0.015	0.031	0.017	0.027	-0.008
Wald χ^2		2167.32***	41738.56***	37736.36***	18992.16***	21237.49***	15739.73**	16520.88***	7499.94***
log L		-4160.56	-1235.60	-1755.35	-1113.08	-1289.84	-1272.29	-1185.11	-1204.40
Number of observations		3,163	3,163	3,095	2,786	2,646	2,476	2,265	2,078
	Censored	1,292	68	309	140	170	211	188	207
	Uncensored	1,871	3,095	2,786	2,646	2,476	2,265	2,078	1,871

4. CONCLUSIONS

The main finding of this study on the Italian Radio, TV & Telecommunications equipment industry is that the rejection of *Gibrat's Law*, common to most previous empirical research and also found here, may be due to market dynamics and selection, that is, to the entry process and the failure of transient smaller firms. Indeed, whilst we find that *Gibrat's Law* must be rejected over a seven-year period in which both incumbent and newborn firms are considered, for both the sub-populations convergence towards a Gibrat-like behavior over time can be detected. In other words, the reshaped and smaller population of surviving firms resulting from market selection exhibits, *within itself*, patterns of growth consistent with *Gibrat's Law*.

Referring to the list of questions proposed in Section 2, we can conclude that *Gibrat's Law* is rejected in general terms (question *a*), but this rejection is due to the presence of a 'fringe' of smaller and younger firms which are gradually selected out by market mechanisms. In other words, over time, some sort of shakeout (see Klepper and Miller, 1995) occurs and the remaining 'core' of surviving firms tends to behave according to the *Law of Proportionate Effect* (question *c*). This evidence is consistent with theoretical models of entry and market selection with learning (see Jovanovic, 1982; Pakes and Ericson, 1998; Cabral, 1997).

The process is even more marked among new entries (question *b*), since the fringe of sub-optimal scale firms is relatively larger. This is why the overall seven-year β_1 is lower than for incumbent firms. Nevertheless, among newborn firms as well, there is evident convergence towards *Gibrat's Law* (question *c*).

In sum, the passage of time enables the market 'to clean' a given population of firms and the surviving industrial core (mature, larger, well-established and most efficient firms) does not seem to depart from a Gibrat-like pattern of growth. Of course, this process of gradual shakeout may be strengthened by economic recession, as was the case in Italian manufacturing during the early 1990s, but nevertheless this result reconciles the recent literature with the very early studies on *Gibrat's Law* (see Hart and Prais, 1956; Simon and Bonini, 1958; Hymer and Pashigian, 1962) which tended to confirm the *Law* on the basis of samples comprising very large, old and well-established firms.

If these results are confirmed by future research, *Gibrat's Law* should no longer be considered a representation of overall industrial dynamics, but rather as a way to describe the growth behavior of mature, large and well-established manufacturing firms.

NOTES

[1] Fotopoulos and Louri (2004) is an example of the first approach, and Goddard, Wilson, and Blandon (2002) of the second.

[2] See for example Becchetti and Trovato (2002), Heshmathi (2001), Fotopoulos and Louri (2004), Almus and Nerlinger (2000), Harhoff, Stahl and Woywode (1998).

[3] As far as this second point is concerned, the paper is an extension of Lotti, Santarelli and Vivarelli (2001).

[4] More clear-cut is instead the picture arising from studies dealing with the service sector, some of which (Audretsch, Klomp, Santarelli and Vivarelli, 2004; Piergiovanni, Santarelli, Klomp and Thurik, 2003) have shown that *Gibrat's Law* cannot be regarded as a law in the strict sense, given that heterogeneous patterns of behaviour *do* emerge in the case of small scale (hospitality) services.

[5] All private Italian firms are obliged to pay national security contributions for their employees to INPS. Consequently, the registration of a new firm as 'active' signals an entry into the market, while the cancellation of a firm denotes an exit from it (this happens when a firm finally stops paying national security contributions). For administrative reasons - delays in payment, for instance, or uncertainty about the actual status of the firm - cancellation may sometimes be preceded by a period during which the firm is 'suspended'. The present paper considers these suspended firms as exiting from the market at the moment of their transition from the status of 'active' to that of 'suspended', while firms which have halted operations only temporarily during the follow-up period, and which were 'active' in January 1994, have been treated as survivors.

[6] Following a random walk (with drift) stochastic process.

[7] We use Φ to denote the cumulative density function of the Normal distribution and φ to denote its density function.

[8] Since Heckman's (1979) estimator may be inefficient and biased for small samples.

[9] Although we are aware that by choosing a cross-section approach for the year by year estimates we are not controlling for heterogeneity, therefore running the risk of obtaining biased results. In this connection, a more efficient procedure would have been represented by the Arellano and Bond (1991) generalized method of moments (GMM) one. However, we decided not to use the GMM procedure because it does not allow the year by year adjustments to be taken into account.

[10] The test statistic is LR = 2 (log L_U - log L_R), where log L_U and log L_R are the log-likelihoods for the unrestricted and restricted versions of the model, that is distributed as a χ^2 statistic with 1 degree of freedom under the null hypothesis that the restriction $\rho = 0$ is valid.

[11] This result has to be taken has a broad indication of a possible pattern of behaviour, given the considerations put forward in footnote 9 above.

[12] The coefficient of this dummy variable is significantly different from zero, thereby pointing up differences in growth patterns between newborn and incumbent firms. The results are not given here, but are available on request.

REFERENCES

Almus, M. and E. A. Nerlinger (2000), "Testing Gibrat's Law for Young Firms. Empirical Results for West Germany", *Small Business Economics*, 15(1), 1-12.

Arellano, M. and S. R. Bond (1991), "Some Tests of Specification for Panel Data: Monte Carlo Evidence and an Application to Employment Equations", *Review of Economic Studies*, 58(2), 277-297.

Audretsch, D. B., L. Klomp, E. Santarelli and A. R. Thurik (2004), "Gibrat's Law: Are the Services Different?", *Review of Industrial Organization*, 24(3), 301-324.

Becchetti, L. and G. Trovato (2002), "The Determinants of Growth for Small and Medium Sized Firms", *Small Business Economics*, 19(3), 291-306.

Cabral, L. (1997), "Entry Mistakes", Centre for Economic Policy Research, *Discussion Paper* No. 1729, November.

Chesher, A. (1979), "Testing the Law of Proportionate Effect", *Journal of Industrial Economics*, 27(4), 403-411.

Fotopoulos, G. and H. Louri (2004), "Corporate Growth and FDI: Are Multinationals Stimulating Local Industrial Development?", *Journal of Industry, Competition and Trade*, 4(2), 163-189.

Gibrat, R. (1931), *Les Inegalites Economiques*, Paris, Librairie du Recueil Sirey.

Giorgetti, M. L. (2003), "Lower Bound Estimation – Quantile Regression and Simplex Methods: An Application to Italian Manufacturing Sectors", *Journal of Industrial Economics*, 51(1), 113-120

Goddard, J., J. Wilson and P. Blandon (2002), "Panel Tests of Gibrat's Law for Japanese Manufacturing", *International Journal of Industrial Organization*, 20(4), 415-433.

Harhoff, D., K. Stahl and M. Woywode (1998), "Legal form, Growth and Exit of West German Firms - Empirical Results for Manufacturing, Construction, Trade and Service Industries", *Journal of Industrial Economics*, 46(4), 453-488.

Hart, P. E. and S. J. Prais (1956), "The Analysis of Business Concentration: A Statistical Approach", *Journal of the Royal Statistical Society*, 119, series A, 150-191.

Heckman, J. J. (1979), "Sample Selection Bias as a Specification Error", *Econometrica*, 47(2), 153-161.

Heshmati, A. (2001), "On the Growth of Micro and Small Firms: Evidence from Sweden", *Small Business Economics*, 17(3), 213-228.

Hymer, S. and P. Pashigian (1962), "Firm Size and the Rate of Growth", *Journal of Political Economy*, 70(4), 556-569.

Jovanovic, B. (1982), "Selection and Evolution of Industry", *Econometrica*, 50, 649-670.

Klepper, S. and J. H. Miller (1995), "Entry, Exit, and Shakeouts in the United States in New Manufactured Products", *International Journal of Industrial Organization*, 13(4), 567-591.

Lotti, F. and E. Santarelli (2004), "Industry Dynamics and the Distribution of Firm Sizes: A Non-parametric Approach", *Southern Economic Journal*, 70(3), 443-466.

Lotti, F., E. Santarelli and M. Vivarelli (2001), "The Relationship Between Size and Growth: The Case of Italian Newborn Firms", *Applied Economics Letters*, 2001, 8(7), 451-454.

Pakes, A. and R. Ericson (1998), "Empirical Implications of Alternative Models of Firm Dynamics", *Journal of Economic Theory*, 79(1), 1-45.

Peters, M., R. C. Cressy and D. J. Storey (1999), *The Economic Impact of Ageing on Entrepreneurship and SMEs*, Warwick/Zoetermeer, Warwick Business School and EIM Policy and Business Research.

Piergiovanni, R., E. Santarelli, L. Klomp and A. R. Thurik (2003), "Gibrat's Law and the Firm Size/Firm Growth Relationship in Italian Small Scale Services", *Revue d'Economie Industrielle*, No. 102, 69-82.

Roberts, B. M. and S. Thompson (2003), "Entry and Exit in a Transition Economy: The Case of Poland", *Review of Industrial Organization*, 22(3), 225-243.

Simon, H. A. and Ch. P. Bonini (1958), "The Size Distribution of Business Firms", *American Economic Review*, 58(4), 607-617.

Storey, D. J. (2003), "Entrepreneurship, Small and Medium Sized Enterprises and Public
    Policies," in Z. J. Acs and D. B. Audretsch, *Handbook of Entrepreneurship Research*,
    Boston, Kluwer, 473-514.
Sutton, J. (1998), *Technology and Market Structure*, Cambridge (MA), The MIT Press.

Chapter 8
ENTREPRENEURSHIP, INNOVATION, AND THE EVOLUTION OF INDUSTRIAL DISTRICTS

Enrico Santarelli
University of Bologna, and Max Planck Institute of Economics, Jena

1. INTRODUCTION[1]

This chapter focuses on some crucial aspects of the development of industrial districts in the Emilia Romagna region of Italy, where this type of spatial agglomeration of industrial firms (on which see Brenner, 2004) has flourished since the period immediately after the Second World War. Industrial districts specializing in manufacturing are so intimately bound up with modern economic growth in this region that the typical organization of industrial activities characterized by the widespread presence of such spatial clusters and of Small and Medium Sized Enterprises (SMEs) is usually labeled, after Brusco (1982), the "Emilian model". Accordingly, this chapter is aimed at investigating in-depth the various mechanisms through which the externalities associated to the working of industrial districts are actually disseminated across local firms. In particular, it analyses with case studies and econometric analysis the prediction that innovative activity favors those firms or industries in the manufacturing aggregate which have direct access to knowledge producing inputs.

In Section 2.1, in depth analysis of the biomedical cluster allows considerations to be drawn about the importance of entrepreneurship in the *early* development of a district lately dominated by Multi National Corporations (MNCs). Analysis of the ceramic tile cluster carried out in Section 2.2 shows the importance of large, leading firms in the *recent* development of local agglomerations, whereas comparison of the economic performance of a sample of firms in the ceramic tile district and one in the whole industry in Italy shows that over the 1998-2000 period the former performed better than the latter in terms of average annual growth rate of the value of total sales, whereas non-district firms displayed a most favorable dynamics in terms of net income, return on equity, and cash flow.

Then performed (Section 3) is an econometric analysis aimed at comparing the technological strength (in terms of patents registered with the European Patent Office) of innovative firms located within and outside industrial districts in Emilia Romagna. The analysis deals with the population of firms with their headquarters in the region that registered at least one patent with the European Patent Office. Results from panel model estimates show that being located within an industrial district resulted in a technological advantage during the overall 1986-1995 period. The concluding section makes some considerations on the future of spatially concentrated industrial districts *vis-à-vis* the diffusion of Information and Communication Technologies (ICT).

2. EVIDENCE FROM CASE STUDIES

The revival of the industrial district as a unit of investigation in economic analysis owes a great debt to the Italian economists Giacomo Becattini (1979, 1990), and Sebastiano Brusco (1982, 1986), who respectively describe the industrial district as *i)* a local system characterized by the active integration between a *community of people* and a *community of industrial firms*; and *ii)* a flexible specialization system - typical of the Emilia Romagna, Marche, Toscana, and Veneto regions of Italy - characterized by the widespread presence of firms with fewer than 200 employees that by subcontracting many stages of production to other (equally small) firms are able to mobilize a labor-force ten times larger than the labor-force on their wage-books. These local systems are characterized by a strong incentive to invest in advanced production machinery which is usefully employed thanks to a strong polarization of skills. Accordingly, Brusco (1986, p. 90) identifies a further and highly significant feature of industrial districts, namely "the presence, in an area that produces a certain commodity, of *firms that produce the machinery necessary for the production of the commodity*" (italics added).

This 'romantic' portrait, mostly centered around the key role played by SMEs in traditional industries substantially immune from competition by mass-production industries, has been partly changed following the works by Gianni Lorenzoni and his co-authors (Lorenzoni and Ornati, 1988; Lazerson and Lorenzoni, 1999), who focused in-depth on the recent evolution of industrial districts. Lorenzoni contends that "focal firms" - defined as those firms that occupy strategically central positions in the industrial district thanks to the great number of relationships that they have with both customers and suppliers - look decisive in expanding the district's horizons by enabling incorporation of new technologies, organizational skills, and markets (Lazerson and Lorenzoni, 1999, p. 362). These firms are strategic centers that favor the emergence of a form of hierarchy more akin to the generation and transfer of new knowledge (Lorenzoni and Baden-Fuller, 1995; Boari and Lipparini, 1999).

Emilia Romagna is one of the most economically advanced Italian regions and is characterized by a well developed industrial structure and the widespread presence of a large number of industrial districts – mostly specialized in medium-low and medium-high technology manufacturing productions. Another important feature of the region is its system for supporting cooperative relations among small firms in order to create value added products that secure global markets. This results in a diversified "cluster" in which small firms operating in cooperative networks are able to push down transaction costs and to increase their likelihood of succeed in highly competitive international markets. For these reasons, Emilia Romagna is an ideal observatory for a comparative study of the degree of technological innovativeness of district- and non-district firms. In the next Section, qualitative investigation of a high-technology and a medium-technology industrial district, the bio-medical and the ceramic tile ones, will shed light on how location in district may or may not help firms' innovative behavior.

2.1 The Biomedical District of Mirandola

The biomedical district of Mirandola represents a challenge to the commonly held view of industrial districts in Italy (Biggiero, 2002). In fact, it differs from the traditional industrial districts as regards its main features: *i)* it was 'initiated' by a typical Schumpeterian entrepreneur; *ii)* it performs high-tech activities (namely, the production of health-care products, with the exception of those for pharmaceutical use); *iii)* it is characterized by the presence of subsidiaries of foreign firms.

A pharmacist by training, as early as 1962 Mario Veronesi began to prepare the ground for what was eventually to become the Mirandola district. In the course of his work with local hospitals, Mr. Veronesi saw a nascent market for plastic disposable, initially produced in the garage of his house. During the years that followed, he founded numerous companies (including Miraset, Sterilplast, Dasco, Bellco, Dideco, and Dar) to supply the medical market with components for infusion, hemodialysis, oxygenation, and related applications (cf. Lichtman, 2002).

Since the beginning, following Mr. Veronesi's intuition on the favorable prospects for growth in this market, the district specializes in the production of disposable sterilized products (and the relative equipment) for hemodialysis, infusion, and the circulation of the blood outside the body in general (47% of value added) - an activity in which it is the international leader - cardio-surgical devices (16.2%), sterilized disposable products for respiratory use in anesthesia and reanimation (13.2%). It is localized in 15 municipal areas comprised in the territory of the province of Modena. More than 50 percent of firms (36 out of 70) and 90 percent of employment are in the area of Mirandola (Table 1), where the district originated. With respect to the industry as a whole, the Mirandola district accounts for more than 16 percent of total employment in Italy. Approximately 50 percent of local firms are small subcontractors, all of them with fewer than 50 employees. Among firms producing for the final market, 'local' ones, which account for 70 percent of the total number of firms of this type, all have fewer than 50 employees. Total employment in the district is 3,660 employees, with total sales exceeding €500 million, of which 59 percent derive from exports (mostly to the other E.U. countries and the United States). Exports are led by the excellent performance of the leading firm (the Swedish-owned Gambro-Dasco), which is expanding its market shares in non-E.U. European countries and increased its total sales by 30 percent between 1997 and 2000 (R&I, 2001).

Table 1 - The biomedical industry in the Mirandola district

	1997	2000	2001
Total sales (million Euro)	400	515	570
% of sales from export	49.8	60.7	57.0
Number of firms	74	70	71
of which subcontractors	*39*	*35*	*35*
Number of employees	3,209	3,660	3,941

Source: R&I (2001).

A further peculiarity of the Mirandola district with respect to the traditional view of industrial districts as comprising small firms that developed in opposition to large firms is the presence within it of multinational corporations (MNCs) and large national companies[2]. These companies have taken over the most important firms started by Mr. Veronesi and specialize in the production of both disposable goods and machinery. Thus, contrary to the usual idea of FDIs as driven by the availability of credit facilities, reduced labor costs or foreign market penetration, in the case of the Mirandola biomedical district, foreign firms making acquisitions have been attracted by possibilities to access to locally-available skills, technology, and know-how.

This phenomenon has resulted in a relatively high degree of seller concentration, with the first four producers (Gambro-Dasco, Mallinckrodt, B. Braun Carex, and Biofil) accounting for 63 percent of employment and 73 percent of total sales. Among the 10 non-district firms (only 4 of which are domestic firms) 6 have between 50 and 249 employees, whereas 4 have more than 250. These firms account for nearly 83 percent of total production, and employ 75 percent of total workers. They entered the district after 1980, through the acquisition of incumbent local firms founded by Mr. Veronesi together with two partners. Consistently with the view of focal firms put forward by Lorenzoni and his co-authors, entry by MNCs and large national companies fostered the adoption of process innovations (such as the introduction of the first CAD systems) and quality control procedures, as well as the more careful selection of materials. Besides, it brought in the synergies and the superior coordination skills of the group organization[3], and eventually acted as a driver for innovation and growth of al firms in the district (Boari and Lipparini, 1999). The quality-upgrading effect resulting from the emergence of these leading firms and groups set in motion a learning process among local firms and subcontractors, which in turn made major improvements to their procedures. The Mirandola district operates as a group of companies able to take a product from design to prototype to development of specialized machinery[4], to production, and beyond. Dozens of highly specialized firms offer services such as molding, extrusion, subcontracting, assembly, sterilization, instrument manufacture, and consulting (cf. Lichtman, 2002).

Product innovation is the crucial competitive factor for firms in this industry. However, since only 43 percent of firms in the district produce for market clients, the innovation process in the Mirandola area is mostly the result of close co-operation and interaction among firms, characterized by the presence of a hierarchical structure within which larger firms promote the achievement of higher levels of efficiency and competitiveness (Boari and Lipparini, 1999). Thus, not only are the largest bio-medical firms actively involved in innovative activities, but they also include both local independent firms and subcontractors in the overall innovation process. The resulting local system of innovation is one in which MNCs and large national companies control the strategic phases of R&D, design, production of machinery with embodied technological change, and final control, whereas small local firms are responsible for the intermediate phase of production and handle the assembly process. One has in this respect to consider carefully the impact of non-economic factors in fostering such networking processes. In particular, the construction and maintenance of "trust" occupies a crucial function, and it is the pillar upon which local clusters can be built and maintained (cf. Dei Ottati, 1994; Meech and Marsh, 2003). Following Rocco, Finholt, Hofer, Herbsleb (2001), two main categories of "trust" can be identified: *cognitive trust* and *emotional trust*. The former is related to the competences of the parts in the transactions, that should be of a similar order of magnitude; the latter is instead related to the intentions and identifies the possible sources of moral hazard which are likely to characterize each transaction. Crucial in the networking process that lead to the creation of the Mirandola district is production of specialized machinery and devices for specialized machinery which set off a learning process involving all the players (either foreign or domestic, either producing for the final market or subcontractors) in the biomedical district. In this process, production machinery - mostly for the assembly of plastic disposable- represents *dedicated assets* in Williamson's (1985) sense, namely resources designed for specific purposes and which cannot be easily re-deployed to alternative uses. In effect, the innovative process technologies employed in the Mirandola district are so specific to the production of certain disposable goods that their design and development requires close cooperation among all the firms involved in the local biomedical *filiere*[5]. Interaction among producers and users of machinery and capital equipment is therefore a factor favoring the creation of specific knowledge which contributes to the overall technological competitiveness of the district. It is therefore not surprising that, according to Ceris (cf. CNEL/Ceris-Cnr, 1997), the second specialization of the Mirandola district is in the production of specialized industrial machinery.

To summarize, the Mirandola district displays the features of an "organizational community" (as defined by Lipparini and Lomi, 1999) in which the district's various areas of competence constitute a sort of *tacit knowledge* which diffuses among all local players. The glue that joins everything together and enables the circulation of information among all firms in the local arena is *a)* the coordination skills brought in by the advent of exogenous forces (*multinationals* from other countries and large national companies) and *b)* the interaction between producers and users of machinery[6]. The case of the "biomedical valley" in the Emilia Romagna region proves that it is the 'right' agglomeration of firms and industries at local level that is crucial for helping firms' innovative activities in districts.

2.2. The Ceramic Tile District of Sassuolo

When comparing the distinctive features of two industrial clusters that dominate the global ceramic tile industry - Sassuolo in Italy and Castellón in Spain - Meyer-Stamer, Maggi and Seibel (2001) stress that whereas it is the capital goods producers that drive technical change and innovation in the Italian district, what drives competitive advantage in the Spanish one is innovation in downstream activities. Meyer-Stamer, Maggi and Seibel's paper also helps reassessment of the competitiveness of tile clusters in the developing world. Tile firms in Brazil's leading cluster, located in Santa Catarina, benefit from the fierce rivalry amongst Italian producers (most of which are located in the Sassuolo district), amongst Spanish producers and between Italian and Spanish producers. Although Brazilian firms are technology followers, they are innovative in downstream activities, experimenting with concepts that are not yet used by Italian or Spanish manufacturers.

As well known, Italy has been the leader in the ceramic tile industry since the Middle Ages. Today, the industry is mostly located around the town of Sassuolo, in the province of Modena. The industry is made up of companies of various sizes, most of them SMEs, ranging from small crafts enterprises producing hand made products according to centuries-old traditions to large publicly traded corporations producing the latest in porcelain material. According to Assopiastrelle, the employers' association for the Italian tile industry, Italy accounts for 40 percent of the entire world trade in ceramic tiles, employing approximately 37,000 people and manufacturing more than 630 million square meters of tile annually in nearly 600 firms. A relatively low level of concentration characterizes this industry, with the largest 5 firms accounting for about 17 percent of total production (cf. Prometeia, 2002).[7] Only 29 firms have total sales exceeding €50 million (21 of which in the Sassuolo district!), whereas 353 micro-firms fall below the €2 million threshold. Italian producers of ceramic tiles are deeply integrated in international trade, with 70 percent of total sales represented by exports to foreign markets. According to CNEL/Ceris-Cnr (1997), the second specialization of the Sassuolo district is the production of specialized machinery for the ceramic tile industry. The Sassuolo district started up during the 1950s as an industrial agglomeration within which vertically integrated firms were also directly involved in the development and refinement of production machinery and raw materials. It was however only in the 1960s that, as a consequence of the specialization and division of labor among district firms, a group of specialized suppliers of machinery and capital equipment came into being (cf. Russo, 1985). Another important organizational change in the industry occurred during the late 1980s, when the leading firm[8] and the industrial group became the main forces of growth in the local system.

Nowadays, this industrial cluster still maintains its leadership in the production of ceramic tiles, although its recent economic performance has been only slightly better than that of other Italian firms not located in the same area. In fact, comparison of the economic performances of two samples of ceramic tiles producers, one located in the Sassuolo district, the other outside the district, gives a somewhat controversial picture (Table 2), although within a generally positive framework. Both samples exhibit favorable dynamics of total sales, with district firms performing on average better in the four final years of observation. Conversely, non-district firms performed better than firms in the Sassuolo district in terms of Net income, gross operating surplus, ROE, and Cash flow. District firms were instead characterized by a more aggressive investment strategy which should result in a greater likelihood that they will benefit from embodied technological change more than non-district firms in the following years[9]. Nevertheless, the non-substantially different economic performances of district and non-district firms is also connected to the capacity of the former to leave the narrow boundaries of the local system and becoming more integrated with the latter. This might be indication of the emergence of the "multi-located" district (as originally defined by Santarelli, 1988; cf. also Chiarvesio, Di Maria and Micelli, 2004) as a productive aggregate in which an appropriate network of suppliers, within- and between-sector externalities, contracting and subcontracting with other firms belonging to the same or related industries, spillovers and knowledge originating from outside the local system are crucial for innovation activities.

Table 2- The economic performances of Italian firms in the ceramic tile industry

DISTRICT FIRMS (SASSUOLO)	1995	1996	1997	1998	1999	2000
Sales	15.5	-1.5	6.0	7.1	5.6	11.0
Net income (%)*	4.6	2.0	2.2	2.8	3.4	1.9
Gross Operating Surplus	16.2	11.8	12.5	12.7	13.3	11.7
ROE (after tax)	12.8	5.3	5.9	7.7	9.3	5.3
Fixed investments (%)*	10.4	6.5	5.2	8.0	7.1	5.9
Cash flow (%*)	11.2	8.2	8.6	8.7	9.5	8.2
NON-DISTRICT FIRMS	1995	1996	1997	1998	1999	2000
Sales	14.0	-0.3	5.7	3.2	5.2	8.6
Net income (%)*	5.1	3.0	3.1	4.0	4.5	3.1
Gross Operating Surplus	16.2	12.9	13.6	14.4	15.7	14.1
ROE (after tax)	12.3	6.6	7.1	8.8	9.7	6.5
Fixed investments (%)*	9.7	7.2	4.6	5.7	7.9	6.1
Cash flow (%)*	10.6	8.9	9.2	9.9	10.4	10.1

* all values are in percent of total sales.
Source: Prometeia (2002).

By integrating in the same perspective space and product relationships, this view proves useful in the explanation of the transition of local systems from the "Marshallian district" to the "satellite platform" (Markusen, 1996) in which the focal firms outsource non-strategic parts of the overall production process to manufacturers located outside the original borders of the district (cf. Becchetti and Castelli, 2005). Extending Markusen reasoning, one may define the new multi-located "Hub-and Spoke District" as a network of service and industrial SMEs (spokes) working for large companies (hubs) not necassarily located within the same portion of territory. This kind of agglomeration might have been favored by the Information & Communication Technology (ICT) revolution, which provided viable alternatives to the face-to-face communication that characterized the spatially concentrated industrial district. In this connection, the transaction cost advantages resulting from exploitation of ICT enable the re-location process of productive activities to be implemented without determining any significant additional cost for the firm.

3. EVIDENCE FROM ECONOMETRIC ANALYSIS

3.1. From the Case Studies to the Econometric Analysis

The two case studies discussed in Section 2 give a somewhat controversial indication concerning the allegedly superior performance of district firms with respect to their non-district counterparts. In particular, the data presented in Table 2 show that in the 1990s the overall economic performance of non-district firms was not much worse than that of district firms in the same industry. Comparative analysis of the degree of technological innovativeness of both district- and non-district firms might shed some light on whether being located within an industrial district is in itself a factor enhancing the performance and ameliorating the competitiveness of manufacturing firms.

Firstly, one might argue that firms located in industrial districts *did* benefit significantly, as regards their innovative activities, from the agglomeration economies that characterize local clusters. Although when all firms pursue an aggressive innovation and patent policy the differences between district- and non-district firms are likely to result less clear-cut than in periods in which innovation strategies do not occupy a key role in the management's agenda.

Secondly, one can contend that the availability of faster means of communication following the diffusion of ICT rendered the alternative between a *core* and a *periphery* (in the sense of Krugman, 1991) location less crucial in the last two decades. In this case, agglomeration economies of the district type might not affect significantly the innovative performance at the firm level.

Finally, as suggested by the case study of the ceramic tile industry, it is likely that the industries of specialization in the regional economy are increasingly becoming *traded* industries (Porter, 2003) which sell products across regions and, mostly, to other countries. This implies that they do not base their decision to locate within or outside the narrowly defined industrial district on resources but on broader competitive considerations. In this case, no statistically significant relationship between district location and innovative performance should arise.

On the basis of the above discussion, this section provides a simple econometric test of the relationship between clustering and innovation. Employed for this purpose is a database developed at Aster (the Agency for

Technological Transfer of the Emilia Romagna region) through its "Technology Watch" project carried out in cooperation with the National Research Council of Italy, the University of Bologna, and ENEA (the Italian National Agency for New Technologies, Energy and the Environment). The database contains micro-level data on patenting activity by firms located in the region that have registered at least one patent with the European Patent Office between 1978 and 1997, and includes balance sheet figures (taken from Centrale dei Bilanci) besides a full range of qualitative and quantitative information. The original database was checked in order to detect inconsistencies in individual tracks due to administrative factors, and cancellations due to firm transfers, mergers and take-overs. Some descriptive statistics are reported in Table 3.

Table 3 – Summary statistics

	Mean	Standard Deviation	Min	Max	Average Annual Change (%)
	1986-1995				
SIZE (Number of employees)	266.00	364.90	26.10	1,686.70	1.0638
PPE (Property, plant and equipment)	13,496.40	20,073.30	448.30	77,371.50	1.1332
ΔGOS (Gross Operating Surplus)	0.37	0.38	0.04	1.96	
Patents	2.50	4.50	0.10	19.20	
STRUCTURALCHARACTERISTICS (YES/NO)	ABS. VALUE		YES % VALUE		
DIST (Industrial district)	10		29.4		
MULTI (Multi-plant)	10		29.4		
GROUP (Industrial group)	14		41.2		
EXP (Export)	29		85.3		
SSUP (Specialized suppliers)	12		35.3		
SDOM (Supplier dominated)	17		50.0		
SINT (Scale intensive)	3		8.8		
SB (Science based)	*2*		*5.9*		
Number of firms	34		100.0		

Although it is commonly accepted in the literature dealing with industrial districts that patents - as well as R&D expenditures - are not crucial for the most innovative firms operating within industrial districts (cf., for example, Garofoli, 2002), it is maintained here (consistently with the findings by Acs, Anselin and Varga, 2002) that they nonetheless represent the most reliable, and easily comparable across firms, indicator of the outcome of formal and informal innovative activities[10]. In fact, their limited heuristic value notwithstanding, patents are widely employed in the studies of the output side of the overall innovation process (for a critical survey, cf. Piergiovanni and Santarelli, 1996).

3.2. Patents, Firm Size, and Firm Location

Analysis of the innovative performance of firms in the Emilia Romagna regions took account of all firms with at least one patent registered with the European Patent Office (EPO). In particular, the analysis dealt with the patent activity of firms in industrial districts compared to a control sample of non-district firms that had also patented with EPO. In this connection, the use of data comprising 'high quality' patents, such as those provided by EPO, represents a viable alternative to the data collected through the national patent system. Nevertheless, it remains true that firms of different sizes have a different propensity to use patent protection and that firms in traditional industries are more likely to develop non-patentable innovations than are firms in technologically progressive industries. As a consequence, in this more than in other cases, the empirical results are likely to reflect the partial inadequacy of the innovation data that are employed.

The period considered was 1979 to 1997, which was characterized by the increasing integration of Emilia Romagna firms into the global economy, with a significant process of partial relocation of manufacturing activities in least developed and transition economies (cf. Barba Navaretti, Santarelli and Vivarelli, 2002). Several firm-specific factors were taken into account when attempting to explain inter-firm differences in patenting activity:

- the fact that a firm is/is not located within an industrial district (DIST). Adopted for this purpose was the classification proposed in the CNEL/Ceris-Cnr (1997) report, which is the one most akin to the guidelines developed by the Ministry of Industry;
- firm size (total number of employees in each year during the relevant period) (SIZE);
- total net value of property, plant and equipment (as a proxy for the stock of total fixed assets) (PPE);
- dynamics of the gross operating surplus (as a measure of the economic performance of the firm) (ΔGOS);
- the fact that the firm operates with one or more plants (as a proxy for the organizational structure) (MULTI);
- the fact that the firm is part of an industrial group (GROUP)[11];
- the fact that the firm is an exporting firm (EXP);
- the fact that the firm belongs to one of the categories (specialized suppliers (SSUP), supplier dominated (SDOM), scale intensive (SINT)) in Pavitt's (1984) taxonomy[12].

Firms for which no balance sheet data were available and firms which exited before the end of the period were dropped from the original list of those with at least one patent with EPO. Since complete balance sheet data were available only for the years comprised between 1986 and 1995, the econometric analysis performed in section 4.2 focuses on this period only, taking the total number of patents granted to the firm between 1979 and 1985 as the cumulated stock of patents in the base year 1986. In the database, district firms represent 29.4 percent of the sample, whereas in relation to the sectoral composition of the sample, the largest share is accounted for by supplier dominated firms (in Pavitt's (1984) sense), representing 50.0 percent of total firms. Conversely, science based firms are the least represented, with a share of 5.8 percent in the ten-year period considered. Average size of sample firms is relatively large: 266 employees. However, this does not mean that small firms, that are characteristic of manufacturing industry in the region, are under-represented in the sample. Rather, this is the result of the presence in the sample of a few very large firms.

The rationale for choosing most of the variables listed above is intuitive. First, the district variable allows to determine whether the external economies typical of the district - which have been seen in operation from a qualitative viewpoint in the two case-studies of the Mirandola and the Sassuolo districts - do affect the innovative output of the firm. Accordingly, it was determined for each firm localized in a municipality comprised within a certain industrial district whether the firm's productive specialization was the same as that characterizing the industrial district.

Second, employment size was included in the analysis in order to seek confirmation for the so-called second Schumpeterian hypothesis, according to which innovative capability increases with firm size.[13]

Third, the value of property, plant and equipment is both a measure of firm scale and the stock of capital (including intangibles such as software) which can be usefully employed in the production process, under the hypothesis that the larger the stock of capital the higher the innovative capability of the firm.

Fourth, the gross operating surplus is a measure of the wealth produced by the firm once the variable costs have been subtracted. The idea behind the introduction of this variable is that firms achieving better economic performance are more able to raise the financial resources needed to carry the costs connected with patent registration and protection.

Fifth, multi-plant firms are likely to employ professional managers and to possess more sophisticated organizational capabilities than is usually the case of single-plant firms. Managerial skills are likely to result in the more efficient organization of the innovation process, with a greater likelihood of obtaining patentable inventions.

Sixth, firms belonging to an industrial group are involved in a process of information sharing that is likely to generate positive external economies. As a consequence, also firms devoid of autonomous innovative capability may be able to extract patentable innovations from a combination of knowledge freely available within the group.

Seventh, export-oriented firms have to cope with international competition. Thus, in order to obtain larger shares of foreign markets they are forced to undertake innovative activities likely to result in more patents.

Eight, for more than twenty years Pavitt's (1984) classification of firms according to their attitude towards innovation has been one of the most widely used taxonomies of innovating firms. Since all but two (biomedical) of the firms in the sample used for the present study are in the scale-intensive, specialized supplier, and supplier dominated categories of Pavitt's scheme, the use of dummy variables for such categories may be helpful in identifying whether belonging to one category or another affects the likelihood of obtaining more patents.

3.3. Results from Panel Model Estimates

The availability of longitudinal data for 34 firms and 10 years allowed estimation of a panel model. Thus, the analysis started by postulating restrictions on the parameters, namely overall homogeneity of both slopes and intercepts. Since this hypothesis was not rejected by the data, the next step was to perform a pooled regression by means of Generalized Least Squares Estimators[14].

The functional form of the model was the following:

$$y_{it} = \alpha_{it}^* + \beta_{it}' \mathbf{x}_{it} + u_{it},$$ (1)

where i denotes the firms, t the years comprised in the analysis, α_{it}^* is a 1x1 scalar constant representing the effects of variables peculiar to the ith firms, $\beta_{it}' = (\beta_{1it}, \beta_{2it}, ..., \beta_{Kit})$ is a $1 \times K$ vector of constants, $\mathbf{x}_{it}' = (x_{1it}, x_{2it}, ..., x_{Kit})$ a $1 \times K$ vector of exogenous variables, the regressors employed in the analysis, and u_{it} is the error term with mean zero and variance σ_u^2.

The following specification (2) of the model was then tested:

$$PAT_{it} = \beta_0 + \beta_1 DIST_{it} + \beta_2 SIZE_{it} + \beta_3 PPE_{it} + \beta_4 SIZE_{it} + \beta_5 GOS_{it} + \beta_6 MULTI_{it} +$$
$$+ \beta_7 GROUP_{it} + \beta_8 EXP_{it} + \beta_9 SSUP_{it} + \beta_{10} SDOM_{it} + +\beta_{11} SINT_{it} + \varepsilon_{it}$$ (2)

where the index i represents firm ($i = 1,...,34$), the index t stands for year ($t = 1986,..., 1995$), and ε_{it} is the usual error term with usual properties. The results in Table 4 show a negative, although slightly significant, impact of location within an industrial district on patenting, and also larger firm size seems to be an impediment rather than a stimulus to patenting[15]. Conversely, belonging to an industrial group, a higher value of property, plant and equipment, and the fact that the firm operates with more than one plant are all factors that positively affect patenting. The negative and significant coefficients of the three dummy variables for Pavitt's taxonomy instead suggest that patenting is an activity more typical of science-based firms than of specialized supplier, supplier dominated, and scale intensive ones.

Table 4- Estimation results for model (2) 1986-1995

DEPENDENT VARIABLE: PAT (NUMBER OF PATENTS)			
Variables	Coeff.	Stand. Err.	Prob.
Intercept	4.078***	0.935	0.0000
DIST (Industrial district)	-0.552**	0.190	0.0040
SIZE (Number of employees)	-0.001*	0.000	0.0148
PPE (Property, plant and equipment)	6.09E-05***	9.19E-06	0.0000
ΔGOS (Gross Operating Surplus)	-0.025	0.032	0.4393
MULTI (Multi-plant)	2.262***	0.305	0.0000
GROUP (Industrial group)	0.271*	0.144	0.0614
EXP (Export)	-0.092	0.135	0.4966
SSUP (Specialized suppliers)	-3.362***	0.933	0.0004
SDOM (Supplier dominated)	-3.231***	0.926	0.0006
SINT (Scale intensive)	-4.137***	0.954	0.0000
Number of observations			*340*
F test			*21.137*
R^2 Adjusted			*0.373*

***, **, * mean statistically significant at 99%, 95%, and 90% confidence level, respectively.

In general, the results obtained from the panel estimates are consistent with the second hypothesis put forward in Section 3.1 above about the non-crucial role of location in industrial districts as a driver of innovation after the 1980s. This finding supports the idea that a transition from agglomeration to multi-location, a changed attitude towards patenting, the increasing irrelevance of the choice between a core and a periphery location, and the transformation of district industries in traded industries selling abroad are all factors that contributed to challenge the previous technological advantage of district firms[16].

4. CONCLUSIONS

The long-term evolution of industrial districts, in particular those in Emilia Romagna, has been punctuated by increasing enlargements of the type and number of activities carried out by firms belonging to this industrial agglomeration. What has remained unchanged is the circulation of information and the close relationships among firms that led to increasing inter- and infra-sectoral integration. In this connection, the emergence of Schumpeterian entrepreneurship and that of specialized suppliers of capital equipment in the 1960s, the advent of leading firms belonging to industrial groups during the late 1980s, and, likely, the efficient relocation of the most labor-intensive phases of the overall production process consequent upon the availability of more reliable devices for exchange of information, are the crucial events in the history of industrial districts in Emilia Romagna. The resulting "multi-located" district (as defined by Santarelli, 1988) of the last two decades is therefore nothing but a new form of industrial agglomeration in the age of globalization: whereas spatial concentration is no longer the most crucial factor enabling the prosperity of the modern district, its distinctive organizational features and the flows of information that it is able to set in motion are substantially unchanged. What Harrison (1994) saw as a point of strength of MNCs - namely, the ability to relocate manufacturing throughout the world to exploit diminishing tariff and transportation costs besides escaping increasing competition by low-wage countries - is now a point of strength also of industrial districts.

NOTES

[1] I am indebted to Thomas Brenner, Emanuele Giovannetti, Francesca Lotti, Roy Thurik, Marco Vivarelli, seminar participants at Max Planck Institute of Economics (Jena, September 2004), and, in particular, to Roberta Piergiovanni for their helpful suggestions; to Chiara Cassi for assistance in data collection and statistical computation. All remaining errors are my own.

[2] For a formal treatment of the potential ties between large firms and local economies, in particular in relation to knowledge exchanges, see Bellandi (2001).

[3] The importance of industrial groups as a new form of industrial organization in the Emilia Romagna region has been shown by Brioschi *et al.* (2002)

[4] The relationship between utilizers and producers of specialized industrial machinery is consistent with the results of Glaeser, Kallal, Scheinkman and Schleifer (1992), who stressed the importance of knowledge spillovers occurring *between* rather than *within* industries as a factor explaining the agglomeration in cities.

[5] On the importance of cooperative innovative activities within local clusters, cf. Fritsch (2004).

[6] As implied in Marshall's original formulation of "external economies" (Marshall, 1890), spillovers do not stem from producers of similar products but are related to the input-output or customer-supplier relationship that arise from interaction between firms producing specialized capital equipment and machinery and firms using those devices (Forni and Paba, 2002).

[7] Of the 32 largest producers of ceramic tiles in Italy, 30 are located in Emilia Romagna, either in the Sassuolo district or in the districts of Faenza and Imola.

[8] The largest producer of ceramic tiles in the Sassuolo district is Iris Ceramica. Set up quite recently, in 1961, this company attained market leadership thanks to direct control of production cycles and experience in advanced manufacturing technologies.

[9] This result is indirect indication of the heterogeneity among enterprises belonging to the same district. As shown by Rabellotti and Schmitz (1999), this heterogeneity can be found

in firm size, performance, degree of technological innovativeness, market segment, marketing strategy, links with other focal firms, use of the services of entrepreneurial associations, etc.

[10] In this connection, Santarelli and Sterlacchini (1990) have pointed out that small firms in traditional industries do not carry out structured R&D activities, but nonetheless devote considerable effort to improving their levels of innovative activity.

[11] This information was obtained from the database Infoimprese, provided by the Union of the Chambers of Commerce.

[12] For testing the predictions of Pavitt's taxonomy concerning firms' technological structure also Science Based firms were considered. However, as shown in Table 3, they represent the smallest sub-group of the sample in our study. Thus, the n-1 dummies used for taking into account Pavitt's taxonomy do not comprise this sub-group.

[13] As a consequence of the lower propensity of smaller firms to undertake those R&D activities which have been shown to result in patented innovations.

[14] Of course, several alternative econometric methods could have been employed, including the Poisson regression model and the negative binomial. However, econometric models based on count data would have required analysis also of companies with zero patents, for which balance sheet and other data were not forthcoming from the database.

[15] Although the coefficient of the SIZE variable is statistically significant only at the 90 percent confidence level. In any case, this result is consistent with the empirical regularity emerged from a number of studies concerning the independence of the firm's innovative intensity on the firm's size (cf. Klette and Kortum, 2004).

[16] This finding is also consistent with those by Becchetti and Castelli (2005) showing that adoption of ICT acts as a partial substitute for space and product relationships in firms which do nor benefit of local agglomeration economies

REFERENCES

Acs, Z. J., L. Anselin and A. Varga (2002), "Patents and Innovation Counts as Measures of Regional Production of new Knowledge", *Research Policy*, 31(7), 1069-1085.

Barba Navaretti, G., E. Santarelli and M. Vivarelli (2002), "The Role of Subsidies in Promoting Italian Joint Ventures in Least Developed and Transition Economies", *Applied Economics*, 34(12), 1562-1569.

Becattini, G. (1979), *Scienza economica e trasformazioni sociali*, Firenze, la Nuova Italia.

Becattini, G. (1990), "The Marshallian Industrial District as a Socio-economic Notion", in F. Pyke, G. Becattini and D. Sengenberger (eds.), *Industrial Districts and Inter-firm Cooperation in Italy*, Geneva, ILO.

Becchetti, L. and A. Castelli (2005) "Inside the Blackbox: Economic Performance and Technology Adoption when Space and Product Relationships Matter", *Rivista di Politica Economica*, 95(1-2), 137-176.

Bellandi, M. (2001), "Local Development and Embedded Large Firms", *Entrepreneurship & Regional Development*, 13(3), 189-210.

Biggiero, L. (2002), "The Location of Multinationals in Industrial Districts: Knowledge Transfer in Biomedicals", *Journal of Technology Transfer*, 27(1), 111-122.

Boari, C. and A. Lipparini (1999), "Networks within Industrial Districts: Organising Knowledge Creation and Transfer by Means of Moderate Hierarchies", *Journal of Management and Governance*, 3(3), 339-360.

Brenner, T. (2004), *Local Industrial Clusters, Existence, Emergence and Evolution*, London, Routledge.

Brioschi, F., M. S. Brioschi and G. Cainelli (2002), "From the Industrial District to the District Group: An Insight into the Evolution of Local Capitalism in Italy", *Regional Studies*, 36(9), 1052-2002.

Brusco, S. (1982), "The Emilian Model: Productive Decentralization and Social Integration", *Cambridge Journal of Economics*, 6(1), 167-184.

Brusco, S. (1986), "Small Firms and Industrial Districts: The Experience of Italy", *Economia Internazionale*, 39(2-3-4), 85-97.

Chiarvesio, M., E. Di Maria and S. Micelli (2004) "From Local Networks of SMEs to Virtual Districts? Evidence from Recent Trends in Italy", *Research Policy*, 33(10), 1509-1528.

CNEL/Ceris-Cnr (1997), *Innovazione, piccole imprese e distretti industriali*, Roma, CNEL.

Dei Ottati, G. (1994), "Trust Interlinking Transactions and Credit in the Industrial District", *Cambridge Journal of Economics*, 18(6), 529-546.

Forni, M. and S. Paba (2002), "Spillovers and the Growth of Local Industries", *Journal of Industrial Economics*, 50(2), 151-171.

Fritsch, M. (2004), "Cooperation and the Efficiency of Regional R&D Activities", *Cambridge Journal of Economics*, 28(6), 829-846.

Garofoli, G. (2002), "R&S nei distretti industriali e nei sistemi di piccola impresa", in Quadrio Curzio, A., M. Fortis and G.P. Galli (eds.), *La competitività dell'Italia. Scienza, ricerca, innovazione*, Milano, Edizioni Il Sole 24 Ore.

Glaeser, E., H. Kallal, J. Scheinkman and A. Schleifer (1992), "Growth of Cities", *Journal of Political Economy*, 100(6), 1126-1152.

Harrison, B. (1994), *Lean and Mean: The Changing Landscape of Corporate Power in the Age of Flexibility*, New York, Basic Books.

Klette, T. J. and S. Kortum (2004, "Innovating Firms and Aggregate Innovation", *Journal of Political Economy*, 112(5), 986-1018.

Krugman, P. (1991), *Geography and Trade*, Cambridge (MA), The MIT Press.

Lazerson, M. and G. Lorenzoni (1999), "Resisting Organizational Inertia: The Evolution of Industrial Districts", *Industrial and Corporate Change*, 3(3), 361-377.

Lichtman, B. (2002), "Regional Focus: Northern Italy", EMDM, *Medical Devicelink*, http://www.devicelink.com/emdm/archive/02/09/004.html.

Lipparini, A. and A. Lomi (1999), "Interorganizational Relations in the Modena Biomedical Industry: A Case Study in Local Economic Development", in A. Grandori (ed.), *Interfirm Networks. Organization and Industrial Competitiveness*, London, Routledge, 120-150.

Lorenzoni, G. and O. Ornati (1988), "Constellation of Firms and New Ventures", *Journal of Business Venturing*, 3(1), 41-57.

Lorenzoni, G. and C. W. F. Baden-Fuller (1995), "Creating a Strategic Center to Manage a Web of Partners", *California Management Review*, 37(2), 146-163.

Markusen, A. (1996), "Sticky Places in Slippery Space: A Typology of Industrial Districts", *Economic Geography*, 72(3), 293-313.

Marshall, A. (1890), *Principles of Economics*, London, MacMillan.

Meech, J. F. and S. Marsh (2003), "Social Factors in E-commerce Personalization", Ottawa, Institute for Information Technology, National Research Council of Canada Montreal Road.

Meyer-Stamer, J., C. Maggi and S. Seibel (2001), "Improving Upon Nature: Creating Competitive Advantage in Ceramic Tile Clusters in Italy, Spain and Brazil", *INEF Report* N 54, Duisburg: Institut für Entwicklung und Frieden der Gerhard-Mercator-Universität Duisburg.

Pavitt, K. (1984), "Sectoral Patterns of Technical Change: Towards a Taxonomy and a Theory", *Research Policy*, 13(4), 343-373.

Piergiovanni, R. and E. Santarelli (1996), "Analyzing Literature-based Innovation Output Indicators: The Italian Experience", *Research Policy*, 25(5), 689-711.

Porter, M. E. (2003), "The Economic Performance of Regions", *Regional Studies*, 37(6&7), 549-578.

Prometeia (2002), *Analisi dei microsettori - Piastrelle*, Bologna, Prometeia.

Rabellotti, R. and H. Schmitz (1999), "The Internal Heterogeneity of Industrial Districts in Italy, Brazil and Mexico", *Regional Studies*, 33(2), 97-108.

R&I (2001), *Il distretto biomedicale modenese*, Modena, mimeo.

Rocco, E., T. A. Finholt, E. C. Hofer and J. D. Herbsleb (2001), "Out of Sight, Short of Trust", paper presented at the Founding Conference of the European Academy of Management, Barcelona.

Russo, M. (1985), "Technical Change and the Industrial District: The Role of Interfirm Relations in the Growth and Transformation of Ceramic Tile Production in Italy", *Research Policy*, 14(3), 329-343.

Santarelli, E. (1988), "Distretti multi-localizzati e innovazione nell'industria italiana", *Economia Marche*, 7(2), 161-208.

Santarelli, E. and A. Sterlacchini (1990), "Innovation, Formal vs. Informal R&D, and Firm Size. Some Evidence from Italian Manufacturing Firms", *Small Business Economics*, 2(3), 223-228.

Williamson, O. (1985), *The Economic Institutions of Capitalism: Firms, Markets, Relational Contracting*, New York, The Free Press.

Chapter 9
INNOVATION PREMIUM AND THE SURVIVAL OF ENTREPRENEURIAL FIRMS IN THE NETHERLANDS

Elena Cefis
University of Bergamo, and Utrecht School of Economics, Utrecht University

Orietta Marsili
Rotterdam School of Management, Erasmus University

1. INTRODUCTION[1]

This study explores the effects of innovation on the survival of manufacturing firms in different technological environments in the Netherlands. Previous studies have related the survival of firms to firm-specific characteristics and industry features. Several studies identify firm size and age as determinants of survival. It is accepted as a stylised fact that increasing age and size exert a positive effect on the likelihood that firms will survive (Geroski, 1995). Other studies have focused on the role of innovative activities, looking at the intensity of R&D expenditure (Hall, 1987; Esteve Perez *et al.*, 2004) and indicators of innovative performance (Cefis and Marsili, 2005). In general, these studies find that innovative activities are beneficial for firm survival, regardless of the industry in which firms are active. Across sectors, a number of variables have been associated with the likelihood of survival, such as market size and growth rates (Mata and Portugal, 1994), the characteristics of technology (Audretsch, 1995; Agarwal, 1996; Agarwal, 1998) and the life cycle (Agarwal and Audretsch, 2001). These studies emphasise the heterogeneity of sectors and how the effects of firm specific characteristics vary across them (Audretsch, Santarelli and Vivarelli, 1999).

In this study we analyse the determinants of firms' survival probability by combining firm level and industry level features. We examine the role of innovation within the firm in shaping its survival probability, and contrast this effect across different technological environments; specifically we compare innovative and non-innovative firms in high- and low-tech industries. In addition, we control for the characteristics of the firm, size and age, which are generally pointed to in the literature as being important. Thus, we distinguish between entrepreneurial and established firms in an industry.

The empirical analysis combines economic and demographic data from the Business Register of all firms active in the Netherlands with data on innovation derived from the second Community Innovation Survey (CIS-2). Integration of these two datasets produced a sample of 3,275 firms for which information on innovation, number of employees, date of entry, date of exit and industrial sector were available. The survival probability of a firm was estimated using an approach based on Transition Probability Matrices. We then statistically tested for the significance of differences in survival probability between different categories of firms.

Our results show that, as expected, entrepreneurial firms are more exposed to the risk of failure than established firms, confirming earlier results of the effects of firm age and size on the likelihood of survival. However, entrepreneurial firms benefit relatively more than established firms from a technology rich environment, which in general favours survival. Also, in low-tech industries entrepreneurial firms that innovate have significantly higher (58%) chances of survival than non-innovative firms. In other words, the innovation premium for survival is highest for entrepreneurial firms in low-tech industries.

This study is organised as follows. Section 2 focuses on the determinants of firm survival identified in the related literature. Sections 3 and 4 respectively present the data used in the empirical analysis, and the survival analysis methodology. We discuss the results of the analysis in Section 5. Section 6 concludes.

2. THE DETERMINANTS OF FIRM SURVIVAL

It is well known that the survival probability of firms varies across industrial sectors (Geroski, 1995; Audretsch, Santarelli and Vivarelli, 1999; Audretsch, Houweling and Thurik, 2000). The survival differences across industrial sectors vary less over time when compared to more volatile entry rates. This fact has been interpreted as evidence that barriers to survival are more effective than barriers to entry (Geroski, 1995). These barriers to survival have been related to traditional market structure variables, such as the presence of scale economies, other cost advantages of established firms, and the growth rate of sector specific demand (Audretsch, 1991; Audretsch and Mamhood, 1994; Dunne and Hughes, 1994; Mata and Portugal, 1994; Wagner, 1994). Some studies have highlighted the role of technological conditions in an industry as a determinant of firm survival (Audretsch, 1991; 1995; Agarwal, 1998).

There are two interpretations of the relationship between the level of technological intensity in a sector and the survival probability of firms active in that sector (Agarwal, 1996). One argument maintains that a fast changing environment hampers firm survival. Geroski (1995) argues that it is the ability of new firms to learn about the environment and to adapt their strategies to changes in it, which ultimately determine their chances of survival. Because of the uncertainty associated with innovation (Ericson and Pakes, 1995), the risk of exit is higher for firms in high-tech sectors. Consistent with this interpretation, Mahmood (1992) observes greater hazard rates for new establishments in high-tech industries than in low-tech industries. Also, in high-tech industries the hazard rate is more sensitive to external factors such as scale economies and the intensity of R&D expenditure in the sector. Thus, high levels of innovative activity in a sector render the survival probability of a firm lower and more constrained by structural barriers, such as scale economies.

The second argument sees the technological activities of a sector as being a source of opportunity for innovation for new entrants. Highly innovative sectors may enable new firms to introduce new products and successfully compete with established firms. This increases the likelihood of survival of new firms. In addition, in a fast changing environment the cumulative processes of learning within established firms may be less relevant, and may facilitate the survival of new firms (Agarwal, 1996). In this interpretation, it is not only the existence of a general pool of technological opportunities that matters for survival, but also the ease with which these opportunities can be exploited by new or established firms (Winter, 1984). The 'evolutionary' approach to industrial dynamics characterises these conditions in terms of a 'technological regime'. Following Schumpeter's insight, Nelson and Winter (1982) distinguish two opposing regimes: an entrepreneurial regime (also labelled Schumpeter Mark I) in which new firms are the main drivers of innovation, and a routinised regime (or Schumpeter Mark II) in which established firms are the main sources of innovation. In elaborating Nelson and Winter's model, Marsili (2001) shows that, in general, the chances of survival of established firms increase with the level of technological opportunity within an industry; survival prospects are lower when opportunities can be exploited by entrant firms (that is, when technological entry barriers are low). In addition, the effect is conditional on the age of the firm: survival of young firms increases and survival of older firms decreases as the level of technological opportunity for entrants increases (Dosi, Marsili, Orsenigo, Salvatore, 1995).

Following the 'evolutionary' approach, Audretsch and Mahmood (1994 and 1995), in their study of U.S. manufacturing, separate the two components by taking the total innovation rate in an industry (as a measure of the general level of technological opportunity) and the relative innovation rate of small firms (as indicative of the presence of a an 'entrepreneurial' as opposed to a 'routinised' regime). After controlling for the latter effect, they show that the likelihood of failure of new establishments is greater in highly innovative environments, confirming earlier results where this factor was not controlled for. Thus, these results support the hypothesis that high-tech sectors, because of their high degree of uncertainty, have a negative effect on the survival probabilities of firms.

Audretsch (1995) refines this evidence by demonstrating that the effects of technological conditions vary with firm age. In more innovative industries, new firms have a lower probability of survival within a limited period after entry; but, after a certain number of years (8 years in the cited study) after entry, their probability of survival increases. Similar effects can be found for the level of innovation of small firms in the industry, which approximates the 'entrepreneurial' or 'routinised' nature of the innovation regime. When based on firms' experience, the effects of technology on survival are the opposite to those for newly created firms. Technological opportunities influence firm survival relative to whether the firm is an entrepreneurial or an established firm. High-tech industries negatively affect the survival of newly created firms, but favour the survival of incumbents (Audretsch, Houweling and Thurik, 2000).

However, Agarwal's (1996) empirical study of U.S. manufacturing produces contrasting results to Audretsch (1995). Agarwal classifies a set of industries into the five stages of the product life cycle (PLC) and into technical and non-technical industry categories, based on the intensity of R&D expenditure. She finds that intense technological activities favour the survival of new firms in the 4 years after entry, while this advantage tends to disappear by 12 years after entry. In addition, she shows there is a non-linear relationship between firm age, technological activity and survival. Across all five stages of the PLC, 'infant' firms (6 or less years old) are exposed to greater risk of failure in non-technical industries. In contrast, 'incumbent' firms (older than 6 years) encounter greater risk of failure in technical industries. Focusing on firm size, Agarwal (1998) observed that small firms have greater likelihood of survival in high-tech than low-tech industries. In sum, technological activities seem to enhance the survival probability of new and small firms, while they tend to limit the survival chances of incumbent firms (Agarwal, 1996; Agarwal, 1998).

Despite the role attributed to the technological environment for a firm's survival, there are few studies linking survival to the innovative activities carried out by the firm. Introducing new products and processes is considered to be a key source of competitive advantage in the market (Schumpeter, 1942; Baumol, 2002). With regard to the innovative effort of firms, investing more intensively in R&D activities positively influences their survival prospects (Hall, 1987; Esteve Perez *et al.*, 2004). With regard to innovative performance, in an earlier study (Cefis and Marsili, 2005), we show that innovation does indeed enhance the survival probability of a firm and for young and small firms in the Netherlands, this effect is especially evident.

Our contribution to this field of the literature is to analyse the interaction between firm specific effects of innovation on survival according to the different levels of technological intensity in the external environment.

3. DATA

This study is based on two micro-economic databases collected by the Central Bureau of Statistics Netherlands (CBS): the Business Register database and the CIS-2 in the Netherlands. By combining these datasets, we were able to integrate at firm level, comprehensive data on innovation and the demography of firms.

The Business Register database consists of all firms registered in the Netherlands for fiscal purposes. The database reports number of employees, sector of activity and the date expressed as month of entry and exit in the datasets. Because the dataset includes all registered firms in the population, these dates can be considered as close approximations of the actual dates of entry and exit of firms. For compatibility with the CIS-2, we considered all manufacturing firms present in the Business Register at year 1996. The number of firms in the Business Register at 1996, including firms with zero employees, that is self-employment, is 61,177.

The second wave of the CIS provides information on innovation activities in the Netherlands for the period 1994–1996. This survey includes private sector firms with at least 10 employees. The CIS firms were extracted from those present in the Business Register in order to constitute a stratified random sample, based on size class, region and industrial sector at the 2-digit Standard Industrial Classification (SIC) code level. The number of manufacturing sector respondents to CIS-2 was 3,299 firms, with a response rate of 71 percent.

Our variable of interest is the survival probability of a firm. To estimate this variable, we use the date of exit of a firm from the population of manufacturing firms in the Business Register. The exit date is expressed in months and ranges from January 1996 to December 2003. The dataset thus covers 96 months of possible existence. For each month, we built a dummy variable that was equal to 1 if the firm existed in the database and 0 otherwise.

The first condition that we want to relate to survival probability is the technological environment in which a firm is active. On the basis of the SIC code, each firm is assigned to two broad areas of activity: high-tech manufacturing or low-tech manufacturing. We thus adopt the OECD (2001) classification of industries based on level of technological intensity.

Given some broad technological conditions, our interest is to establish whether the innovative activity of a firm enhances its chances of survival, and whether such an environment shapes this effect. To measure innovation at firm level, we use the CIS-2 for the Netherlands. For this CIS sample of firms, we distinguish between innovators and non-innovators. An innovator is defined as a firm that has introduced in the period 1994–1996 either a product or a process innovation. These variables reflect the respondent's subjective perception of 'being an innovator' and may lead to an overestimation of the actual innovative activity of a firm.

As we assume that technology, and the innovative activity may have different impacts on the survival probability, depending on the age and size of a firm, we built two opposite categories of firms. We define 'entrepreneurial' firms as those that, at 1996, are between 0 and 4 years old (where the age 0 identifies the firms that have entered during the year 1996), and have less than 50 employees. They are both young and small firms. We define 'established' firms those that, at 1996, are 5 or more years old and have more than 50 employees. They are both old and large firms. Firm age and size are derived from the Business Register of the population. The estimate of firm age relies on the entry date, while firm size is measured by number of employees, including the 0 value of self-employment.

By matching the two datasets, we are able to link innovation at the firm level (from the CIS-2 dataset) to firm performance, namely the survival probability (as estimated from the Business Register of the population), while also controlling for the effects of different typologies of firms (entrepreneurial and established) and industries (high-tech and low-tech manufacturing) (both derived from the Business Register). The resulting dataset comprises 3,275 firms.

Table 1 reports the descriptive statistics of the different sets of firms used in the analysis. Firms in low-tech sectors are on average (both mean and median) smaller than firms in high-tech sectors independent of the category of firms reported in Table 1. Innovators are of larger size than non-innovators, both in low-tech and high-tech industries. These characteristics are in line with the more general observation that innovators are larger than non-innovators (Cefis and Marsili, 2004).

4. METHODOLOGY

We used a non-parametric approach based on Transition Probability Matrices to analyse the survival probabilities among different groups of firms. We measure survival probability as the firm probability of remaining in the state in which the firm actually exists, while the probability of exiting the market is given by the probability to go from the state of existence to the one of non-existence.

Table 1 - Descriptive statistics of the number of employees of manufacturing firms at 1996 by sample and industry group

	N	%	Mean	Std. Dev.	Skewness	Kurtosis	Median
ALL FIRMS IN BR							
Low-tech	49,119	80.8	14.2	105.4	53.1	5,205.9	2
High-Tech	11,673	19.2	27.3	395.2	82.6	7,880.3	2
ALL FIRMS IN BR WITH AT LEAST 10 EMPLOYEES							
Low-tech	9,161	74.7	66.4	237.0	24.4	1,067.4	21
High-Tech	3,099	25.3	96.7	762.8	43.0	2,124.3	27
ALL FIRMS IN CIS-2							
Low-tech	2,279	69.6	108.9	228.4	9.9	146.7	52
High-Tech	996	30.4	136.0	322.8	7.6	72.2	59
INNOVATORS IN CIS-2							
Low-tech	1,322	63.7	132.7	249.9	9.2	128.2	69
High-Tech	753	36.3	151.4	327.4	6.3	47.7	67
NON INNOVATORS IN CIS-2							
Low-tech	957	79.8	76.1	190.0	11.7	194.0	33
High-Tech	243	20.3	88.2	303.9	12.9	185.5	35

Source: Business Register (BR), Second Community Innovation Survey (CIS-2).

Among the firms that were in existence when the second wave of CIS data were collected, namely 1996, this being the finite population of firms, at each point in time (after 1996) there is a cross-section distribution of firms that exist and firms that have ceased to exist. The objective is to describe the evolution of this distribution over time, to enable the intra-distribution mobility of firms to be analysed. The intra-distribution mobility gives information about the firm's relative situation, and its movement over time. To study the evolution of this distribution it is necessary to hypothesise a law of motion for the cross-section distribution within a more formal structure. Let F_t denote the distribution of firms at time t; and let us describe the evolution of the distribution using the law of motion:

$$F_{t+m} = P \cdot F_t \qquad (1)$$

where P maps one distribution into another, and tracks where points in F_t end up in F_{t+m}. Equation (1) is a useful first step for analysing the dynamics of $\{ F_t \}$. Operator P of equation (1) can be approximated by assuming a finite state space for firms $S=\{s_1 \; s_2 \; ... \; s_r\}$, where $s_i(i=1,...,r)$ are the possible states. In this case P is simply a Transition Probability Matrix (TPM). P encodes the relevant information about mobility and persistence of firms within the cross section distributions. Therefore, the one-step transition probability is defined by:

$$p_{ij} = P(X_{t+m} = j | X_t = i) \qquad (2)$$

where t denotes discrete moments of time and m different discrete transition periods.

The TPM P is the matrix with p_{ij} as elements measuring the probability of moving from state i to state j in one period m. (Hoel, Port and Stone, 1987).

The focus of our analysis is the probability of firm survival. Therefore, we consider a state space constituted by two states identified by the condition of existence of the firm. More precisely, the first state is defined as the non-existing state (state 0), in which firms are non-active in the market (they have in fact exited the market), and the second is defined as the existing state in which firms are actually present in the market (state 1). The transition probabilities between the two states provide information useful for analysing survival since they measure the probability that a firm remains in existence or exits the market in a particular period.

We estimate the following probabilities:

$$\hat{P}(X_{t+m} = 1 | X_t = 1) = \hat{p} \qquad (3)$$

$$\hat{P}(X_{t+m} = 0 | X_t = 1) = 1 - \hat{p} \qquad (4)$$

The probabilities 3 and are computed on different period lengths (for different m, ranging from 12 to 84 months). These different transition periods allow us to capture the dynamics of the survival probability of firms, and to study how it evolves over time.

It should be noted that in order to perform the persistence analysis we have assumed that firms are homogeneous. In this context, heterogeneity among firms, due to belonging to different sectors or having different sizes or ages, is accounted for by breaking down the overall sample into subsamples according to industrial classification, and size and age classes. Nevertheless, in our subsamples firms are assumed to be homogeneous and, using our methodology, it is not possible to control for heterogeneity at the firm level.

We conducted the analysis dividing the sample into entrepreneurial and established firms, and according to whether they were categorised as high-tech or low-tech manufacturing.

In order to test whether the differences between two estimated probabilities were statistically significant, we applied the following test. Let $\hat{P}_1$ and $\hat{P}_2$ be the survival probabilities estimated in the samples of size n_1 and n_2 (for example the survival probabilities for innovators and non-innovators in the CIS) drawn from their respective populations with probabilities p_1 and p_2. The null hypothesis is that there is no difference between the survival probabilities of the populations, that is $H_0 : p_1 = p_2$, and thus the samples are really drawn from the same population with survival probability p. The test statistic is the difference in the estimated probabilities: $\hat{P}_1 - \hat{P}_2$. Given the fact that the size of our samples is sufficiently large (with at least $n > 80$), under the null hypothesis, the standardised variable

$$Z = \frac{\hat{P}_1 - \hat{P}_2 - 0}{\sigma_{\hat{P}_1 - \hat{P}_2}} \quad \text{is approximately distributed N(0,1), where}$$

$$\sigma_{\hat{P}_1 - \hat{P}_2} = \sqrt{\frac{p_1(1 - p_1)}{n_1} + \frac{p_2(1 - p_2)}{n_2}}$$

Given that p_1 and p_2. are unknown and for the null hypothesis $p_1 = p_2 = p$, the estimator of $\sigma_{\hat{P}_1 - \hat{P}_2}$ is

$$S_{\hat{P}_1 - \hat{P}_2} = \sqrt{P(1 - P)\left(\frac{1}{n_1} + \frac{1}{n_2}\right)}$$

where P is the estimator of the survival probability of the population given by the arithmetic weighted average of p_1 and p_2:

$$P = \frac{n_1 P_1 + n_2 P_2}{n_1 + n_2}.$$

We tested the differences in the survival probabilities of different subgroups of firms and the test results (in parentheses) are reported in Tables 2 and 3.

5. EMPIRICAL RESULTS

We first examine the differences in survival probability of the firms that responded to the CIS-2 of high-tech manufacturing and low-tech manufacturing. Here we focus on the general 'structural' conditions for the survival of entrepreneurial and established firms independent of their specific innovative behaviour.

As expected, in general survival probability is higher for established than for entrepreneurial firms. Indeed, the percentage differences in survival probability between established and entrepreneurial firms increases from 3.1 in the first year to 22.2 in the last year. This shows that firm age and firm size have a positive effect on the survival probability. An earlier study carried out for the entire Dutch manufacturing sector that explored the relationship between firm survival, age and size in more detail, produced similar evidence.

As Figure 1 shows, survival probability is higher in high-tech than in low-tech industries. In general, this holds for both entrepreneurial and established firms, and more particularly, the difference between high tech and low-tech industries increases over time and is higher for entrepreneurial firms than for established firms. Survival probability for an entrepreneurial firm in the high-tech sector is 3.3 percent higher than in the low-tech sector over a one-year period, and 19.8 percent higher over a 7 year period. For an established firm, the differences are smaller, 1.7 percent and 12.7 percent respectively (see Table 2 for the statistical test of significance for the differences in survival probability between high-tech and low-tech industries)[2]. Therefore, while the survival probability for entrepreneurial firms is generally lower than for established firms, entrepreneurial firms benefit more from a high intensity technological environment than do established firms.

We next examine survival in relation to innovators versus non-innovators. In particular, we are interested in comparing the innovation premium between high-tech and low-tech manufacturing, and whether the role of innovation as a strategy for survival differs according to technological intensity of the environment. In addition, we contrast entrepreneurial firms and established firms to see whether a different pattern emerges. At first glance, innovation can be seen to have a positive effect on survival probability. However, its magnitude varies according to the technological characteristics of the environment.

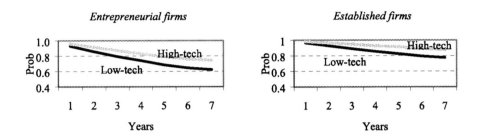

Entrepreneurial firms   Established firms

FIGURE 1 - SURVIVAL PROBABILITIES IN HIGH- AND LOW-TECH INDUSTRIES

Figure 2 depicts the effects of the technology on the survival probabilities of innovators and non-innovators. The survival probabilities of entrepreneurial and established firms are plotted according to their innovative status in low-tech and high-tech industries. Among the entrepreneurial firms, innovators do not seem to be affected by sectoral differences in their survival probability, while non-innovators in high-tech sectors have better survival probability than those in low-tech sectors. It should be noted that for entrepreneurial innovators in the high-tech sector, the chances of survival decrease over the long term, falling to below the level for low-tech sectors. For established firms, those firms in high-tech sectors have higher chances of survival regardless of whether they are innovators or non-innovators.

Table 2 - Differences in survival probability between high-tech and low-tech industries (z-values in parentheses)

| | Number of months | | | | | | |
	12	24	36	48	60	72	84
Entrepreneurial firm	0.028	0.053	0.073	0.082	0.105	0.115	0.124
	(1.76)	(3.46)	(4.99)	(5.84)	(7.87)	(9.05)	(10.43)
Established firm	0.016	0.038	0.057	0.072	0.089	0.101	0.098
	(2.70)	(6.21)	(9.58)	(2.36)	(15.71)	(18.31)	(18.36)

$|z| > 2.58$ statistically significant at 1 percent; $|z| > 1.96$ statistically significant at 5 percent; $|z| > 1.64$ statistically significant at 10 percent.

The next step in the analysis is to establish whether technology environments shape, not only the survival probabilities of firms, but also the magnitude of the effect of innovation on these probabilities. For this purpose, we calculate the innovation premium (the difference in the survival probabilities between innovators and non-innovators) for entrepreneurial and established firms according to the different technological environments. In low-tech industries, innovation is crucial for enhancing survival chances. The innovation premium is particularly relevant for entrepreneurial firms, and is shown to be positive and increasing over the seven year period. From Figure 3 it can be seen that differences in the levels of probabilities are 0.060 over one year, and 0.282 over seven years (see Table 3 for the statistical significance of these differences). This shows that the survival probability is 6.7 percent higher for innovators than for non-innovators in the first year, and 58.0 percent higher in the last year of observation. The effect of innovation is always positive, but less pronounced for established firms and follows a non-monotonic increase along the years.

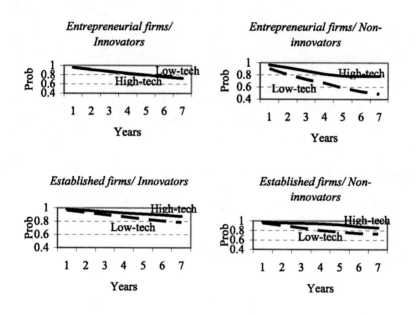

FIGURE 2 - SURVIVAL PROBABILITIES OF ESTABLISHED AND ENTREPRENEURIAL FIRMS BY INNOVATION.

In high-tech sectors, the survival probabilities of innovators and non-innovators are barely distinguishable, either for established or entrepreneurial firms. Figure 3 depicts the two curves of the differences in the levels of probabilities fluctuating around zero, meaning that the innovation premium is very small in the case of both an entrepreneurial and an established firm. Indeed, these differences are not statistically significant, except for the longest transition period in which the difference is negative and significant at 1 percent (see Table 3). In fact, the innovation premium for entrepreneurial firms becomes negative in the 'long run'. As Figure 3 shows, over 6 and 7 years, in high-tech sectors non-innovators have higher chances of survival than innovators. This counterintuitive result might be due to the fact that entrepreneurial innovative firms are more likely to be acquired by other firms than entrepreneurial non-innovative firms. This effect appears over the long run because it can require a certain period of observation to determine whether a new and small firm is successful or not. Therefore, the acquiring firm may 'wait and see' before making the decision to acquire a new and innovative firm. Because we are not able to distinguish among different modes of exit in our current dataset, we cannot conclude if the negative sign of the difference in probabilities reflects a real negative premium of innovation or is instead the effect of the acquisition process.

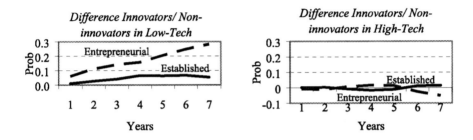

FIGURE 3 - INNOVATION PREMIUM OF ESTABLISHED AND ENTREPRENEURIAL FIRMS.

Table 3 - Differences in survival probability between innovators and non-innovators (z-values in parentheses)

	Number of months						
	12	24	36	48	60	72	84
HIGH-TECH							
Entrepreneurial firm	-0.008	-0.010	0.008	0.017	0.014	-0.026	**-0.051**
	(-0.36)	(-0.44)	(0.35)	(0.78)	(0.64)	(-1.25)	(-2.62)
Established firm	0.002	0.003	-0.008	-0.016	-0.011	0.013	0.015
	(0.13)	(0.24)	(-0.62)	(-1.28)	(-0.94)	(1.04)	(1.25)
LOW-TECH							
Entrepreneurial firm	**0.060**	**0.112**	**0.141**	**0.157**	**0.205**	**0.247**	**0.282**
	(3.08)	(5.93)	(7.91)	(9.39)	(12.86)	(16.53)	(20.11)
Established firm	0.010	**0.027**	**0.042**	**0.066**	**0.063**	**0.067**	**0.053**
	(1.06)	(2.89)	(4.62)	(7.52)	(7.49)	(8.19)	(6.72)

$|z| > 2.58$ statistically significant at 1 percent; $|z| > 1.96$ statistically significant at 5 percent; $|z| > 1.64$ statistically significant at 10 percent. Differences significant at 10 percent are in bold

6. CONCLUSIONS

In this study we examined the difference in survival probability between innovators and non-innovators, which we label the 'innovation premium' for survival, for different types of firms and technological environments. In particular, we compared the innovation premiums for high-tech and low-tech manufacturing to discover whether innovation plays a more important role as a strategy for survival in a rapidly changing environment than in a slowly changing environment. In addition, we analysed whether different patterns emerge when we contrast entrepreneurial firms and established firms, and assuming that innovation plays a distinct role for the two categories of firms.

We carried out an empirical analysis of the survival probabilities with an approach based on TPM. Using data from the Business Register of the population of manufacturing firms in the Netherlands and the CIS-2, we estimated the survival probabilities for different categories of firms. These categories were based on firm age and size, firm specific innovative performance, and industry specific technology intensity.

Among the group of established firms, we observed that firms with the highest survival probabilities are those active in technology intensive environments, regardless of whether they are innovators or non-innovators. On the other hand, in low-tech sectors being an innovator is a decisive factor in firm survival, increasing survival probability by 7.2 percent. This result suggests that the highest premium in survival for an established firm (whether an innovator or not) lies in being active in a high-tech sector. Thus, to increase survival probability, innovation must be complemented by firm specific organisational and commercial capabilities.

Our results show that for entrepreneurial firms it is crucial to either be an innovator or at least to be active in a high-tech sector; in a low-tech sector, innovative activity is a "matter of life or death". Indeed, innovation increases the survival probability of entrepreneurial firms in low-tech sectors by 58 percent compared to non-innovative firms. This is the highest innovation premium amongst all the categories of firms and sectors studied.

NOTES

[1] The empirical part of this research was carried out at the Centre for Research of Economic Microdata at Statistics Netherlands. The views expressed in this paper are those of the authors and do not necessarily reflect the policies of Statistics Netherlands. Support from the University of Bergamo (grant ex 60%, n. 60CEFI03, Dept. of Economics) is gratefully acknowledged.
[2] Table 2 reports the difference in the level of survival probability and its statistical significance. In the text, we also refer to the percentage variation in probability.

REFERENCES

Agarwal, R. (1996), "Technological Activity and Survival of Firms", *Economics Letters*, 52(1), 101-108.

Agarwal, R. (1998), "Small Firm Survival and Technological Activity", *Small Business Economics*, 11(3), 215-224.

Agarwal, R. and D. B. Audretsch (2001), "Does Entry Size Matter? The Impact of the Life Cycle and Technology on Firm Survival", *Journal of Industrial Economics*, 49(1), 21-43.

Audretsch, D. B. (1991), "New-firm Survival and the Technological Regime", *Review of Economics and Statistics*, 73(3), 441-450.

Audretsch, D. B. (1995), "Innovation, Growth and Survival", *International Journal of Industrial Organization*, 13(4), 441-457.

Audretsch, D. B., P. Houweling and A. R. Thurik (2000), "Firm Survival in the Netherlands", *Review of Industrial Organization*, 16(1), 1-11.

Audretsch, D. B. and T. Mahmood (1994), "The Rate of Hazard Confronting new Firms and Plants in U.S. Manufacturing", *Review of Industrial Organization*, 9(1), 41-56.

Audretsch, D. B. and T. Mahmood (1995), "New Firm Survival: New Results Using a Hazard Function", *Review of Economics and Statistics*, 77(1), 97-103.

Audretsch, D. B., E. Santarelli and M. Vivarelli (1999), "Start-up Size and Industrial Dynamics: Some Evidence from Italian Manufacturing", *International Journal of Industrial Organization*, 17(7), 965-983.

Baumol, W. J. (2002), *Free Market Innovation Machine: Analyzing the Growth Miracle of Capitalism*, Princeton, Princeton University Press.

Cefis, E. and O. Marsili (2004), "Survivor: The Role of Innovation in Firm's Survival", Working Paper of the T. Koopmans Institute, USE, Utrecht University, No. 03-18.

Cefis, E. and O. Marsili (2005), "A Matter of Life and Death: Innovation and Firm Survival", *Industrial and Corporate Change*, 14(6), 1-26.

Dosi, G., O. Marsili, L. Orsenigo and R. Salvatore (1995), "Learning, Market Selection and the Evolution of Industrial Structures", *Small Business Economics*, 7(6), 411-436.

Dunne, P. and A. Hughes (1994), "Age, Size, Growth and Survival: U.K. Companies in the 1980s", *Journal of Industrial Economics*, 42(2), 115-139.

Ericson, R. and A. Pakes (1995), "Markov-perfect Industry Dynamics: A Framework for Empirical Work", *Review of Economic Studies*, 62(1), 53-82.

Esteve Perez, S., A. Sanchis LLopis and J. -A. Sanchis LLopis (2004), "The Determinants of Survival of Spanish Manufacturing Firms", *Review of Industrial Organization*, 25(3), 251-273.

Geroski, P. A. (1995), "What do We Know about Entry?", *International Journal of Industrial Organization*, 13(5), 421-440.

Hall, B. H. (1987), "The Relationship between Firm Size and Firm Growth in the U.S. Manufacturing Sector", *Journal of Industrial Economics*, 35(4), 583-606.

Hoel P. G., S. C. Port and C. J. Stone (1987), *Introduction to Stochastic Processes*, Prospect Heights (Illinois), Waveland Press, Inc..

Mahmood, T. (1992), "Does the Hazard Rate for New Plants Vary between Low- and High-tech Industries?", *Small Business Economics*, 4(2), 201-209.

Marsili, O. (2001), *The Anatomy and Evolution of Industries: Technological Change and Industrial Dynamics*, Cheltenham and Northampton, Edward Elgar.

Mata, J. and P. Portugal (1994), "Life Duration of New Firms", *Journal of Industrial Economics*, 42(3), 227-245.

Nelson, R. R. and S. G. Winter (1982), *An Evolutionary Theory of Economic Change*, Cambridge (MA), Belknap Press of Harvard University Press.

OECD (2001), *Science, Technology, and Industry*, Paris, OECD Publishing.

Schumpeter, J. A. (1942), *Capitalism, Socialism and Democracy*, New York, Harper & Row.

Wagner, J. (1994), "The Post-entry Performance of New Small Firms in German Manufacturing Industries", *Journal of Industrial Economics*, 42(2), 141-154.

Winter, S. G. (1984), "Schumpeterian Competition in Alternative Technological Regimes", *Journal of Economic Behavior and Organization*, 5(3-4), 287-320.

Chapter 10
FOREIGN PRESENCE, TECHNICAL EFFICIENCY AND FIRM SURVIVAL IN GREECE: A SIMULTANEOUS EQUATION MODEL WITH LATENT VARIABLES APPROACH

Helen Louri
Department of Economics, Athens University of Economics and Business

Costas Peppas
Department of Economics, Athens University of Economics and Business

Efthymios Tsionas
Department of Economics, Athens University of Economics and Business

1. INTRODUCTION

One of the most interesting issues in the literature of applied industrial organization is firm entry. The procedure of entry is important for the evolution of markets because it affects their structure, and hence the degree of competition and the ensuing profits and consumer welfare[1]. Drawing from this literature research interest in recent years has moved towards the factors that affect firm survival. Numerous studies took into consideration different firm level characteristics such as age, size, location, profitability, leverage, liquidity, as well as sectoral characteristics including market concentration, capital intensity, level of technology and more recently the presence of foreign firms.

The impacts of foreign presence are ambiguous. The benefits include the inflow of superior technical knowledge that is adapted by new firms and leads to increases in local firms' productivity and performance. These spillover effects can come through employment turnover, direct contact of foreign companies with local agents, increased competition between the more productive foreign firms and the less productive domestic rivals or reverse engineering. The costs stem from the fact that foreign firms produce on a lower cost curve than local industry, thereby crowding out more costly domestic rivals. The intense competition that foreign firms bring along may also increase failure probabilities in their markets, if other firms are not equipped to face such a strong competitive pressure.

In addition, interest was directed towards exploring the role of efficiency on the probability of firm survival. Technical efficiency concerns either the production function or the cost function. From the production function point of view a firm is technically efficient if it produces the maximum output possible given the level of inputs. From the cost function point of view a firm is technically efficient if it produces with the minimum cost given the level of output and input prices. Whichever way technical efficiency is measured, it is thought to affect firm performance and hence survival.

The scope of our paper is to explain how firm and sectoral level characteristics such as size, age, financial profile, capital intensity, technical efficiency, market concentration, foreign penetration etc. affect the probability of exit, using data for the Greek manufacturing industry in 1997-2003. Specifically, we focus on the role that technical efficiency and foreign spillover effects have on survival. For this purpose we first employ a CES translog production function to estimate technical efficiency and we then use the hazard function, corresponding to the Exponenial and Weibull distributions, as well as a simple Cox model to estimate the effect that firm and sectoral level variables have on the survival probabilities of Greek manufacturing firms.

2. SURVIVAL LITERATURE

The first studies about the concept of firm survival have been of a theoretical nature. Ghemawat an Nalebuff (1985) concluded that in a declining industry with firms with asymmetric market shares and identical unit costs, the survivability is inversely related to size, i.e., the largest firm is the first to leave and the smallest is the last, because it can "hang on" longer than the large firm. Reynolds (1988) built a dynamic, game theoretic model to examine the plant closing and exit strategies of firms operating in a declining industry. His results support that in single-plant firms, high-cost plants close before low-cost plants in equilibrium. In a multi-plant duopolists case, a larger firm begins closing plants before a smaller firm as long as cost differences across plants are not large. Finally, Whinston (1988) concluded that when we have multi-plant firms, the generalization that the larger ones exit first, does not hold. The pattern of capacity reduction depends on a number of features related to the structure of the industry and the type of decline.

Moving now to empirical evidence, Dunne, Roberts and Samuelson (1988), examined the patterns of firm entry, growth and exit in U.S. manufacturing based on panel data for the period 1963-1982. They found that plant survival is positively associated with plant age and plant size, and that exit rates vary across industries and persist over time. Baden-Fuller (1989), in his research for U.K. steel castings in 1975-1983 found that profitability does influence the exit decision of a firm. He also concluded that diversified firms and firms that also operate in other business, other things equal, are more likely to make the decision to close a plant. Deily (1991) examined the plant closings of integrated steel firms for the period 1977-1987. He found that larger firm size is associated with a reduced likelihood of exit, steel multi-plant firms competing with minimills are more likely to close a plant and, finally, less profitable steel plants are shut down.

Audretsch (1991) examined the survival probabilities of new firms in the U.S., by using data for 1976-1986 and taking into account among other firm characteristics the innovating activity of firms. He found that new-firm survival is positively related with the extent of innovative activity and that short-run survival is positively related with market concentration. In addition, the existence of substantial scale economies and a high capital-labor ratio required by a sector lower firm survival probabilities. These results vary considerably with the time interval considered.

In a later study, Audretsch (1995) used cross sectional data for U.S. manufacturing, and confirmed that scale economies and product differentiation do constitute a barrier to survival. He also concluded that the likelihood of survival and the post-entry growth rates vary systematically from industry to industry. Moreover, he found that in industries where innovative activity of small firms plays an important role, the likelihood of new entrants' survival over a decade is lower than in industries where innovative activity is less important. More specifically, the likelihood of surviving an additional two years for the entrants that have already survived the first few years is actually greater in highly innovative industries. Also, new entrants that manage to adjust and offer a viable product have a higher likelihood of survival in highly innovative environments.

Audretsch and Mahmood (1995) investigated the relationship between firm survival and firm specific characteristics for U.S. new establishments. They found that the exposure of new establishments to risk tends to be greater in highly innovative environments. Furthermore, the likelihood of survival tends to be lower in industries where scale economies play an important role. The hazard rate is significantly lower for firms that have a large start-up size, whereas, it is significantly higher for establishments, which are branches of an existing enterprise than new independent enterprises. In addition, they found that as the gap between the minimum efficient size and start-up size increases, the hazard ratio also rises. A positive relationship between hazard rate and price-cost margin, as well as a greater hazard rate for new firms during periods of higher employment is also confirmed from their work. Finally, they reported a negative relationship among hazard rate and interest rates, size and wages.

Mata, Portugal and Guimaraes (1995), using panel data, examine the longevity of entrants in Portugal. The current (as opposed to initial) size of a firm affects positively both survival and growth rate. Also, size is an important determinant of survival particularly for de novo entrants. Moreover, plants that have grown face a lower probability of exit than otherwise identical units. In addition, past growth matters for survival and the higher the rate of plant creation in the industry, the lower the expected life of newborn units. Finally, a new firm has a higher survival probability if it enters growing industries or industries with little entry activity.

Doms, Dunne and Roberts (1995) examined the relationship among capital intensity, use of advanced manufacturing technology, growth rates and exit probabilities. Using U.S. data they found that capital intensive plants and plants employing advanced technology such as robots, lasers or computer controlled machinery have higher survival rates. Firm size, age and productivity were not sufficient statistics for characterizing the growth and failure patterns.

Santarelli (1998) used panel data for the Italian tourist sector, to estimate the relationship between the survival of tourist firms and their start-up size, on a region by region basis. He found that the relationship had the expected sign, although for some regions and for the country as a whole it didn't turn out to be statistically significant. Fotopoulos and Louri (2000), using data for Greek manufacturing industry in the 1982-92 period found that initial capital, growth and current size affect positively the probability of survival, while leverage (the ratio of debt to total assets) has the opposite effect. In addition, firms located in large urban centers have a higher survival probability following an 'urban incubator' argument.

Also, Santarelli (2000) using a Cox proportional hazard model, studied the link between duration of a new firm and its start-up size, as well as a series of industry-specific characteristics. He applied his model to the Italian financial intermediation industry. He found that regulatory reform in 1990 accelerated industry concentration, since before the regulatory reform, in 1989, entry was possible even for very small firms. In addition, larger new entrants survived longer than their smaller counterparts independently of the features of spatial and structural competition.

Bernard and Jensen (2002), employed two panel data sets of U.S. firms, one from 1987-1992 and a second one from 1992-1997, to examine the role of firm structure in manufacturing plant closure. They found that plants belonging to multi-plant or U.S. multinational firms have lower failure probabilities but this is due to the quality of the plants themselves rather than their nature. Also, age, size and capital intensity affect positively the probability of firm survival. But when they controlled for plant characteristics such us age, size, capital intensity and export status, they found that multi-plant and U.S. multinational firms are much more likely to close a plant.

Bernard and Sjoholm (2003), examined if foreign ownership affects firm survival in a developing country. Using data for Indonesian manufacturing in 1975-1989, they concluded that a foreign owned firm with any degree of foreign ownership had substantially lower failure probabilities than plants with only domestic ownership. But when controlling for plant size and productivity, foreign plants were more likely to close than similar domestic plants.[2]

3. FOREIGN FIRMS AND SPILLOVERS

Caves (1974) was probably the first researcher to report empirical results about spillover effects stemming from the presence of foreign firms in domestic markets. He used cross-sectional data for Canada and Australia and found evidence of positive spillovers affecting domestic firms. His work has since been extended from a number of researchers. Globerman (1979) used cross sectional data and obtained estimates of labor productivity for domestically owned plants in Canada. He found that labor productivity differences across Canadian owned plants are positively related to capital intensity, plant scale economies, labor quality, average hours per employee, and foreign ownership. The differences in labor productivity are derived partly from spillover efficiency benefits associated with foreign direct investment.

Blomstrom (1986) using cross sectional data, found that foreign presence in Mexican industry is positively related to efficiency. Also, foreign entry is related to positive changes only in the ''modern'' part of the industry. Finally, the most important source of spillover efficiency is found to be the competitive pressure induced by foreign firms. Haddad and Harrison (1993) used a firm level panel-data set for Morocco and they examined whether technology spillovers exist in Moroccan manufacturing sector finding evidence for negative spillover effects stemming from multinationals during the period 1985-1990.

Blomstrom and Kokko (1998), in their review article, support that spillover effects exist, that they are substantial between industries, that they depend on the level of capability and competition and that they vary systematically between countries and industries but there is no comprehensive evidence on their exact nature or magnitude. Finally they argue that the impacts of spillovers on the home country are likely to depend on what activities multinational firms retain in their home country and how internationalized the firms are.

Aitken and Harrison (1999) used panel data on Venezuelan plants to find that foreign equity participation is positively correlated with small enterprise plant productivity. They also found that an increase in foreign ownership negatively affects the productivity of domestically owned plants. The net effect of these two offsetting effects is almost negligent for the economy.

Blomstrom and Sjoholm (1999) used cross sectional data for Indonesia and examined firstly, if majority and minority owned establishments differ in terms of productivity levels and secondly, if the degree of spillovers differs with the degree of foreign ownership. They found that labor productivity is higher in foreign-owned establishments and that domestic establishments benefit from spillovers from FDI. Also the degree of foreign ownership does neither affect the level of labor productivity in foreign firms nor the degree of spillovers to the domestic sector. Finally, they found that spillovers were restricted to non-exporting local firms, probably because export oriented firms already face competitive pressure from the world market.

In a separate work for Ireland, Gorg and Strobl (2003) examined the effect of multinational corporations' (MNCs) presence on the survival Irish firms. Using panel data for the period 1973-1996 found that when controlling for plant and sector specific effects, the presence of MNCs has a positive effect only on indigenous plants in high-tech industries, which suggests the presence of technology spillovers. They did not find any positive effect of MNCs presence on survival of firms, which belong to low-tech sectors. They finally found that the presence of MNCs has a negative effect on the survival of other foreign-owned plants in the low-tech sectors. Finally, Dimelis and Louri (2004) based on cross-sectional data for Greek manufacturing industry found that positive spillovers come from firms with minority foreign ownership. Also, they argued that it is mostly small firms that take advantage of these positive spillovers rather than large firms.

4. TECHNICAL EFFICIENCY AND HAZARD MODELS

One of the fundamental implications we also wish to examine in this work is the effect of technical efficiency on the probability of firm survival. To estimate technical efficiency we employ the translog production function model which is a flexible functional form capable of approximating the unknown production function up to second order. We begin with the assumption that each company's production function relates output, Y, to two inputs, capital, K, and labor, L, and a time trend T. We then have $\ln Y = f(\ln K, \ln L, \ln T)$.

The translog production function is:

$$\ln Y = \alpha_0 + \alpha_1 \ln L + \alpha_2 \ln K + a_3 \ln T + \alpha_4 \frac{1}{2}(\ln L)^2 + \alpha_5 \frac{1}{2}(\ln K)^2 +$$

$$+ \alpha_6 \frac{1}{2}(\ln T)^2 + \alpha_7 (\ln L)(\ln K) + \alpha_8 (\ln L)(\ln T) + \alpha_9 (\ln K)(\ln T) + \varepsilon.$$

Obtaining returns to scale and the technical change index is straightforward. For estimation purposes this theoretical model is cast in the form of a linear model with a composed error term, $y_i = x_i'\beta + v_i - u_i$, $i = 1, \ldots, n$, where y_i is the log of production, x_i is a $k \times 1$ vector of log of inputs, β is a $k \times 1$ vector of parameters, v_i is a two-sided error term representing measurement error, and $u_i \geq 0$ is TI.[3] The stochastic assumptions are that $v_i \sim iidN(0, \sigma_v^2)$, $u_i \sim iid|N(0, \sigma_v^2)|$, and (x_i, v_i, u_i) are mutually independent. It is well known that this model can be estimated using the maximum likelihood method. The probability density of the dependent variable given the covariates is.

$$f(y_i | x_i) = (2/\sigma)\phi(-\varepsilon_i/\sigma)\Phi(-\lambda\varepsilon_i/\sigma),$$

where $\lambda = \sigma_u/\sigma_v$, $\sigma^2 = \sigma_v^2 + \sigma_u^2$, $\varepsilon_i = y_i - x_i'\beta$, and Φ denote the standard normal density and distribution functions. The log likelihood function is simply $\ln L = \sum_{i=1}^{N} \ln f(y_i | x_i)$ and standard numerical techniques can be used to obtain the maximum likelihood estimates and their asymptotic standard errors. Estimation of technical efficiency is possible using a result due to Jondrow, Lovell, Materov, and Schmidt (1982) which provides the expected value of u_i given the observed data. This expectation is:

$$E(u_i | y_i, x_i) = \frac{\sigma\lambda}{1 + \lambda^2}\left[\frac{\phi(-\lambda\varepsilon_i/\sigma)}{\Phi(-\lambda\varepsilon_i/\sigma)} - \lambda\varepsilon_i/\sigma\right].$$

After estimating technical efficiency, we proceed to estimate the probability of firm failure (hazard). It is, however, necessary first to understand the estimation issues involved and this necessitates a full presentation of the econometric model. We consider the following stochastic production frontier with unbalanced panel data:

$$y = \mathbf{x}_{it}'\beta + v_{it} - u_{it}, \tag{1}$$
$$t = 1,...,T_i, \ i = 1,...,n,$$

where $\mathbf{x}_{it}$ is a $k \times 1$ vector of inputs, β is a $k \times 1$ vector of parameters, v_{it} is a two sided disturbance reflecting measurement error, and u_{it} is a non-negative disturbance representing technical inefficiency. Estimation techniques for (1) are well known in the literature under various distributional assumptions about the one sided error component.[4]

In this paper we are interested in modeling survival of firms and its connection with firm performance reflected in technical inefficiency. While many studies, as mentioned in section 2, have been concerned with survival, very few have been concerned with the role of technical inefficiency.[5]

Given a random variable T with probability distribution $f(t)$, and the survival function $S(t) = 1 - F(t)$, where $F(t)$ is the distribution function, the hazard rate can be defined

$$\lambda(t) = \lim_{\varepsilon \to 0} \frac{\Pr[t \le T \le t + \varepsilon | T \ge t]}{\varepsilon} = \frac{f(t)}{S(t)}. \tag{2}$$

Many models have been proposed in the literature for the hazard rate or the survival function, viz. the Exponential, Weibull, lognormal, and log-logistic.[6] For example the Exponential model has $\log S(t) = -\lambda t$, where $\lambda > 0$ is a parameter, the constant hazard rate. The probability density is given by $f(t) = \lambda \exp(-\lambda t)$. For the Weibull model, the hazard rate is $\lambda(t) = \lambda p(\lambda t)^{p-1}$. The probability density function is $f(t) = \lambda p(\lambda t)^{p-1} \exp\left[-(\lambda t)^p\right]$ and the survival function is $F(t) = \exp\left[-(\lambda t)^p\right]$.

The data available for firm i are $D_i = \{y_{it}, \mathbf{x}_{it}, T_i, \mathbf{z}_i, I_i; t = 1,...,T_i\}$, $i = 1,...,n$, where I_i is an indicator variable equal to 1 if the firm ceased to exist at some date $\tau \ge T_i$, and zero otherwise, and z_i is an $m \times 1$ vector of covariates that are thought to be determinants of survival on prior grounds. The firms that survived are also known as "censored". It will be useful to define the set of censored observations, $C = \{i : I_i = 0\}$ (the set of survived firms) and the set of firms that ceased to exist, $U = \{i : I_i = 1\}$, which is the set of uncensored firms.

When the stochastic production frontier in (1) is estimated, a measure of technical inefficiency, say $\hat{u}_{it}$, can be obtained using the Jondrow, Lovell, Materov and Schmidt (1982) formula. This is simply the expected value of u_{it} given the data. The intention here is to estimate the survival function in (2) when the parameter λ depends on the covariates z_i - an $m \times 1$ vector - and certain covariates include *functions of technical inefficiency*, viz.

$$\log \lambda_i = z_i' \gamma_1 + h(u_{it})' \gamma_2, \tag{3}$$

where $h(u_{it})$ is a $q \times 1$ vector of *functions*. In the simplest case, $q = 1$, we can choose $h(u_{it}) = \bar{u}_i = T_i^{-1} \sum_{t=1}^{T_i} u_{it}$, average technical inefficiency but higher empirical moments may be included to investigate aspects of the way in which technical inefficiency impacts on survival. From the way (2) is formulated it is clear that the hazard parameter λ cannot vary over time since we examine survival from the point of view of a time period that is posterior to the sample period induced by (1). For that reason, the h functions must be time averages or involve certain similar operations implicit in their definition.

Proceeding as if u_{it} is known or estimated, the log-likelihood function of the model is

$$\ln L(\theta; D) = \sum_{i \in U} \ln f(T_i | \theta) + \sum_{i \in C} \ln S(T_i | \theta), \tag{4}$$

where: θ is the vector of all unknown parameters in the model and, for the Exponential case, $f(t_i) = \lambda_i \exp(-\lambda_i t_i)$, where λ_i was defined in (3). Substituting in (4) we get

$$\ln L(\theta; D) = \sum_{i \in U} [\log \lambda_i - \lambda_i T_i] - \sum_{i \in C} \lambda_i T_i. \tag{5}$$

The log-likelihood function in (5) can be estimated using standard numerical techniques. The problem with this approach is that technical inefficiency is not known and has to be estimated. To proceed we assume that $v_{it} \sim IN(0; \sigma_v^2)$, $u_{it} \sim IN(0; \sigma_u^2)$, that they are mutually independent and independent of all variables in x_{it} and z_{it}. Moreover, we assume that

$\{y_{it}; t = 1,...,T_i\}$ and T_i are independent for all $I = 1,...,n$. The endogenous variables in our model are y_{it} and $T_i T_j$. Our model is given by the following assumptions:[7]

1. Conditional on $\mathbf{x}_{it}$ and u_{it} we have $y_{it} \sim IN(\mathbf{x}'_{it}\boldsymbol{\beta} - u_{it}; \sigma_v^2)$.

2. Conditional on I_i the probability density of T_i is $f(T_i; \mathbf{u}_i, \gamma)^{1-I_i}$ $S(T_i; \mathbf{u}_i, \gamma)^{I_i}$, where $\gamma = [\gamma'_1, \gamma'_2]'$.

3. Conditional on $\mathbf{x}_{it}$, u_{it} and I_i, the random variables T_i and $\mathbf{y}_i = [y_{i1},..., y_{i,T_i}]'$ are independent.

4. The random variables u_{it} are distributed independently according to a half-normal distribution, $u_{it} \sim |N(0, \sigma_u^2)|$, and are independent of $\mathbf{y}_i$ and T_i conditional on $\mathbf{x}_{it}$, $\mathbf{z}_{it}$ and I_i.

The central object of interest is the joint distribution of endogenous variables which, in this instance, is given by

$$f(\mathbf{y}_i, T_i | \mathbf{x}_{it}, \mathbf{z}_{it}, I_i, \theta) = \int_{R_+^{T_i}} (2\pi\sigma_v^2)^{-T_i/2} (\pi\sigma_u^2/2)^{-T_i/2} \exp\left[-\frac{\sum_{t=1}^{T_i}(y_{it} - \mathbf{x}'_{it}\boldsymbol{\beta} + u_{it})^2}{2\sigma_v^2} + \right.$$

$$\left. -\frac{\sum_{t=1}^{T_i}(u_{it})^2}{2\sigma_u^2} \right] \cdot f(T_i; \mathbf{u}_i, \gamma)^{1-I_i} S(T_i; \mathbf{u}_i, \gamma)^{I_i} d\mathbf{u}_i \qquad (6)$$

where $f(T_i; \mathbf{u}_i, \gamma)$ and $S(T_i; \mathbf{u}_i, \gamma)$ represent the density and survival function respectively where the dependence on $\mathbf{u}_i = [u_{i1},..., u_{iT_i}]$ and the parameter vector θ is made explicit. This expression can be derived as follows. Clearly,

$$f(\mathbf{y}_i, T_i | \mathbf{x}_{it}, \mathbf{z}_{it}, I_i, \theta) = \int_{R_+^{T_i}} f(\mathbf{y}_i, \mathbf{u}_i, T_i | \mathbf{x}_{it}, \mathbf{z}_{it}, I_i, \theta) d\mathbf{u}_i =$$

$$= \int_{R_+^{T_i}} f(\mathbf{y}_i, T_i | \mathbf{x}_{it}, \mathbf{z}_{it}, I_i, \theta, \mathbf{u}_i) f(\mathbf{u}_i | \mathbf{x}_{it}, \mathbf{z}_{it}, I_i, \theta) d\mathbf{u}_i$$

From the half-normality distributional assumption, we have

$$f\left(\mathbf{u}_i\middle|\, \mathbf{x}_{it},\mathbf{z}_{it},I_i,\mathbf{\theta}\right)=\left(\pi\sigma_u^2/2\right)^{-T_i/2}\exp\left[-\frac{\sum_{t=1}^{T_i}u_{it}^2}{2\sigma_u^2}\right],\ i=1,...,n\ .$$

The distribution $f(\mathbf{y}_i,T_i|\,\mathbf{x}_{it},\mathbf{z}_{it},I_i,\mathbf{\theta},\mathbf{u}_i)$ can be easily obtained from the fact that conditional on $x_{it},z_{it},I_i,\theta,u_{it}$, the y_{it} is normally distributed and the fact that $\{y_{it};t=1,...,T_i\}$ and T_i are independent for all $i=1,...,n$.

The problem is that even when the **h** function consists of average technical inefficiency the multivariate integral in (6) cannot be computed in closed form. This integral, however, is essential in formulating the log-likelihood function of the model, which is given by

$$\ln L(\mathbf{y},\mathbf{T};\mathbf{X},\mathbf{Z},\mathbf{I},\mathbf{\theta})=\sum_{i=1}^{n}\log f(\mathbf{y}_i,T_i|\,\mathbf{x}_{it},\mathbf{z}_{it},I_i,\mathbf{\theta})\,. \tag{7}$$

The problem, of course, becomes worse when the **h** function includes *complicated components* like for example $T_i^{-1}\sum_{t=1}^{T_i}(u_{it}-\overline{u}_i)^2$, or $T_i^{-1}\sum_{t=1}^{T_i}(u_{it}-u_{i,t-1})$, or even $T_i^{-1}\sum_{t=1}^{T_i}\max(0,u_{it}-u_{i,t-1})$, viz. the variability of technical inefficiency, its average *change* over the sampling period, or the average *improvement* in technical inefficiency. All these constitute indispensable components of any serious analysis seeking to make inferences about the extent to which technical inefficiency is important for firm survival.

To implement our models we employ the hazard function of the Exponential and Weibull distributions and follow a two-stage estimation approach. First, the stochastic production frontier is estimated, and second, the survival likelihood is maximized. Functions of technical inefficiency are treated as ordinary regressors after evaluating the **h** functions at the estimates of technical inefficiency derived from the first stage.

For the Exponential distribution the hazard is

$$\lambda(t)=\lambda\,,$$

where $\lambda(t)$: rate at which plants exit at time t given that they have survived in $t-1$, (λ: parameter, t: time). The survival function in this case is the following:

$$S(t) = e^{-\lambda t},$$

In addition, we also employ the Weibull duration model:

$$\lambda(t) = \lambda p (\lambda t)^{p-1},$$

where: $\lambda(t)$: rate at which plants exit at time t given that they have survived in $t-1$ (λ: parameter, p: parameter, t: time). The survival function for this case is the following:

$$S(t) = e^{-(\lambda t)^p}.$$

The hazard function for the Weibull distribution is monotonically increasing or decreasing depending on p.

5. ECONOMETRIC ESTIMATIONS

5.1. Data

The study makes use of 3,142 firms manufacturing firms operating in Greece in period 1997-2003. Individual firm information has been derived from the ICAP directory, which provides financial data based on the published accounts of all Plc. and Ltd. firms in Greece. Information on employment and foreign ownership is also collected and given to us by ICAP.

Table 1 presents a summary of the sample. From the 3,142 firms only 2,893 survived the entire period of interest. Of them 249 'died' before 2003. From the firms that did not survive until 2003, 45 died in 1997, 42 died in 1998, 29 in 1999, 26 in 2000, 41 in 2001 and 66 died in 2002. Table 1 also presents the number of firms that belong to each sector each year. Table 2 presents the products that each sector produces. Foreign participation exists in 163 firms. Table 3 presents the descriptive statistics of the firms that enjoy foreign participation. From them 159 survived the entire period of interest (1997-2003). From the 163 'foreign' firms, 92 exhibit majority foreign ownership (foreign ownership >50%) and 71 exhibit minority foreign ownership (foreign ownership ≤50%).

Table 1 – Survival data (1997-2003) by sector

Sector	1997-1997	1997-1998	1997-1999	1997-2000	1997-2001	1997-2002	1997-2003
40	10	8	8	9	9	17	597
49	0	1	0	1	0	0	17
55	4	6	3	3	9	8	436
59	1	2	0	0	1	2	53
60	3	0	2	3	1	4	166
63	5	4	2	1	3	5	267
72	1	3	0	0	2	1	185
74	1	4	3	0	0	2	96
75	1	1	0	0	0	0	73
76	0	0	0	0	1	1	7
79	6	4	1	2	8	8	329
82	3	2	4	3	4	6	265
88	4	5	2	2	2	7	222
92	3	0	1	2	1	4	66
99	3	2	3	0	1	1	114
Total	45	42	29	26	42	66	2,893

Survived	2,893
Failed	249
Total	3,142

Table 2 - Description of sectors

Sector	Products
40	Food, Agricultural, Beverages
49	Tobacco
55	Textiles, White linen, Fabric made, Garments, Underwear, Accessories
59	Footwear, Leather, Fur
60	Wood, Cork, Furniture
63	Paper, Newspapers, Magazines, Publishing, Printing, Graphic arts
72	Rubber, Plastics
74	Chemical, Gases, Paints, Explosives
75	Medicines, Cosmetics, Detergents
76	Liquefied gas bottling, Petroleum, Coal products
79	Quarries, Mines, Salt works, Non metallic mineral products
82	Primary metal products, Metal products and structures
88	Machinery, Electric and electronic equip., Electric appliances, Lighting fixtures
92	Transportation means
99	Miscellaneous manufactured products

Table 3 – Survival data of foreign firms by country of origin

Country	1997-1997	1997-1998	1997-1999	1997-2000	1997-2001	1997-2002	1997-2003
Australia	0	0	0	0	0	0	1
Austria	0	0	0	0	0	0	2
Belgium	0	0	0	0	0	0	4
Cyprus	0	0	0	0	0	0	16
Denmark	0	0	0	0	0	0	1
England	0	0	0	0	0	1	11
France	0	0	0	0	0	0	16
Germany	0	0	0	0	0	0	17
Ireland	0	0	0	0	0	0	5
Italy	0	0	1	0	0	0	8
Japan	0	0	0	0	0	0	1
Libya	0	0	0	0	0	1	0
Liberia	0	0	0	0	0	0	3
Lichtenstein	0	0	0	0	0	0	2
Luxemburg	0	0	0	0	0	0	14
Netherlands	0	0	0	0	1	0	23
Norway	0	0	0	0	0	0	1
Panama	0	0	0	0	0	0	3
Scotland	0	0	0	0	0	0	1
Spain	0	0	0	0	0	0	3
Sweden	0	0	0	0	0	0	2
Switzerland	0	0	0	0	0	0	16
U.S.	0	0	0	0	0	0	9
Total	0	0	1	0	1	2	159
%>50							92
% ≤ 50							71
Total							163

5.2. Variables

The theoretical analysis, the econometric models employed and the availability of data, drive the choice of independent variables that we use in this work. These are:

LOGSIZE: logarithm of firm total assets;

LOGK/L: the logarithm of the ratio of fixed assets to the number of employees;

LEVERAGE: the ratio of debt to total assets;

LIQUIDITY: the ratio of working capital to total assets;
NPMARG: the ratio of net profits to production (sales);
PROFTA: the ratio of net profits to total assets;
DEBTSAL: the ratio of debt to sales;
SPILL (SPILLOVER EFFECT): the ratio of fixed capital belonging to foreign firms in the industry to total fixed capital of the industry;
HERFINDAHL (CONCENTRATION): measured by Herfindhal Index which is defined as follows: $H = \sum_{i=1}^{n} \left(\frac{x_i}{X_i} \right)^2$, where x_i: employment of n individual plant in the industry; X_i: total employment in the industry.
AGE: the difference between the current year and the first recorded year for the plant;
INEFF (TECHNICAL INEFFICIENCY): as provided by the stochastic production frontier estimation;
$INEFF^2$: inefficiency raised to the power of 2;
DINEFF: the improvement in efficiency. Only positive changes in efficiency are taken into consideration;
FOREIGN>50%: dummy variable taking the value of 1 if foreign ownership in a firm's capital exceeds 50 percent (majority foreign ownership),
FOREIGN≤50%: dummy variable taking the value of 1 if foreign ownership in a firm's capital is less than 50 percent (minority foreign ownership);

From the variables presented above, LOGSIZE, LOGK/L, LEVERAGE, LIQUIDITY, DEBTSAL, AGE, NPMARG, PROFTA, INEFF, $INEFF^2$ and DINEFF and FOREIGN> or ≤50% are firm level variables, whereas SPILL and HERF are sectoral variables.

5.3. Estimation Results

Before proceeding to hazard estimations, we employed the translog production function and estimated the technical efficiency of each firm. The estimation of the translog production function is presented in Table 4. The technical (in)efficiency thus produced is then used in the hazard estimations. Next, we estimate hazard functions for the Weibull and the Exponential distributions, as well a simple Cox hazard model. The results are presented in Tables 5, 6 and 7 and show persistent similarities.

As can be seen in these Tables the variable LOGSIZE is always significant with a negative coefficient, which means that size affects negatively the probability of exit, or has a positive effect on firm survival. This result has been supported by many researchers such as Dunne, Roberts and Samuelson (1988), Deily (1991), Audretch and Mahmood (1995), Mata, Portugal,

Guimaraes (1995), who found a positive relationship between firm size and survival. The coefficient of LOGK/L is also consistently significant with a positive sign, which means that high capital requirements increase the hazard. This result contradicts findings by Doms, Dunne and Roberts (1995) and Bernand and Jensen (2002), but it is in the same line with the results of Audretsch (1991), who supports that substantial high capital-labor ratio tends to lower the likelihood of firm survival. LEVERAGE as well as DEBTSAL have also highly significant and positive coefficients meaning that high levels of debt (requiring high interest payments) reduce the likelihood of survival, a result also found in Fotopoulos and Louri (2000). From the financial variables LIQUIDITY as well as NPMARG and PROFTA have also positive and significant coefficients, meaning that firms with high liquidity and/or high profitability suffer a higher exit rate, a result often discussed in the mergers and acquisitions literature where high liquidity and profitability have been found to induce takeover behaviour on behalf of rivals, consequently endangering the firms'existence.

Table 4 - Translog production function estimation

Parameters	Coefficient	Estimates	Standard Error	Est./s.e.	Probability
Constant	A_0	12.8360	0.2221	57.801	0.0000
lnL	α_1	0.5582	0.0706	7.903	0.0000
lnK	α_2	-0.2290	0.0413	-5.544	0.0000
lnT	α_3	0.0311	0.0243	1.284	0.1991
½(lnL)^2	α_4	0.1327	0.0169	7.840	0.0000
(lnL)(lnK)	α_7	-0.0212	0.0083	-2.566	0.0103
(lnL)(lnT)	α_8	0.0028	0.0042	0.667	0.5047
½(lnK)^2	α_5	0.0379	0.0045	8.374	0.0000
(lnK)(lnT)	α_9	0.0040	0.0024	1.656	0.0978
½(lnT)^2	α_6	-0.0108	0.0029	-3.673	0.0002
	σ_v	0.5572	0.0081	68.557	0.0000
	σ_u	0.8098	0.0238	34.069	0.0000

The impact of the sectoral variable FDI SPILLOVERS on the probability of exit is persistently significant and positive. In sectors with strong foreign presence, competition may be harsher, thus driving firms out of the market. Although it has been found that strong foreign presence impacts positively on the productivity of all (domestic and foreign) firms in a market (Dimelis and Louri, 2002), our results show that the negative side of spillovers, which is increased competition, is prevailing and increases hazard. A negative effect of foreign spillovers to firm survival can also be found in Haddad and Harrison (1993). The other sectoral variable, namely market concentration as represented by the Herfindahl index has also been estimated to affect hazard in a positive way - though not always statistically significant - which means that oligopolistic market structures do not enhance firm survival. It may be that concentration effects are harder for smaller and younger firms in a sector but such diversified behaviour could not be distinguished with our data. It is interesting that AGE has been estimated to have a negative and significant sign on hazard, meaning that older firms have a higher probability of survival probably due to accumulated experience and recognition. The age result is similar in Audretsch (1991 and 1995), Dunne, Roberts and Samuelson (1988) and Bernard and Jensen (2002).

Table 5: Hazard estimations (Weibull distribution)

Parameters	Estimates Weibul 1	Probability Weibull 1	Estimates Weibull 2	Probability Weibull 2	Estimates Weibull 3	Probability Weibull 3
Constant	2.413	0.005	1..939	0.022	1.912	0.025
logsize	-2.115	0.000	-2.010	0.000	-2.023	0.000
logK/L	0.072	0.001	0.081	0.000	0.085	0.000
leverage	0.153	0.000	0.221	0.000	0.224	0.000
liquidity	0.302	0.025	0.317	0.015	0.344	0.013
npmarg	0.049	0.113				
profTA			0.383	0.068	0.384	0.067
debtsal	0.011	0.070	0.005	0.063	0.005	0.064
Foreign>50%	0.119	0.451			0.111	0.486
Foreign≤50%	0.206	0.074			0.195	0.095
spill	0.065	0.001	0.070	0.000	0.067	0.001
Herfindahl	0.271	0.346			0.304	0.287
age	-0.077	0.000	-0.079	0.000	-0.079	0.000
ineff	0.357	0.010	0.461	0.009	0.464	0.009
ineff^2	-0.102	0.254	-0.102	0.226	-0.102	0.230
dineff	0.899	0.171	0.675	0.165	0.678	0.166
Weib p	2.567	0.000	2.556	0.000	2.554	0.000

From the variables measuring the technical (in)efficiency of firms the INEFF variable, has a significant and positive effect on hazard, meaning that technically inefficient firms are less likely to survive. Thus, it is important for firms to improve on their technical skills in order to become more efficient and reduce their probability of failure. Finally, a higher empirical moments of efficiency as measured by the INEFF^2 and DINEFF are not found to exert any significant effects. As far as DINEFF is concerned the results were similar when it was including both positive and negative changes in efficiency as when it was including only improvements.

Table 6: Hazard estimations (exponential distribution)

Parameters	Estimates Exponential 1	Probability Exponential 1	Estimates Exponential 2	Probability Exponential 2	Estimates Exponential 3	Probability Exponential 3
Constant	17.574	0.000	17.085	0.000	16.962	0.000
logsize	-10.412	0.000	-10.329	0.000	-10.396	0.000
logK/L	0.357	0.000	0.366	0.000	0.385	0.000
leverage	0.813	0.000	0.999	0.000	1.008	0.000
liquidity	1.763	0.007	1.674	0.010	1.769	0.006
npmarg	0.054	0.224				
profTA			1.311	0.059	1.262	0.065
debtsal	0.018	0.005	0.017	0.004	0.015	0.007
Foreign>50%	0.056	0.955			0.091	0.927
Foreign≤50%	0.725	0.092			0.641	0.202
spill	0.026	0.002	0.027	0.002	0.025	0.002
Herfindahl	2.189	0.083			2.142	0.089
age	-0.112	0.000	-0.113	0.000	-0.114	0.000
ineff	1.146	0.010	1.421	0.002	1.420	0.002
ineff^2	-0.113	0.347	-0.182	0.153	-0.168	0.167
dineff	0.034	0.937	0.073	0.868	0.082	0.851

Table 7: Hazard estimations (Cox model)

Parameters	Estimates Cox 1	Probability Cox 1	Estimates Cox 2	Probability Cox 2	Estimates Cox 3	Probability Cox 3
Constant						
logsize	-1.026	0.000	-1.029	0.000	-1.028	0.000
logK/L	0.667	0.003	0.723	0.001	0.744	0.001
leverage	0.844	0.000	0.979	0.000	0.979	0.000
liquidity	1.332	0.030	1.311	0.034	1.364	0.027
npmarg	0.124	0.138				
profTA			1.497	0.005	1.407	0.008
debtsal	0.017	0.004	0.014	0.008	0.014	0.008
Foreign>50%	-0.814	0.420			-0.787	0.436
Foreign≤50%	-0.132	0.823			-0.065	0.911
spill	0.032	0.000	0.034	0.000	0.032	0.000
Herfindahl	2.166	0.101			1.743	0.211
age						
ineff	0.747	0.067	0.918	0.029	0.948	0.024
ineff^2	-0.126	0.218	-0.143	0.169	-0.148	0.153
dineff	0.345	0.432	0.514	0.248	0.510	0.254

Finally, the role of foreign ownership in hazard was also estimated. Findings in the empirical literature have shown that foreign firms are more productive than domestic firms, hence foreign ownership could be expected to exercise a positive effect on survival. Initially, foreign ownership was included in our estimations through a dummy taking the value of 1 when a firm had any percentage (from 1% to 100%) of foreign ownership in its capital as recorded in its accounts. Such a variable was not found to be significant in any case and hence it is not reported in our estimations. Bernard and Sjoholm (2003) reported a similar finding. But since firms with majority foreign ownership in their capital could be thought to show a different failure rate than firms with minority foreign interests, their separate effects were also estimated. As can be seen in Tables 5, 6 and 7 the effects of foreign ownership as shown by FOREIGN >50% and FOREIGN ≤50% were not found to be significant in any case, meaning that once other firm characteristics such as size, age, financial profile and structural effects are taken into account the sheer fact of foreign ownership does not exercise any differentiating impact on firm survival.

6. CONCLUSIONS

In this paper we used a panel data set including 3,142 Greek manufacturing firms covering the period 1997-2003 to estimate the effects that specific firm- and market-level variables, drawn from different strands of literature (such as survival, foreign direct investment and technical efficiency analyses) have on firm survival. Our main focus was *a)* the effect of foreign presence both in a sectoral market (through spillover effects) as well as in the ownership of a firm, and *b)* the effect that technical efficiency might have on the probability of firm failure. For this purpose, we employed a simultaneous equation model with latent variables approach. Initially the translog production function to estimate technical efficiency and then fed the resulting estimates of technical (in)efficiency (as well as higher moments of it) to our hazard functions. We reported findings estimated from the Exponential and the Weibull distributions as well as from a Cox hazard model. Our variables show a persistent behaviour across all estimations.

The first basic conclusion is that foreign spillovers exercise a positive impact on hazard, unveiling possibly the increased competitive pressure existing in sectors where foreign firms have a stronger presence, rendering survival probabilities harder. In contrast, foreign firm ownership (majority or minority) does not exercise any significant effect on survival, meaning that foreign firms do not have any distinctive survival advantage (potentially stemming from their foreign parent experience or protection) compared to their local rivals (once their other specific characteristics are accounted for).

The second important result is that technical efficiency affects a firm's hazard negatively, that is it positively influences survival. Following a two-stage estimation approach according to which the stochastic production frontier is first estimated, and the survival likelihood is maximized in a second step, functions of technical inefficiency are treated as ordinary regressors. While the first moment is estimated to be significant for survival, higher moments of efficiency have not been found to play a significant role. This is an interesting finding, pointing to the fact that since technically inefficient firms do not produce the maximum level of output given the amount of inputs used, they may as well be aware of the dangers for survival such a sluggish performance may generate.

An interesting extension of our empirical analysis could follow the direction of deepening our knowledge about the effects that innovation and technology level or technology gaps might have on hazard rates. How export performance affects survival prospects is a related issue that could also be worthwhile to investigate. Whichever way one proceeds, one thing that stands clear is that firm dynamics is a new and fascinating subject with many exploration possibilities.

NOTES

[1] For an exhaustive review of the entry literature see Geroski (1995).
[2] Other studies analysing firm survival include Agarwal (1997), Agarwal and Gort (1996), Audretsch (1994), Audretsch, Houweling and Thurik (2000), Audretsch, and Mahmood (1994), Dunne and Hughes (1994), Mahmood (1992 and 2000).
[3] See Aigner, Lovell, and Schmidt (1977), Meeusen and van den Broeck (1977), and Kumbhakar and Lovell (2000) for a survey.
[4] See for example Aigner, Lovell and Schmidt (1977) and Meeusen and van den Broeck (1977), Kumbhakar and Tsionas (2005a, 2005b and 2006), Tsionas (1999 and 2002). Also for excellent surveys of the literature see Greene (1993 and 2001), Bauer (1990), and Kumbhakar and Lovell (2000). We also refer to Greene (2004) for additional issues involved.
[5] For example Dimara, Skuras, Tsekouras and Tzelepis (2003), and Wheelock and Wilson (1995).
[6] See Kalbfleisch and Prentice (1980, pp. 21-30) and Greene (2000, p. 941).
[7] In the following, we are also conditioning on the parameter vector θ.

REFERENCES

Agarwal, R. (1997), "Survival of Firms Over the Product Life Cycle", *Southern Economic Journal*, 63(4), 571-584.

Agarwal, R. and M. Gort (1996), "The Evolution of Markets and Entry, Exit and Survival of Firms", *Review of Economics and Statistics*, 78(4), 489-498.

Aigner, D. J., C .A. K. Lovell and P. Schmidt (1977), "Formulation and Estimation of Stochastic Frontier Production Function Models", *Journal of Econometrics*, 6(1), 21-37.

Aitken J. B. and E. A. Harrison (1999), "Do Domestic Firms Benefit from Direct Foreign Investment? Evidence from Venezuela", *American Economic Review*, 89(3), 605-618.

Audretsch D. B. (1991), "New-firm Survival and the Technological Regime", *Review of Economics and Statistics*, 73(3), 441-450.

Audretsch, D. B. (1994), "Business Survival and the Decision to Exit", *Journal of the Economics of Business*, 1(1), 125-137.

Audretsch, D. B. (1995), "Innovation, Growth and Survival", *International Journal of Industrial Organization*, 13(4), 441-457.

Audretsch, D. B., P. Houweling and A. R. Thurik (2000), "Firm Survival in the Netherlands", *Review of Industrial Organization*, 16(1), 1-11.

Audretsch, D. B. and T. Mahmood (1994), "The Rate of Hazard Confronting New Firms and Plants in U.S. Manufacturing", *Review of Industrial Organization*, 9(1), 41-56.

Audretsch, D. B. and T. Mahmood (1995), "New Firm Survival: New Results Using a Hazard Function", *Review of Economics and Statistics*, 77(1), 97-103.

Baden-Fuller, C. W. F. (1989), "Exit from Declining Industries and the Case of Steel Castings", *Economic Journal*, 99(398), 949-961.

Bauer, P. W. (1990), "Recent Developments in the Econometric Estimation of Frontiers", *Journal of Econometrics*, 46(1-2), 39-56.

Bernard B. A. and J. B. Jensen (2002), "The Deaths of Manufacturing Plants", *National Bureau of Economic Research*, Working Paper No. 9026.

Bernard B. A. and F. Sjoholm (2003), "Foreign Owners and Plant Survival", *National Bureau of Economic Research*, Working Paper No. 10039.

Blomstrom M. (1986), "Foreign Investment and Productive Efficiency: the Case of Mexico", *Journal of Industrial Economics*, 35(1), 97-112.

Blomstrom M. and A. Kokko (1998), "Multinational Corporations and Spillovers", *Journal of Economic Surveys*, 12(2), 1-31.

Blomstrom M. and F. Sjoholm (1999), "Technology Transfer and Spillovers: Does Local Participation with Multinationals Matter?", *European Economic Review*, 43(4-6), 915-923.

Caves R. E. (1974), "Multinational Firms, Competition and Productivity in Host-country Markets", *Economica*, 41(162), 176-193.

Deily, E. M. (1991), "Exit Strategies and Plant-closing Decisions: The Case of Steel", *Rand Journal of Economics*, 22(2), 250-263.

Dimara, E., D. Skuras, K. Tsekouras and D. Tzelepis (2003), "Firm Efficiency and Survival", paper presented at the 2nd Hellenic Workshop on Productivity and Efficiency Measurement, University of Patras, Greece.

Dimelis, S. and H. Louri (2002), "Foreign Ownership and Production Efficiency: A Quantile Regression Analysis", *Oxford Economic Papers*, 54(3), 449-469.

Dimelis, S. and H. Louri (2004), "Foreign Direct Investment and Technology Spillovers: Which Firms Really Benefit?", *Weltwirtschaftliches Archiv*, 140(2), 230-253.

Doms, M., T. Dunne and J. M. Roberts (1995), "The Role of Technology Use in the Survival and Growth of Manufacturing Plants", *International Journal of Industrial Organization*, 13(4), 523-542.

Dunne, P. and A. Hughes (1994), "Age, Size, Growth and Survival: UK Companies in the 1980s", *Journal of Industrial Economics*, 42(2), 115-140.

Dunne, T., J. M. Roberts and L. Samuelson (1988), "Patterns of Firm Entry and Exit in U.S. Manufacturing Industries", *Rand Journal of Economics*, 19(4), 495-515.

Fotopoulos, G. and H. Louri (2000), "Location and Survival of New Entry", *Small Business Economics*, 14(4), 311-321.

Geroski, P. A. (1995), "What Do We Know about Entry?", *International Journal of Industrial Organization*, 13(4), 421-440.

Ghemawat, P. and B. Nalebuff (1985), "Exit", *RAND Journal of Economics* 16(2), 184-194.

Globerman, S. (1979), "Foreign Direct Investment and Spillover Efficiency Benefits in Canadian Manufacturing Industries", *Canadian Journal of Economics*, 12(1), 42-56.

Gorg, H. and E. Strobl (2003), "Multinational Companies, Technology Spillovers and Plant Survival", *Scandinavian Journal of Economics*, 105(4), 581-595.

Greene, W. H. (1993), "The Econometric Approach to Efficiency Analysis", in H. O. Fried, C. A. K. Lovell and S. S. Schmidt (eds.), *The measurement of productive efficiency: Techniques and Applications*, Oxford, Oxford University Press, 68-119.

Greene, W. H. (2000), *Econometric Analysis*, New York, Prentice Hall.

Greene, W. H. (2001), "New Developments in the Estimation of Stochastic Frontier Models with Panel Data", Department of Economics, Stern School of Business, New York University.

Greene, W. H. (2004), "Distinguishing Between Heterogeneity and Inefficiency: Stochastic Frontier Analysis of the World Health Organization's Panel Data on National Health Care Systems", *Journal of Health Economics*, 13(10), 959-980.

Haddad, M. and E. A. Harrison (1993), "Are There Positive Spillovers from Direct Foreign Investment? Evidence from Panel Data for Morocco", *Journal of Development Economics*, 42, 51-74.

Jondrow, J., C. A. K. Lovell, I. S. Materov and P. Schmidt (1982), "On the Estimation of Technical Inefficiency in the Stochastic Frontier Production Function Model", *Journal of Econometrics*, 19, 233-38.

Kalbfleisch, J. D. and R. L. Prentice (1980), *The Statistical Analysis of Failure Time Data*, New York, Wiley.

Kumbhakar, S. C. and C. A. K Lovell (2000), *Stochastic Frontier Analysis*, Cambridge and New York, Cambridge University Press.

Kumbhakar, S. C. and E. G. Tsionas (2005a), "Measuring Technical and Allocative Inefficiency in the Translog Cost System: a Bayesian Approach", *Journal of Econometrics*, 126(2), 355-384.

Kumbhakar, S. C. and E. G. Tsionas (2005b), "The Joint Measurement of Technical and Allocative Inefficiency: An Application of Bayesian Inference in Nonlinear Random Effects Models", *Journal of the American Statistical Association*, 100(471),736-747.

Kumbhakar, S. C. and E. G. Tsionas (2006), "Estimation of Stochastic Frontier Production Functions with Input-Oriented Technical Efficiency", *Journal of Econometrics*, 2005, 126(2), 355-384.

Mahmood, T. (1992), "Does the Hazard Rate of New Plants Vary between High- and low-tech Industries?", *Small Business Economics*, 4(3), 201-210.

Mahmood, T. (2000), "Survival of Newly Founded Businesses: A Log-logistic Model Approach", *Small Business Economics*, 14(3), 223-237.

Mata J., P. Portugal and P. Guimaraes (1995), "The Survival of New Plants: Start-up Conditions and Post-entry Evolution", *International Journal of Industrial Organization*, 13(4), 459-481.

Meeusen, W. and J. van den Broeck (1977), "Efficiency Estimation from Cobb-Douglas Production Functions with Composed Error", *International Economic Review*, 18(2), 435-444.

Reynolds, S. S. (1988), "Plant Closings and Exit Behavior in Declining Industries", *Economica*, New Series, 55(220), 493-503.

Santarelli, E., (1998), "Start-up Size and Post-entry Performance: The Case of Tourism Services in Italy", *Applied Economics*, 30(2), 157-163.

Santarelli, E. (2000), "The Duration of New Firms in Banking: An Application of Cox Regression Analysis", *Empirical Economics*, 25(2), 315-325.

Tsionas, E. G. (1999), "Full Likelihood Inference in Normal-gamma Stochastic Frontier Models", *Journal of Productivity Analysis*, 13(2), 179-201.

Tsionas, E. G. (2002), "Stochastic Frontier Models with Random Coefficients", *Journal of Applied Econometrics*, 17(2), 121-147.

Wheelock, D. C. and P. W. Wilson (1995), "Explaining Bank Failures: Deposit Insurance, Regulation, and Efficiency", *Review of Economics and Statistics*, 77(4), 689-700.

Whinston, D. M. (1988), "Exit with Multiplant Firms", *The Rand Journal of Economics*, 19(4), 568-588.

Chapter 11
ENTREPRENEURSHIP, INDUSTRIAL RESTRUCTURING AND UNEMPLOYMENT IN PORTUGAL

Rui Baptista
Instituto Superior Técnico, Technical University of Lisbon , and Max Planck Institute of Economics, Jena

André van Stel
Erasmus University Rotterdam, EIM Business and Policy Research, Zoetermeer, and Max Planck Institute of Economics, Jena

A. Roy Thurik
Erasmus University Rotterdam, EIM Business and Policy Research, Zoetermeer, and Max Planck Institute of Economics, Jena

1. INTRODUCTION

In recent years, the relationship between entrepreneurship, as reflected by the business ownership (or self-employment) rate, and unemployment has received increasing attention from academics and policy-makers in European countries. Europe and other industrialized regions of the globe have experienced considerable industrial re-structuring in the last three decades, changing from traditional manufacturing industries towards new and more complex technologies such as electronics, software and biotechnology. Audretsch and Thurik (2001 and 2004) argue that the role of new firms in technological development has been enhanced by a reduced importance of scale economies and an increasing degree of uncertainty in the world economy, creating more room for innovative entry.

The present chapter examines the dynamics of the relation between variations in self-employment and unemployment rates for Portugal in the period 1974-2002. A comparison with the pattern observed for OECD countries is the starting point of our investigation. Portugal represents a particularly interesting case for examination of the dynamics of this relationship, given the specifics of the firm size distribution of the

Portuguese economy. In particular, the Portuguese industrial structure is dominated by what may be termed "micro-businesses", *i.e.* firms with less than ten employees. Moreover, the proportion of micro-businesses in the Portuguese economy has increased during the period under analysis. This suggests that, while the Portuguese economy features high levels of business ownership coupled with a small average size of firms, new firm growth rates are likely to be low and that, therefore, the industrial re-structuring effects brought about by increases in business ownership rates probably do not have a significant impact on the reduction of unemployment.

The following sections start by looking at relevant and recent background literature concerning the dynamics driving the relation between entrepreneurship/business ownership and unemployment; we then focus on the evolution of the Portuguese economy for the period under analysis, examining specifically the business ownership and unemployment rates. This provides the necessary backdrop for the discussion of the empirical results. The empirical approach used is then outlined and results are presented, focusing particularly on the pattern of residuals that results from the application to Portuguese data of a model estimated for 23 OECD countries. Departing from the question of how well the model fits the Portuguese data, we attempt to provide explanations for the differences found between the dynamics of the relationship between variations in the self-employment and unemployment rates observed for OECD countries in general and for Portugal in particular.

2. THE RELATION BETWEEN ENTREPRENEURSHIP AND UNEMPLOYMENT

There are many views on the relationship between unemployment and entrepreneurial activity. See Audretsch, Carree, van Stel and Thurik (2005). Occupational choice theory suggests that increased unemployment will lead to an increase in start-up activity on the grounds that the opportunity cost of starting a firm has decreased.[1] However, there are counter effects. The unemployed tend to possess lower endowments of human capital and entrepreneurial talent required to start and sustain a new firm. This would suggest that high unemployment may be associated with a low degree of entrepreneurial activity. High unemployment rates may also imply lower levels of personal wealth which in turn would reduce the likelihood of becoming self-employed (Hurst and Lusardi, 2004). High levels of unemployment may correlate with stagnant economic growth leading to a low number of entrepreneurial opportunities (Audretsch, Thurik, Verheul and Wennekers, 2002).

There is also a literature claiming that start-up activity influences unemployment. New firm start-ups hire employees, resulting in subsequent decreases in unemployment.[2] Furthermore, increased entrepreneurial activity may impact country-wide economic performance in various ways (van Stel, Carree and Thurik, 2005). Entrepreneurs may introduce important innovations by entering markets with new products or production processes (Acs and Audretsch, 2003). Entrepreneurs may increase productivity by increasing competition.[3] They may improve our knowledge of what is technically viable, what consumers prefer and how to acquire the necessary resources by introducing variations of existing products and services in the market. The resulting learning process speeds up the discovery of the dominant design for product-market combinations. The learning does not solely apply to the experimenting entrepreneur. Knowledge spillovers play an important role in this process (Audretsch and Keilbach, 2004). Lastly, they may be inclined to work longer hours and more efficiently as their income is strongly linked to their working effort. Also, their reputation and their social status is directly related to these efforts. See Carree and Thurik (2003) for a survey of the effects of entrepreneurship on economic growth.

We conclude that there are many interrelations between entrepreneurial activity and unemployment. Unraveling the relationship between entrepreneurship and unemployment is crucial, because policy is frequently based on assumptions that do not reflect the ambiguities described. Audretsch, Carree, van Stel and Thurik (2005) try to reconcile the ambiguities found in the relationship between unemployment and start-up activity. They introduce a two-equation vector auto-regression model where changes in unemployment and self-employment are linked to subsequent changes in those variables for a panel of 23 OECD countries. The present chapter reviews this empirical model and presents and interprets the residuals for Portugal.[4]

3. THE EVOLUTION OF THE PORTUGUESE ECONOMY

Figure 1 below displays the evolution of the rates of GDP growth, unemployment, and business ownership in Portugal in the period 1972-2004. To properly assess the evolution of the Portuguese economy during this period it is essential to take into consideration two major external shocks which imparted significant effects on economic growth, as well as on unemployment and business ownership rates. These shocks were i) the oil crisis of 1973, followed by the revolution of 1974 and ii) the entry into the European Union (E.U.) in 1986.

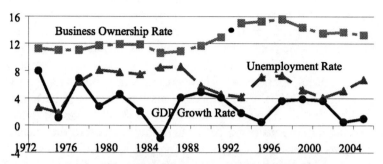

Sources: COMPENDIA Database, OECD and Bank of Portugal
FIGURE 1 - UNEMPLOYMENT, BUSINESS OWNERSHIP AND GDP GROWTH IN PORTUGAL:
1972-2004

Until 1974 Portugal was a colonial power, living under a one party regime and holding considerable portions of Africa. Since the early 1960s, Portugal had been facing colonial wars on several fronts. During the 1960-1973 period, the Portuguese economy increasingly focused on international trade with Western European partners, and less on trade with the colonies. Following the post-war growth cycle in Western Europe, Portugal experienced relatively high economic growth rates. Despite the concentration of economic power in a small number of financial and industrial conglomerates benefiting from government protection, the Portuguese business ownership rate in 1972 was relatively high when compared to the rest of Europe. Most of this self-employment was, however, based on low productivity agriculture and very small retail businesses intended only for subsistence (life style entrepreneurship). Emigration and the mobilization of armed forces shrunk the work force. Together with economic growth, this brought about very low levels of unemployment.

During 1972-1973, Portugal suffered the effects of the rise in overall industrial costs resulting from the increase in oil prices triggered by OPEC. Economic growth slowed down considerably in most OECD countries, thus reducing the demand for Portuguese goods and opportunities for Portuguese workers abroad. In April 1974, a non-violent revolution led by army officers ended the one party regime and made the African colonies independent, leading to a massive inflow of more than half a million refugees. In the period up to late 1975 most property rights were abolished and the main industries and financial services were nationalized. The stock market was virtually eliminated.

The last vestiges of such radical changes were only removed in the early 1980s, in order to pave the way for privatization and E.U. integration, which occurred in 1986. Meanwhile, Portugal underwent two structural adjustment programs overseen by the IMF due to severe current account deficits. As a result of such an assortment of external shocks, the Portuguese economy grew at a very slow rate, experiencing periods of recession. Government intervention supporting many companies facing financial difficulties, coupled with legislation against dismissals and significant increases in public sector employment prevented the unemployment rate from rising to higher levels than those displayed in Figure 1. While high unemployment and economic instability may have made self-employment more attractive, thus contributing to a rise in business ownership, government policies protecting jobs and increasing the economic role of the public sector yielded the opposite effect, leading to a reduction in business ownership.

After Portugal joined the E.U. in 1986, the main focus of development policy became the promotion of socio-economic cohesion through the granting of funding directed at the improvement of physical and educational infra-structure, as well as providing incentives and financial help for private investment. Funding was awarded for investments in start-up firms, the expansion of incumbents, and also for investment in R&D and environmental improvements. Larger firm size was perceived as crucial to ensure competitiveness in the E.U. market. Hence a significant proportion of funding was directed at capacity increases by relatively large incumbents. While this might have restricted the size of start-ups, it did not preclude a significant increase in the business ownership rate. In fact, while large investments in infra-structure and productive capacity brought about a significant decrease in unemployment from the outset of E.U. integration, relatively small average firm size and low entry barriers in most non regulated industries also increased possibilities for self-employment.

So, while the global recession of the early 1990s caused an increase in unemployment, the business ownership rate kept growing, in part due to the de-regulation of markets brought about by privatization and E.U. rules. However, as unemployment rates started to subside in the mid-1990s, so did business ownership rates. It can be argued that, as the Portuguese economy became more integrated in the E.U. market, consolidation and "shakeout"[5] occurred in some markets thus leading to a reduction in the business ownership rate.

4. MEASURING THE RELATION BETWEEN ENTREPRENEURIAL ACTIVITY AND UNEMPLOYMENT

In Audretsch, Carree, van Stel and Thurik (2005) it is explained why the dynamic interrelationship between entrepreneurial activity and unemployment is complex and, in particular, that the direction of causality between the two variables is not clear *a priori*. As a response to the ambiguity inherent in the unemployment-entrepreneurship relationship, the previous sections suggest two testable hypotheses: *i*) that increases in entrepreneurial activity lead to a decrease in subsequent unemployment; *ii*) that increases in unemployment lead to an increase in subsequent entrepreneurial activity.

In order to gain insight in the causal linkages involved in the relationship, Audretsch, Carree, van Stel and Thurik (2005) estimate a vector auto-regression (VAR) model (Sims, 1980). This means that a vector of dependent variables is explained by one or more lags of the vector of dependent variables, i.e., each dependent variable is explained by one or more lags of itself and of the other dependent variables. They estimate a two equation VAR model with the change in unemployment and the change in entrepreneurial activity as dependent variables. Furthermore, they use time dummies as exogenous explanatory variables.[6] These dummies correct for business cycle effects over the sample period that are common for the countries covered by the data set. Their model reads as follows:

$$U_{it} - U_{i,t-L} = \alpha + \sum_{j=1}^{J} \beta_j (E_{i,t-jL} - E_{i,t-(j+1)L}) +$$

$$+ \sum_{j=1}^{J} \gamma_j (U_{i,t-jL} - U_{i,t-(j+1)L}) + \sum_{t=1}^{T} \delta_t D_t + \varepsilon_{1it} \tag{1}$$

$$E_{it} - E_{i,t-L} = \kappa + \sum_{j=1}^{J} \lambda_j (U_{i,t-jL} - U_{i,t-(j+1)L}) +$$

$$+ \sum_{j=1}^{J} \mu_j (E_{i,t-jL} - E_{i,t-(j+1)L}) + \sum_{t=1}^{T} v_t D_t + \varepsilon_{2it}, \tag{2}$$

where U is unemployment, E is entrepreneurial activity, i is a country-index, L is the time span in number of years, J is the number of time lags included and D_t are time dummies. The expected sign of the joint impact of the β coefficients is negative and the expected sign of the joint impact of the λ coefficients is positive. The inclusion of lagged dependent variables on the right hand side in the VAR model allows for a test for the direction of causality.[7]

The model is tested using a data panel for 23 OECD countries between 1974 and 2002. For the unemployment data, U, standardized unemployment rates from *OECD Main Economic Indicators* are used. Entrepreneurial activity, E, is measured as self-employment and these data are taken from the COMPENDIA 2002.1 data set of EIM in Zoetermeer, The Netherlands. The COMPENDIA data set harmonizes self-employment data as published in *OECD Labor Force Statistics* making use of various (country-specific) sources to make the self-employment data as comparable as possible across countries and over time.[8] The definition used in COMPENDIA is the number of non-agricultural self-employed (unincorporated as well as incorporated) as a fraction of the labor force. See Figure 1 for the development of the self-employment rate in Portugal and van Stel (2005) for further details about this data base.

Equations (1) and (2) are estimated using weighted least squares. Audretsch, Carree, van Stel and Thurik (2005) consider changes in self-employment and unemployment over periods of four years, i.e., L equals 4. Furthermore, they test for different time lags, in order to gain insight in the lag structure between unemployment and entrepreneurship. Inclusion of more lags seems more compelling because the employment impact of entrepreneurship is not instantaneous. Rather it requires a number of years for the firm to grow.[9]

Using four-yearly data to avoid overlapping periods (given that $L=4$), the authors test for the shape of the lag structure and find that the model variant using two lags is statistically optimal. The results are presented in Table 1. The variables of interest are bold-printed in the upper part of the table. The control variables (i.e., the lagged dependents) are in the lower part.

Table 1 - Estimating the relation between U and E for 23 OECD Countries (115 observations)

Dependent:	U_t-U_{t-4}	Dependent:	E_t-E_{t-4}
Constant	0.674	Constant	-0.243
(in %-points)	(1.4)	(in %-points)	(1.5)
$E_{t-4}-E_{t-8}$	0.091	$U_{t-4}-U_{t-8}$	0.067 *
	(0.3)		(2.2)
$E_{t-8}-E_{t-12}$	-1.13 **	$U_{t-8}-U_{t-12}$	0.090 **
	(3.8)		(2.8)
$U_{t-4}-U_{t-8}$	-0.246 **	$E_{t-4}-E_{t-8}$	0.329 **
	(2.7)		(3.5)
$U_{t-8}-U_{t-12}$	-0.027	$E_{t-8}-E_{t-12}$	0.167
	(0.3)		(1.7)
R^2	0.403	R^2	0.385
P-value Granger causality test	0.000 **	P-value Granger causality test	0.006 **

Note: Absolute t-values are between brackets. Coefficients for year dummies are not reported.
 Significant at 0.05 level. ** Significant at 0.01 level.
Source: Audretsch, Carree, van Stel and Thurik (2005)

From the left part of the table we see that entrepreneurial activity significantly lowers unemployment but that it takes a lag of eight years before the ("entrepreneurial") effect capitalizes. Only after some time, the new entrants actually contribute to economic growth, either by growing themselves or stimulating incumbent firms to perform better because of the increased competition.

Table 1 also shows that changes in unemployment have a positive impact on subsequent self-employment. This is the "refugee" effect of unemployment stimulating start-up and self-employment rates. Note however that the "refugee" effect is considerably smaller than the "entrepreneurial effect", i.e., the sum of the coefficients in the right (bold-printed) part of Table 1 is much smaller compared to the (absolute) sum in the left part. Finally, from the Granger statistics we conclude that both directions of causality are in order, i.e., unemployment actually causes self-employment (p-value 0.006) while self-employment also causes unemployment (p-value 0.000).

5. ANALYZING THE RESIDUALS FOR PORTUGAL

Based on the results in Table 1 we are now able to analyze the residuals for Portugal during the period 1986-2002.[10] Using data for observed unemployment and business ownership rates for Portugal in the period 1974-2002, it is straightforward to calculate the estimated values of the residuals for Portugal from the coefficients estimated for equations (1) and (2): Z_{1t} for the unemployment rate – equation (1) – and Z_{2t} for the business ownership rate – equation (2):

$$Z_{1t} = U_t^O - U_t^P \tag{1a}$$

$$Z_{2t} = E_t^O - E_t^P \tag{2a}$$

where U_t^O and E_t^O are the observed unemployment and business ownership rates, while U_t^P and E_t^P are the unemployment and business ownership rates predicted by the model in equations (1) and (2), respectively. The values obtained for the residual terms tell us whether the model under-estimates (positive residual) or over-estimates (negative residual) the variations in unemployment and business ownership rates.

5.1. Unemployment Equation (1 and 1a)

The residuals, as well as the observed and predicted unemployment rates, for Portugal are displayed in Figures 2 and 3. We see that the estimated residuals appear to be unsystematic in that positive and negative values alternate. The residuals are negative – indicating an over-estimation of the unemployment rate – for the periods of 1990 and 1994; while for 1986, 1998 and 2002, the model provides lower predicted values for the unemployment rate than those actually observed (positive residuals). The residuals are particularly large for 1990 – which registered an unemployment rate of 4.6 percent, while the model predicted 7.2 percent - and for 2002, when the observed unemployment rate was over 5 percent, while the predicted value was a little above 2 percent.

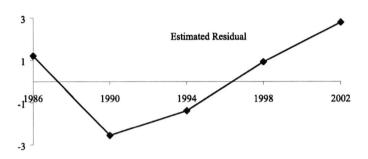

FIGURE 2: ESTIMATED RESIDUALS FOR PORTUGAL 1986-2002 IN %-POINTS (EQUATION 1A)

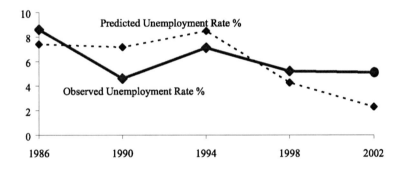

FIGURE 3: OBSERVED AND PREDICTED UNEMPLOYMENT RATES IN PORTUGAL 1986-2002

It seems likely that part of the discrepancies observed between real and predicted unemployment in Portugal could be explained by macroeconomic fluctuations that followed Portugal's entry in the EU, as will be explained below.

As it was briefly argued in the first section of this chapter, the nature of entrepreneurship and the socio-economic environment in Portugal differ from those in most other OECD countries. Figure 4 displays the average business ownership rates for the 23 OECD countries under analysis for the

1972-2004 period. While Portugal displays one of the highest average rates of business ownership, a large percentage of firms are micro-businesses, with less than 10 employees, reflecting a dominance of what may be deemed as "subsistence entrepreneurship" or, using the taxonomy made common by the Global Entrepreneurship Monitor (Acs, Arenius, Hay and Minniti, 2005), "necessity-based entrepreneurial activity." This kind of entrepreneurial activity has remained very important in Portugal when compared with other developed countries (Acs, Arenius, Hay and Minniti, 2005).

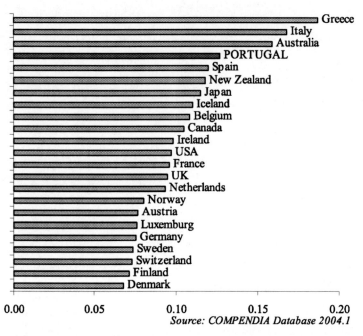

Source: COMPENDIA Database 2004.1

FIGURE 4: AVERAGE BUSINESS OWNERSHIP RATES FOR 23 OECD COUNTRIES – 1972-2004

Using a data source specific for Portugal – the Longitudinal Matched Employer-Employee Microdata set – LMEEM (see Escária and Madruga 2002) – based on information gathered by the Portuguese Ministry of Labor and Solidarity covering all business units with at least one wage-earner in the Portuguese economy, it is possible to shed some additional light on the nature of the size distribution of new firms in Portugal. Figures 5 and 6 display the size distribution of firms in the Portuguese economy in the 1990s and the average net entry rates per size class during the same period.

From Figures 5 and 6, it is possible to establish that, as pointed out earlier in the chapter, the proportion of micro-firms in the Portuguese economy seems to be increasing, as the larger size classes display negative entry rates. Even though the structure of economic activity in Portugal has largely switched from agriculture to services between the 1970s and the 1990s, the persistently small average size of firms means that new firm survival and growth rates are likely to be low.[11] Hence, the industrial restructuring effects brought about by increases in business ownership rates probably will not have significant repercussions on the reduction of future unemployment.

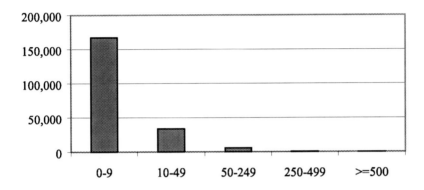

FIGURE 5 - SIZE DISTRIBUTION OF INCUMBENTS (STOCK OF FIRMS) IN THE PORTUGUESE ECONOMY (NO OF EMPLOYEES) – AVERAGE 1991-2000

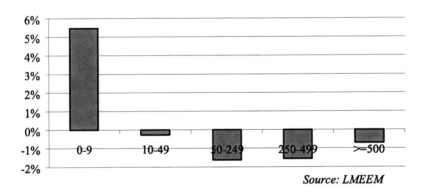

Source: LMEEM

FIGURE 6: NET ENTRY RATES PER SIZE CLASS (NO OF EMPLOYEES) – AVERAGE 1991-2000

Following a methodology similar to that used by Fritsch and Mueller (2004), Baptista, Escária and Madruga (2005) examined the lag structure of the long term effects of new business formation on employment for the Portuguese regions for 1982-2002. Their results, while displaying a lag structure similar to that of Germany, showed that positive long term effects of regional start-ups on future employment are smaller and take longer to occur in Portugal. Since the authors controlled for regional industrial structures of incumbents and new entrants, differences between countries in the magnitude of these long term effects of new business formation on employment are probably due to differences in the "quality" of entrants, which may be indicated by their potential for future growth. It is likely that the relatively high prevalence of subsistence entrepreneurship/necessity-based entrepreneurial activity in Portugal are associated with low firm growth rates, thus leading to lower effects of new business formation on employment growth. Indeed the relatively low labor productivity levels[12] in Portuguese businesses, related to the low education attainment of the working age population (IAPMEI, 2005, p. 15), are not conducive to the positive long term employment effects of new business formation as described in Section 4.

All this suggests that the model estimated in the present paper should systematically over-estimate the (negative) impact of increasing business ownership rates on unemployment, i.e., one should expect observed unemployment in Portugal to be consistently higher than predicted unemployment and so there should be a consistently positive estimated residual. Such a hypothesis, however, does not hold for 1990 and 1994. The pattern of residuals therefore suggests that other economic factors should be taken into account when explaining the model's performance for this period.

As was pointed out earlier, the first wave of cohesion funding which followed entry into the E.U. in 1986 was mostly directed at infra-structure enhancements and production capacity increases. This has generally led to an increase in capital intensity across the Portuguese economy. Probably scale increases by incumbents and the proliferation of public works contributed significantly to foster an unemployment rate below the levels predicted by the model. The dynamics provided by E.U. funding are likely to have provided a positive effect on employment that was unrelated to developments in business ownership rates in previous periods, thus explaining why the unemployment rate in 1990 and 1994 is significantly below the model's predictions.

This leaves only the large positive residual in 2002 to be clarified. In Section 3 it was explained that following the entry of Portugal into the E.U. in 1986, business ownership rates increased due to the de-regulation of markets brought about by privatization and E.U. rules. The increased business ownership rates after 1986 are visible in Figure 1. The results in the left panel of Table 1 imply that, with a lag of eight years, this increase should lead to a reduction in unemployment. Hence, according to the model the increase in business ownership between 1986 and 1994 should have led to a decrease in unemployment between 1994 and 2002. However, from Figure 3 we see that, although the unemployment rate decreased somewhat between 1994 and 1998, it did not change between 1998 and 2002. Hence, the predicted negative effect on unemployment did not occur in reality. This is consistent with the result found by Baptista, Escária and Madruga (2005) that positive long term employment effects of new firms are smaller in Portugal compared to other OECD countries and take longer to occur. This suggests that, although a significant proportion of the new firm entry may have been opportunity-based following E.U.-entry, the new firms do not (yet) contribute to employment creation at the aggregate level. Also, the negative effect on unemployment of the cohesion funding had probably extinguished by the end of the 1990s. Taken together these two phenomena might explain the large positive residual in 2002. This is also consistent with the earlier observation that the proportion of micro-firms in the Portuguese economy has increased during the last decade of the previous century (see Figures 5 and 6).

5.2. Self-employment Equation (2 and 2a)

The residuals, as well as the observed and predicted self-employment rates for Portugal are displayed in Figures 7 and 8. The residuals are positive – indicating an under-estimation of the business ownership rate – for the periods of 1990 and 1994; while for 1986 and 1998 the model provides higher predicted values for the self-employment rate than those actually observed (negative residuals). For 2002 the residual is close to zero. The unsystematic nature of the estimated residuals underlines the validity of the model formed by Equations (1) and (2) since, ideally, the disturbances should be independently distributed. Again part of the discrepancies observed between real and predicted unemployment in Portugal could be explained by macro-economic fluctuations that followed Portugal's entry in the E.U.

As was shown above, high rates of business ownership and a predominance of micro-businesses are distinguishing characteristics of the Portuguese economy. It was argued that this is probably associated with the high significance of necessity-based entrepreneurial activity. Such kind of entrepreneurial efforts result from a lack of better alternatives for subsistence. The prevalence of this kind of entrepreneurial activity suggests that there should be a strong positive effect of increases in unemployment rates on self-employment rates, as the newly unemployed would tend to look at self-employment as a viable subsistence choice.

The features of Portuguese industrial dynamics suggest therefore that the model estimated from data on 23 OECD countries should systematically under-estimate the effect of increases in the unemployment rate on increases in the self-employment rate, i.e., that residuals should be positive. From

Figure 1 we see that significant increases in the unemployment rate occurred only in the mid-1970s and the early 1990s. Considering the lags in the model this should – according to the hypothesis formulated above – have led to positive residuals in 1986, 1998 and 2002.

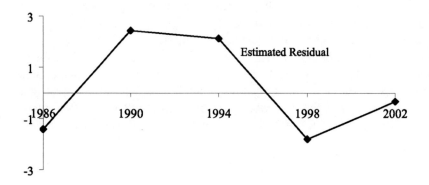

FIGURE 7: ESTIMATED RESIDUALS FOR PORTUGAL 1986-2002 IN %-POINTS (EQUATION 2A)

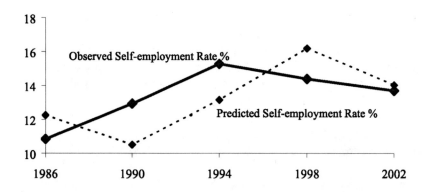

FIGURE 8: OBSERVED AND PREDICTED SELF-EMPLOYMENT RATES IN PORTUGAL 1986-2002

However, from Figure 7 we see that residuals are negative in these periods. This can be explained by counteracting effects on the business ownership rates in these periods, which were already described in Section 3. In the period prior to E.U.-entry (1982-1986) government policies protecting jobs and stimulating the public sector prevented the business ownership rate from rising while from the mid-1990s onwards consolidation and "shakeout" occurred in some markets following the first waves of cohesion funding after E.U.-entry. We argue that if these counteracting effects would not have occurred the residuals might have been positive in these periods, consistent with the hypothesis of increasing unemployment rates having a stronger impact on self-employment rates in Portugal compared to other OECD countries.

For the years 1990 and 1994 we find relatively large positive residuals (Figure 7). Similar to the negative residuals in the unemployment equation for these periods (Figure 2) the reason for this is probably the E.U.-entry in 1986. From the outset of E.U. integration, business ownership rates in Portugal increased significantly, as displayed in Figure 1. While, as pointed out above, the first waves of cohesion funding were applied mostly for infra-structural projects and growth of incumbents, several factors acted towards favoring an increase in start-ups and, therefore, business ownership rates. Among these factors, the growth in financial services associated with de-regulation (which had started in 1982) played a significant role by improving credit conditions for new businesses. Moreover, European integration opened up new geographic markets and created new business opportunities, some of which were exploited by new businesses. It is likely that the general atmosphere of confidence in future development favored a growth in business ownership rates that could not be anticipated by the model. However, as explained in Section 5.1, the contribution to economic development of the increased start-up activity may have been limited.

Finally we note that, from 1996 onwards, after a cycle of significant growth which started in the mid-1980s, the Portuguese business ownership rate started declining as a result of both industry consolidation and the failure of many of the start-ups that appeared in the previous decade. As a result, the model's prediction for the self-employment rate 2002 is actually very close to the observed rate, suggesting that the Portuguese industrial structure – at least with regard to the effect of variations in unemployment on variations in self-employment – is approaching behavioral patterns similar to those of the average of the OECD countries, although it is still too early to confirm this hypothesis.

6. CONCLUSIONS

The Portuguese industrial structure is strongly characterized by the dominance of micro-businesses and by the significance of necessity-based entrepreneurial activity, i.e., business ownership that arises from the lack of a better alternative for subsistence, and not from opportunity recognition and exploitation. Hence, a large proportion of Portuguese business owners tend to possess lower endowments of human capital and entrepreneurial talent required to start and sustain a new firm, suggesting that the effect of

238   *Entrepreneurship, Industrial Restructuring and Unemployment in Portugal*

entrepreneurial activity on unemployment reduction will be smaller in Portugal than in the average of the OECD countries analyzed.

One can therefore argue that, while the specific nature of the Portuguese industrial structure and self-employment do account for differences between the model's predictions of the rate of unemployment induced by variations in self-employment, and the rates of unemployment actually observed, these differences are more likely to be systematically positive, sanctioning the view that entrepreneurial activity in Portugal has smaller negative effects on future unemployment than in other developed countries. The negative residuals experienced in 1990 and 1994 – which seem to contradict this hypothesis – are likely to result from the strong positive effect on employment rates that was set off by entry in the E.U. and the impact of cohesion funding on public works and incumbent growth.

The same logic can be applied to the opposite relationship, i.e., the effect of increases in unemployment rates on business ownership rates. The significance of necessity-based entrepreneurial activity in Portugal suggests that the effect on variations in unemployment rates should be greater in Portugal than for the average of the OECD countries analyzed. One would therefore expect systematic positive residuals, sanctioning the view that a large proportion of self-employment in Portugal results from a lack of better alternatives (and not from opportunity recognition), increasing significantly as a result of increases in unemployment rates. Contrary to this hypothesis we found negative residuals for two of the periods. However we explained that these were due to specific counter effects that occurred in these periods in Portugal thereby providing support for the hypothesis that residuals may be systematically positive for Portugal.

Having carefully analyzed the residuals for both model equations it can then be concluded that differences between Portugal and other developed countries should be consistent in the following respects:

i)   Systematically positive residuals for the (negative) effect of increases in self-employment rates on unemployment rates, suggesting that entrepreneurial activity in Portugal has a smaller positive effect on employment creation than in other OECD countries;

ii) Systematically positive residuals for the effect of variations in unemployment rates on self-employment rates, suggesting that a larger proportion of entrepreneurial activity in Portugal results from a lack of employment alternatives in the business sector than in other OECD countries.

These conclusions do not mean, however, that business ownership in Portugal is excessive or should be discouraged. Stimulating entrepreneurship lifts the dependency on possibly sluggish and transient resources like scale, scope and experience, and intensifies the dependency on resources like adjustment and effectiveness. The latter resources are likely to be more robust against uncertainty and change than the former (Audretsch and Thurik, 2001 and 2004). Stimulating entrepreneurship implies stimulating diversity, which is fundamental for small firms to survive market selection processes.

While the results and conclusions suggest that some significant proportion of entrepreneurial activity in Portugal does not arise from opportunity recognition and is not aimed at growth and market selection, it can also be expected that entrepreneurial efforts will evolve in that direction and that industrial dynamics in Portugal will converge towards the pattern displayed by other OECD countries. The small residual in the self-employment equation for 2002 gives some support for this hypothesis. Some other support for this hypothesis can be found in the wide variety of initiatives undertaken in recent years by universities and public institutions to promote a culture of technology-based entrepreneurship and support innovative start-ups towards a knowledge-based economy[13]. Further enhancement of such activities and of the science and technology base underpinning their development, as well as growing support from the private sector, may contribute to an industrial restructuring process where a higher proportion of new firm start-ups play a significant role in bringing down unemployment.

NOTES

[1] There is an extensive literature about occupational choice and the self-employment option. See Parker (2004) for a survey.

[2] For instance, see Lin, Manser and Picot (1998).

[3] For instance, see Geroski (1989); Nickell (1996) and Nickell, Nicolitsas and Dryden (1997).

[4] Similar analyses of residuals are provided by Thurik and Verheul (2003) for Spain; Thurik (2003) for the U.K.; and van Acht, Stam, Thurik and Verheul (2004) for Japan.

[5] Klepper (1996) discusses the "shakeout" phenomenon in which, following an initial wave of entry, a phase of consolidation is observed in most markets, whereby a dominant product design emerges and scale economies become more prevalent.

[6] The inclusion of country dummies in the model was rejected by standard likelihood ratio tests. Indeed in Section 5 we will see that the estimated residuals for Portugal are unsystematic in that positive and negative values alternate.

[7] The Granger (1969) approach to the question of whether x causes y is to see how much of the current y can be explained by past values of y and then to see whether adding lagged values of x can improve the explanation. y is said to be Granger-caused by x if x helps in the prediction of y, or equivalently if the coefficients on the lagged x's are statistically significant. This can be tested using a simple F-test on the lagged x's.

[8] The harmonizations mainly concern corrections for the number of incorporated self-employed (harmonization across countries) and corrections for trend breaks (harmonization over time). The 23 countries included in COMPENDIA are the (old) E.U.-15 as well as Iceland, Norway, Switzerland, U.S., Japan, Canada, Australia and New Zealand.

[9] Audretsch, Carree, van Stel and Thurik (2005) refer to Geroski (1995), Beesley and Hamilton (1984) and Fritsch and Mueller (2004) for empirical examples of this lag.

[10] Note from Table 1 that the model contains a lag of 12 years. Hence the oldest year for which the unemployment and self-employment rates are predicted by the model is 1986.

[11] See Caves (1998) for a review of the determinants of new form survival and growth.

[12] Portuguese labor productivity represented 50 percent of E.U. average in 2004 (IAPMEI, 2005, p. 6).

[13] See, for instance, IAPMEI (2005), p. 24, as well as http://www.neotec.gov.pt/, http://www.adi.pt/Nest.htm, and http://www.green-wheel.net/.

REFERENCES

Acs, Z. J., and D. B. Audretsch (2003), "Innovation and Technological Change," in Z. J. Acs and D. B. Audretsch (eds.), Handbook of Entrepreneurship Research, Boston/Dordrecht: Kluwer Academic Publishers, 55-79.

Acs, Z. J., P. Arenius, M. Hay and M. Minniti (eds.) (2005), *Global Entrepreneurship Monitor – 2004 Summary Report*, Babson College and London Business School.

Acht, J. van, J. Stam, A. R. Thurik and I. Verheul (2004), "Business Ownership and Unemployment in Japan", Papers on Entrepreneurship, Growth and Public Policy #09-2004, Max Planck Institute of Economics, Jena, Germany.

Audretsch, D. B., M. A. Carree, A. J. van Stel and A. R. Thurik (2005), "Does Self-Employment Reduce Unemployment?", Papers on Entrepreneurship, Growth and Public Policy #07/2005. Max Planck Institute of Economics, Jena, Germany.

Audretsch, D. B., A. R. Thurik, I. Verheul and S. Wennekers (2002), *Entrepreneurship: Determinants and Policy in a European-US Comparison*, Boston/Dordrecht, Kluwer Academic Publishers.

Audretsch, D. B. and A. R. Thurik (2001), "What is New about the New Economy: Sources of Growth in the Managed and Entrepreneurial Economies," *Industrial and Corporate Change*, 10(1), 267-315.

Audretsch, D. B. and A. R. Thurik (2004), "The Model of the Entrepreneurial Economy," *International Journal of Entrepreneurship Education*, 2(2), 143-166.

Audretsch, D. B. and M. Keilbach (2004), "Entrepreneurship Capital and Economic Performance," *Regional Studies*, 38(8), 949-959.

Baptista, R., V. Escária and P. Madruga (2005), "Entrepreneurship, Regional Development and Job Creation: the Case of Portugal", Papers on Entrepreneurship, Growth and Public Policy #06/2005. Max Planck Institute of Economics, Jena, Germany.

Beesley, M. E. and M. T. Hamilton (1984), "Small Firms' Seedbed Role and the Concept of Turbulence", *Journal of Industrial Economics*, 33(2), 217-231.

Carree, M. A. and A. R. Thurik (2003), "The Impact of Entrepreneurship on Economic Growth," in D. B. Audretsch and Z. J. Acs (eds.), *Handbook of Entrepreneurship Research*, Boston/Dordrecht, Kluwer Academic Publishers, 437-471.

Caves, R. E. (1998), "Industrial Organization and New Findings on the Turnover and Mobility of Firms," *Journal of Economic Literature*, 36(4), 1947-1982.

Escária, V. and P. Madruga (2002), "The Construction of a Longitudinal Matched Employer-Employee Microdata Data Set", Mimeo, CIRIUS, ISEG, Technical University of Lisbon.

Fritsch, M., and P. Mueller (2004), "The Effects of New Business Formation on Regional Development over Time", *Regional Studies*, 38(8), 961-975.

Geroski, P. A. (1989), "Entry, Innovation, and Productivity Growth," *Review of Economics and Statistics*, 71(4), 572-578.

Geroski, P. A. (1995), "What Do We Know About Entry?", *International Journal of Industrial Organization*, 13(5), 421- 440.

Granger, C. W. J. (1969), "Investigating Causal Relations by Econometric Models and Cross-Spectral Methods," *Econometrica*, 37(3), 424-438.

Hurst, E. and A. Lusardi (2004), "Liquidity Constraints, Household Wealth and Entrepreneurship," *Journal of Political Economy*, 112(2), 319-347.

IAPMEI (2005), *Portuguese Economic Profile*, mimeo.

Klepper, S. (1996), "Entry, Exit, Growth, and Innovation over the Product Life Cycle," *American Economic Review*, 86(3), 562-583.

Lin, Z. M., E. Manser and G. Picot (1998), "The Role of Self-Employment in Job Creation in Canada and the U.S.", OECD-CERF-CILN International Conference on Self-Employment, Burlington, Ontario, Canada.

Nickell, S. J. (1996), "Competition and Corporate Performance," *Journal of Political Economy*, 104(4), 724-746.

Nickell, S. J, P. Nicolitsas and N. Dryden (1997), "What Makes Firms Perform Well?", *European Economic Review*, 41(3-5), 783-796.

Parker, S. C. (2004), The *Economics of Self-Employment and Entrepreneurship*, Cambridge: Cambridge University Press.

Sims, Ch. A. (1980), "Macroeconomics and Reality," *Econometrica*, 48(1), 1-48.

Stel, A. J. van (2005), "COMPENDIA: Harmonizing Business Ownership Data Across Countries and Over Time", *International Entrepreneurship and Management Journal*, 1(1), 105-123.

Stel, A. J. van, M. A. Carree and A. R. Thurik (2005), "The Effect of Entrepreneurial Activity on National Economic Growth", *Small Business Economics*, 24(3), 311-321.

Thurik, A. R. (2003), "Entrepreneurship and unemployment in the U.K.", *Scottish Journal of Political Economy*, 50(2), 264-290.

Thurik, A. R. and I. Verheul (2003), "The Relationship between Entrepreneurship and Unemployment: the Case of Spain," in: D. Urbano (ed.), Entrepreneurship (Creación de Empresas), Barcelona, Servei de Publicacions de la UAB, 521-547.

Chapter 12
TRANSFERRING THE RISK OF FAILURE.
ENTREPRENEURSHIP AND FIRM DYNAMICS
IN TURKISH MANUFACTURING

Erol Taymaz
Middle East Technical University, Ankara

Ali Güneş
State Institute of Statistics, Ankara

Kenan Orhan
State Institute of Statistics, Ankara

1. INTRODUCTION

Firm and industry dynamics have received considerable attention in recent years. There are numerous theoretical and empirical studies that shed light on the processes of entry, exit, and growth of firms. These studies show that, in almost all countries and sectors, the probability of failure is quite high. Establishing a new firm is a very risky activity.

Although there are a number of debated issues, the empirical literature has been successful in clarifying a number of stylized facts about firm dynamics (Geroski, 1995; Caves, 1998). First, entry is common. Large numbers of firms are established each year. Second, new firms usually start small. Entrants are much smaller than incumbents. Third, failure is also common. Most entrants fail in a few years.

In an evolutionary way of thinking, the processes of entry and exit are regarded as wasteful but necessary for keeping the dynamism of industries. Many researchers have studied firm- and industry-specific factors that determine the likelihood of survival. Two variables have received considerable attention in theoretical and empirical studies: firm size and age. Most of the studies found that current and start-up size has a significant impact on survival probability. Large (and rapidly growing) firms are more likely to survive (for a small set of empirical studies, see Dunne, Roberts and

Samuelson, 1989; Mata and Portugal, 1994; Mata, Portugal and Guimaraes, 1995; Santarelli, 1998; Baldwin, Bian, Dupuy and Gellatly, 2000; Segarra and Callejon, 2002; Geroski, Mata and Portugal, 2003; Disney, Haskel and Heden, 2003; Taymaz, 2005; however, Wagner (1994), Audretsch, Santarelli and Vivarelli (1999) and Santarelli and Vivarelli (2002) found no effect of the start-up size on survival probability). Although firm age and size are positively correlated, and size has a significant positive impact on survival probability, the effect of firm age on survival is found to be significant even after controlling for firm size. There are various explanations for the effects of firm size and age. It is suggested that new firms start small because of difficulties in getting funding from external sources (the so-called imperfect capital market hypothesis), or prefer to start small to reduce the (sunk) costs of entry into an uncertain environment (the real options theory). Since small firms may have higher costs (if they operate at sub-optimal scale or pay higher interest on their debt), and they lack market power, they have low probability of success. If firm age is related with (both market and technological) experience, we may expect a positive correlation between age and survival probability conditional on firm size.[1]

Although the emphasis has been on size and age, empirical studies are rich in terms of firm- and industry-specific variables used to explain industrial dynamics, and, specifically, the exit (survival) process. Researchers have studied the effects of a variety of factors, such as market structure, technological conditions, financial structures, geographical aspects, etc. However, we believe that there is a crucial missing factor: the perception of the entrepreneur about business opportunities, and his/her reaction to market conditions. We, economists and econometricians, know that failure rates of new firms are high, and failure may well come at a very high cost: personal losses as well as financial costs (loss of savings, social status, etc.). Of course, we should expect that entrepreneurs are also aware of these facts, and, therefore, they should take precautionary measures to reduce the costs of (potential) failure. Because of intrinsic characteristics of business environment, an entrepreneur cannot eliminate all the risk, but he/she can transfer a part of risks to other agents. In this study, we analyze three mechanisms that can be used by entrepreneurs to transfer the risks of failure: i) borrowing from external sources (transferring the risk to creditors), ii) reducing sunk costs (by renting/leasing building, machinery and equipment, transferring the risk to investors), and iii) lowering the base wage and compensating workers by bonus-type payments (transferring the risk to workers). These mechanisms (except the first one) have not received enough attention in the literature, and we found that they play a very important role in explaining survival dynamics.

The rest of the paper is organized as follows. A short discussion on risk transferring mechanisms is presented in Section 2. The data sources and main variables of interest are explained in Section 3. We test whether entrepreneurs are able to transfer some of the risks of failure to other agent by estimating a hazard function for new firms. Section 4 presents the model and estimation results. The last section summarizes main findings.

2. MECHANISMS FOR RISK TRANSFER

There are numerous studies that document the fact that business failures are common. Entrepreneurs, who may have also experienced failures in their earlier attempts, know very well that the probability of failure is not insignificant.[2] Therefore, one may expect that entrepreneurs should take some measures that can reduce the probability and cost of failure. We can envisage three measures that the entrepreneur can use: financing investment and operation through external funds ('debt mechanism'), reducing the fixed costs of firing and lay-offs ('wage mechanism'), and leasing the fixed capital ('leasing mechanism').

2.1. Debt Mechanism

The effects of external finance on the establishment and subsequent survival of firms have been studied extensively.[3] There are two strands of literature that are related to our topic. The first literature deals with the role of external finance and liquidity constraints in establishing new firms. This issue was studied systematically the first time by Evans and Jovanovic (1989). They suggested that liquidity constraints are binding even in the U.S., and own capital is essential for starting a business.[4] Liquidity constraints restrict the size of the firm established by those with insufficient funds. Although the Evans-Jovanovic model does not explicitly address the link between external funding and survival, it has some implications: if the liquidity constraint is effective, financially constrained firms will be smaller than the optimal level, and tend to be in a disadvantageous position vis-à-vis those established by wealthy entrepreneurs.

The second literature deals with the default risk under adverse selection and moral hazard in debt financing (interactions between banks and borrowers), and was begun by the work of Stiglitz and Weiss (1981). They showed that the adverse selection effect arises if the interest rate acts as a device to screen 'bad borrowers' from 'good borrowers'. In such a case, higher interest rates induce firms to undertake projects with lower probabilities of success but higher payoffs when successful.

Adverse selection can be used to explain the link between survival and external financing. Firms have usually limited liability on the debt they own: the owners are not responsible for debts that could exceed the capital they have invested in the firm.[5] Therefore, as shown by Gollier, Koehl and Rochet (1997), the optimum exposure to risk of the limited liability firm becomes always larger than under full liability, i.e., firms can take more risky activities if they are debt financed.

Limited liability has two major effects on firm dynamics. First, limited liability encourages entry by providing a kind of wealth insurance for potential risk averse entrepreneurs. Second, firms can enter into high risk projects that offer high returns. Those firms that borrow heavily will be less likely to survive because they will tend to perform risky activities. Thus, the extent of limited liability will determine both the rates of entry and exit.

These predictions are also supported by empirical studies. For example, Fan and White (2003) showed in the U.S. case that higher bankruptcy exemption levels lead to more entrepreneurial activity.[6] They estimated that "the probability of households owning businesses is 35 percent higher if they live in states with unlimited rather than low exemptions." [7]

The failure rate is likely to be higher if the bankruptcy law provides higher exemptions (lower default risk). Persad (2005), in his study on the effects of loans provided under the U.S. Small Business Administration 7(a) program, suggests that the default rate may rise because of two factors: adverse selection (if borrowers stand to lose less in the event of default, borrowers with riskier projects might apply), and moral hazard (borrowers with the same class of project risk exert less effort required to maintain solvency). He finds strong evidence that adverse selection rather than moral hazard explains higher default rates. Since adverse selection problems are quite sizable, he suggests that "the potential benefits of higher exemptions and guarantees in fostering entrepreneurship should be weighed against potential misallocation of credit and a higher cost to taxpayers."

To sum up, the effect of debt financing on failure probability may operate via three distinct channels:[8] *1*) If liquidity constraint is binding, those entrepreneurs without sufficient own wealth may establish firms operating at sub-optimal scale, and face with cost disadvantages against large firms. Therefore, those that have to borrow more are likely to have lower survival probability. Note, however, that this effect may turn out to be insignificant if the firm size is controlled for. If liquidity constraint is not binding, all firms will be established at the optimum scale irrespective of entrepreneurs' wealth, and debt financing would have no effect on survival probability. *2*) Debt financing will add a burden on operating costs, and the firm will be more likely to exit under unfavorable market conditions. The effect will be stronger if the cost of financing (the interest rate) increases by the level of leverage (debt/assets ratio). *3*) With or without liquidity constraints, adverse selection and limited liability may cause entrepreneurs to demand more loans for riskier activities because the loss due to failure will be limited. If the entrepreneur observes an increase in business risks, he/she may tend to rely more on debt financing to pass over some of the risks to the creditors. This is basically the risk transfer mechanism we refer to.

There are a few studies that explicitly analyzed the effects of external financing on survival probability. Fotopoulos and Louri (2000) found that the degree of the debt burden of a firm as measured by the leverage ratio (the ratio of current and medium to long term liabilities over total assets) is "obstructive for the operation and eventually the existence of new firms" in Greek manufacturing in the 1982–1992 period. Ushijima (2005) also found that Japanese plants in the U.S. belonging to more leveraged parents and having increased reliance on debts are less likely to survive. Vartia (2004) studied the impact of financial status on entry and exit dynamics of Finnish manufacturing plants. She used a number of financial ratios in her regression analysis and found that entrants and exits have higher debt to assets ratio than incumbents, and the debt burden (debt/asset ratio) decreases the probability of survival, whereas the coverage ratio (cash flow/interest expenses) enhances the survival probability. Åstebro and Bernhardt (2003) studied whether new small businesses having a bank loan are more likely to survive than those having no bank loan by using the Characteristics of Business Owners surveys collected by the U.S. Bureau of the Census. Although those having a bank loan had, on average, lower survival rates, a probit regression model of start-up company survival including variables on a number of industry and firm characteristics such as owner's human capital, loan sources, and wealth showed that having a bank loan has a positive impact on survival probability conditional on other explanatory variables. Åstebro and Bernhardt's findings are different than those of other researchers, but the variable they used is a dummy variable that does not reflect the burden of debt.

2.2. Wage Mechanism

There are two competing explanations on the link between wages and business failures. First, some researcher (for example, see Hamermesh, 1988) suggested that the risk of business failure (or the risk of lay-offs) will generate higher wages, because the fear of unemployment has to be compensated in competitive labor markets (the compensating differentials hypothesis). Thus, if the firm operates in risky markets, workers will also face with the risk of losing their jobs, and will demand higher wages. Second, it is suggested that (for example, see Blanchflower, 1991) if wages are determined in bilateral bargain, the risk of being fired as a result of business failure will generate lower wages (the bargaining concessions hypothesis). Workers who wish to retain their jobs will accept lower wages to reduce the probability of bankruptcy.

Empirical studies found some evidence supporting the bargaining concessions hypothesis. For example, Blanchflower (1991) found that "fear of unemployment substantially depresses pay, more in non-union workplaces than union workplaces". In a recent study, Carneiro and Portugal (2003) estimated a simultaneous-equations model of firm closing and wage determination by using individual level data. Their findings indicate that the fear of job loss generates bargaining concessions instead of compensating differentials. Therefore, firms employing mostly minimum wage earners are more vulnerable to adverse demand shocks due to their inability to adjust wages downward. In the 'firm-closing equation, they found that higher wages lead to higher rates of failure. Campbell, Carruth, Dickerson and Green, (2004) used 'subjective' measures of unemployment fear that predicts well future unemployment. They also found that high fears of unemployment are found to be associated with significantly lower levels of wage growth for men, but have no significant link with wage growth for women.

These studies analyze the link between the *level* of wages and business failures, but the *composition* of payments to workers could also be important. For example, wages payments in Turkey have four main components: regular wage, overtime payments, bonuses and premiums, and social contributions and payments in kind. Regular wage is a predetermined gross wage (including workers' social security contribution) that is paid to workers over regular intervals. Overtime wage includes gross payments for overtime work. Bonuses and premiums are extra-payments for workers that are based on individual or collective performance (for example, employee productivity, company profits, etc.). Social contributions and payments in kind include all other contributions provided by the firms to employees such as free meal, clothing, etc. The composition of wage payments is important because it determines the firing cost. In the Turkish case, the firm is required to pay one-month's wage for each year of employment as severance pay in the case of non-fault dismissals, and the 'wage' used to calculate the severance pay does not include occasional payments such as overtime payments, bonuses and premiums. Therefore, the firm can reduce firing (and failure) costs by simply varying the *composition* of wages in favor of occasional payments even if it means an increase in the *level* of net wages. In such a case, the firm will transfer the risk of failure to workers who can accept the offer if there are asymmetries in information available to the firm and workers. This is the wage mechanism that can be used by firms to transfer the risks of failures to workers.

2.3. Leasing Mechanism

It is well know, at least since Dixit's (1989) classical article on "Entry and Exit Decisions under Uncertainty", that even small sunk costs can lead to hysteresis' in investment decisions and firm dynamics. An entrepreneur will take into consideration irreversible/sunk costs before starting a new business. He/she will establish a new firm if the expected product price exceeds the variable cost plus the interest on the entry cost and exit if the price is less than the variable cost minus the interest on the exit cost. The level of entry and exit costs is determined by the sunk costs of investment.

The entrepreneur can avoid some of the entry and exit costs by using various financial instruments to start the business. 'Leasing' is one of the options to avoid the capital cost involved in investment.[9] In leasing, the equipment is an asset of the leasing company (the investor/lessor) rather than the user firm (the lessee), and the firm will not bear most of the (sunk) investment costs in the case of failure. By leasing the investment goods, the entrepreneur can reduce its entry and exit costs, and make exit easier. In other words, exit (failure) could be more likely if the firm leases heavily. This is the leasing mechanism that can be used by the entrepreneur to start and to close down a business less costly.

3. THE DATA AND THE MODEL

We hypothesize that those firms operate under risky conditions tend to transfer their failure risks to creditors (by borrowing), to investors (by leasing) and to workers (by changing the composition of wages). If the risk of failure is higher, the firm will tend to transfer a larger part of the risks. Therefore, we would expect that firms that heavily borrow, lease a larger part of their equipment, and pay relatively low regular wages (and prefer more bonus-type occasional payments) will be less likely to survive. The hypothesis will be tested by estimating a Cox proportional hazards model as follows:

$$h(t_i) = exp(-X_{it}\beta)/h_o(t_i) \tag{1}$$

where $h(t_i)$ is the hazard function (the probability that the firm i will exit at time t), h_o the 'baseline' hazard, X a vector of explanatory variables, and β the vector of parameters to be estimated.

We use four variables as proxy for risk transfer behavior. BONUS is measured by the share of bonus-type payments, social contributions and payments in kind in total gross wage.[10] This variable is used to capture the effects of risk transfer to workers. If the entrepreneur anticipates a high risk of failure, he/she will tend to substitute occasional payments (such as bonuses, premiums, etc.) to reduce firing (and, therefore, exit) costs. Second variable, INTEREST, is the ratio of interest payments to sales revenue. Since there is no data available on debt stock and the value of assets, this variable is used as a proxy for indebtedness or debt burden of the firm. As noted before, higher value of interest implies that the firm operates in a risky environment in which the probability of survival is lower. There are two variables for the leasing mechanism. LEASING is the ratio between leasing expenditures on machinery and equipment and sales, and RENT the ratio between rent payments (for building) and sales.

These two variables are expected to have positive (negative) impact on the hazard (survival) probability.

There are some other factors that could influence the hazard probability. The (log) number of employees, LL, is used to control for firm size. Since there could be a (log) non-linear relationship between survival probability and firm size, the quadratic term of the LL variable, LL2, is also included in the model. As noted in the previous section, the wage level could have an impact on survival probability, too. The (log) level of wages relative to the industry average, RELWAGE, is used to check if wages have any influence on survival. Average employment growth rate since entry (LGR) is added into the model to control for the effects of learning and past performance, whereas capital intensity variable (KL, log value of real depreciation allowances per employee) is expected to control for capital intensity and sunk costs. The share of female employees (WOMEN) is a proxy for the characteristics of production ('feminized' activities) and the composition of the labor force. Since female workers are paid lower than male workers, firms employing mostly female workers will not be able to adjust wages downward, and will tend to exit under adverse conditions.

There are two sector- and region-specific control variables. REGGR is measured as annual regional industrial output growth[11], and is used to capture the effects of demand shifts. If the demand increases rapidly, firms in that market will be more likely to survive. The sectoral entry rate, ENTRATE, is defined as the share of new entrants in total number of firms in the same industry. If entry makes competition tougher, the hazard probability will be higher.

The data source is the *Annual Surveys of Manufacturing Industry* conducted by the State Institute of Statistics (SIS). The survey covers all private establishments employing 10 or more people and all public establishments. We use the data for the period 1992-2001. At the time of writing this paper, the data after 2001 were not yet available. Since there is a change in the survey questionnaire for small firms employing 10-24 people in 1992, we do not use the data for pre-1992 period. (The SIS conducted the Census of Manufacturing Industries in 1992.) There are about 11,000 firms[12] each year in the period 1992-2001. Since the initial (1992) and end (2001) years' data are used to define entrants and exits, the analysis is performed for the period 1993-2000.

Figure 1 presents the data on survival rates for small (those firms smaller than the geometric mean of the sample) and large firms. As it is the case in all other countries, the hazard rate is quite high in Turkish manufacturing industries. About half of small entrants (i.e., those firms that employed 10-48 people when they were first established) exit from the market in less than five years. The survival rate is somewhat higher for large entrants (66 percent survives until the age of five), and the equality of survivor functions is rejected at the 1 percent level by the log-rank test, i.e., there is a statistically significant difference in survival rates of small and large firms.

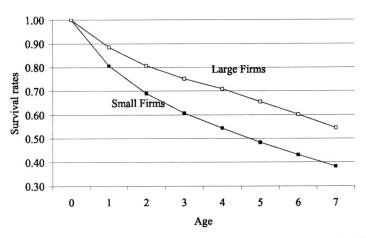

FIGURE 1 – SURVIVAL RATES FOR SMALL AND LARGE FIRMS, 1993-2001

The average values of risk transfer variables by firm size and age are shown in Table 1. The share of bonus-type payments in total gross wage (the BONUS variable) monotonically increases by firm size. The share of bonus-type payments is only 2 percent for new firms employing 10-24 people whereas it is more than 20 percent for those start-ups employing more than 500 people. The strong correlation between bonus-type payments and firm size indicates that large firms tend to use these types of payments for other purposes as well. It seems that older (5-years old) large firms reduce the share of bonus-type payments to some extent, but there is not much difference between young and old small entrants. Low share of bonus-type payments in small entrants is also due to the fact that most of small entrants never pay bonuses, whereas this type of payment is common among large firms.

Table 1 – The extent of risk, by firms size and age in percentage, 1993-2000

| | Current size (number of employees) | | | | | |
	10-24	25-49	50-149	150-249	250-499	>500
NEW FIRMS (AGE 0)						
Bonus payments	2.0	3.5	6.4	12.0	16.9	20.8
Interest payments	1.1	1.8	3.3	3.7	4.3	3.9
Leasing payments	0.1	0.3	0.3	0.2	0.5	0.3
Rents	0.8	0.8	0.6	0.4	0.3	0.2
5-YEARS OLD FIRM (AGE 5)						
Bonus payments	2.4	3.3	6.7	11.9	12.2	15.8
Interest payments	2.1	2.1	3.6	5.3	3.1	4.5
Leasing payments	0.2	0.3	0.3	0.4	0.3	0.3
Rents	0.8	0.8	0.6	0.3	0.3	0.3

Interest payments to sales ratio (the INTEREST variable) also increases by firm size for small and medium-sized firms up to a certain threshold (250 employees). Moreover, as the firm gets older, the interest rate ratio tends to increase, albeit to a small extent. It is equal to only 1.1 percent for small start-ups (employing 10-24 people), and increases to 2.1 percent for small, 5-years old firms.[13] For those firms that employ more than 500 people, the share of interest payments in sales is 3.9 percent, and it gradually rises to 4.5 percent in five years. Although these figures seem to be low, one should also look at the share of interest payments in value added. Since the average share of value added in sales is about 30-35 percent, new Turkish manufacturing firms transfer about 10 percent of their value added as interest payments to financial institutions.

Leasing payments/sales and rents/sales ratios (the average values of LEASING and RENT variables) are quite small. Leasing payments are around 0.1 percent of sales for small entrants employing 10-24 people, and reaches to mere 0.3 percent for large entrants employing more than 500 people. The proportion of firms that use leased machinery and equipment is also low (about 5 percent for small entrants, and 30 percent for large entrants). Moreover, there is not any noticeable change in the leasing ratio over the life of new firms. We observe a completely different pattern for rent payments for buildings. Small firms are more likely to rent buildings: the ratio of rent payments to sales decreases by firm size, from 0.8 percent for the smallest entrant category to 0.2 for the largest entrant category, and the ratio does not change much over time, at least during the first five years of new firms.

New firms (at age zero and five) and the incumbent firms[14] are compared in Table 2. The stylized fact on the size of entrants is observed in the Turkish case as well. Entrants are small, much smaller than the incumbents. The number of people employed by an average entrant is almost 50 percent less than the number of people employed by an average incumbent. As may be expected, the share of bonus-type payments and interest payments/sales ratio are significantly higher in incumbents than new firms, whereas the incumbents seem to rely less on leased machinery and equipment and rented buildings than the new firms do. Incumbents pay higher wages (20 percent more than the start-ups), but, as Brown and Medoff (2003) observe, the difference could be insignificant when other firm characteristics (most importantly, firm size) is controlled for. Those new firms that survive grow quite rapidly. If a new firm survives until age five, it will achieve, on average, 8 percent employment growth each year.

Table 2 - Descriptive statistics (1993-2000 average values)

| | | Entrants | | | Incumbent |
		Age 0	Age 5	All obs.	All obs.
BONUS	Bonus-type payments wage bill	3.45	4.69	3.96	9.67
INTEREST	Interest payments/sales	1.64	2.71	2.06	2.76
LEASING	Leasing payments for machhinery/sales	0.19	0.23	0.23	0.15
RENTS	Rent payments for building/sales	0.74	0.70	0.71	0.55
LL	Number of employees [a]	24.26	39.48	29.88	50.92
RELWAGE	Relative wages	-15.27	-5.45	-11.50	6.47
LGR	Average employment growth rate since entry		8.24	8.55	
KL	Depreciation allowances per employee (1997 prices) [a]	17.32	21.38	19.10	19.61
WOMEN	Share of female employees	19.69	20.47	20.29	19.38
REGGR	Regional industrial growth rate	21.90	15.66	17.23	7.51
ENTRATE	Sectoral entry rate	30.91	8.62	16.31	8.92
N	Number of observations	10,140	1,410	31,520	56,025

[a] geometric average

There is not much difference in terms of capital intensity and the share of female workers. New firms are established in those regions/sectors where the demand increases rapidly, and certain sectors attract more entry. The annual regional industrial growth rate is very high for start-ups, more than 20 percent, whereas the average growth rate for incumbents that operate in all regions and sectors reflects the average industrial growth rate in the country (7.5 percent). As noted before and shown in Figure 1, small firms have lower survival probability than large firms but, contrary to our *a priori* expectations, large firms tend to use some of the risk transfer mechanisms (bonus-type payments and external funding) more intensively. The strong correlation between firm size and the share of bonus-type payments and interest payments suggests that there could be other factors that encourage firms to use these instruments. For example, it could be more difficult for large firms to monitor the intensity of work at the workplace, and, therefore, large firms may tend to use more extensively performance-based bonus-type payments. Moreover, if the capital markets are not perfect, then it may be easier for large firms to get funding from the financial system so that large firms could have higher ratio of interest payments to sales. Thus, in order to understand the links between risk transfer mechanisms and survival prospects, we need to control for other factors like the firm size. In the following section, we will study if firms do use these mechanisms in a multivariate context by estimating a Cox proportional hazard function.

4. DETERMINANTS OF SURVIVAL: ESTIMATION RESULTS

We have estimated the Cox proportional hazard function (Equation 1) for all establishments established in the period 1993-2000 in Turkish manufacturing industries.[15] There are about 7,500 establishments established in that time period and almost 40 percent of them exited from the market in the same period. There are, on average, 3.5 observations per establishment.

The first model estimated includes only four risk transfer variables (BONUS, INTEREST, LEASING and RENTS, see Model 1 in Table 3). The BONUS and LEASING variables have negative and statistically significant coefficients, whereas RENTS has a positive and significant coefficient. In other words, those firms that pay (proportionally) more bonus-type payments and interest are more likely to survive, whereas those paying more rent are more likely to exit. The negative coefficient for the BONUS variable reminds us the fact that it is positively correlated with firm size, and its effect on survival incorporates the size effects as well. The INTEREST variable has positive but insignificant coefficient.

When the firm size variables are controlled for in Model 2 (log number of employees and its square, LL and LL2 variables), the coefficient of the BONUS variable switches its sign but becomes statistically insignificant. The interest variable has now a significant positive coefficient: as expected, high interest payments/sales ratio leads to high hazard probability. The LEASING parameter still have negative and significant coefficient that indicate that leasing machinery and equipment reduces the probability of business failure. A comparison between Model 1 and Model 2 shows clearly that the firm size needs to be controlled for to understand the effects of risk transfer variables on hazard (survival) probabilities.

Table 3 – Cox Proportional Hazard model estimation results

	Model 1		Model 2		Model 3		Model 4	
	Coeff.	Std. dev.	Coeff.	Std. dev.	Coeff.	Std. dev.	Coeff.	Std. dev.
BONUS	-1.34	0.23**	0.02	0.23	0.65	0.24***	-0.62	0.76
INTEREST	0.20	0.29	1.33	0.26***	1.35	0.27***	1.34	0.90
LEASING	-10.63	2.47***	-4.99	2.19**	-3.5	2.09*	13.51	12.91
RENTS	9.12	0.99***	6.22	1.01***	2.5	1.14**	2.51	1.14**
LL			-2.38	0.13***	-2.3	0.15***	-2.22	0.15***
LL2			0.23	0.02***	0.23	0.02***	0.22	0.02***
RELWAGE					-0.3	0.04***	-0.30	0.04***
LGR					-0.44	0.06***	-0.44	0.06***
KL					-0.15	0.01***	-0.15	0.01***
WOMEN					0.34	0.07***	0.34	0.07***
REGGR					-0.11	0.04***	-0.11	0.04***
ENTRATE					0.36	0.16**	0.37	0.16***
KL*LEASING							-5.40	4.20
LL*BONUS							0.36	0.21*
LL*INTEREST							0.00	0.24
Number of observations	21,294		21,294		20,434		20,434	
Number of firms	7,494		7,494		7,314		7,314	
Number of failures	2,971		2,971		2,776		2,776	
Wald test	279.3***		1159.0***		1549.5***		1558.0***	
Log pseudo-likelihood	-25,084		-25,084		-25,084		-25,084	

Note: all models include time dummies. Robust standard errors are used. ***,** and * mean statistically significant at 1%, 5% and 10% level, respectively.

The third model includes all other control variables, which have all statistically significant coefficients (at least at the 5 percent level). The relative wage variable (RELWAGE) has a negative coefficient: those firms that pay lower wages are more likely to fail. As Blanchflower (2001) suggests, fear of unemployment due to business risks and failures reduces wages. Thus, our data supports the bargaining concessions hypothesis. The growth rate of the firm has a positive (negative) impact on survival (exit) probability. This finding is consistent with that of Troske (1996) who found that "firm exit is characterized by failing mean growth rates and mean relative firm size for a number of periods prior to exit".

Capital intensive firms are less likely to exit (the capital/labor ratio variable, KL) whereas those that rely on home-based, feminized activities (the WOMEN variable) have higher hazard rates. The growth rate of regional demand (REGGR) has the expected positive impact on survival prospects. The "revolving door" metaphor seems to be valid as well: if a large number of new firms enter into the market (ENTRATE), their exit rates will get higher as well.

The estimates for risk transfer variables in Model 3, which is the preferred model, provide strong support for our hypothesis. The BONUS, INTEREST, and RENTS variables have positive and statistically significant coefficients. In other words, *ceteris paribus*, those firms that tend to pay (proportionally) more bonus-type payments, interest payments and rents have higher failure probability. The only exception is the LEASING variable: it has a negative coefficient that is statistically different from zero at 10 percent significance level. It seems that leasing machinery and equipment enhances survival probability, possibly by reducing the cost of capital.

Leasing could play a more important role if capital intensity and sunk costs are higher. Although there is no data available to measure sunk costs of investment, one may suggest that they are correlated with capital intensity. We test the interactions between capital intensity and leasing by adding the interaction term into our model (the KL*LEASING variable). Similarly, risk transfer through bonus-type payments and interest payments could depend on firm size: large firms may tend to use these mechanism more intensively because they are likely to be constrained by more rigid employment practices, and they can relatively easily borrow from financial institutions. Two additional interaction terms, LL*BONUS and LL*INTEREST are used to check if there is a difference between small and large firms in terms of using these two risk transfer mechanism.

When three interaction variables are included in the model, all three risk transfer variables (LEASING, BONUS and INTEREST) become insignificant because of multicollinearity problem. Among the interaction terms, only the LL*BONUS variable has a statistically significant coefficient (but at only 10 percent level). Moreover, the log-likelihood test for joint significance of interaction variables does reject the null hypothesis that the coefficients of three interaction terms are all equal to zero ($\chi^2_{(3)} = 4.30$, smaller than the critical value at 10 percent level, 6.25). Thus, we conclude that the interaction terms do not increase the explanatory power of the third model.

5. CONCLUSIONS

There is an extensive literature that studies firm and industry dynamics (the processes of entry, exit, and growth). Empirical studies show that new firms start small, and small and young firms are less likely to survive. In all countries, a large proportion of new firms survive only a few years. However, the empirical literature has not paid sufficient attention to how entrepreneurs act in response to business risks, and has a tendency to ignore strategic reactions.

In this paper, we suggest that entrepreneurs are also aware of the stylized facts uncovered by economists and econometricians, and they take measures to reduce the costs of (potential) exit. This study is focused on three mechanisms that can be used by entrepreneurs to transfer the risks of failure: borrowing from external sources (transferring the risk to creditors), reducing sunk costs (by renting/leasing building, machinery and equipment, transferring the risk to investors), and lowering the regular wage and compensating workers by bonus-type payments (transferring the risk to workers). Our empirical analysis has shown that those firms that tend to pay

- more bonuses and premiums (over the regular wage) to their workers,
- more interest to their creditors, and
- more rent to their landlords

are more likely to exit. We also found that leasing machinery and equipment has a positive impact on survival prospects. Our findings provide evidence for the hypothesis that entrepreneurs in Turkish manufacturing industries are able to transfer some of the risks of failure to creditors, investors, and workers.

Evolutionary economists have shown, at least since the early writings of Schumpeter, that the processes of entry and exit are wasteful but necessary for keeping the dynamism of industries. Entry and exit constitute essential components of any experimentally-organized economy (Eliasson, 1991). The possibilities for transferring and diffusing the risks of failure will certainly encourage (potential) entrepreneurs to establish new firms, but any measure that artificially prolong the life of firms that are doomed to fail will weaken the selection process and raise social costs. Risk transfer mechanisms that involve severe informational asymmetries could be detrimental to effective functioning of the selection process.

NOTES

[1] The positive correlation between age and survival probability (conditional on firm size) can also be explained by selection bias driven by variations in firm quality, as in the case of the U.S. iron and steel shipbuilding. Thompson (2005) shows, in a recent study, that "the shipbuilding industry exhibits the usual joint dependence of survival on age and size, but this dependence is eliminated after controlling for heterogeneity by using pre-entry

experience as a proxy for firm quality." Cooley and Quadrini (2001) developed an industry dynamics model in which "the combination of persistent shocks to technology and financial frictions can account for the simultaneous dependence of firm dynamics on size and on age".

[2] Of course, as Camerer and Lovallo (1999) explain, entrepreneurs may overestimate the probability of success.

[3] We do not study here the related literature on investment under uncertainty with perfect and imperfect capital markets (for comprehensive reviews, see Hubbard, 1998; Carruth, Dickerson and Henley, 2000).

[4] For a critical assessment of Evans-Jovanovic paper, see Cressy (2000). For a recent study and review of the literature, see Åstebro and Bernhardt (2003).

[5] In the case of sole proprietorship, business debts are also personal debts. However, even in such a case, the loss has a lower bound because of exemptions recognized by personal bankruptcy laws.

[6] The U.S. data offer an opportunity for studying the effects of bankruptcy liabilities because bankruptcy exemption levels are set by the states and vary widely. For international evidence on the effects of bankruptcy regulations, see Claessens and Klapper (2005).

[7] Since higher exemptions lead to more entrepreneurial activity especially in high risk sectors, suppliers may hesitate to provide loans because lending becomes more risky. Thus, as Berkowitz and White (2004) found , "if small firms are located in states with unlimited rather than low homestead exemptions, they are more likely to be denied credit, and when loans are made, they are smaller and interest rates are higher."

[8] If the creditors can identify good, low risk projects, then those fims that receive loans could have higher survival probability. Here we assume that the entrepreneurs have better information about their business prospects.

[9] Leasing can be favorable compared to outright purchasing of investment goods due to tax regulations. But this issue is beyond the scope of our analysis.

[10] We experimented with only the share of bonus-type payments in total gross wage but the results were qualitatively the same.

[11] 'Region' is defined at the province level. 'Industry' and 'sector' refers to ISIC (Revision 2) 4-digit industries.

[12] The data are collected at the establishment level, which is the main decision-making unit. We use the terms 'establishment' and 'firm' interchangeably.

[13] The proportion of small start-ups (employing 10-49 people) that borrowed external funding is about 35 percent, whereas for large start-ups, the same rate is more than 60 percent. Although the survey does not differentiate between different types of debt, it is likely to cover only interest payments to formal financial institutions. If this is the case, the proportion of small firms using bank credit in Turkey is similar to the proportions observed in the U.S. and Canada. For financial status of small firms in Canada and the U.S., see Baldwin, Gellatly and Gaudreault (2002), and Small Business Administration (2003), respectively.

[14] 'Incumbent' refers to those firms that were established before 1993.

[15] As noted before, the data do not include micro-establishments employing less than 10 people.

REFERENCES

Åstebro, T. and I. Bernhardt (2003), "Start-up Financing, Owner Characteristics, and Survival", *Journal of Economics and Business,* 55(3), 303-319.
Audretsch, D. B., E. Santarelli,. and M. Vivarelli, (1999), "Start-up Size and Industrial Dynamics: Some Evidence from Italian Manufacturing", *International Journal of Industrial Organization,* 17(7), 965-983.
Baldwin, J. R., L. Bian, R. Dupuy and G. Gellatly (2000), *Failure Rates for New Canadian Firms: New Perspectives on Entry and Exit,* Ottawa, Statistics Canada.
Baldwin, J. R., G. Gellatly and V. Gaudreault (2002), *Financing Innovation in New Small Firms: New Evidence from Canada,* Ottawa, Statistics Canada.
Berkowitz, J. and M. J. White (2004), "Bankruptcy and Small Firms' Access to Credit", *Rand Journal of Economics,* 35(1), 69-84.
Blanchflower, D. G. (1991), "Fear, Unemployment and Pay Flexibility", *Economic Journal,* 101, 483-496.
Brown, C. and J. L. Medoff (2003), "Firm Age and Wages", *Journal of Labor Economics,* 21(4), 677-697.
Camerer, C. and D. Lovallo (1999), "Overconfidence and Excess Entry: An Experimental Approach", *American Economic Review,* 89(1), 306-318.
Campbell, D., A. Carruth, A. Dickerson and F. Green (2004), "Job Insecurity and Wages", Department of Economics, University of Kent, mimeo.
Carneiro, A. and P. Portugal (2003), *Wages and the Risk of Displacement,* Banco de Portugal Economic Research Department Working Paper No: 10-03.
Carruth, A., A. Dickerson and A. Henley (2000), "What do We Know about Investment under Uncertainty?", *Journal of Economic Surveys,* 14(1), 119-153.
Caves, R. E. (1998), "Industrial Organization and New Findings on the Turnover and Mobility of Firms", *Journal of Economic Literature,* 36(4), 1947-1982.
Claessens, S. and L. F. Klapper, (2005), "Bankruptcy around the World: Explanations of its Relative Use", *American Law and Economics Review,* 7(2), 253-283.
Cooley, T. F. and V. Quadrini (2001), "Financial Markets and Firm Dynamics," *American Economic Review,* 91(6), 1287-1310.
Cressy, R. (2000), "Credit Rationing or Entrepreneurial Risk Aversion? An Alternative Explanation for the Evans and Jovanovic Finding", *Economics Letters,* 66(3), 235-240.
Disney, R., J. Haskel and Y. Heden (2003), "Entry, Exit and Establishment Survival in U.K. Manufacturing", *Journal of Industrial Economics,* 51(1), 91-112.
Dixit, A. (1989), "Entry and Exit Decisions under Uncertainty", *Journal of Political Economy,* 97(4), 620-638.
Dunne, T., J. M. Roberts and L. Samuelson (1989), "The Growth and Failure of U.S. Manufacturing Plants", *Quarterly Journal of Economics,* 104(4), 671–698.
Eliasson, G. (1991), "Modeling the Experimentally Organized Economy: Complex Dynamics in an Empirical Micro-Macro Model of Endogenous Economic Growth", *Journal of Economic Behavior and Organization,* 16(2), 153-182.
Evans, D. S. and B. Jovanovic (1989), "An Estimated Model of Entrepreneurial Choice under Liquidity Constraints", *Journal of Political Economy,* 97(5), 808-827.
Fan, W. and M. J. White (2003), "Personal Bankruptcy and the Level of Entrepreneurial Activity", *Journal of Law and Economics,* 46(3), 453-567.
Fotopoulos, G. and H. Louri, H. (2000), "Location and Survival of New Entry", *Small Business Economics,* 14(3), 311-321.
Geroski, P. A. (1995), "What Do We Know About Entry?", *International Journal of Industrial Organization,* 13(4), 421-440.

Geroski, P. A., J. Mata and P. Portugal, (2003), *Founding Conditions and the Survival of New Firms*, paper presented at the 30th Annual Conference of the EARIE, Helsinki, August 24-26.

Gollier, C., P. Koehl and J. Rochet, (1997), "Risk-Taking Behavior with Limited Liability and Risk Aversion", *Journal of Risk and Insurance*, 64(3), 347-380.

Hamermesh, D. (1988), "Plant Closings and the Value of the Firm", *Review of Economics and Statistics*, 70(5), 580-586.

Hubbard, R. G. (1998), "Capital-Market Imperfections and Investment", *Journal of Economic Literature*, 36(2), 193-225.

Mata, J. and P. Portugal, (1994), "Life Duration of New Firms", *Journal of Industrial Economics*, 42(2), 227-245.

Mata, J., P. Portugal, and P. Guimaraes, (1995), "The Survival of New Plants: Start-up Conditions and Post-entry Evolution", *International Journal of Industrial Organization*, 13(5), 459-481.

Persad, S. (2005), *Quantifying the Disciplinary Effect of Collateral*, paper presented at the 2005 FMA Annual Meeting, Chicago, October 12 – 15.

Santarelli, E. (1998), "Start-up Size and Post-Entry Performance: The Case of Tourism Services in Italy", *Applied Economics*, 30(2), 157-163.

Santarelli, E. and M. Vivarelli, (2002), "Is Subsidizing Entry an Optimal Policy", *Industrial and Corporate Change*, 11(1), 39-52.

Segarra A. and M. Callejon, (2002), "New Firms' Survival and Market Turbulence: New Evidence from Spain", *Review of Industrial Organization*, 20(1), 1-14.

Small Business Administration (2003), *Financing Patterns of Small Firms: Findings from the 1998 Survey of Small Business Finance*, SBA.

Stiglitz, J. L. and A. Weiss, (1981), "Credit Rationing in Markets with Imperfect Information", *American Economic Review*, 71(3), 393-410.

Taymaz, E. (2005), "Are Small Firms Really Less Productive?", *Small Business Economics*, 25(5), 429-445.

Thompson, P. (2005), "Selection and Firm Survival: Evidence from the Shipbuilding Industry, 1825–1914", *Review of Economics and Statistics*, 87(1), 26-36.

Troske, K. R. (1996), "The Dynamic Adjustment Process of Firm Entry and Exit in Manufacturing and Finance, Insurance, and Real Estate", *Journal of Law & Economics*, 39(4), 705-735.

Ushijima, T. (2005), "Internal Capital Market and the Growth and Survival of Japanese Plants in the United States", *Journal of the Japanese and International Economies*, 19(3), 366-385.

Vartia, L. (2004), *Assessing Plant Entry and Exit Dynamics and Survival - Does Firms' Financial Status Matter?*, Unpublished paper, European University Institute.

Wagner, J. (1994), "The Post-Entry Performance of New Small Firms in German Manufacturing Industries", *Journal of Industrial Economics*, 42(2), 141-154.

Chapter 13
WHAT IS THE BEST POLICY FOR INNOVATIVE ENTREPRENEURSHIP?

Roberta Piergiovanni
ISTAT, Roma

Enrico Santarelli
University of Bologna, and Max Planck Institute of Economics, Jena

1. INTRODUCTION

It is evident from the title of this chapter that we consider innovation and entrepreneurship to be powerful and interrelated forces which shape the paths of economic development and represent a major goal of any policy aimed at improving a country's competitiveness. This means that, in our view, entrepreneurial firms with favorable prospects for growth do not simply contribute to job creation and social cohesion. They are also important because of their impact in terms of innovative and competitive power, in particular when they possess the right human capital endowment and an educated workforce able to implement new technologies (see Audretsch, Thurik, Verheul and Wennekers, 2002, Ch. 1).

In what follows, we shall attempt to show that the concepts associated with the three keywords mentioned above – innovation (Section 2), entrepreneurship (Section 3), and human capital (Section 4) – can be also used as reference concepts around which to sharpen our understanding of some crucial features of the productive system of a medium-technology country, namely Italy, which is taken here as an ideal 'laboratory' in which to identify important areas representing the final and intermediate objectives of entrepreneurship and innovation policies.

2. INNOVATION

We begin with the first keyword: *innovation*. We already know from some of the previous chapters (e.g., the sixth by Audretsch and Elston and the ninth by Cefis and Marsili) that the innovative capability of entrepreneurial firms is a crucial dimension of competitiveness, since it may result either in new products being brought to the marketplace or in higher productivity levels being reached through the adoption of improved machinery and capital equipment with embodied technological change. In this regard, the widespread presence of high-technology entrepreneurial start-ups in recent years has produced accelerated rates of technological change in countries such as the United States and the Netherlands. Conversely, if we look at Italy, it is evident that its system of innovation is a weak one, in particular because of its low capacity to undertake R&D and other innovation-related activities.

Table 1 shows, for each technology class in manufacturing, the R&D intensity and the share of value added to total value added in manufacturing. The individual categories are broken down according to whether they are characterized by a high, medium-high, medium-low or low R&D intensity. Comparing the six countries in the table reveals that, in relation to the high-tech aggregate, Italy is clearly backward, with R&D intensity in this category amounting to about half that in the other countries.

The empirical evidence becomes even more worrisome if we move to the medium-high tech category, although for the medium-low and the low tech ones it appears that all countries, and not just Italy, do not invest greatly in R&D, given that in these categories innovative capability in general and R&D expenditures in particular tend to be of scant if any significance.

Table 1 – R&D intensity (R&D expenditures as a share of value added) and share of value added to GDP by technological category

Type of technology	France	Germany	Italy	U.K.	Japan	U.S.
R&D INTENSITY						
High	0.26	0.23	0.12	0.21	0.24	0.18
Medium-high	0.10	0.11	0.03	0.08	0.12	0.07
Total high and medium-high	0.35	0.34	0.16	0.29	0.36	0.25
Medium-low	0.03	0.02	0.01	0.02	0.04	0.02
Low	0.01	0.01	0.00	0.01	0.02	0.01
Total medium-low and low	0.04	0.03	0.01	0.02	0.05	0.03
Manufacturing	0.40	0.37	0.17	0.31	0.41	0.27
VALUE ADDED IN PERCENTAGE OF GDP (x100)						
High	2.50	2.40	2.00	3.20	3.70	5.00
Medium-high	4.30	8.70	5.40	4.20	6.80	6.10
Total high and medium-high	6.80	11.10	7.40	7.40	10.50	11.10
Medium-low	3.40	4.80	5.80	3.90	4.50	4.50
Low	4.90	4.60	6.90	6.40	5.60	6.30
Total medium-low and low	8.30	9.48	12.69	10.28	10.16	10.83
Manufacturing	15.10	20.60	20.10	17.70	20.70	21.90

Source: own calculations on the OECD Science and Technology Indicators.

Inspection of the lower frame of Table 1 shows that, in terms of share of value added to GDP, Italy is more specialized in medium-low and low tech manufacturing than the other five countries.

This overview of the ability of Italian firms to invest in R&D points to two preliminary conclusions. The first concerns high-tech industries. Here Italy already possesses some productive capacity, albeit slightly lower than that of the other countries considered, but Italian firms experience significant difficulties in undertaking R&D activities, whereas this weakness is absent in comparative terms in those industries for which R&D is not a crucial competitive factor.

The other side of the coin is the outcome of innovative activities: if R&D expenditures represent a measure of the effort made by a firm to obtain innovation, the number of patents gives us a proxy for its innovative output. Inspection of the figures on patents registered with the United States Patents and Trademark Office (USPTO) allows comparison of the long-term trends in patenting by the same six countries examined for the previous table. Table 2 shows that Italy has the smallest share of USPTO patents among the most industrialized countries. Of course, this result reflects the specialization of the country in low-tech industries, but it is nevertheless indicative of the weakness of Italian firms in high-tech ones. The technological backwardness of Italy is also confirmed if the number of patents is weighted for the size of the country.

Table 2 – Total patents (USPTO):across-country comparison (1963-2001)

Country	Patents	%	Growth rate of the number of patents (1996-2001)	Patents/resident population (x1,000)
Italy	35,856	1.2	7.3	0.6
France	93,258	3.2	7.7	1.6
Germany	24,259	8.3	10.6	2.8
U.K.	105,644	3.6	10.1	1.7
Japan	485,961	16.6	7.6	3.6
U.S.	1,957,669	67.0	7.5	7.7
Total	2,920,978	100.0	7.8	4.4

Source: own elaborations from the USPTO database.

The third column of Table 2 shows the dynamics of patents over time as indicated by the growth rate of the number of patents. Again, Italy lags behind the other countries. Its backwardness is particularly evident with respect to two of the three other large E.U. countries, namely Germany and the U.K. Hence, in general, although the innovative capability of Italy reflects the productive specialization of the country, it appears to be sluggish when compared with that of the other most advanced countries in the world.

Focusing on a narrower subset of high-technology industries – that comprising the Information and Communication Technology (ICT) aggregate and biotechnologies – furnishes the geographical picture arising for Italy (Figure 1). Most noteworthy in the biotechnology industry are firms with their headquarters in the Lombardia region, followed by those in Lazio and Toscana; while firms headquartered in the remaining seventeen regions display a scant capacity to develop new innovations. Nor does the picture change substantially if we examine the ICT aggregate (Figure 2): there is still a very promising situation in Lombardia and, to some extent, Piemonte, whereas all the other regions are backward.

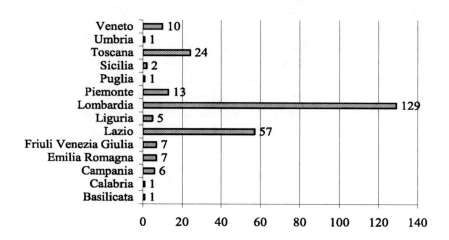

FIGURE 1 - REGIONAL DISTRIBUTION OF BIOTECH PATENTS (USPTO)

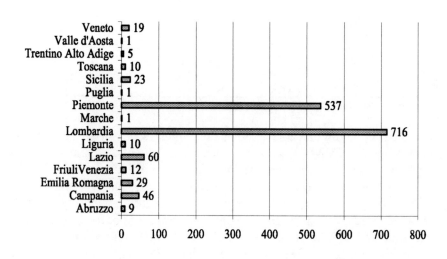

FIGURE 2 - REGIONAL DISTRIBUTION OF ICT PATENTS (USPTO)

3. ENTREPRENEURSHIP

The second keyword used in the introduction of this chapter was: *entrepreneurship*. It is widely believed in the European Union, and particularly in Italy, that higher entry rates denote a larger availability of entrepreneurial forces with which to foster economic growth and structural change (for a critical view of this approach see Santarelli and Vivarelli, 2002; Lotti and Santarelli, 2004).

However, before waxing too enthusiastic over high values of entry rates, one should consider the importance of "entry mistakes" (as defined by Cabral, 1997) – this being an expression which refers to the fact that, in every period and every industry, more firms enter the market than it is able to sustain. Such mistakes are due to lags in observation of rivals' entry decisions; or they occur merely because entry investments take time and in general they result in the inefficient allocation of resources to subjects unable to contribute to the competitiveness of a country, region, or industry. This theory is consistent with the "revolving door" metaphor put forward by Audretsch (1995) (see also Audrestch and Fritsch, 2002; and Love, 1996) - and confirmed by the findings of Taymaz, Güneş and Orhan in Chapter 12 - according to which if a large number of new firms enter into the market their exit rates will get higher as well.

To complicate matters, over the last twenty years subsidies to support new-firm creation have been a quite commonly used instrument of European industrial policy, prompting the following question: are such incentives really useful or do they lead to significant substitution and deadweight effects? In fact, a subsidy may cancel (or at least reduce) the revealed differences between less efficient and more efficient firms and disturb both market selection and the learning process undergone by entrepreneurs. In more detail, subsidizing entry may be risky for at least three reasons.

Firstly, because less efficient firms are artificially supported and do not leave the market, regardless of the entrepreneur's scant revealed capabilities. Secondly, furnishing subsidies conditional on an above-average start-up size may also generate market distortions, since most of the beneficiaries (larger newborn firms) would survive and grow even without the subsidy. Thirdly, the entrepreneur's learning process about his/her own capabilities is biased by the subsidy, and even the most efficient founders may overestimate their market chances.

Of course, there may be marked differences in labor-market conditions across regional or local entities in one and the same country. These economic differences are often unwanted and of a structural nature, and they may last for multiple decades. Governments may seek to reduce such regional inequalities by subsidizing new economic activity in the poorer regional or local entities, or by enhancing entrepreneurial skills in society and fostering entrepreneurial awareness in young people. A typical circumstance in which this kind of intervention is the preferred policy is that characterized by a combination of high unemployment and a low propensity to start new businesses (see Santarelli, Carree and Verheul, 2005).

3.1. Sources and Determinants of Entrepreneurship in Italy

In the light of the above considerations, the data on net entry in Italy in the first quarter of 2005 should be viewed positively: at last, the difference between registrations and cancellations of firms with/from the Registro Imprese of the Chambers of Commerce now displays a negative sign (see Unioncamere, 2005)! Given that a large fraction of new entries represent just structural turbulence, this finding suggests that entry is becoming a little bit more selective. Nevertheless, during the 1998-2004 period as a whole, the number of registered firms continued to increase, reaching the astonishingly high number of 6 million firms at the end of 2004 (Table 3).

Table 3 – Firms registered by sector of economic activity (1998-2004)

Sector	1998		2004		Growth rate 1998-2004
	Registered	%	Registered	%	
Distributive trades	1,506,295	27.3	1,581,818	26.4	5.0
Agriculture	1,092,525	19.8	972,940	16.2	-10.9
Construction	621,180	11.3	771,432	12.9	24.2
Manufacturing	740,492	13.4	752,188	12.5	1.6
Real estate, computer services, etc.	460,949	8.4	581,272	9.7	26.1
Hotels and restaurants	256,180	4.6	285,118	4.8	11.3
Other services	220,995	4.0	240,039	4.0	8.6
Transports and communication	201,630	3.7	212,943	3.6	5.6
Monetary and financial intermediation	90,589	1.6	108,008	1.8	19.2
Health, etc.	19,844	0.4	25,213	0.4	27.1
Education	13,848	0.3	18,939	0.3	36.8
Other (non classified)	292,056	5.3	447,840	7.5	53.3
Total	5,516,983	100.0	5,997,749	100.0	8.7

Source: Unioncamere (2005)

However, if we break this impressive figure on new firm formation down by industry, apart from the largely expected negative balance of agriculture, we find that the increase in the number of registrations is unevenly distributed across sectors. In particular, the substantial stagnation of manufacturing is rather evident, whereas there is remarkable growth in the number of registrations for certain service sector industries, namely those linked with health, education, financial and monetary intermediation. This result is indicative that new entrepreneurship is focusing more on intangibles and less on tangibles, doing so as a consequence of the structural changes brought about by the relocation of traditional manufacturing productions to the developing and transition economies. For these reasons, this shift from manufacturing to certain service sectors is not devoid of positive implications, because it can be seen as preliminary evidence of changing patterns of specialization from old to (relatively) new activities which make more intensive use of skilled labor.

Another interesting aspect of firm demographics concerns the determinants of the overall process of new-firm formation. In this respect, one might want to answer questions such as the following: Is new firm formation a 'defensive' process set in motion by unemployed workers (self-employment) with previous jobs in the industry/geographic area concerned? Or are entrepreneurs attracted by the above average profits to be earned by operating a firm in a fast-growing industry?

Explanation of the unemployment/entrepreneurship relationship is at least twofold. It can be related to the opposing views summarized by the unemployment push and the demand pull hypotheses, which respectively assert that: *1*) Unemployed workers tend to become self-employed entrepreneurs in the same industry; *2*) Workers employed in a given industry start their own businesses in the same industry when the latter exhibits a favorable performance. The debate on the links between unemployment and new-firm formation (on which see Carree, 2002) can be traced back to Frank Knight (1921), who stressed that at any time individuals must choose among three different ways to allocate their time and: being unemployed, self-employed, and employed. According to Knight, it is the relative price of each of these activities that affects the individual's final decision, although a positive relation is highly likely to arise between self-employment and unemployment. This latter idea of a link between unemployment and a 'defensive' type of entrepreneurship was later refined by Oxenfeldt (1943), who outlined an occupational choice framework based on the assumption that individuals confronted with a greater likelihood of becoming unemployed, or with low prospects for wage-employment, tend to become self-employed. This framework was formally modeled by Lucas (1978), who introduced the hypothesis that agents are differentiated by their entrepreneurial skill, and by Kihlstrom and Laffont (1979), who constructed a competitive equilibrium entrepreneurial model under uncertainty in which individuals possess labor which they can supply as workers to a competitive labor market or use as entrepreneurs in running a firm: in equilibrium, more risk-averse individuals become employed workers, while the less risk-averse become entrepreneurs, and this generates a stable dynamic process of firm entry and exit.

From this perspective, some considerations can be put forward concerning both the start-up process and the small average size of Italian firms. Firstly, the small size of Italian firms has long been considered more an opportunity than a threat, given their tendency to locate in industrial districts – a type of industrial organization that favors the exploitation of both static and dynamic economies of scale and enables SMEs to overcome most of their disadvantages with respect to their larger counterparts. Because industrial districts are losing their comparative advantage as a result of globalization, and given the fact that monetary policy is no longer a prerogative of national authorities, a restructuring process is now necessary. As a consequence, the Italian economy is affected by a size constraint on competitiveness, which implies that Italian firms should endeavor to increase their size and change their organizational structure as rapidly as possible, for example by forming or becoming part of industrial groups.

One of the tasks of the Unioncamere Observatory on New Firms has been to analyze a sample of new entries since the end of the 1990s, the aim being to identify – by means of direct interviews – the motivations behind decisions to start up new firms (Table 4).

Table 4 – Entrepreneurial motivation in Italian new-born firms

Motivation	%
SCHUMPETERIAN	47.8
Entrepreneurial success	36.9
Family tradition	6.2
Innovative idea	4.7
YOUNGHIAN	23.4
Previous knowledge of the industry	12.7
Dissatisfaction with previous employment	8.0
Subcontractors	2.7
OPPORTUNIST	9.6
Market opportunities	9.2
Subsidies	0.4
INTRINSICALLY MARGINAL	16.1
OTHER	3.1

Source: own calculations on Unioncamere data

The firms in the sample were divided into four categories: those started because of good prospects for success or to exploit an innovative idea (Schumpeterian motivation); those started as the result of a 'natural' process of specialization and division of labor among firms (Younghian motivation; following Young, 1928); those started to exploit market niches or to gain access to public subsidies (opportunistic motivation); and finally 'intrinsically marginal' firms started as the result of a self-employment motivation and without significant probabilities of survival. Nearly 50 percent of the entrepreneur respondents defined their firm as

'Schumpeterian' and as started in order to become successful and create or perpetuate a family tradition. On breaking this category down, however, it emerges that only a small fraction (4.7%) of these allegedly Schumpeterian firms were started to exploit an innovative idea. This finding is indication that entrepreneurship coupled with innovation is still quite a secondary feature of the overall process of new firm formation in Italy, leaving room for adequate policies targeting innovation entrepreneurship (see Section 5 below).

3.2. The Importance of Self-employment in Italy

More rigorous analysis, for the 103 Italian provinces and for seven years, used the Movimprese dataset provided by the Union of Italian Chambers of Commerce (Unioncamere). An econometric test was performed to capture the impact of the prevailing conditions on the labor market and in the local economy on new firm formation in the Italian provinces between 1998 and 2003. In this case, we concentrated only on persons (unemployed or employed) starting a new business in the province in which they lived. For this purpose, the following model of the determinants of entry was estimated:

$$E_{it} = a_t L_{i,t-1} + b U_{i,t-1} + c VA_{i,t-1} + \varepsilon_{it}^E \tag{1}$$

The index i represents the province ($i = 1,...,103$) and the index t stands for the year ($t = 1998,..., 2003$). We use symbol E_{it} for net entry. Total labor force, the sum of employed and unemployed, is represented by L_{it}, while the symbol for the provincial number of unemployed is U_{it}, whereas VA_{iit} is the symbol for value added per capita in the province. The first determinant of entry in equation (1) is the total labor force in the previous year. For each person in the labor force, (self-)employed or unemployed, there is a probability a_t that (s)he will start an enterprise. This probability is made time-dependent because entry regulations in Italy were relaxed during the years considered. The second determinant is the number of unemployed. There is an additional probability b for the likelihood of the unemployed starting a firm (note that this may also be negative). Hence, the hypothesis that unemployment has a positive (push) effect on entry is simply whether $b > 0$. The third determinant is value added per capita in the province. There is an additional probability c for the likelihood that residents of provinces with better overall economic performances will start a new firm (pull effect). For the purposes of the empirical analysis, the dependent variable E_{it} was constructed for each province by subtracting the number of exiting firms in each year from that of new entries in the same year, while the labor force, the unemployment, and the value added per capita variables were inserted with their values in the previous year. Time and industry dummies were also included in the estimates.

Inspection of the determinants of net entry shows that the unemployment rate is the variable exerting the most statistically significant impact on the dynamics across provinces of this indicator, while the other variables exert no statistically significant impact on net entry (Table 5). Self-employment is therefore a major factor in new-firm formation across the Italian provinces, a finding which highlights the substantially defensive nature of entrepreneurship in Italy.

Table 5 – Empirical results from estimation of equation (1)

Variable	Coefficient	St. error	t-statistics	Prob.
Constant	0.0087	0.0028	1.0201	0.0022
L	0.0001	0.0001	1.0200	0.3077
U	0.0003	0.0007	4.2990	0.0000
VA	-0.0003	0.0001	-2.3660	0.0180
Adj. R^2	0.36			
N	721			

4. HUMAN CAPITAL

The third of the above keywords was: *human capital*. As pointed out by Zoltan Acs in Chapter 5, new firm formation rates are positively related to the level of human capital, and more educated people are more likely to acquire useful knowledge spillovers from others who are involved in research activities.

Whilst our findings for innovation and entrepreneurship were both positive and negative, there is evidence in regard to human capital that some significant improvements are taking place. The Unioncamere data set out in Table 6 signal that demand by Italian firms for more skilled labor has slightly increased in the most recent period. In particular, compared to 2003, although the share of highly skilled workers in total employment is still low in absolute terms, it has grown markedly, whereas the share of blue collars and low-skilled workers has decreased.

This is an encouraging result, and it is consistent with the long-term trend of the last two decades not only in Italy but also in the other developed countries (see Piva, Santarelli and Vivarelli, 2005). Both during the 1980s and the 1990s, along with the ICT revolution, all the most advanced countries experienced marked acceleration in the substitution of skilled labor for unskilled labor. Italy, too, seems therefore to move in the same direction, with the most recent data showing that this 'skill-bias' pattern is becoming increasingly pronounced.

In general, the skill-bias is mainly due to two determinants: technological change and organizational change. In the former case, the underlying hypothesis is that the new technologies are complementary to highly-skilled labor, whereas they are alternative to less skilled labor; hence, if a firm introduces and/or develops new technologies, it will display a greater preference to hire skilled human capital, while expelling a part of its less skilled counterpart.

Table 6 – Evolution of the skill structure of Italian firms (% of employed workers)

	31.12.2001	31.12.2002	31.12.2003
Managers and executives	1.2	1.3	1.3
Highly-skilled workers (including researchers)	4.4	4.3	5.7
Technical personnel	19.2	19.2	20.7
Clerical workers	11.9	11.4	11.6
Sales and marketing personnel	14.2	14.4	14.7
Skilled manual workers	23.5	23.2	22.2
Manual workers	16.2	16.4	15.3
Other unskilled personnel	9.3	9.7	8.6
TOTAL	100.0	100.0	100.0

Source: Unioncamere (2005)

The second hypothesis rests upon the alleged complementarity between highly-skilled human capital and the introduction into the firm of flexible and holistic forms of organization. These latter include organizational changes associated with just-in-time production, management of breakdowns, quality control, work teams and quality circles which require collective effort by labor, and practices of multi-task organization that require workers to perform a wider variety of tasks within a given occupation and to rotate among different jobs.

There is a further hypothesis which concerns a combined superadditive effect of technological change and organizational change. In the case of Italy, the analysis of a sample of manufacturing firms carried out by Piva, Santarelli and Vivarelli (2005) shows that the upskilling trend of employment appears to be mainly a function of the reorganisational strategies adopted by firms, possibly combined with technological change. Moreover, shopfloor reorganization appears to have slightly favored more skilled workers, whereas blue-collar workers seem very vulnerable to the joint effect of reorganization and the implementation of new technologies. Thus, organisational change at the shopfloor level mainly entails the redundancy of blue-collars, while it weakly increases demand for white-collars.

5. CONCLUSIONS

What is the overall picture of the Italian economy *vis-à-vis* the restructuring process set in motion in recent years by globalization? Italy exhibits elements of endemic weakness in relation to the ability of its firms to implement innovation strategies: there is a low propensity to invest in R&D, in particular in those industries in which this would be worthwhile, and regional imbalances emerge in terms of innovative capability. Entrepreneurial talents are certainly widespread, but they are mostly defensive in nature and do not appear to be utilized for the pursuit of growth strategies. By contrast, as far as human capital in concerned, a positive evolution in demand for more skilled labor is indicative that something is moving in a promising direction. Although it has to be recalled that - as put forward by Acs in Chapter 5, and Grilo and Thurik in Chapter 4 - the most favorable environmental conditions for innovative entrepreneurship are usually found in those regions that are characterized by high levels of both highly skilled and unskilled workers, with the latter supplying low level services to the former.

These results can be taken as reference points for some policy suggestions. It is time that Italy (and Europe) put an end to the abuse of subsidies in support of new firm formation, after nearly twenty years during which entrepreneurship has been seen as an intermediate target for employment policies. In effect, the E.U. countries have been prompted by worries about their widening employment gaps with respect to the U.S. to disburse huge amounts of public money to artificially 'seed' new firms (Santarelli and Vivarelli, 2002). The moment has now come to use entrepreneurship policies as an instrument of an industrial policy explicitly aimed at promoting structural change. In this sense, they cannot be implemented independently of innovation policies: taking inspiration from what has been achieved in the U.S. and in some Asian "tigers" (see Mathews and Cho, 2000) - with the role played in fostering innovative entrepreneurship on the one side by venture capitalists and business angels, and on the other by the state as a 'collective entrepreneur' able to mobilize scarce but scattered resources for the development of strategic industries - it would be better to focus selectively on entrepreneurship and to target only those start-ups based on innovative projects and with good prospects of survival and growth.

This implies that what is really needed is not so much extraordinary and uncoordinated policies in support of innovation and entrepreneurship, as a series of coordinated policies able to promote innovative entrepreneurship and structural change. But such change also requires major effort to introduce policies targeted on human capital. We emphasized in Section 4 the favorable dynamics of demand for highly skilled human capital, in particular with an adequate endowment of general knowledge, social and communication skills, and 'learn how to learn' capabilities. The experience of other countries tells us that this kind of human capital achieves the best performance once it reaches the labor market. As shown by Krueger and Kumar (2004a and 2004b), the U.S. is more competitive than Europe in this respect as well, in particular in its provision of general tertiary education. But general education enabling workers to operate new production technologies is costly to obtain. Accordingly, a change of perspective in education strategies can only be promoted by means of direct policy intervention: it is not by chance that the ratio of general to skill-specific, vocational education subsidies in post-secondary school is equal to 2.55 in the U.S., while it is 1 in Germany and Italy.

Unfortunately, and paradoxically, over the last ten years or so the Italian (and the European) system of secondary and tertiary education has instead continued to move in the opposite direction. In the widespread unawareness that skill-specific education works well, as it actually did in the 1960s and 1970s, only when available technologies change slowly, but is useless when new technology emerge at a more rapid pace, as during the information age of the 1980s and 1990s, education policies in Italy (and Europe) have continued to target specialized education. To counteract this dangerous tendency, it is greatly to be recommended that both the secondary and tertiary education levels refocus their goals and become more closely involved in the creation of general and adaptable skills rather than specific competencies. In particular, the universities should engage more vigorously in top-quality research and transfer its results to the 'product' that they really bring to the market: that is, their graduates. In the case of countries like Italy, university graduates should embody those general and basic competencies – refined in close connection with the research undertaken in university departments – that make them more easily adaptable to the skills needs of a labor market in continuous evolution, and of firms facing the challenges raised by global competition.

As suggested by Baptista, van Stel and Thurik in Chapter 11, joint initiatives undertaken by universities and public institutions to promote a culture of technology-based entrepreneurship and to support innovative start-ups in a knowledge-based economy may also enhance employment, growth and innovation in accordance with the European Union's Lisbon strategy. Further enhancement of such activities and of the science and technology base underpinning their development, as well as greater support from the private sector, may contribute to an industrial restructuring process where a larger proportion of new firm start-ups plays a significant role in fostering innovation and reducing unemployment.

REFERENCES

Audretsch, D. B. (1995), *Innovation and Industry Evolution*, Cambridge (MA), The MIT Press.

Audretsch, D. B., A. R. Thurik, I. Verheul and S. Wennekers (eds.) (2002), *Entrepreneurship: Determinants and Policy in a European-U.S. Comparison*, Boston, Dordrecht and London, Kluwer.

Audretsch, D. B. and M. Fritsch (2002), "Growth Regimes over Time and Space", *Regional Studies*, 36(2), 113-124.

Cabral, L. (1997), "Entry Mistakes", Centre for Economic Policy Research, Discussion Paper No. 1729, November.

Carree, M. A. (2002), "Does Unemployment Affect the Number of Establishments? A Regional Analysis for U.S. States", *Regional Studies*, 36(4), 389-398.

Kihlstrom, R. E. and J. -J. Laffont (1979), "A General Equilibrium Entrepreneurial Theory of Firm Formation Based on Risk Aversion", *Journal of Political Economy*, 87(4), 719-748.

Knight, F. H. (1921), *Risk, Uncertainty, and Profit*, Boston, Houghton Mifflin.

Krueger, D. and K. B. Kumar (2004a), "US-Europe Differences in Technology-driven Growth: Quantifying the Role of Education", *Journal of Monetary Economics*, 51(2), 161-190.

Krueger, D. and K. B. Kumar (2004b), "Skill-specific rather than General Education: A Reason for U.S.-Europe Growth Differences?", *Journal of Economic Growth*, 9(2), 167-207.

Lotti, F. and E. Santarelli (2004) "Industry Dynamics and the Distribution of Firm Sizes: A Non-parametric Approach", *Southern Economic Journal*, 70(3), 443-466.

Love, J. H. (1996), "Entry and Exit: A County-level Analysis", *Applied Economics*, 28(4), 441-451.

Lucas, R. E., Jr. (1978), "On the Size Distribution of Business Firms", *Bell Journal of Economics*, 9(2), 508-523.

Mathews, J. and D. -S. Cho (2000), *Tiger Technology: The Creation of a Semiconductor Industry in East Asia*, Cambridge, Cambridge University Press.

Oxenfeldt, A. R. (1943), *New Firms and Free Enterprise: Pre-War and Post-War Aspects*, Washington (DC), American Council on Public Affairs.

Piva, M., E. Santarelli and M. Vivarelli (2005), "The Skill Bias Effect of Technological and Organisational Change: Evidence and Policy Implications", *Research Policy*, 2005, 34(2), 141-157.

Santarelli, E. and M. Vivarelli (2002), "Is Subsidizing Entry an Optimal Policy?", *Industrial and Corporate Change*, 11(1), 39-52

Santarelli, E., M. Carree and I. Verheul (2005), "Unemployment and Firm Entry and Exit: An Update on a Controversial Relationship", METEOR Research Memoranda, University of Maastricht, December.

Unioncamere (2005), *Rapporto Italia 2005*, Roma, Unioncamere.

Young, A. A. (1928), "Increasing Returns and Economic Progress", *Economic Journal*, 38(152), 527-542.

AUTHOR INDEX

SUBJECT INDEX

Box-Cox quantile regression; 54;
72
Business services; 117; 118;
123;124
Chesher's method; xv; xx; 42; 53;
55; 57; 58; 63; 64; 68; 70;
152; 163;
Cox hazard model; xviii; 141;
147; 200; 202; 213; 216;
217; 221; 249; 254; 255
Entrepreneurship; vi; vii; ix; x;
xiv; xv; xvi; xix; xx; 70;
75-78; 80-84; 86; 87; 89;
91-102; 105; 106; 109-
113; 115; 121; 125; 132;
150; 153; 154; 165; 178;
223-226; 228; 229; 231;
232; 234; 238; 239; 240;
241; 243; 246; 261; 265;
266; 267; 269; 270; 272;
273; 274
Entry and exit of firms; ix; x; xiv;
xv; xvi; xvii; xviii; xix;
xx; 2-7; 9; 13; 14; 16-20;
23; 24; 39; 41; 61; 71; 72;
75; 101; 107; 110; 111;
115; 123; 141; 147; 150;
151; 155; 161; 162; 163;
169; 184; 186; 187; 188;
197; 199; 201; 202; 203;
218; 219; 220; 223; 232;
233; 235; 239; 241; 243;
246; 247; 249; 250; 253;
256; 257; 259; 260; 265;
266; 267; 269; 270; 274
Equilibrium; xv; 2; 3; 12-20; 23;
24; 25; 27; 28; 31; 34; 36;
37; 39; 100; 200; 267;
274
European Union; ix; xiv; xvi; xix;
76; 77; 78; 82; 83; 86; 89;
92-97; 100; 102; 168;
225; 226; 227; 234; 235;
237; 238; 240; 263; 265;
272; 273;
Germany; vii; viii; x; xi; xiv; xvii;
59; 62; 65; 67; 69; 70; 71;
87; 90: 100; 132; 135-
148; 162; 212; 232; 233;
262; 263; 273
Gibrat's Law; xx; 48; 53; 54; 56;
59; 60; 61; 63; 71; 72;
141; 147; 154; 163
Static analysis of Gibrat's
Law; 42-52;
Greece; ix; x; xi; xiv; 66; 67; 87;
91; 97; 199-221; 232;
Hospitality sector; 44; 45; 48; 52;
56; 57; 63; 162; 221
Industrial district; vi; vxii; xviii;
165-179; 190; 191; 192;
268
Innovation; vi; vii; viii; ix; xiv;
xv; xviii; xix; xx; 38; 70;
71; 72; 83; 111; 115; 132;
140; 141; 147; 165; 169;
170; 172-178; 180-189;
192; 193; 194; 195; 196;
197; 218; 219; 225; 240;
241; 259; 261-264; 269;
270; 272; 273; 274
Italy; viii; ix; x; xi; xiv; xvii; xix;
41; 46; 59; 65; 66; 67; 69;
87; 91; 97; 149; 150; 151;
152; 165-168; 170; 171;
179; 180; 181; 182; 212;
221; 232; 261-266; 269;
270-273
Logit model; 49; 63; 65; 81; 97;

Printed in the United States
68438LVS00002B/90